My Diary
North and South

William Howard Russell (*From* Vanity Fair, *"Men of the Day, No. 96," 16 January 1875. Courtesy of the New York Public Library*)

WILLIAM HOWARD RUSSELL

My Diary
North and South

Edited by **Eugene H. Berwanger**

Temple University Press
Philadelphia

Library of Congress Cataloging-in-Publication Data

Russell, William Howard, Sir, 1820–1907.
My diary, North and South.

1. United States—Description and travel—1848–1865.
2. United States—History—Civil War, 1861–1865.
3. Confederate States of America—Description and travel.
4. Russell, William Howard, Sir, 1820–1907—Journeys—United States.
I. Berwanger, Eugene H.
II. Title.
E167.R96 1987b   973.7   87-10206
ISBN 0-87722-522-2

Manufactured in the United States of America

Contents

Six

Seven

Preface

I was first drawn to William Howard Russell's diary after reading his description of Abraham Lincoln: "a tall, lank, lean man with pendulous arms"; a man whose "mouth is absolutely prodigious," whose nose had an inquiring anxious air; a man who appeared stern but who was able to smile good-humoredly. Further reading proved that Russell's pen portrait of the president was just one of many contained in the book. He also vividly portrayed other Union and Confederate leaders of the Civil War era, including William H. Seward, General George B. McClellan, General Irwin McDowell, Jefferson Davis, and General P. G. T. Beauregard. Nor did Russell ignore average citizens. Besides recounting their physical appearance, he wrote of their manners, values, and habits in detail.

Because of Russell's ability to use words so effectively, his diary is a distinctive record of Americans in 1861. It is an exceptional source, too, inasmuch as Russell was one of the few individuals to travel in both the North and South and to interview so many leading politicians, military leaders, and average citizens. An outgoing individual himself, Russell made friends easily, drawing them out and encouraging them to discuss national affairs as well as local issues. Moreover, his interests were wide-ranging. Even though he came to the United States as a war correspondent for the London *Times,* Russell did not focus on military events alone. He was as fascinated by the institution of slavery and racial attitudes as he was by American views of democracy. He found the reactions of women to secession and military conflict somewhat amusing but also appalling for their vehemence. He was stunned by the lack of respect that common citizens had for civilian and military leaders in both North and South. Nor was it just people that captured Russell's imagination. He could convey as much enthusiasm in describing cities, railroads, and river traffic as in discussing the people and their ideals.

Russell, an Englishman, was an outsider looking in. Unlike Americans who lived in the South or the North, he did not feel the need to justify either side. In the beginning of the diary he expressed his hope to remain impartial, and for the most part he did. Total impartiality, however, was not always possible. Because he abhorred slavery, Russell found it difficult to sympathize with the southern cause. While he thought George B. McClellan a personable individual, Russell concluded from his own experiences in reporting wars that the American general was inept. An aristocrat himself, Russell found upper-class American values more appealing; the manners and sophistication of the more average people he found wanting.

Russell's diary also shows the international aspect of the Civil War. His remarks about southern insistence that the need for cotton would force Britain to aid the Confederacy, about conversations among members of the diplomatic corps in Washington, and about the eagerness of Europeans to participate in or observe military clashes prove both foreign awareness and interest in the American war.

Perhaps another noteworthy feature of Russell's diary was his tendency to question mid-nineteenth-century American values. In a country that lauded its democratic form of government, he found many people who found disagreeable the idea of universal suffrage. If America was a haven for the outcasts of Europe in the 1850s and 1860s, the newcomers were neither well-liked nor respected. And if northerners expressed a distaste for slavery, this feeling did not imply sympathy for blacks as people. Moreover, Russell came to conclude that Americans, North and South, were too quick to underrate their foes while boasting of their own military ability.

This edition is approximately one-third the length of the original diary published in 1863. I have retained most of the passages focusing on the Civil War and the manners and ideals of the American people. For the most part, the deleted material dealt with Russell's observations on past American history or his extensive comments on diplomacy and economic affairs. My editors have been most generous in allowing me to include visual materials to enhance the text. These include a map locating cities and military installations to which Russell referred at length and photographs of leading individuals mentioned. Taken together, the text and illustrations offer an accurate and penetrating picture of Americans during their first year of Civil War.

Eugene H. Berwanger
Fort Collins, Colorado

Acknowledgments

I wish to express my appreciation to the following people for their aid in identifying obscure individuals in South Carolina, Louisiana, and in England: Professor Jason H. Silverman of Winthrop College, Rock Hill, South Carolina; Rose Lambert, Librarian, Louisiana State Museum, New Orleans; Milton Gustafson, Chief, Diplomatic Records Branch, National Archives, Washington, D. C.; Professor John White, The University of Hull, England; and Professor Brian Holden Reid, King's College, London. And finally to the late Mrs. Joe Patterson Smith of Jacksonville, Illinois, who gave me many of her husband's books; among them was the 1863 London imprint of William Howard Russell's *My Diary North and South.*

My Diary
North and South

Introduction

William Howard Russell was a special correspondent for the London *Times.* His career in journalism began when he withdrew from Trinity College to become a reporter for various newspapers in Dublin. Soon after, Russell's accounts of famine and political discontent in Ireland brought him to the attention of John Delane, editor of the *Times* in London. In 1841 Delane engaged Russell to write exclusive reports for the *Times* on events in Ireland. Within a short time Russell had acquired a following among the British reading public. He was not only able to ferret out the news and report it without seeming bias but also wrote in a forthright and engaging manner. Impressed with Russell's ability, Delane next sent him to cover the Crimean War in 1854, an assignment that gained Russell something of an international reputation. Many of his letters on the Crimea were reprinted in American newspapers, and by the mid-1850s Russell's name enjoyed almost as much recognition in the United States as in Great Britain. Russell had trained himself to be a "war correspondent," explaining troop movements and tactics of warfare to a nonmilitary readership. But he went beyond: he was one of the few English newsmen who, along with detailing maneuvers on the Crimean battlefront, reported descriptive aspects and personalities among the opposing factions. Russell's next assignment was in India, where he reported on the mutiny of 1857–58. Vividly his letters described the horrors of a chaotic and blundering campaign, and his accounts were instrumental in ending the British troops' indiscriminate executions of mutineers. Given Russell's experience in dealing with war and civil disorder, it followed that Delane would again turn to Russell as the southern states began seceding from the Union in 1860 and civil war in the United States appeared likely.

Russell arrived in New York in mid-March 1861, the month in which national attention focused on the Sumter crisis. Quickly he hurried to Washington, D.C., where he renewed friendships with Americans he had met in England and secured introductions to Union political and military leaders whose acquaintance might be useful. A warm reception awaited Russell: Union leaders readily took him into their confidence. Informed on the sectional crisis, Russell sensed the inevitability of a military confrontation. The fate of the Union, he concluded presently, would be decided on the battlefield. And war, when it came, would erupt in South Carolina. Russell wished very much to report it firsthand. He also hoped to interview Confederate leaders, so that his letters to the *Times* would reflect both northern and southern points of view. Therefore, after only a few weeks in Washington, Russell hastened to the South before war might break out and fighting close off access to the region. To his regret, Russell did not witness the bombardment of Fort Sumter; he departed Washington just as the firing began. Yet during the next several months he would interview many Confederate politicians and generals and evaluate their capacity to lead a southern nation.

Russell made a herculean tour of the South, from April 12 to June 20, 1861. Daily he traveled overland, by river and even, at least on one occasion, through a swamp. Resolutely he visited military sites, government chambers, and plantation homes, meeting everywhere with prominent local citizenry. Determinedly he questioned black and white southerners, evaluating their answers within the context of his own observation. To Russell, southern whites appeared confident, even boastful, and anxious to extol the glories of their new southern nation. Not so the blacks. Less readily could Russell draw them out on the quarrel between the North and the South; he marveled at their reluctance to respond to his queries. Although focusing on the sectional dilemma, Russell enhanced his account with generous detail on background aspects of southern life: slavery, the general demeanor of the people, and the physical features of the region through which he was traveling.

In Charleston all doors seemed open to Russell. Mary Boykin Chesnut confided in her diary that certain of the town's leading citizens busied themselves with novels by William Makepeace Thackeray in advance of Russell's visit. By reading Thackeray, English novelist and Russell's friend, they hoped to make the best possible impression on the reporter.[1] While in the city, Russell spoke with prominent secessionists and Unionists, and he walked about Fort Sumter as well, reaching some tentative conclusions about Confederate military capability. From Charleston he traveled to Savannah, Georgia. All too soon he had to push on to Montgomery, Alabama, temporary capital of the Confederacy and focal point of his itinerary in the South.

Montgomery was a disappointment to Russell, despite the cordiality of his southern hosts. Food was poor and accommodations even worse, the most primitive Russell was to encounter in America. Above all Russell was appalled by slave auctions held openly on the streets and the insensitivity of the local population to the slave traffic. Even though it meant declining Jefferson Davis's invitation to dinner, Russell decided to continue on to more cosmopolitan Mobile. Apparently his decision was a good one, for it led to a rather daring encounter with the military and heightened the drama of his tour. In Mobile, he persuaded the owner of a fishing schooner to run him through the Union blockade to Fort Pickens off the coast of Pensacola, Florida. Here Russell had his first real contact with officers of the U.S. Navy; from them he gained the impression that the navy was, without doubt, the superior arm of the U.S. military force.

Russell concluded his journey to the South with a visit to New

[1]C. Vann Woodward, ed., *Mary Chesnut's Civil War* (New Haven: 1981), p. 50; see also Mary Boykin Chesnut, *A Diary from Dixie,* ed. Ben Ames Williams (Boston: 1949), p. 39.

Orleans, several sugar plantations along the Mississippi River, and finally Memphis. In the meantime Virginia had seceded and the Confederates had moved their capital from Montgomery to Richmond. Although he would have liked to visit Richmond to assess the impact of the change, Russell opted instead to return to Washington. Friends there alerted him to an impending battle between Union and Confederate forces in northern Virginia, and this one Russell was determined not to miss. Then too, he could not be assured, were he to remain in the South, that his letters to the *Times* would get through the Union blockade. To Russell it was imperative that he witness military action firsthand and that his letters get to London without delay.

By the time he had completed his tour and reached the nation's capital once again, Russell had spent nearly three months in the Confederacy. He had a fair, rather representative idea about American southerners and the conflict in which they were engaged. Himself an upper-class Briton, Russell shared with his southern hosts an affinity for the manners and life-style of the plantation South. Toward the southern middle and lower white classes he felt less favorably disposed. Their manners Russell described as crude; their inordinate tobacco chewing and spitting he found revulsive. Early on, Russell had credited southern secessionists with a certain tolerance toward individuals expressing Union sympathies. But as he reached New Orleans, he found southerners increasingly less indulgent. Here local officials were impressing British, Irish, and Scottish immigrants into the Confederate army despite their objections. Appeals to the British consul were their only hope, if they could get to him on time.

Throughout his travels, Russell was careful to maintain a neutral attitude both in his conversations with American friends and his reports back to London. His equanimity was but a pose. In his diary, even while in the South, he began voicing clearly pronorthern sentiment. Chiefly he disliked slavery. Toward southern blacks Russell displayed a nascent racism common among the British upper classes: he appeared equivocal in some instances; in others he gave the distinct impression that he regarded blacks as backward. Still he denounced every southern rationalization for exploiting black labor while keeping slaves in a state of ignorance and poverty. ". . . the impression left on my mind by what I had seen in slave States," argued Russell, "is unfavourable to the institution of slavery. . . . I have reason to believe that the more deeply the institution is probed, the more clearly will its unsoundness and its radical evils be discerned. . . . Slavery is a curse . . . a cancer, the ravages of which are covered by fair outward show, and by the apparent health of the sufferer. Never did a people enter a war so utterly destitute of any reason for waging it."

While Russell faulted slavery, primarily, for the impasse between North and South, he was also cognizant of states' rights as a factor. Given the force of states' rights thinking in the South, said he, the Union could never be restored no matter what the outcome on the battlefield. Southern hatred for northerners, especially for those residing in the New England states, was so strong as to preclude successful reunification. Russell's view is understandable in terms of what he had witnessed. New Yorkers, as far as he could determine, seemed detached from the struggle and oblivious to the secession movement; Washington had its share of southern sympathizers both disdainful of the Lincoln government and scornful of the Republican party. Not until he ventured below the Potomac River did Russell encounter any real expression of unity. And the South, he thought, might just prevail: in 1861 the Confederate armies gave every indication of military superiority over the North. Only later would the war, with its devastation, wear down southern morale.

Russell, in his attitude on the United States and the Civil War, held a view not uncommon among upper-class Britons. While he felt a deep respect for the Union, he could not overcome the idea that the American experiment in democracy was about to fail. The English aristocracy could approve a republican form of government only so long as the masses might continue to accept upper-class authority. Otherwise, failure seemed a certainty. Likely no government permitting expanded suffrage and broad participation by all economic groups would survive. Further, Russell saw Americans as bellicose and overconfident in their abilities. William Seward, for example, he found strident on foreign affairs. But was Seward's attitude toward Britain in 1861 really as rigid as Russell had presented it? Likely Russell was more accurately reflecting official British concern for Seward and his avowed expansionism. Perhaps Seward would be more aggressive now that he had been placed in charge of directing Union foreign policy.

As for the South, it was cotton that would win Britain for the

Confederacy. Southerners everywhere agreed that Britain's need for cotton would force her to support the Confederate cause and ultimately break the Union blockade. Again and again, Russell heard the argument, and he was amused. Quite secure in his own pride as an Englishman and knowing that "Britannia ruled the waves," Russell found it inconceivable that any nation, great or small, might force Great Britain to act against its will.

Quite simply, Russell failed to understand the nationalism that was growing stronger in both the North and the South. Southern, or Confederate, nationalism he perceived as a kind of local pride, and he marveled at Seward's claim that Union sentiment in the South remained strong despite the setback of secession. But then, Russell was traveling in areas of the South where pro-Confederate feeling was strongest, and he failed to see any real validity in Seward's assertion. R. K. Webb, the modern-day British historian, would offer another assessment: "Except for slavery, the issues of the war were incomprehensible to the British; they understood liberalism, in a constricted sort of way, but they never really grasped nationalism. Perhaps their own nationalism had been around so long that they could not recognize its analogue elsewhere."[2]

But if Russell erred in this thinking about reunification, he was more astute in perceiving quite another outcome of the war. Well before most Americans were aware of the fact, Russell acknowledged the growing power of the federal government. He foresaw correctly that the central government in Washington would play a much greater role in the political life of the nation during the postwar period.

When Russell's diary was published midway through the Civil War, its political and military heroes had yet to emerge. Nevertheless he rated the various Union and Confederate leaders, even in 1861, much as would historians of a later era. Russell, for his part, could not accept what many in Washington were saying about Lincoln. In Russell's view, Lincoln was neither backwoods politician nor buffoon. From their initial meeting, Russell held Lincoln in high esteem. Clearly he was disappointed when the Lincolns became less friendly

[2]R. K. Webb, *Modern England From the Eighteenth Century to the Present* (New York: 1968), pp. 314–315.

toward him following the publication of his account of Bull Run. About Jefferson Davis, well to the south in Montgomery, Russell could only write, "he did not impress me a as favourably as I expected." Perhaps Davis was more polished than Lincoln, conceded Russell, and more aware of political nuances; still the Confederate chief lacked the "shrewdness, humour, and natural sagacity" that Russell so admired in the Union president.

Russell was equally discerning in his estimation of the generals and their military capacity. He was unmoved by P. G. T. Beauregard, even though the latter went out of his way to take Russell into his confidence. A single meeting with John C. Frémont was sufficient to convince Russell of "the pathfinder's" incompetence. George B. McClellan, he agreed, might well have the ability to organize an army, but he was too cautious. Likely he would be ineffective in battle. As for Benjamin Butler, he served capably at Fort Monroe. But Russell had his reservations: he thought Butler a "prying man, revelling in the exercise of power."

Others caught Russell's attention more favorably. For Irwin McDowell he felt a degree of sympathy. It was through no fault of his own that McDowell had been forced into battle with an army so broadly inexperienced. Upon meeting William T. Sherman, shortly after the Battle of Bull Run, Russell sensed that he was speaking to a man with superior leadership qualities. Admiral Andrew H. Foote shared similar attributes. "It will be hard against the Confederates," adjudged Russell, "when they get such men at work on the rivers and coasts, for they seem to understand their business thoroughly." Russell never had the good fortune to make Robert E. Lee's acquaintance, yet he was aware that both Union and Confederate military officers regarded Lee as one of the most capable generals in the field on either side.

In his travels throughout the Union and the Confederacy, William Russell continued to enjoy a warm welcome by leading military and political figures everywhere. William Seward, Lincoln's secretary of state, hosted the Englishman at dinner on numerous occasions and once invited Russell to his home for an evening of whist with his family. Seward further arranged to have Russell invited to a formal dinner at the White House, where Russell was pleased to find himself seated at the president's table. Jefferson Davis proved equally affable when Russell arrived in the Confederate capital. Generals and fort commanders, whatever their loyalty, readily obliged Russell in discussing the military situation. On one occasion Russell even found himself interviewing McClellan as the general was preparing for bed.

In part it was the appeal of Russell's own cleverness and vitality that brought him friends. Thackeray knew that: he once remarked that he would pay Russell a guinea a day for the pleasure of his wit and "good company" at dinner.[3] Accordingly, Union and Confederate leaders sought the pleasure of his companionship, and more. As he might exert considerable influence back home, both with the British public and with government leaders, they solicited his favor. Russell was not only a voice in England's most powerful newspaper but had a reputation for molding public opinion. When the Aberdeen ministry fell in 1855, Russell and his reports on the cruelty of the British army in the Crimea were cited as the cause. Thus the Confederates, who were courting the Britons for recognition and material aid, considered it important that Russell see them in their best light and be appropriately charitable. The North had equal interest in Russell's reportage. On his whim, Confederate diplomacy might as easily be thwarted.

Russell pleaded immunity, refusing to sympathize openly with either the North or the South. He pledged only, in the *Times*, to record his impressions of the American people and their problems as he saw them. But increasingly his American public became more wary. With nationalistic feeling deepening on both sides, neither Unionists nor Confederates could appreciate Russell's statements when they were too critical or damaging. Southerners were the first to take exception. Mississippians, for example, smarted at Russell's feature on the antiquated practice of dueling in their state and their tendency to settle quarrels by violent means. Apparently it was the mayor of the city of Jackson who had confided all to Russell. Such was the uproar when Russell's article was reprinted in southern newspapers that the mayor was forced to issue a public statement denying that the conversation had ever taken place.

Southerners were especially sensitive to Russell's criticism of slavery, their own "peculiar institution." They knew all too well of the

---

[3]John Black Atkins, "Sir William Howard Russell," in *Dictionary of National Biography* (London: 1901–1959), supp. 1, p. 243.

reservations many Britons had on this issue. And slavery, they knew, was the chief obstacle in the way of their recognition by Britain. Russell's continued unfavorable references could hardly help. Mrs. Chesnut was saddened. "Russell abuses us in his letters from New Orleans," she chided. "People here care a great deal of what Russell says because he 'represents the Times,' and the London Times reflects the sentiment of the English people. How we do cling to the idea of an alliance with England and France."[4]

Others took offense as well. It was Russell's account of the Battle of Bull Run, July 21, 1861, that made him unpopular in the North. Particularly resentful were the troops stationed around Washington.[5] In the days preceding the battle, Union soldiers exhibited much bravado and savored the defeat they were sure to inflict on their enemy. Russell would tell it otherwise. These were not conquering heroes, said he, but rather a disorganized rabble deserting in the midst of battle, fleeing in chaos from imagined southern cavalry units, and altogether disregarding their commanders as they sought personal refuge. Russell made it clear that his impressions were gathered in the area bordering on the fighting and not on the battlefront itself. His departure from Washington had been delayed and Russell did not arrive at Manassas until Union recruits were in full retreat. Impeded by their flight, he simply was not able to push through to McDowell's headquarters. Had it been otherwise, he might have reconstructed the picture differently. Still Russell's account was no more critical than others run in northern newspapers. It is just that his letters on Bull Run were no longer timely when they finally appeared in the United States at the end of August. By then federal soldiers wished to forget their conduct during the battle.

Few northerners were comfortable with his report on Bull Run, and in the aftermath Russell had reason to fear for his safety. Daily he received messages threatening physical harm, and in one instance a soldier thrust a gun at him. Washingtonians who knew him, especially the women, snubbed Russell on the street. Privately, northern army officers had to agree among themselves that Russell's reports

[4]Chesnut, *Diary from Dixie,* p. 73.
[5]Russell wrote two separate letters on the Battle of Bull Run, the first on July 22, 1861, and the second four days later. See *New York Herald,* Aug. 20, 1861, p. 8, and Aug. 24, 1861, p. 2.

were no exaggeration. Others were unforgiving. To the common soldier and the American press, the sobriquet "Bull Run Russell" became synonymous with inaccurate reporting.

The charge was excessive. Generally Russell's letters to the *Times* were regarded as fair and without bias. Ruefully, Mrs. Chesnut conceded the point. "To me it is evident," she wrote in her diary, "that Russell, the Times correspondent, tries to tell the truth, unpalatable as it is to us. . . . His work is very well done for a stranger who comes and in his haste unpacks his three P's—pen, paper, and prejudices—and hurries through his work." This was quite an admission for Mrs. Chesnut, as she was inclined to label the Englishman both "snobbish" and a "licensed slanderer." To the north Horace Greeley, editor of the *New York Tribune,* inveighed against Russell's critics. "He has written nothing which justifies the offensive attacks which have been made upon him by so many of our journals," said the editor reprovingly. Charles Sumner wished to set the record straight. "Let me add," wrote Sumner in a missive to the Englishman, "that I have been astonished at the minuteness of criticism directed against your account of [Bull Run]. . . . If I can judge from what I hear, people are much less sensitive with regard to your errors of fact than with regard to the tone in which you wrote. They feel this is not friendly. . . . that you write down upon us."[6]

The American press was resentful in any case. As Union leaders had welcomed Russell into their inner circle, he gained access to information and innuendo to which others were not privy. He was scornful of American journalism besides. After tolerating Russell's presence a mere six months in the United States, James Gordon Bennett of the *New York Herald* could restrain himself no longer. "But what shall be done with Mr. Russell? He is a snob of the first water," charged Bennett, "and belongs to that class in Great Britain whose sentiments toward us [are unfriendly]. . . . Shall an alien writer, a proved ally of our enemies, whose pen drips gall and whose confidence assist treason, enjoy privileges of which our own citizens are, from necessity, forcibly deprived? Mr. Russell opposes our govern-

[6]Chesnut, *Diary from Dixie,* pp. 39, 124, 155; Woodward, *Mary Chesnut's Civil War,* pp. 50, 227; *New York Tribune,* Aug. 24, 1861; Sumner to Russell, Sept. 16, 1861, in Edward L. Pierce, *Memoir and Letters of Charles Sumner* (Boston: 1893), vol. 4, pp. 42–43.

ment; it should yield him no protection. He hates our country; let him leave it.'"[7]

Despite his capacity to offend his American readership, Russell remained on amicable terms with certain influential individuals in Washington. When he thought he should no longer visit Seward for fear that his presence might prove embarrassing, the secretary inquired about Russell's absence. McClellan gave every indication that he valued Russell's friendship and even sent officers from his own staff to escort Russell during troop reviews. Only Edwin M. Stanton seemed distinctly more reserved, a change that did not portend well for the reporter from the *Times.* It was, according to the Englishman, Stanton's very appointment as secretary of war in January, 1862 that would compromise Russell's own effectiveness as war correspondent.

As McClellan was preparing his strategy in early 1862 for the Peninsula Campaign, Russell determined to travel with the army itself. He was concerned for accuracy of detail in his reports. Apparently the general had no objection, for he issued a pass to Russell just before his own departure. But it was not so easy as that. Guards along the military route denied him passage, refusing to let Russell through without permission from Stanton. Repeatedly he appeared at the War Department, soliciting the necessary document. Just as surely, the secretary refused to see him. Finally, in desperation, Russell appealed to the president. Lincoln's answer was a revelation. It was not his report on Bull Run that was the problem, intimated Lincoln. Rather, it was the pro-Confederate attitude of the London *Times.* In short, Union officials had failed to secure the sympathy of England's most influential newspaper. No longer would they offer any special favors to its emissary.[8]

---

[7] *New York Herald,* Aug. 25, 1861.

[8] John Black Atkins, *The Life of Sir William Howard Russell: The First Special Correspondent* (London: 1911), Vol. 2, pp. 67, 119; see also Rupert Furneaux, *The First War Correspondent: William Howard Russell of the Times* (London: 1944). The statement on Lincoln and the government's attitude toward the *Times* does not appear in the diary. It was taken from Russell's correspondence and published in the Atkins biography. Russell was undoubtedly frustrated by his failure to secure permission to travel with McClellan's army; apparently his quest for a pass from Stanton took up so much time that he did not keep a daily record of his activities during 1862. Instead, he summarized these last weeks of his stay; in the diary he merely wrote that he had appealed to Lincoln and that the president rejected his request.

This turn of events devastated Russell. Unless he could be at the front, he would have no access to essential news sources. He hesitated only briefly. It would serve no purpose to move the base of his operations: were he to follow events from within the Confederacy, he could not hope that his letters would get through the Union blockade. With a sense of sadness and without even consulting his editor, Russell returned to England. His ability to report the Civil War had been curtailed by a decision he could not reverse.

Few people traveled as widely throughout the United States as did William Howard Russell in 1861, and no other journalist interviewed so many Union and Confederate leaders in so short a time. Although on assignment as a war correspondent, Russell reveals a broad, compelling interest in American society and culture as a whole. Clearly he revels in his description of urban Washington and back-country landscape, of dreary slave quarters and upper-class drawing rooms and restaurants in New Orleans. His portrayals of women during this time of crisis are just as vivid as his accounts of military stratagem and attack. To Russell, the efficiency of the Illinois Central Railroad was fully as intriguing as the Union fortifications at Fort Pickens. Few others would have had the audacity to question slaves in front of an overseer about their religious training, or to ask a slave-waiter outright in a public restaurant if his master treated him well. Russell allows himself more candor in his diary than in his letters to the *Times* because his diary is just that—a collection of rich, sometimes random impressions. Undoubtedly he made use of his journal as he composed his letters, but in writing for the press he was selective and condensed his material for better effect. He also deleted references that might cause pain or resentment.

This edition of the diary is based on the 1863 London imprint, which appeared about a year after Russell's departure from Washington. Several months later still, on the eve of the Battle of Gettysburg, a Boston publishing house began circulating an abridged edition of the diary. It was not well received in America. In that period Russell's popularity in the Union slackened even further: rumor had it that Russell was dabbling in unsavory investments all the while he was on tour in the United States. For the most part, historians of the Civil War era ignored *My Diary North and South* until 1954. In that year

Fletcher Pratt published a brief edition, limiting his purview to the military aspects of Russell's text. He deleted much of the descriptive material and many of Russell's observations about domestic life in nineteenth-century America. The Pratt edition has been out of print for more than a decade.

The London edition of 1863, in contrast, comprises two volumes and runs some nine hundred pages in all. At the very core of the relevant material are long digressions unrelated either to the sectional crisis or to American society in 1861. Many of these passages I have chosen not to include; mainly they deal with British-American relations, the diplomatic corps in Washington, and the American Revolution or the War of 1812. Russell even detailed, in his edition, a side trip to Niagara Falls and a hunting vacation in central Illinois.

The original edition contains sixty chapters, each one approximately twenty pages in length. Chapter divisions appear to be arbitrary: some begin midway through a day's entry, obliging the reader to seek his bearings in the previous chapter. Someone—Russell maybe, or perhaps his publisher—simply divided the diary into chapters of even length with little thought to organization. Once I began deleting extraneous material, chapter lengths and divisions became even more confusing. Some chapters were excessively long, others far too short. Ultimately I reorganized the diary by separating it into seven distinct sections, each covering a major portion of Russell's travels or activities.

William Russell probably wrote his diary with a view to its publication. There was precedent: already he had published his diaries from the Crimean War and from his travels in India. Later, his journal on the Franco-Prussian War would appear in print as well. Yet it seems unlikely that either Russell or his publisher edited to any extent the manuscript from his American junket. Capitalization and spelling in the London edition are inconsistent. Commonly capitalized words such as "Republican," "Democrat," and "Union" (when referring to the United States) appear in both upper and lower case; "dispatch" is just as often "despatch." At times he has his own rendition of place names and surnames. Thus "Fort Donelson" becomes "Donaldson," and Samuel Tilden's name appears as "Tylden." I have capitalized words where appropriate and corrected misspellings of names throughout the text. Also, I have removed the hyphens from such words as "to-day," "to-morrow," and "head-quarters"—a nineteenth-century usage that may appear somewhat archaic to the modern reader. In all other instances I have retained Russell's British spelling and his occasional use of foreign phrases.

Editors of diaries and letters often must generously annotate a text where the author has failed to identify individuals or make clear his intent. There are, in fact, some explanatory notes in this edition, but far fewer than one might expect. Russell's style is concise, and he is careful to identify most of the people he mentions. For reference, I have appended biographical notes on the better-known Americans, detailing their activities prior to the Civil War. In the nineteenth-century style, Russell uses only surnames preceded by an appropriate formal title. Again for clarity, I have inserted the given names of these individuals in brackets upon their first mention in the diary.

What follows, then, is Russell's diary. Despite his limited sojourn in the United States, he offered conclusions both thoughtful and astute on the American crisis. Like foreign travelers of any era, Russell saw Americans as they could not see themselves. His assessment was not always free from error or bias; still, his diary provides a fascinating description of Americans on the advent of their Civil War.

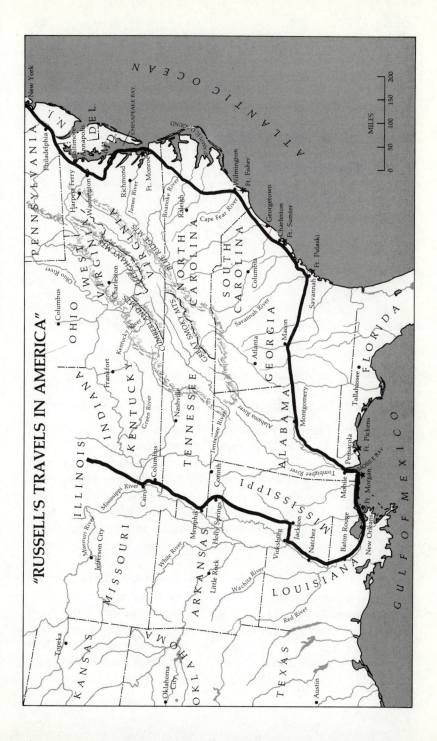

"RUSSELL'S TRAVELS IN AMERICA"

ATLANTIC OCEAN

MILES

0 50 100 150 200

New York

PENNSYLVANIA

N.J.

DEL.

Philadelphia

Baltimore

Annapolis

MD.

CHESAPEAKE BAY

PAMLICO SOUND

Harpers Ferry

Washington

Ft. Monroe

Richmond

VIRGINIA

James River

WEST VIRGINIA

Ohio River

Charleston

Roanok River

Raleigh

Cape Fear River

Wilmington

Ft. Fisher

Georgetown

Charleston

Ft. Sumter

Ft. Pulaski

Columbia

SOUTH CAROLINA

NORTH CAROLINA

BLUE RIDGE MTS.

ALLEGHANY MTS.

CUMBERLAND MTS.

GREAT SMOKY MTS.

Columbus

OHIO

INDIANA

ILLINOIS

KENTUCKY

Frankfort

Kentucky River

Green River

Nashville

TENNESSEE

Tennessee River

Savannah River

Atlanta

Macon

GEORGIA

Savannah

FLORIDA

Tallahassee

ALABAMA

Montgomery

Pensacola

Ft. Pickens

Alabama River

Tombigbee River

Mobile

MOBILE BAY

Ft. Morgan

GULF OF MEXICO

Missouri River

Jefferson City

MISSOURI

Cairo

Mississippi River

White River

Memphis

ARKANSAS

Little Rock

Wachita River

Holly Springs

Corinth

MISSISSIPPI

Jackson

Vicksburg

Natchez

Baton Rouge

New Orleans

LOUISIANA

Red River

Topeka

KANSAS

Oklahoma City

OKLAHOMA

TEXAS

Austin

Description of
the Diary

ONE: New York to Washington (March 3–April 11, 1861)

This portion of the diary focuses on Russell's ocean voyage and his month-long sojourn in New York City and Washington.

Trans-Atlantic crossing: During the boat trip Russell speaks with many American passengers, attempting to gauge their feelings toward secession and the coming crisis. Most of these people are civilians; there are, however, two army officers, both West Point graduates and both returning to the United States to join the southern cause. Russell notes the hostility between northerners and southerners.

New York: Russell describes his general impressions of the city, the racial and cultural makeup of the population, and attitudes of New Yorkers toward secession. He is surprised to learn that many New Yorkers are ambivalent about secession and a few even favor a division of the free and slave states. He meets and converses with a number of editors, including Henry J. Raymond of the *New York Times* and Horace Greeley of the *New York Tribune,* and with other noted Americans: George Bancroft, historian and diplomat, for example. Most of Russell's conversations are concerned with the secession crisis, the new Lincoln administration, or how the creation of a southern nation might affect New York City.

New York to Washington: Russell's description of the trip emphasizes the characteristics of the countryside, but he also records the habits and manners of other passengers.

Washington: Russell describes the city and the people in great detail. Of special interest to him is Willard's Hotel, where most of the guests are office seekers or men hoping to secure high military rank in the U.S. Army. He is astonished by the amount of prosouthern feeling in the city as well as the disdain of many people for the Lincoln government and the Republican party. Russell recounts interviews with political and military leaders, including Winfield Scott, William Seward, and Stephen A. Douglas. He gives much detail on his initial meeting with Lincoln and on a formal dinner at the White House. Russell confers with the three Confederate commissioners sent to Washington to work out peace terms, and he travels to the Washington Naval Yard and Mt. Vernon. The section ends with a comparison of the military and economic potential of the North and the South.

TWO: Baltimore to Savannah (April 12–May 2, 1861)

On April 12, 1861, the day Fort Sumter was fired upon, Russell leaves Washington for Baltimore to travel by boat into Virginia. While in Baltimore he records his impressions of the city and reactions of the people toward the firing on Sumter. From Norfolk to Charleston he travels by train, describing the countryside and general demeanor of both blacks and whites. Particularly interesting are his descriptions of manners, dress, and general indolence and the white people's overwhelming support for the Confederate cause. The farther he travels south, the more Russell becomes aware of increasing poverty and idleness among nonplanters.

Charleston: Here Russell visits forts Sumter and Moultrie and talks to southern leaders, including P. G. T. Beauregard, Governor Francis Pickens of South Carolina, and former U.S. senators James Chesnut and Louis Wigfall. During these conversations, such topics as military preparations, southern nationalism, and Confederate-British relations are discussed. Russell is somewhat taken aback by the large number of slaves in Charleston and efforts to control them. He questions whether blacks are as happy in slavery as Southerners claim; if they are, he asks, why is it necessary to have curfews and patrols? He also visits a rice plantation along the Peedee River in the northern part of South Carolina and makes extensive comments on rice culture and slavery in the region.

Savannah: Russell visits Fort Pulaski, assessing its defenses, and a sea island plantation. He finds Savannah one of the more charming cities in the lower South; upon leaving, he regrets that he has spent so little time there and has seen so few of its attractions.

THREE: The Gulf States (May 3–June 1, 1861)

Russell travels through Georgia and Alabama by train; he is taken aback by the poverty of the region and its people.

Montgomery: In the Confederate capital Russell discusses current affairs with most political and military leaders in the city, including Jefferson Davis. He also attends Varina Davis's reception at the Confederate White House and compares it with a similar reception given by Mary Lincoln in Washington. He records his impression of the city at large, of a slave auction, and of the prospects of the Confederate Nation.

Montgomery to Mobile: Russell is not impressed with Montgomery and leaves for Mobile after a brief stay, traveling by boat on the Alabama River. Aside from his usual comments about the people and their attitudes toward slavery and southern independence, Russell gives an excellent description of how cotton is loaded from the land onto boats by means of movable slides and conveyor belts that permit ships to remain away from the shoreline.

Mobile: The international flavor of this city has a strong effect on Russell, for he writes in detail about its hotels, restaurants, and entertainment as well as his attendance at a "Negro Dance." While in Mobile, he visits Fort Pickens and the Pensacola Navy Yard; here his favorable impression of the fortifications and Union naval officers leads him to predict that Fort Pickens will remain in Union hands throughout the war. He discusses the military situation and slavery with Braxton Bragg, Confederate general, and he interviews Judge

John Campbell, who has recently resigned from the U.S. Supreme Court. In addition, Russell has an opportunity to talk with Josiah Nott, the physician who carried on craniological research designed to prove that blacks were inferior to whites.

New Orleans: Russell writes rather long descriptions of the city, its racially mixed population, and attitudes toward the national crisis. He records his concern about efforts of local officials to impress foreign nationals into the Confederate army and his chagrin at conditions in New Orleans jails. While in the city, he is invited to John Slidell's home and, as a result, recounts typical evening activities in an upper-class southern home.

FOUR: Up the Mississippi (June 2–June 20, 1861)

This trip from New Orleans to Cairo, Illinois, lasts only eighteen days; still, it proves eventful in strengthening Russell's dislike of slavery. He is a guest at several sugar plantations where he observes the lethargy of the white population and the conditions of slave labor and slave quarters. He asks numerous questions of both whites and blacks and concludes that slavery is harsher on sugar plantations than in other parts of the South. Russell also visits Vicksburg, Natchez, and Jackson, Mississippi; he finds all of these cities to be less sophisticated than northern cities and other urban centers he has visited in the South. He is particularly taken with accounts of dueling, about which he hears in Jackson, and with the general lawlessness of Mississippians.

Memphis: Russell notes the frontier atmosphere of the city. Most of the visit is taken up with the touring of military installations. These trips give Russell his first real chance to observe Confederate soldiers, and he decides that southern enlisted men show greater ability to adapt to outdoor life than their northern counterparts and that they display a greater emotional involvement in the cause.

Russell concludes his journey by recording his impressions of the South and its prospects, really a summary of his feelings after traveling through the region. He admits his pronorthern bias because of his dislike of slavery and declares that defense of slavery on the part of Confederates is a chief cause for the war. He then predicts that slavery will disappear no matter what the outcome of the fighting.

FIVE: *Return to Washington (June 21–July 7, 1861)*

Illinois: Russell spends several days in Cairo, where he focuses on military preparations. He is not impressed with the city and finds it as backward as most other Mississippi River towns. From Cairo, Russell takes the Illinois Central Railroad to Chicago. Apparently he saw none of Chicago's political leaders; at least, he fails to mention any by name. He describes the city only briefly, saying that most accounts of its attractions are correct and he cannot improve on them.

New York: Russell meets many of the same people he talked with on his previous visit and is most startled by the change of attitude that has occurred during his absence. The ambivalence about secession and southern independence has vanished, and New Yorkers now reveal much more support for the Union cause. His stay in New York is brief because he wants to be in the national capital when the rumored battle (eventually Bull Run) occurs between the northern and southern armies.

Washington: Russell again makes contact with military leaders and develops a close friendship with General Irwin McDowell. He visits Congress and records his impressions of leading Republican legislators. He also describes Union soldiers, their aversion to authority, their fondness of liquor, and the disorganization within the Army of the Potomac. The section concludes with a discussion of how Americans celebrate the Fourth of July.

SIX: *Bull Run (July 8–July 26, 1861)*

Washington: To prepare himself to evaluate the capabilities of the Union army, Russell makes numerous trips to military installations around the capital; he pays particular attention to McDowell's headquarters at Arlington. Assured that a battle is not imminent, he visits Fort Monroe and writes about its defenses and General Benjamin Butler, its commander. Returning to Washington by way of Annapolis, Russell is stunned to find General McDowell at the railroad depot searching for military units that have not yet arrived in the city. Russell recounts his own efforts to purchase or hire a horse so that he can follow the Union army into battle.

Bull Run: Russell's account of the battle region is vivid and leaves a lasting impression. He notes reactions of Virginia civilians who live between Washington and Manassas, activities of Washingtonians who have come to witness the battle, and confusion among Union soldiers. During the battle Russell becomes separated from his own group and is forced to make his way back to Washington as best he can. This portion of the diary concludes with an account of the gloom that pervades Washington as a result of the Union defeat.

SEVEN: Aftermath (July 27, 1861–April 9, 1862)

Maryland: Because little is happening on the military front, Russell travels outside of Washington. He spends several days at the Carroll plantation in Maryland, where he finds slavery to be less harsh than it is farther south; he contrasts the peculiar institution in Maryland, South Carolina, and Louisiana. He also visits Harpers Ferry and attempts to visit the site of the Battle of Ball's Bluff but is turned back by the weather.

Washington: Russell makes a special effort to gain the confidence of General George B. McClellan who has been named commander of the Army of the Potomac. Russell is invited to accompany McClellan on his various troop reviews, and these trips give him the occasion to meet and assess the leadership potential of numerous Union military commanders. In the latter portion of the diary Russell reports the growing hostility that he is facing because of his letters to the London *Times* describing the Battle of Bull Run, and he recounts his difficulties in trying to obtain a pass to travel with McClellan's army. During his last months in the United States, Russell does not make day-to-day entries in the diary; he summarizes his deteriorating relationship with Secretary of War Edwin Stanton, his failure to impress the secretary, and the reasons for his eventual decision to leave the United States.

One

NEW YORK TO WASHINGTON

(March 3–April 11, 1861)

[March 3–March 15.] On the evening of 3rd March, 1861, I was transferred from the little steam-tender to the deck of the good steamship *Arabia,* and at nightfall we were breasting the long rolling waves of the Atlantic.

The Americans on board were, of course, the most interesting passengers to one like myself, who was going out to visit the great Republic under very peculiar circumstances. There was, first, Major [Robert S.] Garnett, a Virginian who was going back to his State to follow her fortunes. He was an officer of the Regular Army of the United States, who had served with distinction in Mexico; an accomplished, well-read man; reserved, and rather gloomy; full of the doctrine of States' Rights, and animated with a considerable feeling of contempt for the New Englanders, and with the strongest prejudices in favour of the institution of slavery. He laughed to scorn the doctrine that all men were born equal in the sense of all men having equal rights. Some were born to be slaves—others to follow useful mechanical arts—the rest were born to rule and to own their fellow-men. There was next a young Carolinian, who had left his post as attaché at St. Petersburg to return to his State: thus, in all probability, avoiding the inevitable supercession which awaited him at the hands of the new Government at Washington. He represented, in an intensified form, all the Virginian's opinions, and held that Mr. [John] Calhoun's interpretation of the Constitution was incontrovitibly right. There were difficulties in the way of State sovereignty, he confessed; but they were only in detail—the principle was unassailable.

To Mr. [Julian] Mitchell, South Carolina represented a power quite sufficient to meet all the Northern States in arms. "The North will attempt to blockade our coast," said he, "and in that case, the South must march to the attack by land, and will probably act in Virginia." "But if the North attempts to do more than institute a blockade?— for instance, if their fleet attack your seaport towns, and land men to occupy them?" "Oh, in that case, we are quite certain of beating them." Mr. Julian Mitchell was indignant at the idea of submitting to the rule of a "rail-splitter," and of such men as [William H.] Seward and [Simon] Cameron. "No gentleman could tolerate such a Government."

An American family from Nashville, consisting of a lady and her son and daughter, were warm advocates of "gentlemanly" government, and derided the Yankees with great bitterness. But they were by no means as ready to encounter the evils of war, or to break up the Union, as the South Carolinian or the Virginian; and in that respect they represented, I was told, the negative feelings of the Border States, which are disposed to a temporising, moderate course of action, most distasteful to the passionate seceders.

There were also two Louisiana sugar planters on board—one owning 500 slaves, the other rich in some thousands of acres; they seemed to care very little for the political aspects of the question of secession, and regarded it merely in reference to its bearing on the sugar crop and the security of slave property. Secession was regarded by them as a very extreme and violent measure, to which the State had resorted with reluctance; but it was obvious, at the same time, that, in event of a general secession of the slave States from the North, Louisiana could neither have maintained her connection with the North nor have stood in isolation from her sister States.

All these, and some others who were fellow passengers, might be termed [aristocratic] Americans. Garnett belonged to a very old family in Virginia. Mitchell came from a stock of several generations' residence in South Carolina. The Tennessee family were, in speech and thought, types of what Europeans consider true Americans to be. Now take the other side. First there was an exceedingly intelligent, well-informed young merchant of New York. Educated at a university in the Northern States, he had lived a good deal in England and was returning to his father from a course of bookkeeping in the house of his uncle's firm in Liverpool. Without being violent in tone, the young Northerner was very resolute in temper and determined to do all which lay in his power to prevent the "glorious Union" being broken up.

But did the other Americans who shared his views unreservedly approve of American institutions, and consider them faultless? By no means. The New Yorkers especially were eloquent on the evils of the suffrage, and of the license of the press in their own city; and displayed much irritation on the subject of naturalisation. The Irish were useful, in their way, making roads and working hard, for there were few Americans who condescended to manual labour; but it was absurd to give the Irish votes which they used to destroy the influence of native-born citizens.

Another young merchant, a college friend of the former, was just returning from a tour in Europe with his amiable sister. His father was the son of an Irish immigrant, but he did not at all differ from the other gentlemen of his city in the estimate in which he held the Irish element; and though he had no strong bias one way or other, he was quite resolved to support the abstraction called the Union, and its representative fact—the Federal Government. Thus the agriculturist and the trader—the grower of raw produce and the merchant who dealt in it—were at opposite sides of the question— wide apart as the Northern and Southern poles. They sat apart, ate apart, talked apart—two distinct nations, with intense antipathies on the part of the South, which was active and aggressive in all its demonstrations.

The Southerners have a [strong dislike of] the Irish. It appears that the Regular Army of the United States is mainly composed of Irish and Germans. In case of a conflict, which these gentlemen think inevitable, "low Irish mercenaries would," they say, "be pitted against the gentlemen of the South, and the best blood in the States would be spilled by fellows whose lives are worth nothing whatever." Poor Paddy is regarded as a mere working machine, fit, at best, to serve against Choctaws and Seminoles. His facility of reproduction has to compensate for the waste which is caused by the development in his unhappy head of the organs of combativeness and destructiveness. Certainly if the war is to be carried on by the United States Regulars, the Southern States will soon dispose of them, for they do not number 20,000 men, and their officers are not much in love with the new Government. But can it come to war? Mr. Mitchell assured I shall see some "pretty tall fighting."

The most vehement Northerners in the steamer are Germans, who are going to the States for the first time or returning there. They have become satisfied, no doubt, by long process of reasoning, that there is some anomaly in the condition of a country which calls itself the land of liberty, and is at the same time the potent palladium of serfdom and human chattelry. When they are not seasick, which is seldom, the Teutons rise up in all the might of their misery and dirt and, making spasmodic efforts to smoke, blurt out between the puffs, or in moody intervals, sundry remarks on American politics. "These are the swine," quoth Garnett, "who are swept out of German gutters as too foul for them, and who come over to the States and presume to control the fate and wishes of our people. In their own country they proved they were incapable of either earning a living or exercising the duties of citizenship; and they seek in our country a licence denied them in their own, and the means of living which they could not acquire anywhere else."

And for myself I may truly say this, that no man ever set foot on the soil of the United States with a stronger and sincerer desire to ascertain and to tell the truth as it appeared to him. I had no theories to uphold, no prejudices to subserve, no interests to advance, no instructions to fulfill; I was a free agent, bound to communicate to the powerful organ of public opinion I represented, my own daily impressions of the men, scenes, and actions around me, without fear, favour, or affection of or for anything but that which seemed to me to be the truth.

It was on the morning of the fourteenth day that the shores of

New York loomed through the drift of a cold wintry sea, leaden-gray and comfortless, and in a little time more of the coast, covered with snow, rose in sight. Towards the afternoon the sun came out and brightened the waters and the sails of the pretty trim schooners and coasters which were dancing around us. How different the graceful, tautly rigged, clean, white-sailed vessels from the round-stearned, lumpish billyboys and nondescripts of the eastern coast of our isle! Presently there came bowling down toward us a lively little schooner-yacht, very like the once famed *America,* [1] brightly painted in green, sails dazzling white, lofty pounderous masts, no tops. As she came nearer, we saw she was crowded with men in chimney pot black hats and coats, and the like—perhaps a party of citizens on pleasure, cold as the day was. Nothing of the kind. The craft was our pilot boat, and the hats and coats belonged to the hardy mariners who act as guides to the port of New York. Their boat was lowered and was soon under our mainchains; and a chimney pot hat having duly come over the side, delivered a mass of newspapers to the captain which were distributed among the eager passengers.

[March 16.] The entrance to New York, as it was seen by us on 16th March, is not remarkable for beauty or picturesque scenery, and I incurred the ire of several passengers because I could not consistently say it was very pretty. It was difficult to distinguish through the snow the villas and country houses, which are said to be so charming in summer. But beyond these rose a forest of masts close by a low shore of brick houses and blue roofs, above the level of which again spires of churches and domes and cupolas announced a great city. On our left, at the narrowest part of the entrance, there was a very powerful casemated work of fine close stone, built close to the water's edge, and armed on all the faces. On the right hand, crossing its fire with that of the batteries and works on our left, there was another regular stone fort with fortified enceinte, and higher up the channel, as it widens to the city, I could make out a smaller fort on the water's edge. The situation of the city renders it susceptible of powerful defence from the sea-side, and even now it would be hazardous to run the gauntlet of the batteries unless in powerful

---

[1]"The once famed *America*" refers to an American schooner-yacht that defeated fourteen British vessels in a race around the Isle of Wight in 1852.

iron-clad ships favoured by wind and tide, which could hold the place at their mercy. Against a wooden fleet New York is now all but secure, save under exceptional circumstances in favour of the assailants.

At present I find public attention is concentrated on the two Federal forts, Pickens and Sumter, called after two officers of the revolutionary armies in the old war. As [Florida][2] and South Carolina have gone out, they now demand the possession of these forts, as of the soil of their several states and attached to their sovereignty. On the other hand, the Government of Mr. Lincoln considers it has no right to give up anything belonging to the Federal Government, but evidently desires to temporize and evade any decision which might precipitate an attack on the forts by the batteries and forces prepared to act against them. There is not sufficient garrison in either for an adequate defence, and the difficulty of procuring supplies is very great. Under the circumstances every one is asking what the Government is going to do? The Southern people have declared they will resist any attempt to supply or reinforce the garrisons and in Charleston, at least, have shown they mean to keep their word. It is a very strange situation. The Federal Government, afraid to speak and unable to act, is leaving its soldiers to do as they please. In some instances, officers of rank, such as General [David] Twiggs, have surrendered everything to the State authorities,[3] and the teachery and secession of many officers in the army and navy no doubt paralyze and intimidate the civilians at the head of affairs.

Sunday, 17th March.   The first thing I saw this morning was a procession of men, forty or fifty perhaps, trudging through the cold and slush two and two: they wore shamrocks in their hats and green silk sashes emblazoned with crownless harp upon their coats, but it needed not these insignia to tell they were Irishmen, and their solemn mien indicated that they were going to mass. The aspect of the street was irregular, and its abnormal look was increased by the air of the passers-by, who at that hour were domestics—very finely dressed

[2]The 1863 London imprint reads "Alabama."

[3]Twiggs, commander of the Department of Texas, voluntarily surrendered his forces and supplies to Ben McCulloch and the Texas Rangers in February 1861. Dismissed from the United States Army the following month, Twiggs joined the Confederate army and commanded the Louisiana District until his death in 1862.

Negroes, Irish, or German. The coloured ladies made most elaborate toilettes, and as they held up their broad crinolines over the mud looked not unlike double-stemmed mushrooms.

No liveried servants are to be seen about the streets, the doorways, or the area-steps. Black faces in gaudy caps, or an unmistakable "Biddy" in crinoline are their substitutes. The chief charm of [Fifth Avenue] was the living ornature which moved up and down the [pavement]. The costumes of Paris, adapted to the severity of this wintry weather, were draped round pretty, graceful figures which were *svelte* and well poised. Today I am quite satisfied that if the American women are deficient in stature and in that which makes us say, "There is a fine woman," they are easy, well formed, and full of grace and prettiness. Admitting a certain pallor, the face is not only pretty, but sometimes of extraordinary beauty, the features fine, delicate, well defined. Ruby lips, indeed, are seldom to be seen, but now and then the flashing of snowy-white evenly set ivory teeth dispels the delusion that the Americans are—though the excellence of their dentists be granted—naturally ill provided with what they take so much pains, by eating bon-bons and confectionery, to deprive of their purity and colour.

I was introduced to many persons today and was only once or twice asked how I liked New York; perhaps I anticipated the question by expressing my high opinion of the Fifth Avenue. Those to whom I spoke had generally something to say in reference to the troubled condition of the country, but it was principally of a self-complacent nature. "I suppose, sir, you are rather surprised, coming from Europe, to find us so quiet here in New York; we are a peculiar people, and you don't understand us in Europe."

In the afternoon I called on Mr. [George] Bancroft, formerly Minister to England, whose work on America must be rather rudely interrupted by this crisis.[4] Anything with an "ex" to it in America is of little weight—ex-presidents are nobodies, though they have had the advantage, during their four years' tenure of office, of being

[4]It is uncertain what George Bancroft said to Russell about the progress of his multivolume history of the United States; however, volume nine of the twelve-volume series was published at the end of the Civil War. At this point in the war, Bancroft did not accept Lincoln's argument about the illegality of secession; but as the fighting continued, he changed his opinion and occasionally counseled the President on matters of historical precedent.

prayed for as long as they live. So it is of ex—ministers, whom nobody prays for at all. Mr. Bancroft conversed for some time on the aspect of affairs, but he appeared to be unable to arrive at any settled conclusion except that the Republic, though in danger, was the most stable and beneficial form of government in the world, and that as a Government it has no power to coerce the people of the South or to save itself from the danger. I was indeed astonished to hear from him and others so much philosophical abstract reasoning as to the right of seceding, or, what is next to it, the want of any power in the Government to prevent it.

Returning home in order to dress for dinner, I got into a street-railway car, a long low omnibus drawn by horses over a *strada ferrata* [railroad] in the middle of the street. It was filled with people of all classes, and at every crossing some one or other rang the bell and the driver stopped to let out or to take in passengers, whereby the unoffending traveller became possessed of much snow-croppings and mud on boots and clothing. I found that by far a greater inconvenience caused by these street-railways was the destruction of all comfort or rapidity in ordinary carriages.

I dined with a New York banker, who gave such a dinner as bankers generally give all over the world. He is a man still young, very kindly, hospitable, well-informed, with a most charming household—an American by theory, an Englishman in instincts and tastes—educated in Europe, and sprung from British stock. Considering the enormous interests he has at stake, I was astonished to perceive how calmly he spoke of the impending troubles. His friends, all men of position in New York society, had the same dilettante tone and were as little anxious for the future, or excited by the present, as a party of *savants* chronicling the movements of a "magnetic storm."

On going back to the hotel, I met several gentlemen, one of whom said, "the majority of the people of New York, and all the respectable people, were disgusted at the election of such a fellow as Lincoln to be President and would back the Southern States, if it came to a split."

March 19.   In the afternoon a number of gentlemen called and made the kindest offers of service; letters of introduction to all parts of the States; facilities of every description—all tendered with frankness.

I was astonished to find little sympathy and no respect for the newly installed Government. They were regarded as obscure or undistinguished men. I alluded to the circumstance that one of the journals continued to speak of "The President" in the most contemptuous manner and to designate him as the great "Rail-Splitter." "Oh, yes," said the gentleman with whom I was conversing, "that must strike you as a strange way of mentioning the Chief Magistrate of our great Republic, but the fact is, no one minds what the man writes of any one, his game is to abuse every respectable man in the country in order to take his revenge on them for his social exclusion, and at the same time to please the ignorant masses who delight in vituperation and scandal."

In the evening, dining again with my friend the banker, I met several men of position, acquirements, and natural sagacity. Among the guests were the Hon. Horatio Seymour, a former Governor of the State of New York; Mr. [Samuel J.] Tilden, an astute lawyer; and Mr. Bancroft; the result left on my mind by their conversation and arguments was that, according to the Constitution, the Government could not employ force to prevent secession, or to compel States which had seceded by the will of the people to acknowledge the Federal power. In fact, according to them, the Federal Government was the mere machine put forward by a society of Sovereign States, as a common instrument for certain ministerial acts, more particularly those which affected the external relations of the Confederation. I do not think that any of the guests sought to turn the channel of talk upon politics, but the occasion offered itself to Mr. Horatio Seymour to give me his views of the Constitution of the United States, and by degrees the theme spread over the table. I had bought the "Constitution" for three cents in Broadway in the forenoon and had read it carefully, but I could not find that it was self-expounding; it referred itself to the Supreme Court, but what was to support the Supreme Court in a contest with armed power, either of the Government or people? There was not a man who maintained the Government had any power to coerce the people of a State, or to force a State to remain in the Union, or under the action of the Federal Government; in other words, the symbol of power at Washington is not at all analogous to that which represents an established Government in other countries. Although they admitted the Southern leaders had meditated "the

treason against the Union" years ago, they could not bring themselves to allow their old opponents, the Republicans now in power,
to dispose of the armed force of the Union against their brother
Democrats in the Southern States.[5]

Mr. Seymour is a man of compromise, but his views go farther
than those which were entertained by his party ten years ago. Although secession would produce revolution, it was, nevertheless, "a
right," founded on abstract principles, which could scarcely be abro-
gated consistently with due regard to the original compact. One of
the company made a remark which was true enough, I dare say. We
were talking of the difficulty of relieving Fort Sumter—an infallible
topic just now. "If the British or any foreign power were threatening
the fort," said he, "our Government would find means of relieving
it fast enough." In fact, the Federal Government is groping in the
dark; and whilst its friends are telling it to advance boldly, there are
myriad voices shrieking out of its ears, "If you put out a foot you are
lost." There is neither army or navy available, and the ministers have
no machinery of rewards, and means of intrigue, or modes of gaining
adherents known to European administrations. The Democrats behold with silent satisfaction the troubles into which the Republican
triumph has plunged the country, and are not at all disposed to
extricate them. The most notable way of impeding their efforts is to
knock them down with the "Constitution" every time they rise to the
surface and begin to swim out.

New York society, however, is easy in its mind just now, and the
upper world of millionaire merchants, bankers, contractors, and great
traders are glad that the vulgar Republicans are suffering for their
success. Not a man there but resented the influence given by universal suffrage to the mob of the city, and complained of the intolerable
effects of their ascendancy—of the corruption of the municipal bodies, the venality of electors and elected, and the abuse, waste, and
profligate outlay of the public funds. Of these there were many
illustrations given to me, garnished with historiettes of some of the

[5]Up to this time Russell's contacts in New York City seem to have been mainly
financiers and Democrats. Before the firing on Fort Sumter, both groups in the city
advocated compromise or expressed strong pro-Confederate sympathy; bankers feared
the loss of their southern investments in case of war; Democrats advocated states'
rights and some even accepted the idea of peaceful separation.

civil dignitaries, and of their coadjustors in the press; but it did not require proof that universal suffrage in a city of which perhaps three-fourths of the voters were born abroad or of foreign parents, and of whom many were the scum swept off the seethings of European populations, must work most injuriously on property and capital. I confess it is to be much wondered at that the consequences are not more evil; but no doubt the time is coming when the mischief can no longer be borne and a social reform and revolution must be inevitable.

March 20th.   The papers are still full of Sumter and Pickens. The reports that they are or are not to be relieved are stated and contradicted in each paper without any regard to individual consistency.

In the afternoon went down Broadway, which was crowded, notwithstanding the piles of blackened snow by the kerbstones, and the sloughs of mud, and half frozen pools at the crossings. Visited several large stores or shops—some rival the best establishments in Paris or London in richness and in value and far exceed them in size and splendour of exterior. New York has certainly all the air of a "nouveau riche." There is about it an utter absence of any appearance of a grandfather—one does not see even such evidences of eccentric taste as are afforded in Paris and London. There is no curiosity shop, and such efforts as are made to supply the deficiency reveal an enormous amount of ignorance or of bad taste. The new arts, however, flourish; the plague of photography has spread through all the corners of the city, and the shopwindows glare with flagrant displays of the most tawdry art. In some of the large booksellers' shops—Appleton's for example—are striking proofs of the activity of the American press, if not the vigour and originality of the American intellect. I passed down long rows of shelves laden with the works of European authors, for the most part, oh shame! stolen and translated into American type without the smallest compunction or scruple, and without the least intention of ever yielding the most pitiful deodand [compensation] to the authors. Mr. [William] Appleton sells no less than one million and a half of Webster's spelling books a year; his tables are covered with a flood of pamphlets, some for, others against coercion; some for, others opposed to slavery—but when I asked for a single solid, substantial work on the present difficulty, I was told there was not one published worth a cent.

I dined with a littérateur well known in England to many people a year or two ago—sprightly, loquacious, and well-informed, if neither witty nor profound—now a Southern man with Southern proclivities, as Americans say; once a Southern man with such strong anti-slavery convictions, that his expression of them in an English quarterly had secured him the hostility of his own people—one of the emanations of American literary life for which their own country finds no fitting receiver. As the best proof of his sincerity, he has just now abandoned his connection with one of the New York papers on the Republican side, because he believed that the course of the journal was dictated by anti-Southern fanaticism. He is, in fact, persuaded that there will be a civil war and that the South will have much of the right on its side in the contest.[6] At his rooms were Dr. [William] Gwin, a California ex-senator, Mr. [Francis C.] Barlow, and several of the leading men of a certain clique in New York. The Americans complain, or assert, that we do not understand them, and I confess the reproach, or statement, was felt to be well founded by myself at all events when I heard it declared and admitted that "if Mons. [August] Belmont had not gone to the Charleston Convention, the present crisis would never have occurred."[7]

[6]Russell may have been referring to Hinton Rowan Helper, author of *The Impending Crisis of the South: How to Meet It* (1857). After publishing his book, Helper moved to New York City and cooperated with Horace Greeley on an abridgment, which the Republican party then used as political propaganda. Following the failure of a lecture series to publicize his views, Helper accepted the consulship at Buenos Aires from the Lincoln administration. Helper had lived in California during the early 1850s and was likely acquainted with William Gwin. Francis C. Barlow was a member of the *New York Tribune* editorial staff in 1861. I have been unable to locate any article by Helper in "an English quarterly." Russell perhaps confused an actual essay with an extensive review of the *Impending Crisis* published in the (London) *Westminster Review*, vol. 75 (1860–61).

[7]August Belmont of New York strongly advocated the nomination of Stephen A. Douglas in 1860. A delegate to the Democratic national convention at Charleston, Belmont used his influence on the New York delegation to support Douglas's popular sovereignty platform. When the convention adopted the platform, six southern states withdrew, causing a split in the Democratic party. Belmont later raised funds for Douglas's campaign and served as chairman of the Democratic National Committee.

March 22nd. I paid a visit to Mr. Horace Greeley and had a long conversation with him. He expressed great pleasure at the intelligence that I was going to visit the Southern States. "Be sure you examine the slave-pens. *They* will be afraid to refuse you, and you can tell the truth." As the capital and the South form the chief attractions at present, I am preparing to escape from "the divine calm" and the snows of New York. I was recommended to visit many places before I left New York, principally hospitals and prisons. Sing-Sing, the state penitentiary, is "claimed," as the Americans say, to be the first "institution" of its kind in the world. Time presses, however, and Sing-Sing is a long way off.

March 23rd. It is announced positively that the authorities in Pensacola and Charleston have refused to allow any further supplies to be sent to Fort Pickens, the United States fleet in the Gulf, and to Fort Sumter. Everywhere the Southern leaders are forcing on a solution with decision and energy, whilst the Government appears to be helplessly drifting with the current of events, having neither bow nor stern, neither keel nor deck, neither rudder, compass, sails, or steam. Mr. Seward has declined to receive or hold any intercourse with the three gentlemen called Southern Commissioners, who repaired to Washington accredited by the Government and Congress of the seceding States now sitting at Montgomery, so that there is no channel of mediation or means of adjustment left open. I hear, indeed, that Government is secretly preparing what force it can to strengthen the garrison at Pickens and to reinforce Sumter at any hazard; but that its want of men, ships, and money compels it to temporise, lest the Southern authorities should forestall their designs by a vigorous attack on the enfeebled forts.

There is, in reality, very little done by New York to support or encourage the Government in any decided policy, and the journals are more engaged now in abusing each other, and in small party aggressive warfare, than in the performance of the duties of a patriotic press, whose mission at such a time is beyond all question the resignation of little differences for the sake of the whole country and an entire devotion to its safety, honour, and integrity. But the New York people must have their intellectual drams every morning, and it matters little what the course of Government may be, so long as the aristocratic Democrat can be amused by ridicule of the Great Rail Splitter, or a vivid portraiture of Mr. Horace Greeley's old coat, hat, breeches, and umbrella. The coarsest personalities are read with gusto, and attacks of a kind which would not have been admitted into the *Age* or *Satirist* in their worst days, form the staple leading articles of one or two of the most largely circulated journals in the city. "Slang" in its worst Americanised form is freely used in [sensational] headings and leaders, and a class of advertisements which are not allowed to appear in respectable English papers have possession of columns of the principal newspapers, few, indeed, excluding them.

March 25th. I had an invitation to meet several members of the New York press association at breakfast. Among the company were —Mr. Bayard Taylor, with whose extensive notes of travel his countrymen are familiar; Mr. [Henry J.] Raymond, of the *New York Times* (formerly Lieutenant-Governor of the State); Mr. [Frederick Law] Olmsted, the indefatigable, able, and earnest writer, whom to describe simply as an abolitionist would be to confound with ignorant if zealous, unphilosophical, and impracticable men; Mr. [Charles A.] Dana, of the *Tribune;* Mr. [William H.] Hurlbert, of the *Times;* the editor of the *Courier des Etats Unis;* Mr. [Charles L.] Young, of the *Albion,* which is the only English journal published in the States; and others. There was a good deal of pleasant conversation, though every one differed with his neighbour, as a matter of course, as soon as he touched on politics. There was talk of secession and Sumter, the press, politicians, New York life, and so on. The first topic occupied a larger place than it was entitled to because in all likelihood the sporting editor of one of the papers who was present expressed, perhaps, some justifiable feeling in reference to the refusal of the belt to the American. It would be strange to see the great tendency of Americans to institute comparisons with ancient and recognised standards, if it were not that they are adopting the natural mode of judging of their own capabilities. The nation is like a growing lad who is constantly testing his powers in competition with his elders. He is in his youth and nonage, and he is calling down the lanes and alleys to all comers to look at his muscle, or run against or to fight him. It is a sign of youth, not a proof of weakness, though it does offend the old hands and vex the veterans.

One of the gentlemen present said that England might dispute the right of the United States Government to blockade the ports of her own States, to which she was entitled to access under treaty, and might urge that such a blockade was not justifiable; but then, it was argued, that the President could open and shut ports as he pleased; and that he might close the Southern ports by a proclamation in the nature of an Order in Council. It was taken for granted that Great Britain would only act on sordid motives, but that the well-known affection of France for the United States is to check the selfishness of her rival and prevent a speedy recognition.

At six o'clock, P.M., I left the Clarendon and was conveyed over the roughest and most execrable pavements through several miles of unsympathetic, gloomy, dirty streets, and crowded thoroughfares, over jaw-wrenching street-railway tracks, to a large wooden shed covered with inscriptions respecting routes and destinations. I was directed to struggle for my ticket in another little wooden box, from which I presently received the necessary document full of the dreadful warnings and conditions, which railway companies inflict on the public in all free countries. I just got [on] in time to stumble into a long box on wheels, with a double row of uncomfortable seats with a passage down the middle, where I found a place beside Mr. [Henry S.] Sanford, the newly appointed United States Minister to Belgium, who was kind enough to take me under his charge to Washington.

The night was closing in very fast as the train started, but such glimpses as I had of the continuous line of pretty-looking villages of wooden houses, two stories high, painted white, each with its Corinthian portico, gave a most favourable impression of the comfort and prosperity of the people. The rail passed through the main street of most of these hamlets and villages and the bell of the engine was tolled to warn the inhabitants, who drew up to the sidewalks and let us go by. Soon the white houses faded away into faint blurred marks on the black ground of the landscape or twinkled with starlike lights, and there was nothing more to see. The passengers were crowded as close as they could pack, and as there was an immense iron stove in the centre of the car, the heat and stuffiness became most trying, although I have been undergoing the ordeal of the stove-heated New York houses for nearly a week. Once a minute, at least, the door at either end of the carriage was opened, and then closed with a sharp crashing noise that jarred the nerves, and effectually prevented sleep. It generally was done by a man whose sole object seemed to be to walk up the centre of the carriage in order to go out of the opposite door—occasionally it was the work of the newspaper boy with a sheaf of journals and trashy illustrated papers under his arm. Now and then it was the conductor; but the periodical visitor was a young gentleman with a chain and rings, who bore a tray before him and solicited orders for "gum drops," and "lemon drops," which, with tobacco, apples, and cakes, were consumed in great quantities by the passengers.

At ten o'clock, P.M., we crossed the river by a ferry boat to Philadelphia and drove through the streets, stopping for supper a few moments at the La Pierre Hotel. To judge from the vast extent of the streets, of small, low, yet snug-looking houses through which we passed, Philadelphia must contain in comfort the largest number of small householders of any city in the world. At the other terminus of the rail, to which we drove in a carriage, we procured for a small sum, a dollar I think, berths in a sleeping car, an American institution of considerable merit. Unfortunately a party of prize fighters had a mind to make themselves comfortable and the result was anything but conducive to sleep. They had plenty of whiskey, and were full of song and fight, nor was it possible to escape their urgent solicitations "to take a drink," by feigning the soundest sleep. One of these, a big man, with a broken nose, a mellow eye, and a very large display of rings, jewels, chains, and pins, was in very high spirits, and informed us he was "Going to Washington to get a foreign mission from Bill Seward." Another told us he was "Going to the bosom of Uncle Abe" (meaning the President)—"that he knew him well in Kentucky years ago, and a high-toned gentleman he was." Any attempts to persuade them to retire to rest made by the conductors were treated with sovereign contempt, but at last whiskey asserted its supremacy, and having established the point that they "would not sleep unless they . . . pleased," they slept and snored.

[March 26th.] At 6 A.M. we were roused up by the arrival of the train at Washington, having crossed great rivers and traversed cities without knowing it during the night. I looked out and saw a vast mass of white marble towering above us on the left, stretching out in colonnaded porticoes, and long flanks of windowed masonry, and surmounted by an unfinished cupola, from which scaffold and cranes raised their black arms. This was the Capitol. To the right was a cleared space of mud, sand, and fields studded with wooden sheds and huts, beyond which, again, could be seen rudimentary streets of small red brick houses, and some church spires above them.

Emerging from the station, we found a vociferous crowd of blacks, who were the hackney-coachmen of the place; but Mr. Sanford had his carriage in waiting and drove me straight to Willard's Hotel, where he consigned me to the landlord at the bar. Our route lay through Pennsylvania Avenue—a street of much breadth and length, lined with ailanthus trees, each in a whitewashed wooden sentry box, and by most irregularly built houses in all kinds of material, from deal plank to marble—of all heights and every sort of trade. Few shopwindows were open and the principal population consisted of blacks, who were moving about on domestic affairs. At one end of the long vista there is the Capitol; and at the other, the Treasury building—a fine block in marble, with the usual American classical colonnades.

Close to these rises the great pile of Willard's Hotel, now occupied by applicants for office and by the members of the newly assembled Congress. It is a quadrangular mass of rooms, six stories high, and some hundred yards square; and it probably contains at this moment more scheming, plotting, planning heads, more aching and joyful hearts, than any building of the same size ever held in the world. I was ushered into a bedroom which had just been vacated by some candidate—whether he succeeded or not I cannot tell, but if his testimonials spoke truth, he ought to have been selected at once for the highest office. The room was littered with printed copies of letters testifying that J. Smith, of Hartford, Conn., was about the ablest, honestest, cleverest, and best man the writers ever knew. Up and down the long passages doors were opening and shutting for men with papers bulging out of their pockets, who hurried as if for their life in and out, and the building almost shook with the tread of the candidature, which did not always in its present aspect justify the correctness of the original appellation.

It was a remarkable sight and difficult to understand unless seen. From California, Texas, from the Indian Reserves, and the Mormon

Territory, from Nebraska, as from the remotest borders of Minnesota, from every portion of the vast territories of the Union, except from the seceded States, the triumphant Republicans had winged their way to the prey.

There were crowds in the hall through which one could scarce make his way—the writing-room was crowded, and the rustle of pens rose to a little breeze—the smoking-room, the bar, the barbers, the reception room, the ladies' drawing room—all were crowded. At present not less than 2,500 people dine in the public room every day. On the kitchen floor there is a vast apartment, a hall without carpets or any furniture but plain chairs and tables, which are ranged in close rows, at which flocks of people are feeding, or discoursing, or from which they are flying away. The servants never cease shoving the chairs to and fro with a harsh screeching noise over the floor, so that one can scarce hear his neighbour speak. The tumult, the miscellaneous nature of the company, the heated, muggy rooms, not to speak of the great abominableness of the passages and halls, despite a most liberal provision of spittoons, conduce to render these institutions by no means agreeable to a European. Late in the day I succeeded in obtaining a sitting room with a small bedroom attached, which made me somewhat more independent and comfortable—but you must pay highly for any departure from the routine life of the natives. Ladies enjoy a handsome drawing room, with piano, sofas, and easy chairs, all to themselves.

I dined at Mr. Sanford's, where I was introduced to Mr. Seward, Secretary of State; Mr. Truman Smith, an ex-senator much respected among the Republican party; Mr. [Henry B.] Anthony, a senator of the United States; a journalist, a very intelligent looking man, with an Isrealitish cast of face; Colonel [John W.] Foster of the Illinois Railway; and one or two more gentlemen. Mr. Seward is a slight, middle-sized man of feeble build, with the stoop contracted from sedentary habits and application to the desk, and has a peculiar attitude when seated, which immediately attracts attention. A well-formed and large head is placed on a long, slender neck, and projects over the chest in an argumentative kind of way, as if the keen eyes were seeking for an adversary; the mouth is remarkably flexible, large but well formed, the nose prominent and aquiline, the eyes secret, but penetrating, and lively with humour of some kind twinkling

about them; the brow bold and broad, but not remarkably elevated;
the white hair silvery and fine—a subtle, quick man, rejoicing in
power, given to perorate and to oracular utterances, fond of badinage,
bursting with the importance of state mysteries, and with the dignity
of directing foreign policy of the greatest country—as all Americans
think—in the world. After dinner he told some stories of the pressure
on the President for place, which very much amused the guests who
knew the men, and talked freely and pleasantly of many things—
stating, however, few facts positively. In reference to an assertion in
a New York paper that orders had been given to evacuate Sumter,
"That," he said, "is a plain lie—no such orders have been given. We
will give up nothing we have—abandon nothing that has been en-
trusted to us. If people would only read these statements by the light
of the President's inaugural, they would not be deceived." He wanted
no extra session of Congress. "History tells us that kings who call
extra parliaments lose their heads," and he informed the company he
had impressed the President with his historical parallels.

All through this conversation his tone was that of a man very
sanguine and with a supreme contempt for those who thought there
was anything serious in secession. "Why," said he, "I myself, my
brothers, and sisters, have been all secessionists—we seceded from
home when we were young, but we all went back to it sooner or later.
These States will all come back in the same way." I doubt if he was
ever in the South; but he affirmed that the state of living and of
society there was something like that in the State of New York sixty
or seventy years ago. In the North all was life, enterprise, industry,
mechanical skill. In the South there was dependence on black labour,
and an idle extravagance which was mistaken for elegant luxury—
tumble-down old hackney-coaches, such as had not been seen north
of the Potomac for half a century, harness never cleaned, ungroomed
horses, bad cookery, imperfect education. No parallel could be drawn
between them and the Northern States at all.

The company addressed him as "Governor," which led to Mr.
Seward's mentioning that when he was in England he was induced
to put his name down with that prefix in a hotel book, and caused
a discussion among the waiters as to whether he was the "Governor"
of a prison or of a public company. From what he said, however, I
infer that he was satisfied with the reception he had met in London.

William H. Seward
(Library of Congress)

Like most Americans who can afford it, he has been up the Nile. The weird old stream has a great fascination for the people of the Mississippi—as far at least as the first cataract.

March 27th. This morning, after breakfast, Mr. Sanford called, according to promise, and took me to the State Department. In a moderately sized, but very comfortable, apartment, surrounded with book shelves and ornamented with a few engravings, we found the Secretary of State seated at his table and enjoying a cigar; he received me with great courtesy and kindness, and after a time said he would take occasion to present me to the President, who was to give audience that day to the minister of the new kingdom of Italy, who had hitherto only represented the kingdom of Sardinia.

I have already described Mr. Seward's personal appearance; his son, to whom he introduced me, is the Assistant Secretary of State, and is editor or proprietor of a journal in the State of New York, which has a reputation for ability and fairness. Mr. Frederick Seward is a slight, delicate-looking man, with a high forehead, thoughtful brow, dark eyes, and amiable expression; his manner is very placid and modest and, if not reserved, he is by no means loquacious. As we were speaking, a carriage drove up to the door, and Mr. Seward exclaimed to his father, with something like dismay in his voice, "Here comes the Chevalier in full uniform!"—and in a few seconds in effect the Chevalier [Giuseppe] Bertinatti made his appearance in cocked hat, white gloves, diplomatic suit of blue and silver lace, sword, sash, and riband of the Cross of Savoy. I thought there was a quiet smile on Mr. Seward's face as he saw his brilliant companion, who contrasted so strongly with the more than republican simplicity of his own attire. "Fred, do you take Mr. Russell round to the President's, whilst I go with the Chevalier. We will meet at the White House." We accordingly set out through a private door leading to the grounds and within a few seconds entered the hall of the moderate mansion, [the] White House, which has very much the air of a portion of a bank or public office, being provided with glass doors and plain heavy chairs and forms. Passing through one of the doors on the left, we entered a handsome spacious room, richly and rather gorgeously furnished, and rejoicing in a kind of *demi-jour* [half-light], which gave increased effect to the gilt chairs and ormolu ornaments. Mr. Seward and the Chevalier stood in the centre of the room, whilst his son and I remained a little on one side: "For," said Mr. Seward, "you are not supposed to be here."

Soon afterwards there entered, with a shambling, loose, irregular, almost unsteady gait, a tall, lank, lean man, considerably over six feet in height, with stooping shoulders, long pendulous arms, terminating in hands of extraordinary dimensions, which, however, were far exceeded in proportion by his feet. He was dressed in an ill-fitting, wrinkled suit of black, which put one in mind of an undertaker's uniform at a funeral; round his neck a rope of black silk was knotted in a large bulb, with flying ends projecting beyond the collar of his coat; his turned-down shirt-collar disclosed a sinewy, muscular yellow neck, and above that, nestling in a great black mass of hair, bristling and compact like a ruff of mourning pins, rose the strange quaint face and head, covered with its thatch of wild republican hair, of President Lincoln. The impression produced by the size of his extremities, and by his flapping and wide-projecting ears, may be removed by the appearance of kindliness, sagacity, and the awkward bonhomie of his face; the mouth is absolutely prodigious; the lips, straggling and extending almost from one line of black beard to the other, are only kept in order by two deep furrows from the nostril to the chin; the nose itself—a prominent organ—stands out from the face, with an inquiring anxious air, as though it were sniffing for some good thing in the wind; the eyes dark, full, and deeply set, are penetrating, but full of an expression which almost amounts to tenderness; and above them projects the shaggy brow, running into the small hard frontal space, the development of which can scarcely be estimated accurately, owing to the irregular flocks of thick hair carelessly brushed across it. One would say that, although the mouth was made to enjoy a joke, it could also utter the severest sentence which the head could dictate, but that Mr. Lincoln would be ever more willing to temper justice with mercy, and to enjoy what he considers the amenities of life, than to take a harsh view of men's nature and of the world, and to estimate things in an ascetic or puritan spirit. A person who met Mr. Lincoln in the street would not take him to be what is called a "gentleman"; and, indeed, since I came to the United States, I have heard more disparaging allusions made by Americans to him on that account than I could have expected among simple republicans, where all should be equals; but, at the same time, it would not be possible for the most indifferent observer to pass him in the street without notice.

As he advanced through the room, he evidently controlled a desire to shake hands all round with everybody, and smiled good-humouredly till he was suddenly brought up by the staid deportment of Mr. Seward, and by the profound diplomatic bows of the Chevalier Bertinatti. Then, indeed, he suddenly jerked himself back, and stood in front of the two ministers, with his body slightly drooped forward, and his hands behind his back, his knees touching, and his feet apart. Mr. Seward formally presented the minister.

The minister forthwith handed his letter to the President, who gave it into the custody of Mr. Seward and then, dipping his hand into his coat pocket, Mr. Lincoln drew out a sheet of paper, from which he read his reply, the most remarkable part of which was his

President Abraham Lincoln *(Photo by Alexander Gardner, courtesy of Lincoln National Life Foundation, Ft. Wayne, Indiana)*

doctrine "that the United States were bound by duty not to interfere with the differences of foreign governments and countries." After some words of compliment, the President shook hands with the minister, who soon afterwards retired. Mr. Seward then took me by the hand and said, "Mr. President, allow me to present to you Mr. Russell of the London *Times.*" On which Mr. Lincoln put out his hand in a very friendly manner, and said, "Mr. Russell, I am very glad to make your acquaintance, and to see you in this country. The London *Times* is one of the greatest powers in the world—in fact, I don't know anything which has much more power—except perhaps the Mississippi. I am glad to know you as its minister." Conversation ensued for some minutes, which the President enlivened by two or three peculiar little sallies, and I left agreeably impressed with his shrewdness, humour, and natural sagacity.

In the evening I dined with Mr. Seward, in company of his son Mr. Seward, junior, Mr. Sanford, and a quaint, natural specimen of an American rustic lawyer, who was going to Brussels as the Secretary of the Legation. His chief, Mr. Sanford, did not appear altogether happy when introduced to his secretary, for he found that he had a very limited knowledge (if any) of French, and of other things which it is generally considered desirable that secretaries should know.

Very naturally, conversation turned on politics. Although no man can foresee the nature of the crisis which is coming, nor the mode in which it is to be encountered, the faith of men like Mr. Sanford and Mr. Seward in the ultimate success of their principles, and in the integrity of the Republic, is very remarkable; and the boldness of their language in reference to foreign powers almost amounts to arrogance and menace, if not to temerity. Mr. Seward asserted that the ministers of England or of France had no right to make any allusion to the civil war which appeared imminent; and that the Southern commissioners who had been sent abroad could not be received by the Government of any foreign power, officially or otherwise, without incurring the risk of breaking off relations with the Government of the United States. As regards the great object of public curiosity, the relief of Fort Sumter, Mr. Seward maintains a profound silence, beyond the mere declaration, made with a pleasant twinkle of the eye, that "the whole policy of the Government, on that and other questions, is put forth in the President's inaugural, from which there will be no deviation." Turning to the inaugural message, however, there is no such very certain indication, as Mr. Seward pretends to discover, of the course to be pursued by Mr. Lincoln and the Cabinet. To an outside observer, like myself, it seems as if they were waiting for events to develop themselves, and rested their policy rather upon acts that had occurred, than upon any definite principle designed to control or direct the future.

I should here add that Mr. Seward spoke in high terms of the ability, dexterity, and personal qualities of Mr. Jefferson Davis, and declared his belief that but for him the secession movement never could have succeeded as far as it has gone and would, in all probability, indeed, have never taken place at all.

On returning to my hotel I found a card from the President, inviting me to dinner the following day.

March 28th.   I was honoured today by visits from a great number of members of Congress, journalists, and others. Judging from the expressions of most of the Washington people, they would gladly see a Southern Cabinet installed in their city. The cold shoulder is given to Mr. Lincoln and all kinds of stories and jokes are circulated at his expense. People take particular pleasure in telling how he came towards the seat of his Government disguised in a Scotch cap and cloak, whatever they may mean.[8]

In the evening I repaired to the White House. Mrs. Lincoln was already seated to receive her guests. She is of the middle age and height, of a plumpness degenerating to the *embonpoint* [stoutness] natural to her years; her features are plain, her nose and mouth of an ordinary type, and her manners and appearance homely, stiffened, however, by the consciousness that her position requires her to be something more than plain Mrs. Lincoln, the wife of the Illinois lawyer; she is profuse in the introduction of the word "sir" in every sentence, which is now almost an Americanism confined to certain

[8]Lincoln was not proud of the incident. Persuaded by Allen Pinkerton, a Chicago detective, that his life was in danger, Lincoln took an earlier-than-scheduled train into Washington. To conceal his appearance, he wore a soft, slouched hat—called a "Scotch" or "Kossuth" cap—a muffler, and a short, bobtailed overcoat. Democratic and Confederate caricaturists took pleasure in portraying a frightened Lincoln peeping out of a boxcar and looking for his assassins.

classes, although it was once as common in England. Her dress I shall not attempt to describe, though it was very gorgeous and highly coloured. She handled a fan with much energy, displaying a round, well-proportioned arm, and was adorned with some simple jewellery. Mrs. Lincoln struck me as being desirous of making herself agreeable; and I own I was agreeably disappointed, as the secessionist ladies at Washington had been amusing themselves by anecdotes which could scarcely have been founded on fact.

Several of the ministers had already arrived; by and by all had come, and the party only waited for General [Winfield] Scott, who seemed to be the representative man in Washington of the monarchical idea, and to absorb some of the feeling which is lavished on the pictures and memory, if not on the monument, of Washington. Whilst we were waiting, Mr. Seward took me round, and introduced me to the ministers, and to their wives and daughters, among the latter, Miss [Kate] Chase, who is very attractive, agreeable, and sprightly. Her father [Salmon P. Chase], the Finance Minister, struck me as one of the most intelligent and distinguished persons in the whole assemblage; tall, of a good presence, with a well-formed head, fine forehead, and a face indicating energy and power. There is a peculiar droop and motion on the lid of one eye, which seems to have suffered from some injury, that detracts from the agreeable effect of his face; but, on the whole, he is one who would not pass quite unnoticed in a European crowd of the same description.

In the whole assemblage there was not a scrap of lace or a piece of ribbon. Nor were the ministers by any means remarkable for their personal appearance.

Mr. Cameron, the Secretary of War, a slight man, above the middle height, with grey hair, deep-set keen grey eyes, and a thin mouth, gave me the idea of a person of ability and adroitness. His colleague, the Secretary of the Navy, a small man with a great long grey beard and spectacles, did not look like one of much originality or ability; but people who know Mr. [Gideon] Welles declared that he is possessed of administrative power, although they admit that he does not know the stem from the stern of a ship and are in doubt whether he ever saw the sea in his life. Mr. [Caleb B.] Smith, the Minister of the Interior, is a bright-eyed, smart (I use the word in the English sense) gentleman, with the reputation of being one of the most conservative members of the Cabinet. Mr. [Montgomery] Blair, the Postmaster-General, is a person of much greater influence than his position would indicate. He has the reputation of being one of the most determined Republicans in the Ministry; but he held peculiar notions with reference to the black and white races, which, if carried out, would not by any means conduce to the comfort or happiness of free Negroes in the United States.[9] He is a tall, lean man, with a hard, Scotch, practical-looking head—an anvil for ideas to be hammered on. His eyes are small and deeply set and have a rat-like expression; and he speaks with caution, as though he weighed every word before he uttered it. The last of the ministers is Mr. [Edward] Bates, a stout, thick-set, common-looking man, with a large beard, who fills the office of Attorney-General.

In the conversation which occurred before dinner, I was amused to observe the manner in which Mr. Lincoln used the anecdotes for which he is famous. Where men bred in courts, accustomed to the world, or versed in diplomacy, would use some subterfuge, or would make a polite speech, or give a shrug of the shoulders as the means of getting out of an embarrassing position, Mr. Lincoln raises a laugh by some bold west-country anecdote and moves off in the cloud of merriment produced by his joke. Thus when Mr. Bates was remonstrating apparently against the appointment of some indifferent lawyer to a place of judicial importance, the President interposed with, "Come now, Bates, he's not half as bad as you think. Besides that, I must tell you, he did me a good turn long ago. When I took to the law, I was going to court one morning with some ten or twelve miles of bad road before me, and I had no horse. The judge overtook me in his wagon. 'Hollo, Lincoln! Are you not going to the courthouse? Come in and I'll give you a seat.' Well, I got in, and the judge went on reading his papers. Presently the wagon struck a stump on one side of the road; then it hopped off to the other. I looked out, and I saw the driver was jerking from side to side in his seat; so says I, 'Judge, I think your coachman has been taking a little drop too much this morning.' 'Well I declare, Lincoln,' said he, 'I should not much wonder if you are right, for he has nearly upset me half-a-dozen of

[9]Montgomery Blair and his brother, Francis P. Blair, Jr., advocated colonizing blacks outside the borders of the United States.

times since starting.' So, putting his head out of the window, he shouted, 'Why, you infernal scoundrel, you are drunk!' Upon which, pulling up his horses and turning around with great gravity, the coachman said, 'By gorra! that's the first rightful decision you have given for the last twelvemonth.' " While the company were laughing, the President beat a quiet retreat from the neighbourhood of the Attorney-General.

It was at last announced that General Scott was unable to be present, and that, although actually in the house, he had been compelled to retire from indisposition, and we moved in to the banquetting-hall. The first "state dinner," as it is called, of the President was not remarkable for ostentation. No liveried servants, on Persic [Persian] splendor of ancient plate, no *chefs d'oeuvre* [culinary masterpieces] of art glittered round the board. Vases of flowers decorated the table, combined with dishes in what may be called the "Gallo-American" style, with wines which owed their parentage to France, and their rearing and education to the United States, which abound in cunning nurses for such productions. The conversation was suited to the state dinner of a Cabinet at which women and strangers were present. I was seated next to Mr. Bates and the very agreeable and lively secretary of the President, Mr. [John M.] Hay, and except when there was an attentive silence caused by one of the President's stories, there was a Babel of small talk round the table, in which I was surprised to find a diversity of accent almost as great as if a number of foreigners had been speaking English. I omitted the name of Mr. [Hannibal] Hamlin, the Vice-President, as well as those of less remarkable people who were present; but it would not be becoming to pass over the occupant of a post which leads to the Presidency, in event of any occurrence which may remove Mr. Lincoln.

After dinner the ladies and gentlemen retired to the drawing-room, and the circle was increased by the addition of several politicians. I had an opportunity of conversing with some of the ministers, if not with all, from time to time, and I was struck by the uniform tendency of their remarks in reference to the policy of Great Britain. They seemed to think that England was bound by her anti-slavery antecedents to discourage to the utmost any attempt of the South to establish its independence on a basis of slavery, and to assume that they were the representatives of an active war of emancipation.

March 29th, Good Friday.   The religious observance of the day was not quite as strict as it would be in England. The Puritan aversion to ceremonials and formulary observances has apparently affected the American world, even as far south as this.

I had the advantage of a conversation with Mr. Truman Smith who maintained that by the Federal Compact each State had delegated irrevocably the essence of its sovereignty to a Government to be established in perpetuity for the benefit of the whole body. The slave States, seeing that the progress of free ideas and the material power of the North was obtaining an influence which must be subversive of the supremacy they had so long exercised in the Federal Government for their own advantage, had developed this doctrine of States' Rights as a cloak to treason, preferring the material advantages to be gained by the extension of their system to the great moral position which they would occupy as a portion of the United States in the face of all the world.

In the evening I had the pleasure of dining with an American gentleman who has seen much of the world, travelled far and wide, who has read much and beheld more, a scholar, a politician, after his way, a poet, and an ologist.[10] Such men never do or can succeed in the United States; they are far too refined, philosophical, and cosmopolitan. From what I see, success here may be obtained by refined men, if they are dishonest; never by philosophical men, unless they be corrupt; not by cosmopolitan men under any circumstances whatever; for to have sympathies with any people, or with any nation in the world except his own is to doom a statesman with the American public, unless it be in the form of an affectation of pity or good will, intended really as an offence to some allied people. At dinner there was the very largest naval officer I have ever seen in company, although I must own that our own service is not destitute of some good specimens, and I have seen an Austrian admiral at Pola, and the superintendent of the arsenal, to Tophaneh, who were not unfit to be marshals of France. This Lieutenant, named [William] Nelson, was certainly greater in one sense than his British namesake, for he weighed 260 pounds.

[10]A specialist in a branch of learning that ends with the suffix "ology"; for example, geology, anthropology, or psychology.

The Lieutenant was a strong Union man, and he inveighed fiercely, and even coarsely, against the members of his profession who had thrown up their commissions. The superintendent of the Washington Navy Yard is supposed to be very little disposed in favour of this present Government; in fact, Capt. [Franklin] Buchanan may be called a secessionist, nevertheless, I am invited to the wedding of his daughter in order to see the President give away the bride. Mr. Nelson says Sumter and Pickens are to be reinforced. Charleston is to be reduced to order, and all traitors hanged, or he will know the reason why; and, says he, "I have some weight in the country." In the evening, as we were going home, notwithstanding the cold, we saw a number of ladies sitting out on the door steps, in white dresses. The streets were remarkably quiet and deserted; all the coloured population had been sent to bed long ago. The fire bell, as usual, made an alarm or two about midnight.

March 30th. Descended into the barber's shop off the hall of the hotel; all the operators, men of colour, mostly mulattoes or yellow lads, good-looking, dressed in clean white jackets and aprons, were smart, quick, and attentive. It appears that the trade of barber is almost the birthright of the free Negro or coloured man in the United States. There is a striking exemplification of natural equality in the use of brushes, and the senator flops down in the seat and has his noble nose seized by the same fingers which the moment before were occupied by the person and chin of an unmistakable rowdy.

The great employment of four-fifths of the people at Willard's at present seems to be to hunt senators and congressmen through the lobbies. The men who have got places, having been elected by the people, must submit to the people who think they have established a claim on them by their favours. The majority confer power, but they seem to forget that it is only the minority who can enjoy the first fruits of success. There are men at Willard's who have come literally thousands of miles to seek the places which can only be theirs for four years, and who with true American facility have abandoned the calling and pursuits of a lifetime for this doubtful canvas; and I was told of one gentleman, who having been informed that he could not get a judgeship, condescended to seek a place in the Post Office, and finally applied to Mr. Chase to be appointed keeper of a "lighthouse," he was not particular where. In the forenoon I drove to the Washington Navy Yard, in company of Lieutenant Nelson and two friends. It is about two miles outside the city, situated on a fork of land projecting between a creek and the Potomac River, which is here three-quarters of a mile broad.

The Navy Yard is surrounded by high brick walls; in the gateway stood two sentries in dark blue tunics, yellow facings, with eagle buttons, brightly polished arms, and white Berlin gloves, wearing a cap something like a French kepi, all very clean and creditable. Inside are some few trophies of guns taken from us at Yorktown, and from the Mexicans in the land of Cortez. The interior inclosure is surrounded by red brick houses, and stores and magazines, picked out with white stone; and two or three green grass plots, fenced in by pillars and chains and bordered by trees, give an air of agreeable freshness to the place. Close to the river are the workshops; of course there is smoke and noise of steam and machinery. In a modest office, surrounded by books, papers, drawings, and models, as well as by shell and shot and racks of arms of different descriptions, we found Capt. [John A.] Dahlgren, the acting superintendent of the yard, and the inventor of the famous gun which bears his name and is the favorite armament of the American navy. Capt. Dahlgren contends that guns capable of throwing the heaviest shot may be constructed of cast-iron, carefully prepared and moulded so that the greatest thickness of metal may be placed at the points of resistance, at the base of the gun, the muzzle and forward portions being of very moderate thickness.[11]

All inventors, or even adapters of systems, must be earnest, self-reliant persons, full of confidence; Captain Dahlgren has certainly most of these characteristics, but he has to fight with his navy department, with the army, with boards and with commissioners—in fact, with all sorts of obstructors. When I was going over the yard, he deplored the parsimony of the department, which refused to yield to his urgent entreaties for additional furnaces to cast guns.

[11]The Dahlgren gun has been likened to a round-bottomed soda-water bottle turned on its side. The metal at the breech had great thickness and was gradually tapered toward the muzzle. The caliber of the Dahlgren, originally cast at 11 inches, was later enlarged to 20 inches.

No large guns are cast at Washington. The foundries are only capable of turning out brass fieldpieces and boatguns. Compared with our establishments, this dockyard is a mere toy, and but few hands are employed in it.

On returning to the hotel I found a magnificent bouquet of flowers with a card attached to them, with Mrs. Lincoln's compliments, and another card announcing that she had a "reception" at three o'clock. It was rather late before I could get to the White House, and there were only two or three ladies in the drawing-room when I arrived. I was informed afterwards that the attendance was very scanty. The Washington ladies have not yet made up their minds that Mrs. Lincoln is the fashion. They miss their Southern friends and constantly draw comparisons between them and the vulgar Yankee women and men who are now in power. I do not know enough to say whether the affectation of superiority be justified; but assuredly if New York be Yankee, there is nothing in which it does not far surpass this preposterous capital. The impression of homeliness produced by Mrs. Lincoln on first sight is not diminished by closer acquaintance. Few women not to the manner born there are, whose heads would not be disordered, and circulation disturbed, by a rapid transition, almost instantaneous, from a condition of obscurity in a country town to be mistress of the White House. Her smiles and her frowns become a matter of consequence to the whole American world. If she but drive down Pennsylvania Avenue, the electric wire thrills the news to every hamlet in the Union which has a newspaper; and fortunate is the correspondent who, in a special dispatch, can give authentic particulars of her destination and of her dress. The lady is surrounded by flatterers and intriguers, seeking for influence or such places as she can give.

March 31st, Easter Sunday. I dined with Lord [Richard B.] Lyons and members of the Legation; the only stranger present being Senator [Charles] Sumner. Politics were of course eschewed, for Mr. Sumner is Chairman of the Committee on Foreign Relations of the Senate, and Lord Lyons is a very discreet minister; but still there crept in a word of Pickens and Sumter and that was all. Mr. [Gustavus V.] Fox, formerly of the United States Navy and since that a master of a steamer in the commercial marine, has been sent on some mission to Fort Sumter, and has been allowed to visit Major [Robert] Anderson by the authorities at Charleston; but it is not known what was the object of his mission.[12] Everywhere there is secession resignation, in a military sense of the word. The Southern Commissioners declare they will soon retire to Montgomery, and that any attempt to reinforce or supply the forts will be a *casus belli* [cause for war]. There is the utmost anxiety to know what Virginia will do. General Scott belongs to the State, and it is feared he may be shaken if the State goes out. Already the authorities of Richmond have intimated they will not allow the foundry[13] to furnish guns to the seaboard forts, such as Monroe and Norfolk in Virginia. This concession of the autonomy is really a recognition of States' Rights. For if a State can vote itself in or out of the Union, why can it not make war or peace and accept or refuse the Federal Government? In fact, the Federal System is radically defective against internal convulsion, however excellent it is or may be for purposes of external polity. I walked home with Mr. Sumner to his rooms and heard some of his views, which were not so sanguine as those of Mr. Seward, and I thought I detected a desire to let the Southern States go out with their slavery if they so desired it. Mr. Chase, by the way, expressed sentiments of the same kind more decidedly the other day.

April 1st. On Easter Monday, after breakfast with Mr. Olmsted, I drove over to visit Senator [Stephen A.] Douglas. By his ability and

[12]It might be instructive to mention the sequence of events that led to the firing on Fort Sumter. Before Lincoln took office, President Buchanan had attempted to re-enforce the fort with provisions and troops, but Confederates fired on the relief ship and it turned back. On March 5, 1861, Major Anderson informed President Lincoln that he could not hold the fort much longer without provisions. During that month Lincoln, the Cabinet, and General Scott held numerous meetings to discuss the Sumter crisis. In mid-March Lincoln sent Fox to Charleston to assess the situation. Fox, in turn, recommended provisioning the fort, and Lincoln ordered a relief expedition to be prepared and to sail for Sumter on April 6. On that day he informed Governor Pickens of South Carolina that an attempt would be made to supply Sumter with provisions only. Informed of Lincoln's intention, the Confederate government at Montgomery instructed P. G. T. Beauregard, commander at Charleston, to "proceed in such a manner as you may determine, to reduce" the fort. The first shots against Sumter were fired on April 12, 1861, at 4:30 A.M.

[13]The Tredegar Iron Works.

eloquence he has raised himself to the highest position in the State short of the Presidency, which might have been his but for the extraordinary success of his opponent in a fortuitous suffrage scramble. He is called the Little Giant. His sketch of the causes which have led to the present disruption of parties, and the hazard of civil war, was most vivid and able; and for more than an hour he spoke with a vigour of thought and terseness of phrase which, even on such dreary and uninviting themes as squatter sovereignty and the Kansas-Nebraska question, interested a foreigner in the man and the subject. Although his sympathies seemed to go with the South on the question of slavery and territorial extension, he condemned altogether the attempt to destroy the Union.

April 2nd. I started early and performed my pilgrimage to "the shrine of St. Washington," at Mount Vernon, as a foreigner on board called the place. It is an oblong wooden house, of two stories in height, with a colonnade toward the river face, and a small balcony on the top and on the level of the roof, over which rises a little paltry gazebo. There is no attempt at neatness or order about the place; though the exterior of the house is undergoing repair, the grass is unkempt, the shrubs untrimmed—neglect, squalor, and chicken feathers have marked the lawn for their own. The house is in keeping and threatens to fall to ruin. The lower rooms presented nothing worthy of notice—some lumbering, dusty, decayed furniture; a broken harpsichord, dust, cobwebs—no remnant of the man himself. The gardens, too, were tabooed; but through the gate I could see a wilderness of neglected trees and shrubs, not unmingled with a suspicion of a present kitchen-ground.

On the return of the steamer I visited Fort Washington, which is situated on the left bank of the Potomac. I found everything in a state of neglect—gun carriages rotten, shot piles rusty, furnaces tumbling to pieces. The place might be made strong enough on the river front, but the rear is weak, though there is low marshy land at the back. A company of regulars were on duty. The sentries took no precautions against surprise. Twenty determined men, armed with revolvers, could have taken the whole work. Afterwards, when I ventured to make a remark to General Scott as to the carelessness of the garrison, he said: "A few weeks ago it might have been taken by a bottle of whiskey. The whole garrison consisted of an old Irish pensioner."

April 3rd. I had an interview with the Southern Commissioners today, at their hotel.[14] For more than an hour I heard, from men of position and of different sections in the South, expressions which satisfied me the Union could never be restored, if they truly represented the feelings and opinions of their fellow-citizens. They have the idea they are ministers of a foreign power treating with Yankeedom, and their indignation is moved by the refusal of Government to negotiate with them, armed as they are with full authority to arrange all questions arising out of an amicable separation—such as the adjustment of Federal claims for property, forts, stores, public works, debts, land purchases, and the like. One of the Judges of the Supreme Court of the United States, Mr. [John A.] Campbell, is their intermediary, and of course it is not known what hopes Mr. Seward had held out to him; but there is some imputation of Punic faith against the Government on account of recent acts, and there is no doubt the Commissioners hear, as I do, that there are preparations at the Navy Yard and at New York to relieve Sumter, at any rate, with provisions, and that Pickens has actually been reinforced by sea. In the evening I dined at the British Legation and went over to the house of the Russian Minister, M. [Edouard] de Stoeckl, in the evening. The diplomatic body in Washington constitute a small and very agreeable society of their own, in which few Americans mingle except at the receptions and large evening assemblies. As the people now in power are *nove homines* [new men], the wives and daughters of ministers and attachés are deprived of their friends who belonged to the old society

[14]The southern commission consisted of André B. Roman, Louisiana; Martin B. Crawford, Georgia; and John Forsyth, Alabama. Russell apparently met only with Crawford and Forsyth, for on April 5 he notes his introduction to Roman. The commissioners were sent to Washington by Jefferson Davis to work out a peaceful separation between the Confederacy and the Union. Seward refused to negotiate with them directly but used Justice John A. Campbell of the U.S. Supreme Court as an intermediary. Because Seward opposed holding Sumter, he implied through Campbell that the fort would be evacuated—a statement contrary to Lincoln's attitude. The commissioners, playing upon Seward's belief of strong Unionism in the South, encouraged him to believe that reunification of the North and South might be possible in the future. These evasive innuendoes led each side to conclude later that the other had been less than truthful.

in Washington, and who have either gone off to secession, or sympathise so deeply with the Southern States that it is scarcely becoming to hold very intimate relations with them in the face of Government. From the house of M. de Stoeckl I went to a party at the residence of M. [Gabriel Garcia] Tassara, the Spanish Minister, where there was a crowd of diplomats, young and old. Diplomatists seldom or never talk politics, and so Pickens and Sumter were unheard of; but it is stated nevertheless that Virginia is on the eve of secession, and will certainly go if the President attempts to use force in relieving and strengthening the Federal forts.

April 4th.   I had a long interview with Mr. Seward today at the State Department. He set forth at great length the helpless condition in which the President and the Cabinet found themselves when they began the conduct of public affairs at Washington. The last Cabinet had tampered with treason and had contained traitors; a miserable imbecility had encouraged the leaders of the South to mature their plans, and had furnished them with the means of carrying out their design. One minister had purposely sent away the navy of the United States to distant and scattered stations; another had purposely placed the arms, ordnance, and munitions of war in undue proportions in the Southern States, and had weakened the Federal Government so that they might easily fall into the hands of the traitors and enable them to secure war *matériel* of the Union; a minister had stolen the public funds for traitorous purposes—in every port, in every department of the State, at home and abroad, on sea and by land, men were placed who were engaged in this deep conspiracy—and when the voice of the people declared Mr. Lincoln President of the United States, they set to work as one man to destroy the Union under the most flimsy pretexts. The President's duty was clearly defined by the Constitution. He had to guard what he had, and to regain, if possible, what he had lost. He would not consent to any dismemberment of the Union nor to the abandonment of one iota of Federal property —nor could he do so if he desired.

These and many more topics were presented to me to show that the Cabinet was not accountable for the temporising policy of inaction, which was forced upon them by circumstances, and that they would deal vigorously with the secession movement—as vigorously as Jackson did with nullification in South Carolina, if they had the means. But what could they do when such men as Twiggs surrendered his trust and sacrificed the troops to a crowd of Texans; or when naval and military officers resigned *en masse,* that they might accept service in the rebel forces? All this excitement would come right in a very short time—it was a brief madness, which would pass away when the people had opportunity for reflection. Meantime the danger was that foreign powers would be led to imagine the Federal Government was too weak to defend its rights, and that the attempt to destroy the Union and to set up a Southern Confederacy was successful. In other words, again, Mr. Seward fears that, in this transition state between their forced inaction and the *coup* by which they intend to strike down secession, Great Britain may recognize the Government established at Montgomery, and [he] is ready if needs be, to threaten Great Britain with war as the consequence of such recognition. But he certainly assumed the existence of strong Union sentiments in many of the seceded States, as a basis for his remarks, and admitted that it would not become the spirit of the American Government, or of the Federal system, to use armed force in subjugating the Southern States against the will of the majority of the people. Therefore if the majority desire secession, Mr. Seward would let them have it—but he cannot believe in anything so monstrous, for to him the Federal Government and Constitution, as interpreted by his party, are divine, heaven-born. He is fond of repeating that the Federal Government never yet sacrificed any man's life on account of his political opinions, but if this struggle goes on it will sacrifice thousands—tens of thousands, to the idea of a Federal Union. "Any attempt against us," he said, "would revolt the good men of the South, and arm all men in the North to defend their Government."

I dined with Senator Douglas, where there was a large party, among whom were Mr. Chase, Secretary of the Treasury; Mr. Smith, Secretary of the Interior; Mr. [John] Forsyth, Southern Commissioner; and several members of the Senate and Congress. Mrs. [Adele Cutts] Douglas did the honours of her house with grace and charming good nature. I observe a great tendency to abstract speculation and theorising among Americans, and their after dinner conversation is apt to become didactic and sententious. Few men speak better than Senator Douglas: his words are well chosen, the flow of his ideas even and constant, his intellect vigorous, and thoughts well cut, precise, and vigorous—he seems a man of great ambition.

April 5th. Dined with the Southern Commissioners and a small party at Gautier's, a French restauranteur in Pennsylvania Avenue. The gentlemen present were, I need not say, all of one way of thinking; but as these leaves will see the light before the Civil War is at an end, it is advisable not to give their names, for it would expose persons resident in Washington, who may not be suspected by the Government, to those marks of attention which they have not yet ceased to pay to their political enemies. Although I confess that in my judgment too much stress had been laid in England on the severity with which the Federal authorities have acted toward their political enemies, who were seeking their destruction, it may be candidly admitted, that they have forfeited all claim to the lofty position they once occupied as a Government existing by moral force and by the consent of the governed.

As Col. [George E.] Pickett and Mr. [A. D.] Banks are notorious secessionists, and Mr. [Phillip] Phillips has since gone South after the arrest of his wife on account of her anti-Federal tendencies, it may be permitted to mention that they were among the guests. I had pleasure in making the acquaintance of Governor [André B.] Roman. Mr. [Martin J.] Crawford, his brother commissioner, is a much younger man of considerably greater energy and determination but probably of less judgment. The third commissioner, Mr. Forsyth, is fanatical in his opposition to any suggestion of compromise or reconstruction; but, indeed, upon the point, there is little difference of opinion amongst any of the real adherents of the South. Mr. Lincoln they spoke of with contempt; Mr. Seward they evidently regarded as the ablest and most unscrupulous of their enemies; but the tone in which they alluded to the whole of the Northern people indicated the clear conviction that trade, commerce, and pursuit of gain, manufacture, and the base mechanical arts, had so degraded the whole race, they would never attempt to strike a blow in fair fight for what they prized so highly in theory and in words. Whether it be in consequence of some secret influence which slavery has upon the minds of men, or that the aggression of the North upon their institutions had been of a nature to excite the deepest animosity and most vindictive hate, certain it is there is a degree of something like ferocity in the Southern mind toward New England which exceeds belief. I am persuaded that these feelings of contempt are extended toward England. They believe that we, too, have had the canker of peace upon us. One evidence of this, according to Southern men, is the abolition of duelling. This practice, according to them, is highly wholesome and meritorious; and, indeed, it may be admitted that in the state of society which is reported to exist in the Southern States, it is a useful check on such men as it restrained in our own islands in the last century. In the course of conversation, one gentleman remarked that he considered it disgraceful for any man to take money for the dishonor of his wife or his daughter. "With us," he said, "there is but one mode of dealing known. The man who dares tamper with the honour of a white woman knows what he has to expect. We shoot him down like a dog, and no jury in the South will ever find any man guilty of murder for punishing such a scoundrel." An argument which can scarcely be alluded to was used by them, to show that these offences in slave States had not the excuse which might be adduced to diminish their gravity when they occurred in States where all the population were white. Indeed, in this, as in some other matters of a similar character, slavery is their *summum bonum* [ultimate] of morality, physical excellence, and social purity. I was inclined to question the correctness of the standard which they had set up, and to inquire whether the virtue which needed this murderous use of the pistol and the dagger to defend it was not open to some doubt; but I found there was very little sympathy with my views among the company.

The gentlemen at table asserted that the white men in the slave States are physically superior to the men in the free States; and indulged in curious theories in morals and physics to which I was a stranger. Disbelief of anything a Northern man—that is, a Republican—can say, is a fixed principle in their minds. I could not help remarking, when the conversation turned on the duplicity of Mr. Seward and the wickedness of the Federal Government in refusing to give the assurance Sumter would not be relieved by force of arms, that it must be of very little consequence what promises Mr. Seward made, as, according to them, not the least reliance was to be placed on his word. The notion that the Northern men are cowards is justified by instances in which Congressmen have been insulted by Southern men without calling them out, and Mr. Sumner's case was quoted as the type of affairs of the kind between the two sides.

I happened to say that I always understood Mr. Sumner had been attacked suddenly and unexpectedly and struck down before he could rise from his desk to defend himself; whereupon a warm refutation of that version of the story was given, and I was assured that Mr. [Preston] Brooks, who was a very slight man and much inferior in height to Mr. Sumner, struck him a slight blow at first and only inflicted the heavier strokes when irritated by the Senator's cowardly demeanor. In reference to some remark made about the cavaliers and their connection with the South, I reminded the gentlemen that, after all, the descendants of the Puritans were not to be despised in battle, and that the best gentry in England were worsted at last by the trainbands of London, and the "rabbledom" of Cromwell's Independents.[15]

Altogether the evening, notwithstanding the occasional warmth of the controversy, was exceedingly instructive; one could understand from the vehemence and force of the speakers the full meaning of the phrase of "firing the Southern heart," so often quoted as an illustration of the peculiar force of political passion to be brought to bear against the Republicans in the secession contest. Mr. Forsyth struck me as being the most astute, and perhaps most capable of the gentlemen whose mission to Washington seems likely to be so abortive.

April 6th.   Today I paid a second visit to General Scott, who received me very kindly and made many inquiries respecting the events in the Crimea and the Indian mutiny and rebellion. He professed to have no apprehension for the safety of the capital; but in reality there are only some 700 or 800 regulars to protect it and the Navy Yard, and two field batteries, commanded by an officer of very doubtful attachment to the Union. The head of the Navy Yard is openly accused of treasonable sympathies.

Mr. Seward has definitively refused to hold any intercourse what-

---

[15]In English history during the Civil War, 1640–49, "trainband" was a term used to designate citizens from urban areas trained and armed as a supplementary fighting force to the rebel army.

ever with the Southern Commissioners, and they will retire almost immediately from the capital. As matters look very threatening, I must go South and see with my own eyes how affairs stand there before the two sections come to open rupture. Mr. Seward, the other day, in talking of the South, described them as being in every respect behind the age, with fashions, habits, level of thought, and modes of life, belonging to the worst part of the last century. But still he never has been there himself! The Southern men come up to the Northern cities and springs, but the Northerner rarely travels southward. Indeed, I am informed that if he were a well-known abolitionist, it would not be safe for him to appear in a Southern city. I quite agree with my thoughtful and earnest friend, Olmsted, that the United States can never be considered as a free country till a man can speak as freely in Charleston as he can in New York or Boston.

The President, I hear this evening, is alarmed lest Virginia should become hostile, and his policy, if he has any, is temporising and timed. It is perfectly wonderful to hear people using the word "Government" at all, as applied to the President and his Cabinet—a body which has no power "according to the Constitution" to save the country governed or itself from destruction.

In the hotel the roar of the office seekers is unabated. Train after train adds to their numbers. They cumber the passages. The hall is crowded to such a degree that suffocation might describe the degree to which the pressure reaches, were it not that tobacco smoke invigorates and sustains the constitution. As to the conditions of the floor, it is beyond description.

April 7th.   Raining all day, cold and wet. I am tired and weary of this perpetual jabber about Fort Sumter. Men here who know nothing at all of what is passing send letters to the New York papers, which are eagerly read by the people in Washington as soon as the journals reach the city, and then all these vague surmises are taken as gospel and argued upon as if they were facts. The [New York] Herald keeps up the courage and spirit of its Southern friends by giving the most florid accounts of their prospects and making continual attacks on Mr. Lincoln and his Government; but the majority of the New York papers are inclined to resist secession and aid the Government.

April 8th. How it does rain! Last night there were torrents of water in the streets literally a foot deep. It still runs in muddy whirling streams through the channels, and the rain is falling incessantly from a dull leaden sky. The air is warm and clammy. There are all kind of rumours abroad. Sumter, of course, was the main topic. Some reported that the President had promised the Southern Commissioners, through their friend Mr. Campbell, Judge of the Supreme Court, not to use force in respect to Pickens or Sumter. I wrote to Mr. Seward, to ask him if he could enable me to make any definite statement on these important matters. The Southerners are alarmed at the accounts they have received of great activity and preparations in the Brooklyn and Boston navy yards, and declare that "treachery" is meant. I find myself quite incapable of comprehending their position. How can the United States Government be guilty of "treachery" toward subjects of States which are preparing to assert their independence, unless that Government has been guilty of falsehood or admitted the justice of the decision to which the State had arrived?

On returning to my hotel, I found a note from Mr. Seward, asking me to visit him at nine o'clock. On going to his house, I was shown to the drawing room and found there only the Secretary of State, his son, and Mrs. [Anna W.] Seward.[16] I made a *parti carré* [foursome] for a friendly rubber of whist, and Mr. Seward, who was my partner, talked as he played so that the score of the game was not favourable. But his talk was very interesting. "All the preparations of which you hear mean this only. The Government, finding the property of the State and Federal forts neglected and left without protection, are determined to take steps to relieve them from that neglect and to protect them. But we are determined in doing so to make no aggression. The President's inaugural clearly shadows out our policy. We will not go beyond it—we have no intention of doing so—nor will we withdraw from it." After a time Mr. Seward put down his cards and told his son to go for a portfolio which he would find in a drawer on his table. Mrs. Seward lighted the drop light of the gas, and on her husband's return with the paper left the room. The Secretary then

---

[16]Anna Wharton Seward, Frederick's wife, was acting as her father-in-law's official hostess at this time. William Seward's wife, Frances A. Seward, had been in ill health since 1853 and spent much time at the family home in Auburn, New York.

lit his cigar, gave one to me, and proceeded to read slowly and with marked emphasis, a very long, strong, and able dispatch, which he told me was to be read by Mr. [Charles Francis] Adams, the American Minister in London, to Lord John Russell. It struck me that the tone of the paper was hostile, that there was an undercurrent of menace through it, and that it contained insinuations that Great Britain would interfere to split up the Republic, if she could, and was pleased at the prospect of the dangers which threatened it.

At all the stronger passages Mr. Seward raised his voice, and made a pause at their conclusion as if to challenge remark or approval. At length I could not help saying, that the dispatch would, no doubt, have an excellent effect when it came to light in Congress, and that the Americans would think highly of the writer; but I ventured to express an opinion that it would not be quite so acceptable to the Government and people of Great Britain. This Mr. Seward, as an American statesman, has a right to make but a secondary consideration. By affecting to regard secession as a mere political heresy which can be easily confuted and by forbidding foreign countries alluding to it, Mr. Seward thinks he can establish the supremacy of his own Government, and at the same time gratify the vanity of the people. Even war with us may not be out of the list of those means which would be available for [fusing] the broken Union into a mass once more. However, the Secretary is quite confident in what he calls "reaction." "When the Southern States," he says, "see that we mean them no wrong—that we intend no violence to persons, rights, or things—that the Federal Government seeks only to fulfill obligations imposed on it in respect to the national property, they will see their mistake and one after another they will come back into the Union." Mr. Seward anticipated this process will at once begin, and that secession will all be done and over in three months—at least, so he says. It was after midnight ere our conversation was over, much of which of course I cannot mention in these pages.

April 10th. Today I devoted to packing up such things as I did not require and sending them to New York. I received a characteristic note from General Scott, asking me to dine with him tomorrow, and apologising for the shortness of his invitation, which arose from his only having just heard that I was about to leave so soon for the South.

The General is much admired by his countrymen, though they do not spare some "amiable weaknesses"; but, in my mind, he can only be accused of a little vanity, which is often found in characters of the highest standard.

[April 11th.] The General's dinner hour was early, and when I arrived at his modest lodgings, I found a troop of mounted volunteers of the district parading up and down the street. The General, who wore an undress blue frock coat with eagle-covered brass buttons and velvet collar and cuffs, was with Mr. Seward and Mr. Bates, the Attorney-General, and received me very courteously. He was interrupted by cheering from the soldiers in the street and by clamours for "General Scott." Out the General went to them and addressed a few words to his audience in the usual style about "rallying round," and "dying gloriously," and "old flag of our country," and all that kind of thing. Then followed dinner, which did credit to the cook, and wine, which was most excellent, from France, Spain, and Madeira.

To me his conversation was very interesting. Whilst he was speaking, a telegraphic dispatch was brought in, which the General perused with evident uneasiness. He apologised to me for reading it by saying the dispatch was from the President on Cabinet business, and then handed it across the table to Mr. Seward. The Secretary read it, and became a little agitated, and raised his eyes inquiringly to the General's face, who only shook his head. Then the paper was given to Mr. Bates, who read it and gave a grunt, as it were, of surprise.

In order to give the ministers opportunity for a conference, I asked Major [George W.] Cullum to accompany me into the garden and lighted a cigar. As I was walking about in the twilight, I observed two figures at the end of the little enclosure, standing as if in concealment close to the wall. Major Cullum said, "The men you see are sentries I have thought it expedient to place there for the protection of the General. The villains might assassinate him, and would do it in a moment if they could. He would not hear of a guard nor anything of the sort, so, without his knowing it, I have sentries posted all round the house all night." This was a curious state of things for the commander of the American army, in the midst of a crowded city, the capital of the free and enlightened Republic, to be placed in! On our return to the sitting room, the conversation was continued some hour or so longer. I retired with Mr. Seward in his carriage. As we were going up Pennsylvania Avenue—almost lifeless at that time— I asked Mr. Seward whether he felt quite secure against any irruption from Virginia, as it was reported that one Ben McCulloch, the famous Texas desperado, had assembled five hundred men at Richmond for some daring enterprise; some said to carry off the President, Cabinet, and all. He replied that, although the capital was almost defenceless, it must be remembered that the bold bad men who were their enemies were equally unprepared for active measures of aggression.

Two

BALTIMORE TO SAVANNAH

(APRIL 12–MAY 2, 1861)

April 12th. This morning I received an intimation that the Government had resolved on taking decisive steps which would lead to the development of events in the South and test the sincerity of secession. The Confederate general at Charleston, [Pierre G. T.] Beauregard, has sent to the Federal officer in command at Sumter, Major Anderson, to say that all communication between his garrison and the city must cease; and, at the same time, or probably before it, the Government at Washington informed the Confederate authorities that they intended to forward supplies to Major Anderson, peaceably if permitted, but at all hazards to send them. The Charleston people are manning the batteries they have erected against Sumter, have fired on a vessel under the United States flag, endeavouring to communicate with the fort, and have called out and organised a large force in the islands opposite the place and in the city of Charleston.

I resolved therefore to start for the Southern States today, proceeding by Baltimore to Norfolk instead of going by Richmond, which was cut off by the floods. Before leaving, I visited Lord Lyons,

Mr. Seward, the French and Russian ministers; left cards on the President, Mrs. Lincoln, General Scott, Mr. Douglas, Mr. Sumner, and others. There is no appearance of any excitement in Washington. Some ladies said to me that when I came back I would find some nice people at Washington, and that the rail-splitter, his wife, the Sewards, and all the rest of them would be driven to the place where they ought to be: "Varina Davis is a lady, at all events, not like the other. We can't put up with such people as these!" A naval officer whom I met, told me, "if the Government are really going to try force at Charleston, you'll see they'll be beaten, and we'll have a war between the gentlemen and the Yankee rowdies; if they attempt violence, you know how that will end." The Government are so uneasy that they have put soldiers into the Capitol, and are preparing it for defence.

At 6 p.m. I drove to the Baltimore station in a storm of rain. In the train there was a crowd of people, many of them disappointed place-hunters, and much discussion took place respecting the propriety of giving supplies to Sumter by force, the weight of opinion being against the propriety of such a step. The tone in which the President and his Cabinet were spoken of was very disrespectful. One big man, in a fur coat, who was sitting near me, said. "Well, darn me if I wouldn't draw a bead on Old Abe, Seward—aye, or General Scott himself, though I've got a perty good thing out of them, if they do try to use their soldiers and sailors to beat down States' Rights. If they want to go they've a right to go." To which many said, "That's so! That's true!"

When we arrived at Baltimore at 8 p.m., the streets were deep in water. A coachman, seeing I was a stranger, asked me two dollars, or 8s. 4d., to drive to the Eutaw House, a quarter of a mile distance. On my arrival, the landlord, no less a person than a major or colonel, took me aside and asked me if I had heard the news. "No, what is it?" "The president of the Telegraph Company tells me he has received a message from his clerk at Charleston that the batteries have opened fire on Sumter because the Government has sent down a fleet to force in supplies." The news had, however, spread. The hall and bar of the hotel were full, and I was asked by many people whom I had never seen in my life, what my opinions were as to the authenticity of the rumour. There was nothing surprising in the fact that the Charleston people had resented any attempt to reinforce the forts, as I was aware, from the language of the Southern Commissioners, that they would resist any such attempt to the last, and make it a *casus* [an example] and *causa belli* [cause for war].

April 13. I was complimented by the landlord's attention this morning when he came to the room and in much excitement informed me the news of Fort Sumter being bombarded by the Charleston batteries was confirmed. "And now," said he, "there's no saying where it will all end."

After breakfast I was visited by some gentlemen of Baltimore, who were highly delighted with the news, and I learned from them there was a probability of their State joining those which had seceded. The whole feeling of the landed and respectable classes is with the South. The dislike to the Federal Government at Washington is largely spiced with personal ridicule and contempt of Mr. Lincoln. Your Marylander is very tenacious about being a gentleman and what he does not consider gentlemanly is simply unfit for anything, far less for place and authority.

At the black barber's I was meekly interrogated by my attendant as to my belief in the story of the bombardment. He was astonished to find a stranger could think the event was probable. "De gen'lmen of Baltimore will be quite glad ov it. But maybe it'll come bad after all." I discovered my barber had strong ideas that the days of slavery were drawing to an end. "And what will take place then, do you think?" "Wall, sare, 'spose coloured men will be good as white men." That is it. They do not understand what a vast gulf flows between them and the equality of position with the white race. He said the town slaveowners were very severe and harsh in demanding larger sums than the slaves could earn. The slaves are sent out to do jobs, to stand for hire, to work on the quays and docks. Their earnings go to the master, who punishes them if they do not bring home enough. Sometimes the master is content with a fixed sum, and all over that amount which the slave can get may be retained for his private purposes.

At dark I started for Norfolk, in the steamer *Georgianna.*

Sunday, April 14. A night of disturbed sleep, owing to the ponderous thumping of the walking beam close to my head, the whizzing of steam, and the roaring of the steam trumpet to warn vessels out of the way—mosquitoes, too, had a good deal to say to me in spite of my dirty gauze curtains. Soon after dawn the vessel ran alongside the jetty at Fortress Monroe, and I saw indistinctly the waterface of the work which is in some danger of being attacked, it is said, by the Virginians. There was no flag on the staff above the walls and the place looked dreary and desolate. It has a fine bastioned profile, with moat and armed lunettes—the casemates were bricked up or occupied by glass windows, and all the guns I could make out were on the parapets. A few soldiers were lounging on the jetty, and after we had discharged a tipsy old officer, a few Negroes, and some parcels, the steam pipe brayed—it does not whistle—again, and we proceeded across the mouth of the channel and James River toward Elizabeth River, on which stand Portsmouth and Gosport.

On my way to the upper deck, I observed the bar was crowded by gentlemen engaged in consuming, or waiting for, cocktails or mint juleps. The latter, however, could not be had just now in such perfection as usual, owing to the inferior condition of the mint. In the matter of drinks, how hospitable the Americans are! I was asked to take as many as would have rendered me incapable of drinking again;

Moat and Seaward Face of Fortress Monroe *(From* Harper's Pictorial History of the Civil War *(New York: Harper & Bros., 1868), Vol. 1, p. 125. Courtesy of the New York Public Library)*

my excuse on the plea of inability to grapple with cocktails and the like before breakfast was heard with surprise, and I was urgently entreated to abandon so bad a habit.

The steamer in a few minutes came alongside a dirty, broken down, wooden quay, lined with open booths, on which a small crowd, mostly of Negroes, had gathered. Our vessel was in a narrow creek; at one side of the town—in the centre of the stream the old *Pennsylvania.* Below us, lay the *Merrimac,* apparently in ordinary. The only man-of-war fit for sea was a curiosity—a stumpy bluff-bowed, Dutch-built-looking sloop, called the *Cumberland.* Two or three small vessels, dismasted, were below the *Merrimac,* and we could just see the building sheds in which were one or two others on the stocks. A fleet of oyster boats anchored, or in sailless observance of the Sunday, dotted the waters. There was an ancient and fishlike smell about the town worthy of its appearance and of its functions as a seaport. As the vessel came close alongside there was the usual greeting between friends, and many a cry, "Well, you've heard the news? The Yankees out of Sumter! Isn't it fine!" There were few who did not participate in that sentiment but there were some who looked black as night and said nothing.

The steam ferry [which plies to Norfolk at the other side of the creek] was a ricketty affair. The inflection of tobacco juice on the board was remarkable. Although it was but seven o'clock [A.M.], every one had his quid in working order, and the air was filled with yellowish-brown rainbows and liquid paraboles, which tumbled in spray or in little flecks of the weed on the foul decks. As it was Sunday, some of the numerous flagstaffs which adorn the houses in both cities displayed the United States bunting; but nothing could relieve the decayed air of Norfolk. An execrable, tooth-cracking drive ended at last in front of the Atlantic Hotel, where I was doomed to take up my quarters. It is a dilapidated, uncleanly place, with tobacco-stained floor, full of flies and strong odours. The waiters were all slaves: untidy, slip-shod, and careless creatures. I was shut up in a small room, with the usual notice on the door, that the proprietor would not be responsible for anything, and that you were to lock your doors for fear of robbers, and that you must take your meals at certain hours. After a poor meal, in a long room filled with "citizens," all of them discussing Sumter, I went out into the street.

The people, I observe, are of a new and marked type—very tall, loosely yet powerfully made, with dark complexions, strongly marked features, prominent noses, large angular mouths in square jaws, deep-seated bright eyes, low, narrow foreheads—and are all of them much given to ruminate tobacco. The bells of the churches were tolling. "What is it?" exclaimed I to one. "Come along, the telegraph's in at the *Day Book.* The Yankees are whipped!" and so continued. I came at last to a crowd of men, struggling, with their faces toward the wall of a shabby house, increased by fresh arrivals, and diminished by those who, having satisfied their curiosity, came elbowing forth in a state of much excitement, exultation, and perspiration. "It's all right enough!" "Didn't I tell you so?" "Bully for Beauregard and the Palmetto State!" I shoved on and read at last the programme of the cannonade and bombardment, and of the effects upon the fort, on a dirty piece of yellowish paper on the wall. It was a terrible writing. At all the street corners men were discussing the news with every symptom of joy and gratification. Now I confess I could not share in the excitement at all. The act seemed to me the prelude to certain war.

I walked up the main street, and turned up some of the alleys to have a look at the town. Everywhere Negroes, male and female, gaudily dressed or in rags. Not a word were they talking about Sumter. "Any news today?" said I to a respectable looking Negro in a blue coat and brass buttons, wonderful hat, and vest of amber silk, check trousers, and very broken-down shoes. "Well, sare, I think nothin' much occur. Der hem a fire at Squire Nichol's house last night; leastway so I hear, sare." Squire, let me say parenthentically, is used to designate justices of the peace. Was it a very stupid *pococurante* [doltish person], or a very cunning, subtle Sambo?

Monday, April 15.   Up at dawn. Crossed by ferry to Portsmouth and arrived at railway station, which was at no place in particular, in a street down which the rails were laid. The superintendent gave me permission to take a seat in the engine car, to which I mounted accordingly, was duly introduced to and shook hands with the engineer and the stoker, and took my seat next [to] the boiler. The stoker fired up, the engine rattled along over the rugged lane between the trees which now began to sweep around us from the horizon where they rose like the bank of a river or the shores of a sea, and presently we plunged into the gloom of the primaeval forest, struggling as it were, with the last wave of the deluge. The strange tract we are passing through is the "Dismal Swamp," a name which must have but imperfectly expressed its horrors before the railway had traversed its outskirts, and the canal, which is constructed in its midst, left traces of the presence of man in that remnant of the world's exit from the flood. In the centre of this vast desolation there is a large loch, called "Lake Drummond," in the jungle and brakes around which the runaway slaves of the plantations long harboured and once or twice assembled bands of depredators, which were hunted down, broken up, and destroyed like wild beasts.

[The superintendent], a young man of some twenty-seven years of age, was an excellent representative of the young American—full of intelligence, well read, a little romantic in spite of his practical habits and dealing with matters of fact, much attached to the literature, if not to the people, of the old country. He asked me about Washington politics with as much interest as if he had never read a newspaper. I made a remark to that effect. "Oh, sir, we can't believe," exclaimed he, "a word we read in our papers. They tell a story one day, to contradict it the next. We never know when to trust them, and that's one reason, I believe, you find us all so anxious to ask questions and get information from gentlemen we meet travelling." Of the future he spoke with apprehension; "but," said he, "I am here representing the interests of a large number of Northern shareholders, and I will do my best for them. If it comes to blows after this, they will lose all, and I must stand by my own friends down South, though I don't belong to it."

So we rattle on, till the scene, at first so attractive becomes dreary and monotonous, and I tire of looking out for larger turtles and more alligators. The silence of these woods is oppressive. There is no sign of life where the train passes through the water, except among the amphibious creatures. After a time, however, when we draw out of the swamp and get into a dry patch, wild, ragged-looking cattle may be seen staring at us through the trees or tearing across the rail, and herds of porkers, nearly in the wild-boar stage, scuttle over the open.[1]

---

[1]Russell has passed into North Carolina at this point in his journey; his account of pro-Confederate sentiment and activity in the state, which follows, is interesting inasmuch as North Carolina was still in the Union on April 15, 1861, and the state did not secede until May 20.

Presently we came in sight of a flag fluttering from a lofty pine which had been stripped of its branches, throwing broad bars of red and white to the air, with a blue square in the upper quarter containing seven stars. "That's our flag," said the engineer, who was a quiet man much given to turning steam cocks, examining gauges, wiping his hands in fluffy impromptu handkerchiefs, and smoking tobacco. "That's our flag! And long may it wave—o'er the land of the free and the home of the ber-rave!" As we passed, a small crowd of men, women, and children, of all colours, in front of a group of poor broken-down shanties or log huts, cheered—to speak more correctly —whopped and yelled vehemently. The cry was returned by the passengers in the train. "We're all the right sort hereabout," said the engineer. "Hurrah for Jeff Davis!" The right sort were not particularly flourishing in outward aspect, at all events. The women, palefaced, were tawdry and ragged; the men, yellow, seedy looking. For the first time in the States, I noticed barefooted people.

Again, over another log village, a Confederate flag floated in the air; and the people ran out, Negroes and all, and cheered as before. The new flag is not so glaring and gaudy as the Stars and Stripes; but, at a distance, when the folds hang together, there is a considerable resemblance in the general effect of the two. If ever there is a real *sentiment du drapeau* [feeling for the flag] got up in the South, it will be difficult indeed for the North to restore the Union. These pieces of coloured bunting seem to twine themselves through heart and brain.

The stations along the roadside now gradually grew in proportion, and instead of a small sentry box beside a wood pile there were three or four wooden houses, a platform, a booking office, an "exchange" or drinking room, and general stores, like the shops of assorted articles in an Irish town. These stations have very grand names and the stores are dignified by high-sounding titles; nor are "billiard saloons" and "restaurants" wanting. We generally found a group of people waiting at each, and it really was most astonishing to see well-dressed, respectable looking men and women emerge out of the "dismal swamp" and out of the depths of the forest, with silk parasols and crinoline, bandboxes and portmanteaux, in the most civilised style. There were always some Negroes, male and female, in attendance on the voyagers, handling the baggage or the babies, and looking comfortable enough, but not happy. The only evidence of the good spirits and happiness of these people which I saw was on the part of a number of men who were going off from a plantation for the fishing on the coast. They and their wives and sisters, arrayed in their best—which means their brightest colours—were grinning from ear to ear as they bade good-by. The Negro likes the mild excitement of sea fishing, and in pursuit of it he feels for the moment free.

At Goldsboro, which is the first place of importance on the line, the wave of the secession tide struck us in full career. The station, the hotels, the street through which the rail ran was filled with an excited mob all carrying arms, with signs here and there of a desire to get up some kind of uniform—flushed faces, wild eyes, screaming mouths, hurrahing for "Jeff Davis" and "the Southern Confederacy," so that the yells overpowered the discordant bands which were busy with "Dixie's Land." Here was the true revolutionary furor in full sway. The men hectored, swore, cheered, and slapped each other on the backs; the women, in their best, waved handkerchiefs and flung down garlands from the windows. All was noise, dust, and patriotism.

It was a strange sight and a wonderful event at which we were assisting. These men were a levy of the people of North Carolina called out by the Governor of the State[2] for the purpose of seizing upon forts Caswell and Macon, belonging to the Federal Government, and left unprotected and undefended. The enthusiasm of the "citizens" was unbounded, nor was it quite free from a taint of alcohol. Many of the volunteers had flint firelocks, only a few had rifles. All kinds of headdress were visible, and caps, belts, and pouches of infinite variety. A man in a large wide-awake with a cock's feather on it, a blue frockcoat with a red sash, and a pair of cotton trousers thrust into his boots, came out of Griswold's Hotel with a sword under his arm, and an article, which might have been a napkin of long service, in one hand. He waved the article enthusiastically, swaying to and fro on his legs, and ejaculating "H'ra for Jeff Dav's—H'ra for S'thern E'r'rights!" and tottered over to the carriage through the crowd amid the violent vibration of all the ladies' handkerchiefs in the balcony. Just as he got into the train, a man in uniform dashed after him and caught him by the elbow, exclaiming,

[2]John W. Ellis.

"Them's not the cars, General! The cars this way, General!" The military dignitary, however, felt that if he permitted such liberties in the hour of victory he was degraded forever, so, screwing up his lips and looking grave and grand, he proceeded as follows: "Sergeant, you go be ———. I say these are my cars! They're *all* my cars! I'll send them where I please—to ——— if I like, sir. They shall go where I please—to New York, sir, or New Orleans, sir! and—sir, I'll arrest you." This famous idea distracted the General's attention from his project of entering the train, and muttering, "I'll arrest you," he tacked backwards and forwards to the hotel again.

As the train started on its journey, there was renewed yelling, which split the ear—a savage cry many notes higher than the more ringing cheer. At the wayside inn, where we dined—*pièce de résistance* being pig—the attendants, comely, well-dressed, clean Negresses were slaves—"worth a thousand dollars each." I am not favourably impressed by either the food or the mode of living, or the manners of the company. One man made very coarse jokes about "Abe Lincoln" and "Negro wenches," which nothing but extreme party passion and bad taste could tolerate. Several of the passengers had been clerks in Government offices at Washington and had been dismissed because they would not take the oath of allegiance. They were hurrying off full of zeal and patriotism to tender their services to the Montgomery Government.

At nightfall the train stopped at Wilmington, and I was shot out on a platform under a shed to do the best I could. In a long, lofty, and comfortless room, like a barn, which abutted on the platform, there was a table covered with a dirty cloth on which lay little dishes of pickles, fish, meat, and potatoes, at which were seated some of our fellow passengers. The equality of all men is painfully illustrated when your neighbour at table eats with his knife, dips the end of it into the salt, and disregards the object and end of napkins. But it is carried to a more disagreeable extent when it is held to mean that any man who comes to an inn has a right to share your bed. I asked for a room, but I was told that there were so many people moving about just now that it was not possible to give me one to myself; but at last I made a bargain for exclusive possession. Rest, however, there was little or none. I might have as well slept on the platform of the railway station outside. Trains coming in and going out shook the room and the bed on which I lay and engines snorted, puffed, roared, whistled, and rang bells close to my keyhole.

[April 16.] Early next morning, soon after dawn, I crossed the Cape Fear River, on which Wilmington is situated, by a steam ferry boat. On the quay lay quantities of shot and shell. "How came these here?" I inquired. "They're anti-abolition pills," said my neighbour; "they've been waiting here for two months back, but now that Sumter's taken, I guess they won't be wanted." To my mind, the conclusion was by no means legitimate. From the small glance I had of Wilmington, with its fleet of schooners and brigs crowding the broad and rapid river, I should think it was a thriving place. Confederate flags waved over the public buildings, and I was informed that the forts had been seized without opposition or difficulty.[3] I can see no sign here of the "affection to the Union," which, according to Mr. Seward, underlies all "secession proclivities."

As we traversed the flat and uninteresting country through which the rail passes, Confederate flags and sentiments greeted us everywhere; men and women repeated the national cry; at every station militia men and volunteers were waiting for the train, and the everlasting word "Sumter" ran through all the conversation in the cars.

The Carolinians are capable of turning out a fair force of cavalry. At each stopping place I observed saddle horses tethered under the trees and light driving vehicles drawn by wiry muscular animals, not remarkable for size but strong looking and active. Some farmers in blue jackets, and yellow braid and facings, handed round their swords to be admired by the company. A few blades had flashed in obscure Mexican skirmishes—one, however, had been borne against "the Britishers." I inquired of a fine, tall, fair-haired young fellow whom they expected to fight. "That's more than I can tell," quoth he. "The Yankees ain't such cussed fools as to think they can come here and whip us, let alone the British." "Why, what have the British got to do with it?" "They are bound to take our part; if they don't we'll just give them a hint about cotton, and that will set matters right." This was said very much with the air of a man who knows what he

[3]These forts included Fort Fisher and several minor military posts located along the Cape Fear estuary.

is talking about, and who was quite satisfied "he had you there." I found it was still displeasing to most people, particularly one or two of the fair sex, that more Yankees were not killed at Sumter. All the people who address me prefixed my name, which they soon found out, by "Major" or "Colonel"—"Captain" is very low, almost indicative of contempt. The conductor who took our tickets was called "Captain."

At the Peedee River the rail is carried over marsh and stream on trestle work for two miles. "This is the kind of country we'll catch the Yankees in, if they come to invade us. They'll have some pretty tall swimming, and get knocked on the head, if ever they gets to land. I wish there was ten thousand of the cusses in it this minute." At Nichol's Station on the frontiers of South Carolina, our baggage was regularly examined at the custom house, but I did not see any one paying duties. As the train approached the level and marshy land near Charleston, the square block of Fort Sumter was seen rising above the water and the "Stars and Bars" flying over it,[4] and the spectacle created great enthusiasm among the passengers. The smoke was still rising from an angle of the walls. Outside the village-like suburbs of the city a regiment was marching for old Virginny amid the cheers of the people—cavalry were picketed in the fields and gardens—tents and men were visible in the byways.

It was nearly dark when we reached the station. I was recommended to the Mills House, and on arriving there found Mr. [Samuel] Ward, whom I had already met in New York and Washington, and who gave me an account of the bombardment and surrender of the fort. The hotel was full of notables. I was introduced to ex-Governor [John L.] Manning, Senator [James] Chesnut, Hon. [William] Porcher Miles, on the staff of General Beauregard, and to Colonel [James] Lucas, aide-de-camp to Governor [Francis W.] Pickens. I was taken after dinner and introduced to General Beauregard, who was engaged, late as it was, in his room at the headquarters writing dispatches. The General is a small, compact man, about thirty-six years of age, with a quick and intelligent eye and action, and a good deal of the Frenchman in his manner and look. He received me in the most

[4]Russell's use of the term "Stars and Bars" is somewhat premature, because the familiar Confederate battle flag had not yet been designed.

cordial manner and introduced me to his engineer officer, Major [William H.] Whiting, whom he assigned to lead me over the works next day.

After some general conversation I took my leave; but before I went, the General said, "You shall go everywhere and see everything; we rely on your discretion and knowledge of what is fair in dealing with what you see. Of course you don't expect to find regular soldiers in our camps or very scientific works." I answered the General that he might rely on my making no improper use of what I saw in this country, but "unless you tell me to the contrary, I shall write an account of all I see to the other side of the water, and if, when it comes back, there are things you would rather not have known, you must not blame me." He smiled, and said, "I dare say we'll have great changes by that time."

That night I sat in the Charleston Club with John Manning. There were others present, like Mr. Chesnut, and Mr. Porcher Miles. We

General Pierre G. T. Beauregard *(Mathew Brady Collection, National Archives)*

talked long, and at last angrily, as might be between friends, of political affairs.

I own it was a little irritating to me to hear men indulge in extravagant broad menace such as came from their lips. I was obliged to handle the question quietly at first. "Suppose the Yankees, as you call them, come with such preponderance of men and *matériel,* that they are three to your one, will you not be forced to submit?" "Never. The Yankees are cowardly rascals. We have proved it by kicking and cuffing them till we are tired of it; besides, we know John Bull very well. He will make a great fuss about non-interference at first, but when he begins to want cotton he'll come off his perch." I found this was the fixed idea everywhere. The doctrine of "cotton is king," to them is a lively all powerful faith without distracting heresies or schisms. The dependence of such a large proportion of the English people on this sole article of American cotton is fraught with the utmost danger to our honour and to our prosperity. Here were these Southern gentlemen exulting in their power to control the policy of Great Britain, and it was small consolation to me to assure them they were mistaken.

About 8:30 P.M. a deep bell began to toll. "What is that?" "It's for all the coloured people to clear out of the streets and go home. The guards will arrest any who are found out without passes in half an hour." There was much noise in the streets, drums beating, men cheering, and marching, and the hotel is crammed full of soldiers.

April 17.   The streets of Charleston present some such aspect of those of Paris in the last revolution. Crowds of armed men singing and promenading the streets. The battle-blood running through their veins—that hot oxygen which is called "the flush of victory" on the cheek; restaurants full, revelling in barrooms, club-rooms crowded, orgies and carousing in tavern or private house, in taproom, from cabaret—down narrow alleys, in the broad highway. Sumter has set them distraught; never was such a victory; never such brave lads; never such a sight. There are pamphlets already full of the incident. It is a bloodless Waterloo or Solferino.

After breakfast I went down to the quay, with a party of the General's staff to visit Fort Sumter. The senators and governors turned soldiers wore blue military caps, with "palmetto" trees embroidered thereon; blue frockcoats, with upright collars, and shoulder straps edged with lace and marked with two silver bars to designate their rank of captain; gilt buttons with the palmetto in relief; blue trousers with a gold lace cord, and brass spurs—no straps. The day was sweltering, but a strong breeze blew in the harbour, and puffed the dust of Charleston, coating our clothes and filling our eyes with powder. The streets were crowded with lanky lads, clanking spurs, and sabres, with awkward squads marching to and from with drummers beating calls, and ruffles, and points of war; around them groups of grinning Negroes delighted with the glare and glitter, a holiday and a new idea for them—secession flags waving out of all the windows. As we walked down toward the quay, where the steamer was lying, numerous traces of the unsettled state of men's minds broke out in the hurried conversations of the various friends who stopped to speak for a few moments. "Well, governor, the old Union is gone at last!" "Have you heard what Abe is going to do?" "I don't think Beauregard will have much more fighting for it. What do you think?" And so on.

Near the quay there is a very fine building in white marble, which attracted our notice. It was unfinished, and immense blocks of the glistening stone destined for its completion lay on the ground. "What is that?" I inquired. "Why, it's a custom house Uncle Sam was building for our benefit, but I don't think he'll ever raise a cent for his treasury out of it." "Will you complete it?" "I should think not. We'll lay on few duties; and what we want is free-trade, and no duties at all, except for public purposes. The Yankees have plundered us with their custom houses and duties long enough." An old gentleman here stopped us. "You will do me the greatest favour," he said to one of our party who knew him, "if you will get me something to do for our glorious cause. Old as I am, I can carry a musket—not far, to be sure, but I can kill a Yankee if he comes near." When he had gone my friend told me the speaker was a man of fortune, two of whose sons were in camp at Morris Island, but that he was suspected of Union sentiments as he had a Northern wife, and hence his extreme vehemence and devotion.

There was a large crowd around the pier. As we got on deck, I was presented to many judges, colonels, and others of the mass of society on board, and "after compliments," I was generally asked in the first place, what I thought of the capture of Sumter, and in the second, what England would do when the news reached the other side. Already the Carolinians regard the Northern States as an alien and detested enemy, and entertain, or profess, an immense affection for Great Britain.

The shore opposite Charleston is more than a mile distant and is low and sandy, covered here and there with patches of brilliant vegetation and long lines of trees. It is cut up with creeks, which divide it into islands, so that passages out to the sea exist between some of them for light craft, though the navigation is perplexed and difficult. The city lies on a spur or promontory between the Ashley and the Cooper rivers, and the land behind it is divided in the same manner by similar creeks, and is sandy and light, bearing, nevertheless, very fine crops and trees of magnificent vegetation. The steeples, the domes of public buildings, the rows of massive warehouses and cotton stores on the wharfs, and the bright colours of the houses, render the appearance of Charleston, as seen from the river front, rather imposing. From the mastheads of the few large vessels in harbour floated the Confederate flag. Looking to our right, the same standard was visible, waving on the low, white parapets of the earthworks which had been engaged in reducing Sumter.

That much-talked-of fortress lay some two miles ahead of us now, rising up out of the water near the middle of the passage out to sea between James Island and Sullivan's Island. It struck me at first as being like one of the smaller forts off Cronstadt,[5] but a closer inspection very much diminished its importance; the material is brick, not stone, and the size of the place is exaggerated by the low background and by contrast with the sea-line. The land contracts on both sides opposite the fort, a projection of Morris Island, called "Cummings Point," running out on the left. There is a similar promontory from Sullivans Island, on which is erected Fort Moultrie, on the right from the sea entrance. Castle Pinckney, which stands on a small island at the exit of the Cooper River, is a place of no importance, and it was too far from Sumter to take any share in the bombardment; the same remarks apply to Fort Johnson on James Island, on the right bank of the Ashley River below Charleston. The works which did the mis-

[5] A Russian naval base located in the Gulf of Finland.

chief were the batteries of sand on Morris Island, at Cummings Point, and Fort Moultrie. The floating battery, covered with railroad iron, lay a long way off and could not have contributed much to the result.

As we approached Morris Island, which is an accumulation of sand covered with mounds of the same material, on which there is a scanty vegetation alternating with salt water marshes, we could perceive a few tents in the distance among the sand-hills. The sandbag batteries and an ugly black parapet, with guns peering through portholes as if from a ship's side, lay before us. Around them men were swarming like ants, and a crowd in uniform were gathered on the beach to receive us as we landed from the boat of the steamer, all eager for news, and provisions, and newspapers, of which an immense flight immediately fell upon them. A guard with bayonets crossed in a very odd sort of manner, prevented any unauthorised persons from landing. They wore the universal coarse gray jacket and trousers with worsted braid and yellow facings, uncouth caps, lead buttons stamped with the palmetto tree. Their unbronzed firelocks were covered with rust. The soldiers lounging about were mostly tall, well-grown men, young and old, some with the air of gentlemen; others coarse, long-haired fellows, without any semblance of military bearing, but full of fight and burning with enthusiasm, not unaided, in some instances, by coarser stimulus.

The whole of the island was full of life and excitement. Officers were galloping about as if on a field day or in action. Commissariat carts were toiling to and fro between the beach and the camps, and sounds of laughter and revelling came from the tents. These were pitched without order, and were of all shapes, hues, and sizes, many being disfigured by rude charcoal drawings outside and inscriptions such as "The Live Tigers," "Rattlesnake's Hole," "Yankee Smashers," &c. The vicinity of the camps was in an intolerable state, and on calling the attention of the medical officer who was with me to the danger arising from such a condition of things, he said with a sigh, "I know it all. But we can do nothing. Remember they're all volunteers and do just as they please."

In every tent was hospitality and a hearty welcome to all comers. Cases of champagne and claret, French *pâtés,* and the like, were piled outside the canvas walls, when there was no room for them inside.

In the middle of these excited gatherings I felt like a man in the full possession of his senses coming in late to a wine party. "Won't you drink with me, sir, to the—(something awful)—of Lincoln and all Yankees?" "No! if you'll be good enough to excuse me." "Well, I think you're the only Englishman who won't." Our Carolinians are very fine fellows, but a little given to the Bobadil [flamboyant] style —hectoring after a cavalier fashion, which they fondly believe to be theirs by hereditary right. They assume that the British crown rests on a cotton bale, and the Lord Chancellor sits on a pack of wool.

Secession is the fashion here. Young ladies sing for it; old ladies pray for it; young men are dying to fight for it; old men are ready to demonstrate it. The founder of the school was St. Calhoun. Here his pupils carry out their teaching in thunder and fire. States' Rights are displayed after its legitimate teaching, and the Palmetto flag and the red bars of the Confederacy are its exposition. The utter contempt and loathing for the venerated Stars and Stripes, the abhorrence of the very words United States, the intense hatred of the Yankee on the part of these people, cannot be conceived by anyone who has not seen them. I am more satisfied than ever that the Union can never be restored as it was and that it has gone to pieces, never to be put together again in the old shape, at all events, by any power of earth.

After a long and tiresome promenade in the dust, heat, and fine sand, through the tents, our party returned to the beach, where we took boat, and pushed off for Fort Sumter. The Confederate flag rose above the walls. On near approach the marks of the shot against the *pain coupé* [merlons] and the embrasures near the salient were visible enough; but the damage done to the hard brickwork was trifling, except at the angles: the edges of the parapets were ragged and pockmarked, and the quay wall was rifted here and there by shot; but no injury of a kind to render the work untenable could be made out. The greatest damage inflicted was, no doubt, the burning of the barracks, which were culpably erected inside the fort, close to the flank wall facing Cummings Point.

As the boat touched the quay of the fort, a tall, powerful-looking man came through the shattered gateway, and with uneven steps strode over the rubbish towards a skiff which was waiting to receive him, and into which he jumped and rowed off. Recognising one of my companions as he passed our boat, he suddenly stood up and with a leap and a scramble tumbled in among us, to the imminent danger of upsetting the party. Our new friend was dressed in the blue frockcoat of a civilian, round which he had tied a red silk sash—his waistbelt supported a straight sword, something like those worn with Court dress. His muscular neck was surrounded with a loosely fastened silk handkerchief; and wild masses of black hair, tinged with grey, fell from under a civilian's hat over his collar; his unstrapped trousers were gathered up high on his legs, displaying ample boots, garnished with formidable brass spurs. But his face was one not to be forgotten—a straight, broad brow, from which the hair rose up like the vegetation on a river bank, beetling black eyebrows—a mouth coarse and grim, yet full of power, a square jaw—a thick argumentative nose—a new growth of scrubby beard and moustache —these were relieved by eyes of wonderful depth and light, such as I never saw before but in the head of a wild beast. If you look some day when the sun is not too bright into the eye of the Bengal tiger in the Regent's Park, as the keeper is coming round, you will form some notion of the expression I mean. It was flashing, fierce, yet calm —with a well of fire burning behind and spouting through it, an eye pitiless in anger, which now and then sought to conceal its expression beneath half-closed lids, and then burst out with an angry glare, as if disdaining concealment.

This was none other than Louis T. Wigfall, Colonel in the Confederate army and Senator from Texas in the United States—a good type of the men whom the institutions of the country produce or throw off—a remarkable man, noted for his ready, natural eloquence; his exceeding ability as a quick, bitter debater; the acerbity of his taunts; and his readiness for personal encounter. To the last he stood in his place in the Senate in Washington, when nearly every other Southern man had seceded, lashing with a venomous and instant tongue, and covering with insults, ridicule, and abuse, such men as Mr. [Zachariah] Chandler, of Michigan, and other Republicans: never missing a sitting of the House and seeking out adversaries in the barroom or the gambling tables. The other day, when the fire against Sumter was at its height and the fort, in flames, was reduced almost to silence, a small boat put off from the shore and steered through the shot and the splashing waters right for the walls. It bore the colonel and a Negro oarsman. Holding up a white handkerchief on the end of his sword, Wigfall landed on the quay, clambered through an embrasure, and presented himself before the astonished Federals with a proposal to surrender, quite unauthorised, and "on his own hook," which led to the final capitulation of Major Anderson.

I am sorry to say, our distinguished friend had just been paying his respects *sans bornes* [without limit] to Bacchus or Bourbon, for he was decidedly unsteady in his gait and thick in speech; but his head was quite clear, and he was determined I should know all about his exploit. Major Whiting desired to show me round the work but he had no chance. "Here is where I got in," quoth Colonel Wigfall. "I found a Yankee standing here by the traverse, out of the way of our shot. He was pretty well scared when he saw me, but I told him not to be alarmed but to take me to the officers. There they were huddled up in that corner behind the brickwork, for our shells were tumbling into the yard and bursting like,"—&c. (The Colonel used strong illustrations and strange expletives in narrative.) Major Whiting shook his military head and said something uncivil to me, in private, in reference to volunteer colonels and the like, which gave him relief; whilst the martial Senator—I forgot to say that he has the name, particularly in the North, of having killed more than half a dozen men in duels—(I had an escape of being another)—conducted me through the casemates with uneven steps, stopping at every traverse to expatiate on some phase of his personal experiences, with his sword dangling between his legs and spurs involved in rubbish and soldiers' blankets.

Fort Sumter After the Bombardment *(From* Battles and Leaders of the Civil War *(New York: The Century Co., 1887), Vol. 1, p. 79. Courtesy of the New York Public Library)*

There was a working party of volunteers clearing away the rubbish in the place. It was evident they were not accustomed to labour. And on asking why Negroes were not employed, I was informed: "The niggers would blow us all up, they're so stupid; and the State would have to pay the owners for any of them who were killed and injured." "In one respect, then, white men are not so valuable as Negroes?" "Yes, sir,—that's a fact."

After a time our party went down to the boats in which we were rowed to the steamer that lay waiting for us at Morris Island. Below, in the cabin, there was spread a lunch or quasi-dinner; and the party of Senators, past and present, aides-de-camp, journalists, and flâneurs, were not indisposed to join it. For me there was only one circumstance which marred the pleasure of that agreeable reunion. Colonel and Senator Wigfall, who had not sobered himself by drinking deeply, in the plenitude of his exultation alluded to the assault on Senator Sumner as a type of the manner in which the Southerners would deal with Northerners generally, and cited it as a good exemplification of the fashion in which they would bear their "whipping." It was a strange scene—these men, hot and red-handed in rebellion, with their lives on the cast, trifling and jesting, and carousing as if they had no care on earth—all excepting the gentlemen of the local press, who were assiduous in note and food taking. It was near nightfall before we set foot on the quay of Charleston. The city was indicated by the blaze of lights, and by the continual roll of drums, and the noisy music, and the yelling cheers which rose above its streets. As I walked toward the hotel, the evening drove of Negroes, male and female, shuffling through the streets in all haste, in order to escape the patrol and the last peal of the curfew bell, swept by me.

But listen! There is a great tumult, as of many voices coming up the street, heralded by blasts of music. It is a speech-making from the front of the hotel. Such an agitated, lively multitude! How they cheer the pale, frantic man, limber and dark-haired, with uplifted arms and clenched fists, who is perorating on the balcony! "What did he say?" "Who is he?" "Why it's he again!" "That's Roger Pryor—he says that if them Yankee trash don't listen to reason and stand from under, we'll march to the North and dictate the terms of peace in Faneuil Hall! Yes, sir—and so we will, certa-i-n su-re!" "No matter, for all that, we have shown we can whip the Yankees wherever we meet them—at Washington or down here." How much I heard of all this today—how much more this evening! The hotel is noisy as ever—more men in uniform arriving every few minutes, and the hall and passages crowded with tall, good-looking Carolinians.

April 18th.   Second and third editions and extras! News of secession meetings and of Union meetings! Every one is filled with indignation against the city of New York, on account of the way in which the news of the reduction of Fort Sumter has been received there. New England has acted just as was expected but better things were anticipated on the part of the Empire City. There is no sign of shrinking from a contest: on the contrary, the Carolinians are full of eagerness to test their force in the field. "Let them come!" is their boastful *mot d'ordre* [cry].

The anger which is reported to exist in the North only adds to the fury and animosity of the Carolinians. They are determined now to act on their sovereign rights as a state, cost what it may, and uphold the ordinance of secession. The answers of several State Governors to President Lincoln's demand for troops have delighted our friends. Beriah Magoffin, of Kentucky, declares he won't give any men for such a wicked purpose; and another gubernatorial dignitary laconically replied to the demand for so many thousand soldiers, "Nary one." [John] Letcher, Governor of Virginia, has also sent a refusal. From the North comes news of mass meetings, of hauling down secession colours, mobbing secession papers, of military bodies turning out, banks subscribing and lending.

Jefferson Davis has met President Lincoln's proclamation by a counter manifesto, issuing letters of marque and reprisal—on all sides preparation for war. The Southern agents are buying steamers, but they fear the Northern States will use their navy to enforce a blockade, which is much dreaded, as it will cut off supplies and injure the commerce on which they so much depend. Assuredly Mr. Seward cannot know anything of the feeling of the South, or he would not be so confident as he was that all would blow over and that the States, deprived of the care and fostering influences of the general Government, would get tired of their secession ordinances, and of their experiment to maintain a national life, so that the United States will be re-established before long.

I went over and saw General Beauregard at his quarters. He was busy with papers, orderlies, and dispatches, and the outer room was crowded with officers. His present task, he told me, was to put Sumter in a state of defence and to disarm the works bearing on it, so as to get their fire directed on the harbour approaches, as "the North in its madness" might attempt a naval attack on Charleston. His manner of transacting business is clear and rapid. Two vases filled with flowers on his table, flanking his maps and plans; and a little hand bouquet of roses, geraniums, and scented flowers lay on a letter which he was writing as I came in, by way of paper weight. He offered me every assistance and facility, relying, of course, on my strict observances of a neutral's duty. I reminded him once more, that as the representative of an English journal, it would be my duty to write freely to England respecting what I saw; and that I must not be held accountable if on the return of my letters to America, a month after they were written, it was found they contained information to which circumstances might attach an objectionable character. The General said, "I quite understand you. We must take our chance of that, and leave you to exercise your discretion."

In the evening I dined with our excellent Consul, Mr. [Robert] Bunch, who had a small and very agreeable party to meet me. One very venerable old gentleman, named [Benjamin] Huger (pronounced as Hugeē), was particularly interesting in appearance and conversation. He formerly had some official appointment under the Federal Government, but had gone out with his State and had been confirmed in his appointment by the Confederate Government. Still he was not happy at the prospect before him or his country. "I have lived too long," he exclaimed; "I should have died 'ere these evil days arrived." What thought, indeed, must have troubled his mind when he reflected that his country was but little older than himself; for, he was one who had shaken hands with the framers of the Declaration of Independence. But though the tears rolled down his cheeks when he spoke of the prospect of civil war, there was no symptom of apprehension for the result, or indeed of any regret for the contest, which he regarded as the natural consequence of the insults, injustice, and aggression of the North against Southern rights.

Only one of the company, a most lively, quaint, witty old lawyer named [James] Petigru, dissented from the doctrines of secession; but he seems to be treated as an amiable harmless person, who has a weakness of intellect or a "bee in his bonnet" on this particular matter.

It was scarcely very agreeable to my host or myself to find that no considerations were believed to be of consequence in reference to England except her material interests, and that these worthy gentlemen regarded her as a sort of appanage to their cotton kingdom. "Why, sir, we have only to shut off your supply of cotton for a few weeks, and we can create a revolution in Great Britain. There are four millions of your people depending on us for their bread, not to speak of the many millions of dollars. No, sir, we know that England must recognise us," &c.

These tall, thin, fine-faced Carolinians are great materialists. Slavery perhaps has aggravated the tendency to look at all the world through parapets of cotton bales and rice bags, and though more stately and less vulgar, the worshippers here are not less prostrate before the "almighty dollar" than the Northerners. Again cropping out of the dead level of hate to the Yankee, grows its climax in the profession from nearly every one of the guests, that he would prefer a return to British rule to any reunion with New England. "The names in South Carolina show our origin—Charleston, and Ashley, and Cooper, &c. Our Gadsden, Sumter, and Pinckney were true cavaliers," &c. They did not say anything about Peedee or Tombigbee, or Sullivans Island, or the like. We all have our little or big weaknesses.

On my way home again I saw the sentries on their march, the mounted patrols starting on their ride, and other evidences that though the slaves are "the happiest and most contented race in the world," they require to be taken care of like less favoured mortals. The city watch-house is filled every night with slaves, who are confined there till reclaimed by their owners, whenever they are found out after nine o'clock, P.M., without special passes or permits. Guns are firing for the Ordinance of Secession of Virginia.[6]

April 19th.   An exceeding hot day. The sun pours on the broad sandy street of Charleston with immense power, and when the wind blows down the thoroughfare it sends before it vast masses of hot

[6]Virginia seceded on April 17, 1861.

dust. The houses are generally detached, surrounded by small gardens, well provided with verandahs to protect the windows from the glare, and are sheltered with creepers and shrubs and flowering plants, through which flit humming-birds and fly-catchers. In some places the streets and roadways are covered with planking, and as long as the wood is sound they are pleasant to walk or drive upon.

I paid a visit to the markets; the stalls are presided over by Negroes, male and female; the coloured people engaged in selling and buying are well clad; the butchers' meat by no means tempting to the eye, but the fruit and vegetable stalls well filled. Fish is scarce at present, as the boats are not permitted to proceed to sea lest they should be whipped up by the expected Yankee cruisers, or carry malcontents to communicate with the enemy.

I again called on General Beauregard and had a few moments' conversation with him. He told me that an immense deal depended on Virginia, and that as yet the action of the people in that State had not been as prompt as might have been hoped, for the President's proclamation with a declaration of war against the South, in which all would be ultimately involved. He is going to Montgomery to confer with Mr. Jefferson Davis. I have no doubt there is to be some movement made in Virginia. Whiting is under orders to repair there, and he hinted that he had a task of no common nicety and difficulty to perform. He is to visit the forts which had been seized on the coast of North Carolina and probably will have a look at Portsmouth. It is incredible that the Federal authorities should have neglected to secure this place.

Later I visited the Governor of the State, Mr. Pickens, to whom I was conducted by Colonel Lucas, his aide-de-camp. His palace was a very humble shed-like edifice with large rooms, on the doors of which were pasted pieces of paper with sundry high-reading inscriptions, such as "Adjutant-General's Dept., Quartermaster-General's Dept., Attorney-General of State," &c., and through the doorways could be seen men in uniform, and grave, earnest people busy at their desks with pen, ink, paper, tobacco, and spittoons. The Governor, a stout man, of big head, and a large important looking face, with watery eyes and flabby features, was seated in a barrack-like room furnished in the plainest way and decorated by the inevitable portrait of George Washington, close to which was the "Ordinance of Secession of the State of South Carolina" of last year.

Governor Pickens is considerably laughed at by his subjects, and I was amused by a little middy who described with much unction the Governor's alarm on his visit to Fort Pickens, when he was told that there were a number of live shells and a quantity of powder still in the place. He is said to have commenced one of his speeches with "Born insensible to fear," &c. To me the Governor was very courteous, but I confess the heat of the day did not dispose me to listen with due attention to a lecture on political economy with which he favoured me. I was told, however, that he had practised with success on the late Czar when he was United States Minister to St. Petersburg, and that he does not suffer his immediate staff to escape from having their minds improved on the relations of capital to labour, and on the vicious condition of capital and labour in the North.

The Governor writes very good proclamations, nevertheless, and his confidence in South Carolina is unbounded. "If we stand alone, sir, we must win. They can't whip us." A gentleman named [John J.] Pringle, for whom I had letters of introduction, has come to Charleston to ask me to his plantation, but there will be no boat for the port till Monday and it is uncertain then whether the blockading vessels, of which we hear so much, may not be down by that time.

April 20th.   I visited the editors of the *Charleston Mercury* and the *Charleston Courier* today at their offices. The Rhett family have been active agitators for secession, and it is said they are not over well pleased with Jefferson Davis for neglecting their claims to office. The elder, a pompous, hard, ambitious man, possesses ability. He is fond of alluding to his English connections and predilections, and is intolerant of New England to the last degree. I received from him, ere I left, a pamphlet of his life, career, and services.[7]

I called on several of the leading merchants and bankers. With all it was the same story. Their young men were off to the wars—no business doing. In one office I saw an announcement of a company

---

[7]The Charleston *Mercury* was edited by Robert Barnwell Rhett, Jr., the Charleston *Daily Courier* by Aaron Willington. Russell's reference to the "elder" is undoubtedly to Robert B. Rhett, Sr., a leading southern fire-eater.

for a direct communication by steamers between a southern port and Europe. "When do you expect that line to be opened?" I asked. "The United States cruisers will surely interfere with it." "Why, I expect, sir," replied the merchant, "that if those miserable Yankees try to blockade us and keep you from our cotton, you'll just send their ships to the bottom and acknowledge us. That will be before autumn, I think." It was in vain I assured him he would be disappointed. "Look out there," he said, pointing to the wharf, on which were piled some cotton bales, "there's the key will open all our ports, and put us into John Bull's strong box as well."

I dined today at the hotel, notwithstanding many hospitable invitations, with Messrs. Manning, Porcher Miles, and Pringle. Mr. [William H.] Trescot, who was Under-Secretary-of-State in Mr. [James] Buchanan's Cabinet, joined us, and I promised to visit his plantation as soon as I have returned from Mr. Pringle's. We heard much the same conversation as usual, relieved by Mr. Trescot's sound sense and philosophy. He sees clearly the evils of slavery, but is, like all of us, unable to discover the solution and means of averting them.

The secessionists are in great delight with Governor Letcher's proclamation, calling out troops and volunteers, and it is hinted that Washington will be attacked and the nest of black Republican vermin which haunt the capital driven out. Agents are to be at once dispatched to get up a navy, and every effort made to carry out the policy indicated in Jeff Davis's issue of letters of marque and reprisal. Norfolk harbour is blocked up to prevent United States ships getting away; and at the same time we hear that the United States officer commanding at the arsenal at Harpers Ferry has retired into Pennsylvania, after destroying the place by fire. How "old John Brown" would have wondered and rejoiced had he lived a few months longer!

April 21st. In the afternoon I went with Mr. Porcher Miles to visit a small farm and plantation some miles from the city, belonging to Mr. [George I.] Crafts.[8] Our arrival was unexpected but the planter's welcome was warm.

We wandered through tangled brakes and thick Indian-like jun-

[8]The Crafts plantation was located in St. Andrew's Parish, just across the Ashley River from Charleston.

gle, filled with disagreeable insects, down to the edge of a small lagoon. At the rear of the cottage-like residence (to the best of my belief built of wood), in which the planter's family lived, was a small enclosure, surrounded by a palisade, containing a number of wooden sheds which were the Negro quarters; after dinner as we sat on the steps, the children were sent for to sing for us. They came very shyly and by degrees, first peeping round the corners and from behind trees, oftentimes running away in spite of the orders of their haggard mammies, till they were chased, captured, and brought back by their elder brethren. They were ragged, dirty, shoeless urchins of both sexes; the younger ones abdominous as infant Hindoos, and wild as if just caught. With much difficulty the elder children were dressed into line; they they began to shuffle their flat feet, to clap their hands, and to drawl out in a monotonous sort of chant something about the "River Jawdam," after which Mrs. [Mary] Crafts rewarded them with lumps of sugar, which were as fruitful of disputes as the apple of discord. A few fathers and mothers gazed at the scene from a distance.

April 22nd.   Today was fixed for the visit to Mr. Pringle's plantation, which lies above Georgetown near the Peedee River. Our party which consisted of Mr. [Nelson] Mitchell, an eminent lawyer of Charleston, Colonel [William] Reed, a neighbouring planter, Mr. Ward of New York, our host, and myself, were on board the Georgetown steamer at seven o'clock, A.M., and started with a quantity of commissariat stores, ammunition, and the like for the use of the troops quartered along the coast. There was, of course, a large supply of newspapers also. At that early hour invitations to the "bar" were not uncommon, where the news was discussed by long-legged, grave, sallow men. There was a good deal of joking about "old Abe Lincoln's paper blockade," and the report that the Government had ordered their cruisers to treat the crew of Confederate privateers as "pirates" provoked derisive and menacing comments. The full impulses of national life were breathing through the whole of this people. There is their flag flying over Sumter, and the Confederate banner is waving on all the sand forts and headlands which guard the approaches to Charleston.

A civil war and persecution have already commenced. "Suspected

Abolitionists" are ill treated in the South, and "Suspected Secessionists" are mobbed and beaten in the North. The news of the attack on Sixth Massachusetts, and the Pennsylvania regiment, by the mob in Baltimore, has been received with great delight;[9] but some long-headed people see that it will only expose Baltimore and Maryland to the full force of the Northern States.

There is about Georgetown an air of quaint simplicity and old-fashioned quiet, which contrasts refreshingly with the bustle and tumult of American cities. While waiting for our vehicle we enjoyed the hospitality of Colonel Reed, who took us into an old-fashioned, angular, wooden mansion, more than a century old.

At length we were ready for our journey and, in two light covered gigs, proceeded along the sandy track which, after a while, led us to a road cut deep in the bosom of the woods where silence was only broken by the cry of a woodpecker, the scream of a crane, or the sharp challenge of the jay.

It was five o'clock before we reached our planter's house—White House Plantation. My small luggage was carried into my room by an old Negro in livery, who took great pains to assure me of my perfect welcome, and who turned out to be a most excellent valet. A low room hung with coloured mezzotints, windows covered with creepers, and an old-fashioned bedstead and quaint chairs, lodged me sumptuously; and after such toilette as was considered necessary by our host for a bachelor's party, we sat down to an excellent dinner, cooked by Negroes and served by Negroes, and aided by claret mellowed in Carolinian suns, and by Madeira brought down stairs cautiously from the cellar between the attic and the thatched roof.

Our party was increased by a neighbouring planter and after dinner the conversation returned to the old channel—all the frogs praying for a king—anyhow a prince—to rule over them. Our good host is anxious to get away to Europe, where his wife and children are, and all he fears is being mobbed at New York, where Southerners are exposed to insult, though they may get off better in that respect than black Republicans would down South. Some of our guests talked of

[9]This disturbance occurred on April 19, 1861. The Sixth Massachusetts was mobbed as it passed through Baltimore; four soldiers and twelve civilians were killed in the fighting between the rioters and the troops.

the duello and of famous hands with the pistol in these parts. The conversation had altogether very much the tone which would have probably characterised the talk of a group of Tory Irish gentlemen over their wine some sixty years ago, and very pleasant it was. Not a man—no, not one—will ever join the Union again!

My black friends who attend on me are grave as Mussulman Khitmutgars.[10] They are attired in liveries and wear white cravats and Berlin gloves. At night when we retire, off they go to their outer darkness in the small settlement of Negro-hood, which is separated from our house by a wooden palisade. Their fidelity is undoubted. The house breathes an air of security. The doors and windows are unlocked. There is but one gun, a fowlingpiece, on the premises. No planter hereabouts has any dread of his slaves. But I have seen, within the short time I have been in this part of the world, several dreadful accounts of murder and violence, in which masters suffered at the hands of their slaves. There is something suspicious in the constant never ending statement that "we are not afraid of our slaves." The curfew and the night patrol in the streets, the prisons and watch-houses, and the police regulations prove that strict supervision, at all events, is needed and necessary. My host is a kind man and a good master. If slaves are happy anywhere they should be so with him.

These people are fed by their master. They have half a pound per diem of fat pork and corn in abundance. They rear poultry and sell their chickens and eggs to the house. They are clothed by their master. He keeps them in sickness as in health. Now and then there are gifts of tobacco and molasses for the deserving. There is little labour going on in the fields, for the rice has been just exerting itself to get its head above water. These fields yield plentifully; the waters of the river are fat, and they are let in whenever the planter requires it by means of floodgates and small canals, through which the flats can carry their loads of grain to the river for loading the steamers.

April 23rd.   Later in the day when the sun was a little less fierce, we walked out from the belt of trees round the house on the plantation itself. At this time of year there is nothing to recommend to the

---

[10]Moslem servants in India.

eye the great breadth of flat fields, surrounded by small canals, which look like the bottoms of dried up ponds, for the green rice has barely succeeded in forcing its way above the level of the rich dark earth. The river bounds the estate and when it rises after the rains, its waters, loaded with loam and fertilising mud, are let in upon the lands through the small canals, which are provided with sluices and banks and floodgates to control and regulate the supply.

The Negroes had but little to occupy them now. The children of both sexes, scantily clad, were fishing in the canals and stagnant waters, pulling out horrible looking little catfish. They were so shy that they generally fled at our approach. The men and women were apathetic, neither seeking nor shunning us, and I found that their master knew nothing about them. It is only the servants engaged in household duties who are at all on familiar terms with masters.

One big slouching Negro, who seemed to be a gangsman or something of the kind, followed us in our walk and answered any questions we put to him very readily. It was a picture to see his face when one of our party, on returning to the house, gave him a larger sum of money than he had probably ever possessed before in a lump. "What will he do with it?" Buy sweet things—sugar, tobacco, a penknife, and such things. "They have few luxuries and all their wants are provided for." Took a cursory glance at the Negro quarters which are not very enticing or cleanly. They are surrounded by high palings, and the *entourage* is alive with their poultry.

As the *Nina* starts down the river on her return voyage from Georgetown tonight, and Charleston harbour may be blockaded at any time, thus compelling us to make a long détour by land, I resolve to leave by her in spite of any invitations and pressure from neighbouring planters. At midnight our carriage came round and we started in a lovely moonlight to Georgetown.

The *Nina* was blowing the signal for departure, the only sound we heard all through the night, as we drove through the deserted streets of Georgetown, and soon after three o'clock, A.M., we were on board and in our berths.

April 24th. In the morning we found ourselves in [a] chopping little seaway for which the *Nina* was particularly unsuited, laden as she was with provisions and produce. Eyes and glasses anxiously straining seawards for any trace of the blockading vessels. Every sail scrutinised, but no "Stars and Stripes" visible.

Our captain—a good specimen of one of the inland-water navigators, shrewd, intelligent, and active—told me a good deal about the country. He laughed at the fears of the whites as regards the climate. "Why, here am I," said he, "going up the river, and down the river all times of the year, and at times of day and night when they reckon the air is most deadly, and I've done so for years without any bad effects. The planters whose houses I pass all run away in May, and go off to Europe, or to the piney wood, or to the springs, or they think they'd all die."

The captain says the Negroes on the river plantations are very well off. He can buy enough of pork from the slaves on one plantation to last his ship's crew for the whole winter. The money goes to them, as the hogs are their own. One of the stewards on board had bought himself and his family out of bondage with his earnings. The State in general, however, does not approve of such practices.

At three o'clock, P.M., ran into Charleston harbour and landed soon afterwards.

I saw General Beauregard in the evening; he was very lively and in good spirits though he admitted he was rather surprised by the spirit displayed in the North. "A good deal of it is got up, however," he said, "and belongs to that washy sort of enthusiasm which is promoted by their lecturing and spouting." Beauregard is very proud of his personal strength, which for his slight frame is said to be very extraordinary, and he seemed to insist on it that the Southern men had more physical strength, owing to their mode of life and their education, than their Northern "brethren." In the evening held a sort of *tabaks consilium* [smoker] in the hotel, where a number of officers —Manning, Lucas, Chesnut, [William Ransom] Calhoun, &c.—discoursed of the affairs of the nation. All my friends, except Trescot, I think were elated at the prospect of hostilities with the North, and overjoyed that a South Carolinian regiment had already set out for the frontiers of Virginia.

April 25th. Dined with Mr. Petigru, who had most kindly postponed his dinner party till my return from the plantations, and met there General Beauregard, Judge [Henry C.] King, and others, among whom, distinguished for their *esprit* and accomplishments, were Mrs. [Susan Petigru] King and Mrs. [Caroline Petigru] Carson, daughters of my host. The dislike, which seems innate, to New England is universal and varies only in the form of its expression. It is quite true Mr. Petigru is a decided Unionist but he is the sole specimen of the genus in Charleston, and he is tolerated on account of his rarity. As the witty, pleasant old man trots down the street, utterly unconscious of the world around him, he is pointed out proudly by the Carolinians as an instance of forbearance on their part and as a proof at the same time of popular unanimity of sentiment.

General Beauregard is apprehensive of an attack by the Northern "fanatics" before the South is prepared, and he considers they will carry out coercive measures most rigorously. He dreads the cutting of the levees, or high artificial works, raised along the whole course of the Mississippi, for many hundreds of miles above New Orleans, which the Federals may resort to in order to drown the plantations and ruin the planters.

We had a good-humored argument in the evening about the ethics of burning the Norfolk Navy Yard.[11] The Southerners consider the appropriation of the arms, moneys, and stores of the United States as rightful acts inasmuch as they represent, according to them, their contribution, or a portion of it, to the national stock in trade. When a State goes out of the Union she should be permitted to carry her forts, armaments, arsenals, &c., along with her, and it was a burning shame for the Yankees to destroy the property of Virginia at Norfolk. These ideas, and many like them, have the merit of novelty to English people, who were accustomed to think there were such things as the Union and the people of the United States.

April 26th.   Bade good-by to Charleston at 9:45 A.M. this day to visit Mr. Trescot's Sea Island Plantation. Took our places in the Charleston and Savannah Railway for Pocotaligo [South Carolina], which is the station for Barnwell Island. Our fellow passengers were

[11]When Confederates, on April 20, 1861, moved against the federal naval base at Norfolk, Virginia, Hiram Paulding, the Union commander, attempted to destroy the installation by fire. The scheme failed and southerners salvaged most of the equipment they captured.

all full of politics—the pretty women being the fiercest of all—no! the least good-looking were the most bitterly patriotic, as if they hoped to talk themselves into husbands by the most unfeminine expressions toward the Yankees.

The country is a dead flat, perforated by rivers and watercourses, over which the rail is carried on long and lofty trestle work. But for the fine trees, the magnolias and live oak, the landscape would be unbearably hideous, for there are none of the quaint, cleanly, delightful villages of Holland to relieve the monotonous level or rice swamps and wastes of land and water and mud. At the humble little stations there were invariably groups of horsemen waiting under the trees and ladies with their black nurses and servants who had driven over in the odd-looking old-fashioned vehicles which were drawn up in the shade. Those who were going on a long journey, aware of the utter barrenness of the land, took with them a viaticum and bottles of milk. The nurses and slaves squatted down by their side in the train, on perfectly well-understood terms. No one objected to their presence—on the contrary, the passengers treated them with a certain sort of special consideration and they were on the happiest terms with their charges, some of which were in the absorbent condition of life, and dived their little white faces against the tawny bosom of their nurses with anything but reluctance.

The train stopped at 12:20 [P.M.] at Pocotaligo, and there we found Mr. Trescot and a couple of neighbouring planters. Got into Trescot's gig and plunged into a shady land with wood on each side, through which we drove for some distance. The country, on each side and beyond, perfectly flat—all rice lands—few houses visible—scarcely a human being on the road—drove six or seven miles without meeting a soul. After a couple of hours or so, I should think, the gig turned up by an open gateway on a path or road made through a waste of rich black mud, "glorious for rice," and landed us at the door of a planter, Mr. [Edward B.] Heyward, who came out and gave us a most hearty welcome in the true Southern style. His house is charming, surrounded with trees, and covered with roses and creepers, through which birds and butterflies are flying. Mr. Heyward took it as a matter of course that we stopped to dinner, which we were by no means disinclined to do, as the day was hot, the road was dusty, and his reception frank and kindly. A fine specimen of the planter man;

and, minus his broadbrimmed straw hat and loose clothing, not a bad representative of an English squire at home.

After dinner, at which Mr. Heyward expressed some alarm lest secession would deprive the Southern States of "ice," we continued our journey toward the [Broad] river.

At length, towards sundown, having taken to a track by a forest, we came to a broad muddy river, with steep clay banks. A canoe was lying in the little harbour formed by a slope in the bank, and four stout Negroes, who were seated round a burning log engaged in smoking and eating oysters, rose as we approached and helped the party into the "dug-out," or canoe, a narrow, long, and heavy boat, with wall sides and a flat floor. A row of one hour, the latter part of it in darkness, took us to the verge of Mr. Trescot's estate, Barnwell Island.

"Here we are at last." All I could see was a dark shadow of trees and the tops of rushes by the river side. "Mind where you step and follow me close." And so, groping along through a thick shrubbery for a short space, I came out on the garden and enclosure, in the midst of which the white outlines of a house were visible. Lights in the drawing-room—a lady to receive and welcome us—a snug library—tea, and to bed: but not without more talk about the Southern Confederacy, in which Mrs. [Eliza] Trescot explained how easily she could feed an army, from her experience in feeding her Negroes.

April 27th. Mrs. Trescot, it seems, spent part of her night in attendance on a young gentleman of colour who was introduced into the world in a state of servitude by his poor chattel of a mother. Such kindly acts as these are more common than we may suppose, and it would be unfair to put a strict or unfair construction on the motives of slaveowners in paying such attention to their property. Indeed, as Mrs. Trescot says, "When people talk of my having so many slaves, I always tell them it is the slaves who own me. Morning, noon, and night, I'm obliged to look after them, to doctor them, and attend to them in every way." Property has its duties, you see, madam, as well as its rights.

The planter's house is quite new and was built by himself; the principal material being wood, and most of the work being done by his own Negroes. Such work as window-sashes and panellings, however, was executed in Charleston. A pretty garden runs at the back, and from the windows there are wide stretches of cotton fields visible, and glimpses of the [Broad] river to be seen.

After breakfast our little party repaired to the riverside, and sat under the shade of some noble trees waiting for the boat which was to bear us to the fishing grounds. The wind blew up stream, running with the tide, and we strained our eyes in vain for the boat. The river is here nearly a mile across—a noble estuary rather—with low banks lined with forests, into which the axe had made deep forays and clearings for cotton fields.

It would have astonished a stray English traveller, if, penetrating the shade, he heard in such an out-of-the-way place familiar names and things spoken of by the three lazy persons who were stretched out on the ant-haunted trunks which lay prostrate by the seashore. Mr. Trescot spent some time in London as *attaché* to the United States Legation, was a club man, and had a large circle of acquaintance among the young men about town, of whom he remembered many anecdotes and peculiarities, and little adventures. Since that time he was Under-Secretary-of-State in Mr. Buchanan's Administration and went out with secession. He is the author of a very agreeable book on a dry subject, *The History of American Diplomacy*, which is curious enough as an unconscious exposition of the anti-British jealousies, and even antipathies, which have animated American statesmen since they were created. In fact, much of American diplomacy means hostility to England, and the skilful employment of the anti-British sentiment at their disposal in their own country and elsewhere.

April 28th.   In the morning a child brings in my water and boots —an intelligent, curly-headed creature, dressed in a sort of sack, without any particular waist, barefooted. I imagined it was a boy till it told me it was a girl. I asked if she was going to church, which seemed to puzzle her exceedingly; but she told me finally she would hear prayers from "uncle" in one of the cottages. This use of the words "uncle" and "aunt" for old people is very general. Is it because they have no fathers and mothers? In the course of the day, the child, who was fourteen or fifteen years of age, asked me "whether I would not buy her. She could wash and sew very well, and she thought missus wouldn't want much for her." The object she had in view leaked out at last. It was a desire to see the glories of Beaufort, of which she had heard from the fishermen; and she seemed quite wonderstruck when she was informed I did not live there and had never seen it. She has never been outside the plantation in her life.

After breakfast we loitered about the grounds, strolling through the cotton fields, which had as yet put forth no bloom or flower, and coming down others to the thick fringes of wood and sedge bordering the marshy banks of the island. The silence was profound, broken only by the husky midday crowing of the cocks in the Negro quarters.

In the afternoon I took a short drive "to see a tree," which was not very remarkable, and looked in at the Negro quarters and the cotton mill. The old Negroes were mostly indoors, and came shambling out to the doors of their wooden cottages, making clumsy bows at our approach but not expressing any interest or pleasure at the sight of their master and the strangers. They were shabbily clad in tattered clothes, bad straw hats and felt bonnets, and broken shoes. The latter are expensive articles, and Negroes cannot dig without them. Trescot sighed as he spoke of the increase in price since the troubles broke out.

The huts stand in a row, like a street, each detached, with a poultry house of rude planks behind it. The mutilations which the poultry undergo for the sake of distinction are striking. Some are deprived of a claw, others have the wattles cut, and tails and wings suffer in all ways. No attempt at any drainage or any convenience existed near them, and the same remark applies to very good houses of white people in the South. Heaps of oyster shells, broken crockery, old shoes, rags, and feathers were found near each hut. The huts were all alike windowless, and the apertures, intended to be glazed some fine day, were generally filled up with a deal board. The roofs were shingle, and the whitewash which had once given the settlement an air of cleanliness was now only to be traced by patches which had escaped the action of the rain. I observed that many of the doors were fastened by a padlock and chain outside. "Why is that?" "The owners have gone out, and honesty is not a virtue they have towards each other. They would find their things stolen if they did not lock their doors." Mrs. Trescot, however, insisted on it that nothing could exceed the probity of the slaves in the house, except in regard to sweet things, sugar and the like; but money and jewels were quite safe. It is obvious that some reason must exist for this regard to the distinctions twixt meum and tuum in the case of masters and mistresses, when it does not guide their conduct towards each other, and I think it might easily be found in the fact that the Negroes could scarcely take money without detection. Jewels and jewellery would be of little value to them; they could not wear them, could not part with them. The system has made the white population a police against the black race, and the punishment is not only sure but grievous. Such things as they can steal from each other are not to be so readily traced.

One particularly dirty looking little hut was described to me as "the church." It was about fifteen feet square, begrimed with dirt and smoke, and windowless. A few benches were placed across it, and "the preacher," a slave from another plantation, was expected next week. These preachings are not encouraged in many plantations. They "do the niggers no good"—"they talk about things that are going on elsewhere, and get their minds unsettled," and so on.

On our return to the house I found that Mr. Edmund Rhett, one of the active and influential political family of that name, had called —a very intelligent and agreeable gentleman, but one of the most ultra and violent speakers against the Yankees I have yet heard. He declared there were few persons in South Carolina who would not sooner ask Great Britain to take back the State than submit to the triumph of the Yankees. "We are an agricultural people, pursuing our own system, and working out our own destiny, breeding up women and men with some other purpose than to make them vulgar, fanatical, cheating Yankees—hypocritical, if as women they pretend to real virtue; and lying, if as men they pretend to be honest. We have gentlemen and gentlewomen in your sense of it. We have a system which enables us to reap the fruits of the earth by a race which we save from barbarism in restoring them to their real place in the world as labourers, whilst we are enabled to cultivate the arts, the graces, and accomplishments of life, to develop science, to apply ourselves to the duties of government, and to understand the affairs of the country."

This is a very common line of remark here. The Southerners also take pride to themselves, and not unjustly, for their wisdom in keeping in Congress those men who have proved themselves useful and capable. "We do not," they say, "cast able men aside at the caprices of a mob or in obedience to some low party intrigue, and hence we are sure of the best men, and are served by gentlemen conversant with public affairs, far superior in every way to the ignorant clowns who are sent to Congress by the North. Look at the fellows who are sent out by Lincoln to insult foreign courts by their presence." I said that I understood Mr. Adams and Mr. [William] Dayton[12] were very respectable gentlemen, but I did not receive any sympathy; in fact, a neutral who attempts to moderate the violence of either side, is very like an ice between two hot plates. Mr. Rhett is also persuaded that the Lord Chancellor sits on a cotton bale. "You must recognise us, sir, before the end of October." In the evening a distant thunder storm attracted me to the garden, and I remained out watching the broad flashes and sheets of fire worthy of the tropics till it was bedtime.

April 29th. This morning up at 6 A.M., bade farewell to our hostess and Barnwell Island, and proceeded with Trescot back to the Pocotaligo station, which we reached at 12:20. The country through which we passed was flat and flooded as usual, and the rail passed over dark deep rivers on lofty trestle work, by pinewood and dogwood tree, by the green plantation clearing, with much bank, dyke, and tiny canal mile by mile, the train stopping for the usual freight of ladies, and Negro nurses, and young planters, all very much of the same class, till at three o'clock, P.M., the cars rattled up alongside a large shed, and we were told we had arrived at Savannah.

Here was waiting for me Mr. Charles Green. The drive through such portion of Savannah as lay between the terminus and Mr. Green's house soon satisfied my eyes that it had two peculiarities. In the first place, it had the deepest sand in the streets I have ever seen; and next, the streets were composed of the most odd, quaint, green-windowed, many-coloured little houses I ever beheld, with an odd population of lean, sallow, ill-dressed unwholesome-looking whites, lounging about the exchanges and corners, and a busy, well-clad,

[12]Charles Francis Adams and William Dayton were the American ambassadors to Great Britain and France.

gaily-attired race of Negroes, working their way through piles of children, under the shade of the trees which bordered all the streets. The fringe of green and the height attained by the live oak, pride of India, and magnolia, give a delicious freshness and novelty to the streets of Savannah, which is increased by the great number of squares and openings covered with something like sward, fenced round by white rail, and embellished with noble trees to be seen at every few hundred yards. It is difficult to believe you are in the midst of a city, and I was repeatedly reminded of the environs of a large Indian cantonment—the same kind of churches and detached houses, with their plantations and gardens not unlike. The wealthier classes, however, have houses of the New York Fifth Avenue character: one of the best of these, a handsome mansion of rich red sandstone, belonged to my host, who coming out from England many years ago, raised himself by industry and intelligence to the position of one of the first merchants in Savannah.

Mr. Green drove me through the town, which impressed me more than ever with its peculiar character. We visited Brigadier General [Alexander] Lawton, who is charged with the defences of the place against the expected Yankees, and found him just setting out to inspect a band of volunteers, whose drums we heard in the distance and whose bayonets were gleaming through the clouds of Savannah dust, close to the statue erected to the memory of one Pulaski, a Pole, who was mortally wounded in the unsuccessful defence of the city against the British in the War of Independence. He turned back and led us into his house. The hall was filled with little round rolls of flannel. "These," said he, "are cartridges for cannon of various calibres, made by the ladies of Mrs. [Sarah] Lawton's 'cartridge class.'" There were more cartridges in the back parlour, so that the house was not quite a safe place to smoke a cigar in. The General has been in the United States Army, and has now come forward to head the people of this State in their resistance to the Yankees.

We took a stroll in the park, and I learned the news of the last few days. The people of the South, I find, are delighted at a snubbing which Mr. Seward had given to Governor [Thomas] Hicks, of Maryland, for recommending the arbitration of Lord Lyons, and he is stated to have informed Governor Hicks that "our troubles could not be referred to foreign arbitration, least of all to that of the representative of a European monarchy." The most terrible accounts are given of the state of things in Washington. Mr. Lincoln consoles himself for his miseries by drinking. Mr. Seward follows suit. The White House and capital are full of drunken border ruffians, headed by one Jim Lane of Kansas.[13] But, on the other hand, the Yankees, under one [Benjamin F.] Butler, a Massachusetts lawyer, have arrived at Annapolis, in Maryland, secured the *Constitution,* man-of-war, and are raising masses of men for the invasion of the South all over the States. The most important thing, as it strikes me, is the proclamation of the Governor of Georgia, forbidding citizens to pay any money on account of debts due to Northerners till the end of war.[14] General Robert E. Lee has been named commander-in-chief of the forces of the Commonwealth of Virginia, and troops are flocking to that State from Alabama and other States. Governor [John W.] Ellis has called out 30,000 volunteers in North Carolina, and Governor [Henry] Rector, of Arkansas, has seized the United States military stores at Napoleon. There is a rumor that Fort Pickens has been taken also but [it] is very probably untrue. In Texas and Arkansas the United States Regulars have not made an attempt to defend any of the forts.

In the midst of all this warlike work, volunteers drilling, bands playing, it was pleasant to walk in the shady park, with its cool fountains, and to see the children playing about—many of them, alas! "Playing at soldiers"—in charge of their nurses. Returning, sat on the verandah and smoked a cigar, but the mosquitoes were very keen and numerous. My host did not mind them, but my cuticle will never be sting-proof.

April 30th. At 1:30 P.M. a small party started from Mr. Green's to visit the cemetery at Bonaventure, to which every visitor to Savannah must pay his pilgrimage; *difficiles aditus primos habet* [a difficult approach at first]—a deep sandy road which strains the horses and

---

[13]Following the bombardment of Fort Sumter, Senator James H. Lane of Kansas brought his "Frontier Guard," a Kansas military unit, to Washington. Assigned to protect the White House, the guard spent several nights in the East Room before housing accommodations could be found. The unit disbanded during the summer of 1861.

[14]On April 26, 1861, Joseph E. Brown, governor of Georgia, issued an order repudiating debts that the state and citizens owed to northern financial houses.

the carriages; but at last "the shell road" is reached—a highway several miles long, consisting of oyster shells—the pride of Savannah, which eats as many oysters as it can to add to the length of this wonderful road. There is no stone in the whole of the vast alluvial ranges of South Carolina and maritime Georgia, and the only substance available for making a road is the oyster shell.

In the evening Mr. Green gave a dinner to some very agreeable people. The Georgians are not quite so vehement as the South Carolinians in their hate of the Northerners; but they are scarcely less determined to fight President Lincoln and all his men. And that is the test of this rebellion's strength. I did not hear any profession of a desire to become subject to England, or to borrow a prince of us; but I have nowhere seen stronger determination to resist any reunion with the New England States. "They can't conquer us, Sir!" "If they try it, we'll whip them."

May Day.   When at last we got down to the riverside I found Commodore [Josiah] Tattnall and Brigadier Lawton in full uniform waiting for me.

The [Savannah] river is about the width of the Thames below Gravesend, very muddy, with a strong current, and rather fetid. That effect might have been produced from the rice swamps at the other side of it, where the land is quite low and stretches away as far as the sea in one level green, smooth as a billiard cloth. The bank at the city side is higher, so that the houses stand on a little eminence over the stream, affording convenient wharfage and slips for merchant vessels.

Of these there were few indeed visible—nearly all had cleared out for fear of the blockade; some coasting vessels were lying idle at the quay side, and in the middle of the stream near a floating dock the *Camilla* was moored, with her club ensign flying. These are the times for bold ventures, and if Uncle Sam is not very quick with his blockades there will be plenty of privateers and the like under C.S.A. colours looking out for his fat merchantmen all over the world.

The steamer which was waiting to receive us had the Confederate flag flying, and Commodore Tattnall told me he had just "come over from the other side." I was much interested in the fine white-headed, blue-eyed, ruddy-cheeked old man—who suddenly found himself blown into the air by a great political explosion, and in doubt and wonderment was floating to shore, under a strange flag in unknown waters. He was full of anecdote too, as to strange flags in distant and well-known names. The gentry of Savannah had a sort of Celtic feeling towards him in regard to his old name, and seemed determined to support him.

He has served the Stars and Stripes for three-fourths of a long life —his friends are in the North, his wife's kindred are there, and so are all his best associations—but his State has gone out. How could he fight against the country that gave him birth! The United States is no country in the sense we understand the words. It is a corporation or a body corporate for certain purposes, and a man might as well call himself a native of the common council of the city of London, or a native of the Swiss Diet, in the estimation of our Americans, as say he is a citizen of the United States; though it answers very well to say so when he is abroad or for purposes of a legal character.

When I was venturing to point out to General Lawton the weakness of Fort Pulaski, placed as it is in low land, accessible to boats and quite open enough for approaches from the city side, he said, "Oh, that is true enough. All our seacoast works are liable to that remark, but the Commodore will take care of the Yankees at sea, and we shall manage them on land." These people all make a mistake in referring to the events of the old war. "We beat off the British fleet at Charleston, by the militia—ergo, we'll sink the Yankees now." They do not understand the nature of the new shell and heavy vertical fire, or the effect of projectiles from great distances falling into open works. The Commodore afterwards, smiling, remarked, "I have no fleet. Long before the Southern Confederacy has a fleet that can cope with the Stars and Stripes my bones will be white in the grave."

We got back by eight o'clock, P.M., after a pleasant day. What I saw did not satisfy me that Pulaski was strong or Savannah very safe.

May 2nd. Breakfasted with Mr. [William] Hodgson. There were in attendance some good-looking little Negro boys and men dressed in liveries, and they must have heard our discussion, or rather allusion, to the question which would decide whether we thought they are human beings or black two-legged cattle, with some interest, unless indeed the boast of their master, that slavery elevates the character and civilises the mind of a Negro, is another of the false pretences on which the institution is rested by its advocates.

I revisited some of the big houses afterwards, and found the merchants not cheerful, but fierce and resolute. There is a considerable population of Irish and Germans in Savannah, who to a man are in favour of the Confederacy and will fight to support it. Indeed, it is expected they will do so, and there is a pressure brought to bear on them by their employers which they cannot well resist. The Negroes will be forced into the place the whites hitherto occupied as labourers —only a few useful mechanics will be kept—and the white population will be obliged by a moral force draughting to go to the wars. The kingdom of cotton is most essentially of this world and it will be fought for vigourously. On the quays of Savannah, and in the warehouses, there is not a man who doubts that he ought to strike his hardest for it, or apprehends failure. And then, what a career is before them! All the world asking for cotton, and England dependent on it. What a change since Whitney first set his cotton gin to work in this State close by us! Georgia, as a vast country only partially reclaimed, yet looks to a magnificent future. In her past history the Florida wars and the treatment of the unfortunate Cherokee Indians, who were expelled from their lands as late as 1838, show the people who descended from old Oglethorpe's band were fierce and tyrannical, and apt at aggression; nor will slavery improve them. I do not speak of the cultivated, the hospitable citizens of the large towns, but of the bulk of the slaveless whites.

Three

THE GULF STATES
(MAY 3–JUNE 1, 1861)

May 3rd. I bade good-by to Mr. Green, who with several of his friends came down to see me off at the terminus or "depot" of the Central Railway, on my way to Montgomery—and looked my last on Savannah, its squares and leafy streets, its churches, and institutes with feeling of regret that I could not see more of them, and that I was forced to be content with the outer aspect of the public buildings. I had been serenaded and invited out in all directions, asked to visit plantations and big trees, to make excursions to famous and beautiful spots, and specially warned not to leave the State without visiting the mountain district in the northern and western portion; but the march of events called me to Montgomery.

From Savannah to Macon, 191 miles, the road passes through level country only partially cleared. That is, there are patches of forest still intruding on the green fields, where the jagged black teeth of the destroyed trees rise from above the maize and cotton. There were but few Negroes visible at work nor did the land appear rich, but I was told the rail was laid along the most barren part of the country. The

Indians had roamed in these woods little more than twenty years ago —now the wooden huts of the planters' slaves and the larger edifice with its verandah and timber colonnade stood in the place of their wigwam.

Among the passengers to whom I was introduced was the Bishop of Georgia, the Rev. Mr. [Stephen] Elliott, a man of exceeding fine presence, of great stature, and handsome face, with a manner easy and graceful, but we got on the unfortunate subject of slavery, and I rather revolted at hearing a Christian prelate advocating the institution on scriptural grounds.

This affectation of Biblical sanction and ordinance as the basis of slavery was not new to me, though it is not much known at the other side of the Atlantic. I had read in a work on slavery that it was permitted by both the Scriptures and the Constitution of the United States, and that it must, therefore, be doubly right. The miserable sophists who expose themselves to the contempt of the world by their paltry thesicles on the divine origin and uses of slavery are infinitely more contemptible than the wretched bigots who published themes long ago on the propriety of burning witches or on the necessity for the offices of the Inquisition.

Whenever the Southern Confederacy shall achieve its independence—no matter what its resources, its allies, or its aims—it will have to stand face to face with civilised Europe on this question of slavery, and the strength which it derived from the aegis of the Constitution—"the league with the devil and covenant with Hell"— will be withered and gone.[1]

I am well aware of the danger of drawing summary conclusions off-hand from the windows of a railway, but no one can doubt the evidence of his senses when he sees from the windows of the carriage that the children are barefooted, shoeless, stockingless—that the people who congregate at the wooden huts and grog-shops of the stations are rude, unkempt, but great fighting material too—that the villages are miserable places, compared with the trim, snug settlements one saw in New Jersey from the carriage windows. Slaves in the field looked happy enough—but their masters certainly were

[1]This is Russell's garbled version of William Lloyd Garrison's famous quotation calling the United States Constitution "a covenant with death, an agreement with hell" because it permitted slavery to exist in the South.

rough-looking and uncivilised—and the land was but badly cleared. But then we were traversing the least fertile portions of the State—a recent acquirement—gained only one generation since.

The train halted at a snug little wood-embowered restaurant, surrounded by trellis and latticework, and in the midst of a pretty garden, which presented a marked contrast to the "surroundings" we had seen. The dinner, served by slaves, was good of its kind and the charge not high. On tendering the landlord a piece of gold for payment, he looked at it with disgust, and asked, "Have you no Charleston money? No Confederate notes?" "Well, no! Why do you object to gold?" "Well, do you see, I'd rather have our own paper! I don't care to take any of the United States gold. I don't want their stars and their eagles; I hate the sight of them." The man was quite sincere—my companion gave him notes of some South Carolina bank.

It was dark when the train reached Macon, one of the principal cities of the State. We drove to the best hotel, but the regular time for dinner hour was over and that for supper not yet come. The landlord directed us to a subterranean restaurant, in which were a series of crypts closed in by dirty curtains, where we made a very extraordinary repast, served by a half-clad little Negress, who watched us at the meal with great interest through the curtains—the service was of the coarsest description; thick French earthenware, the spoons of pewter, and knives and forks steel or iron, with scarce a pretext of being cleaned. On the doors were the usual warnings against pickpockets and the customary internal police regulations and ukases. Pickpockets and gamblers abound in American cities, and thrive greatly at the large hotels and the lines of railways.

May 4th. In the morning I took a drive about the city, which is loosely built in detached houses over a very pretty undulating country covered with wood and fruit trees. Many good houses of dazzling white, with bright green blinds, verandahs, and doors, stand in their own grounds or gardens. In the course of the drive I saw two or three signboards and placards announcing that "Smith & Co. advanced money on slaves, and had constant supplies of Virginian Negroes on sale or hire." These establishments were surrounded by high walls enclosing the slave pens, or large rooms in which the slaves are kept for inspection. The train for Montgomery started at 9:45 A.M., and I had no time to stop and visit them. It is evident we are approaching the Confederate capital, for the candidates for office begin to show and I detected a printed testimonial in my room in the hotel. The country, from Macon in Georgia to Montgomery in Alabama, offers no features to interest the traveller which are not common to the districts already described. It is, indeed, more undulating, and somewhat more picturesque or less unattractive, but, on the whole, there is little to recommend it except the natural fertility of the soil. The people are rawer, ruder, bigger—there is the same amount of tobacco chewing and its consequences—and as much swearing or use of expletives. The men are tall, lean, uncouth, but they are not peasants. There are, so far as I have seen, no rustics, no peasantry, in America; men dress after the same type, differing only in finer or coarser material; every man would wear, if he could, a black satin waistcoat and a large diamond pin stick in the front of his shirt, as he certainly has a watch or a gild or gold chain of some sort or other. The mean white affects the style of the large proprietor of slaves or capital as closely as he can; he reads his papers—and, by-the-by, they are becoming smaller and more whitey-brown as we proceed—and takes his drink with the same air—takes up as much room, and speaks a good deal in the same fashion.

The people are all hearty secessionists here—the Bars and Stars are flying at the road-stations and from the pine tops, and there are lusty cheers for Jeff Davis and the Southern Confederacy. Troops are flocking towards Virginia from the Southern States in reply to the march of volunteers from Northern States to Washington; but it is felt that the steps taken by the Federal Government to secure Baltimore have obviated any chance of successfully opposing "Lincolnites" going through that city.[2] There is a strong disposition on the part of the Southerners to believe they have many friends in the North, and they endeavour to attach a factious character to the actions of the Government by calling the volunteers and the war party in the North "Lincolnites," "Lincoln's Mercenaries," "Black Republicans," "Abolitionists," and the like. The report of an armistice, now denied by Mr. Seward officially, was for some time current, but it is plain that the South must make good its words and justify its acts by the sword.

[2]On April 27, 1861, Lincoln suspended the privilege of the writ of *habeas corpus* (an action practically equivalent to declaring martial law) in parts of Maryland, including Baltimore; shortly thereafter, Federal troops moved into the city.

General Scott would, it was fondly believed, retire from the United States Army, and either remain neutral or take command under the Confederate flag, but now that it is certain he will not follow any of these courses, he is assailed in the foulest manner by the press and in private conversation. Heaven help the idol of a democracy!

At one of the junctions General Beauregard, attended by Mr. Manning and others of his staff, got into the car and tried to elude observation, but the conductors take great pleasure in unearthing distinguished passengers for the public, and the General was called on for a speech by the crowd of idlers. The General hates speechmaking, he told me, and he had besides been bored to death at every station by similar demands. But a man must be popular or he is nothing. So, as next best thing, Governor Manning made a speech in the General's name, in which he dwelt on Southern Rights, Sumter, victory, and abolitiondom, and was carried off from the cheers of his auditors by the train in the midst of an unfinished sentence. There were a number of blacks listening to the Governor, who were appreciative.

Towards evening, having thrown out some slight outworks against accidental sallies of my fellow passengers' saliva, I went to sleep, and woke up at 11 P.M. to hear we were in Montgomery. A very ricketty omnibus took the party to the hotel, which was crowded to excess. The General and his friends had one room to themselves. Three gentlemen and myself were crammed into a filthy room which already contained two strangers, and as there were only three beds in the apartment, it was apparent that we were intended to "double up considerably," but after strenuous efforts, a little bribery and cajoling, we succeeded in procuring mattresses to put on the floor, which was regarded by our neighbours as a proof of miserable aristocratic fastidiousness. Had it not been for the flies, the fleas would have been intolerable, but one nuisance neutralised the other. Then, as to food—nothing could be had in the hotel—but one of the waiters led us to a restaurant where we selected from a choice bill of fare which contained, I think, as many odd dishes as ever I saw, some unknown fishes, oyster-plants, 'possums, raccoons, frogs, and other delicacies, and eschewing toads and the like, really made a good meal off dirty plates on a vile tablecloth, our appetites being sharpened by the best of condiments.

Colonel Pickett has turned up here, having made his escape from

Washington just in time to escape arrest—travelling in disguise on foot through out-of-the-way places till he got among friends.

I was glad, when bedtime approached, that I was not among the mattress men. One of the gentlemen in the bed next [to] the door was a tremendous projector in the tobacco juice line: his final rumination ere he sank to repose was a masterpiece of art—a perfect liquid pyrotechny, Roman candles and falling stars. A horrid thought occurred as I gazed and wondered. In case he should in a supreme moment turn his attention my way—I was only seven or eight yards off, and that might be nothing to him—I hauled down my mosquito curtain at once and watched him till, completely satiated, he slept.

May 5th.   Very warm, and no cold water, unless one went to the river. The hotel baths are not promising. This hotel is worse than Mill's House or Willard's. The feeding and the flies are intolerable. One of our party comes in to say that he could scarce get down to the hall on account of the crowd, and that all the people who passed him had very hard, sharp bones. He remarks thereupon to the clerk at the bar, who tells him that the particular projections he alludes to are implements of defence or offence, as the case may be, and adds, "I suppose you and your friends are the only people in the house who haven't a bowie-knife, or a six-shooter, or Derringer about them." The house is full of Confederate Congressmen, politicians, colonels, and placemen with or without places, and a vast number of speculators, contractors, and the like, attracted by the embryo government. Among the visitors are many filibusterers. I hear a good deal about the association called the Knights of the Golden Circle, a Protestant association for securing the Gulf provinces and states, including— which has been largely developed by recent events—them in the Southern Confederacy, and creating them into an independent government.[3]

Montgomery has little claims to be called a capital. The streets are very hot, unpleasant, and uninteresting. I have rarely seen a more

---

[3]The Knights of the Golden Circle was a tenuous and shadowy organization formed in 1854 for the purpose of creating a slave empire out of the southern states, Mexico, and several Central American countries and provinces. During the war the organization changed its objective and supposedly moved to the northern states where it obstructed the war effort. There is little evidence to support the claim of some historians that the KGC was an effective opposition force in the midwestern states.

dull, lifeless place; it looks like a small Russian town in the interior. The names of the shopkeepers indicate German and French origin. I looked in at one or two of the slave magazines. A certain degree of freedom is enjoyed by some of the men, who lounge about the doors and are careless of escape or liberty, knowing too well the difficulties of either.

The South has at present little or no manufactures, takes everything from the Yankee outside or the mean whites within her gates, and despises both. Both are reconciled by interest. The one gets a good price for his manufacture and the fruit of his ingenuity from a careless, spendthrift proprietor; the other hopes to be as good as his master some day and sees the beginning of his fortune in the possession of a Negro. The United States has been represented to the British and Irish emigrants by the free States—the Northern States and the great West—and the British and German emigrant who finds himself in the South, has drifted there through the Northern States, and either is a migratory labourer or hopes to return with a little money

Montgomery, Alabama *(From* Harper's Pictorial History of the Civil War *(New York: Harper & Bros., 1868), Vol. 1, p. 122. Courtesy of the New York Public Library)*

to the North and West, if he does not see his way to the possession
of land and Negroes.

After dinner at the hotel table, which was crowded with officers
and where I met Mr. Howell Cobb and several senators of the new
Congress, I spent the evening with Colonel [George A.] Deas,
Quartermaster-General,[4] and a number of his staff, in their quarters. As I was walking over to the house, one of the detached villa-
like residences so common in Southern cities, I perceived a crowd of
very well dressed Negroes, men and women, in front of a plain
brick building which I was informed was their Baptist meeting-
house, into which white people rarely or never intrude. These were
domestic servants, or persons employed in stores, and their general
appearance indicated much comfort and even luxury. I doubted if
they were all slaves.

May 6th. The environs of Montgomery are agreeable—well-
wooded, undulating, villas abounding, public gardens, and a large
Negro and mulatto suburb. It is not usual, as far as I can judge, to see
women riding on horseback in the South, but on the road here we
encountered several.

After breakfast I walked down with Senator Wigfall to the Capitol
of Montgomery—one of the true Athenian Yankeeized structures of
this novo-classical land, erected on a site worthy of a better fate and
edifice. By an open cistern, on our way, I came on a gentleman
engaged in [a slave auction] disposing of some living ebony carvings
to a small circle, who had more curiosity than cash, for they did not
all respond to the energetic appeals of the auctioneer.

The sight was a bad preparation for an introduction to the legislative assembly of a Confederacy, which rests on the Institution as the
cornerstone of the social and political arch which maintains it. As-
saulted by reason, by logic, argument, philanthropy, [and] progress
directed against his peculiar institutions, the Southerner at last is

---

[4]Deas was acting adjutant general of the Confederacy in 1861. Russell probably
referred to him as quartermaster general because the duties of a quartermaster general under the British military system and those of an adjutant general in a nineteenth-century U.S. military unit were similar.

driven to a fanaticism—a sacred faith which is above all reason or logical attack in the propriety, righteousness, and divinity of slavery.

The chaplain, a venerable old man, loudly invoked curses on the heads of the enemy, and blessings on the arms and councils of the New State. When he was done, Mr. Howell Cobb, a fat, double-chinned, mellow-eyed man, rapped with his hammer on the desk before the chair on which he sat as speaker of the assembly, and the house proceeded to business. I could fancy that, in all but garments, they were like the men who first conceived the great rebellion which led to the independence of this wonderful country—so earnest, so grave, so sober, and so vindictive—at least, so embittered against the power which they consider tyrannical and insulting.

The word "liberty" was used repeatedly in the short time allotted to the public transaction of business and the reading of documents; the Congress was anxious to get to its work, and Mr. Howell Cobb again thumped his desk and announced that the house was going into "secret session," which intimated that all persons who were not members should leave. I was introduced to what is called the floor of the house, and had a delegate's chair, and of course I moved away with the others, and with the disappointed ladies and men from the galleries, but one of the members, Mr. [Robert Barnwell] Rhett, I believe, said jokingly: "I think you ought to retain your seat. If the *Times* will support the South, we'll accept you as a delegate." I replied that I was afraid I could not act as a delegate to a Congress of Slave States. And, indeed, I had been much affected at the slave auction held just outside the hotel, on the steps of the public fountain, which I had witnessed on my way to the Capitol. The auctioneer, who was an ill-favoured, dissipated-looking rascal, had his "article" beside him on, not in, a deal packing-case—a stout young Negro badly dressed and ill-shod, who stood with all his goods fastened in a small bundle in his hand, looking out at the small and listless gathering of men, who, whittling and chewing, had moved out from the shady side of the street as they saw the man put up. The chattel character of slavery in the States renders it most repulsive. What a pity the nigger is not polypoid—so that he could be cut up in [chunks], and each [chunk] reproduce itself!

A man in a cart, some volunteers in coarse uniforms, a few Irish labourers in a long van, and four or five men in the usual black coat, satin waistcoat, and black hat, constituted the audience, whom the auctioneer addressed volubly: "A prime field hand! Just look at him —good-natured, well-tempered; no marks, nary sign of bad about him! En-i-ne hunthered—only nine hun-ther-ed and fifty dol'rs for 'em! Why, it's quite rad-aklous! Nine hundred and fifty dol'rs! I can't raly—That's good. Thank you, sir. Twenty-five bid—nine hun-therd and seventy-five dol'rs for this most useful hand." The price rose to one thousand dollars, at which the useful hand was knocked down to one of the black hats near me. The auctioneer and the Negro and his buyer all walked off together to settle the transaction, and the crowd moved away.

"That nigger went cheap," said one of them to a companion, as he walked towards the shade. "Yes, Sirr! Niggers is cheap now—that's a fact." I must admit that I felt myself indulging in a sort of reflection whether it would not be nice to own a man as absolutely as one might possess a horse—to hold him subject to my will and pleasure, as if he were a brute beast without the power of kicking or biting—to make him work for me—to hold his fate in my hands: but the thought was for a moment. It was followed by disgust.

Yesterday I was much struck by the intelligence, activity, and desire to please of a good-looking coloured waiter, who seemed so light-hearted and light-coloured I could not imagine he was a slave. So one of our party, who was an American, asked him: "What are you, boy—a free nigger?" Of course he knew that in Alabama it was most unlikely he could reply in the affirmative. The young man's smile died away from his lips, a flush of blood embrowned the face for a moment, and he answered in a sad, low tone: "No, sir! I b'long to Massa Jackson," and left the room at once. As I stood at the upper window of the Capitol, and looked on the wide expanse of richly wooded, well-cultivated land which sweeps round the hill side away to the horizon, I could not help thinking of the misery and cruelty which must have been borne in tilling the land and raising the houses and streets of the dominant race before whom one nationality of coloured people has perished within the memory of man. The misery and cruelty of this system are established by the advertisements for run-away Negroes, and by the description of the stigmata of their persons—whippings and brandings, scars and cuts—though these, indeed, are less frequent here than in the border States.

On my return, the Hon. W[illiam] M. Browne, Assistant Secretary of State, came to visit me—a cadet of an Irish family, who came to America some years ago, and having lost his money in land speculations, turned his pen to good account as a journalist, and gained Mr. Buchanan's patronage and support as a newspaper editor in Washington. There he became intimate with the Southern gentlemen, with whom he naturally associated in preference to the Northern members; and when they went out, he walked over along with them. He told me the Government had already received numerous—I think he said 400—letters from shipowners applying for letters of marque and reprisal. Many of these applications were from merchants in Boston, and other maritime cities in the New England States. He further stated that the President was determined to take the whole control of the army, and the appointments to command in all ranks of officers into his own hands.

The press is fanning the flame on both sides; it would be difficult to say whether it or the telegraphs circulate lies most largely; but then as the papers print the telegrams they must have the palm. The Southerners are told there is a reign of terror in New York—that the 7th New York Regiment has been captured by the Baltimore people —that Abe Lincoln is always drunk—that General Lee has seized Arlington Heights, and is bombarding Washington. The New York people are regaled with similar stories from the South. The coincidence between the date of the skirmish at Lexington and of the attack on the Sixth Massachusetts Regiment at Baltimore is not so remarkable as the fact that the first man who was killed at the latter place was a direct descendant of the first of the colonists who was killed by the royal soldiery. Baltimore may do the same for the South which Lexington did for all the Colonies. Head shaving, forcible deportations, tarring and feathering are recommended and adopted as specifics to produce conversion from erroneous opinions. The President of the United States has called into service of the Federal Government 42,000 volunteers, and increased the Regular Army by 22,000 men, and the navy by 18,000 men. If the South secede, they ought certainly to take over with them some Yankee hotel keepers. This "Exchange" is in a frightful state—nothing but noise, dirt, drinking, wrangling.

May 7th.   Today the papers contain a proclamation by the President of the Confederate States of America, declaring a state of war between the Confederacy and the United States, and notifying the issue of letters of marque and reprisal. I went out with Mr. Wigfall in the forenoon to pay my respects to Mr. Jefferson Davis at the State Department. Mr. Seward told me that but for Jefferson Davis the secession plot could never have been carried out. No other man of the party had the brain, or the courage and dexterity, to bring it to a successful issue. All the persons in the Southern States spoke of him with admiration, though their forms of speech and thought generally forbid them to be respectful to any one.

There before me was "Jeff Davis's State Department"—a large brick building, at the corner of a street, with a Confederate flag floating above it. The door stood open, and "gave" on a large hall whitewashed, with doors plainly painted belonging to small rooms, in which was transacted most important business, judging by the names written on sheets of paper and applied outside, denoting bureaux of the highest functions. A few clerks were passing in and out, and one or two gentlemen were on the stairs, but there was no appearance of any bustle in the building.

We walked straight upstairs to the first floor, which was surrounded by doors opening from a quadrangular platform. On one of these was written simply, "The President." Mr. Wigfall went in and after a moment returned and said, "The President will be glad to see you; walk in, sir." When I entered, the President was engaged with four gentlemen, who were making some offer of aid to him. He was thanking them "in the name of the Government." Shaking hands with each he saw them to the door, bowed them and Mr. Wigfall out, and turning to me said, "Mr. Russell, I am glad to welcome you here, though I fear your appearance is a symptom that our affairs are not quite prosperous," or words to that effect. He then requested me to sit down close to his own chair at his office table, and proceeded to speak on general matters, adverting to the Crimean War and the Indian Mutiny, and asking questions about Sebastopol, the Redan, and the Siege of Lucknow.

I had an opportunity of observing the President very closely; he did not impress me as favourably as I had expected, though he is certainly a very different looking man from Mr. Lincoln. He is like

Jefferson Davis *(Library of Congress)*

a gentleman—has a slight, light figure, little exceeding middle height, and holds himself erect and straight. He was dressed in a rustic suit of slate-coloured stuff, with a black silk handkerchief round his neck; his manner is plain and rather reserved and drastic; his head is well formed, with a fine full forehead, square and high, covered with innumerable fine lines and wrinkles, features regular, though the cheek-bones are too high, and the jaws too hollow to be handsome; the lips are thin, flexible, and curved, the chin square, well defined; the nose very regular, with wide nostrils; and the eyes deep set, large and full—one seems nearly blind, and is partly covered with a film, owing to excruciating attacks of neuralgia and tic. Wonderful to relate, he does not chew, and is neat and clean-looking, with hair trimmed, and boots brushed. The expression of his face is anxious, he has a very haggard, care-worn, and pain-drawn look, though no trace of anything but the utmost confidence and the greatest decision could be detected in his conversation. He asked me some general questions respecting the route I had taken in the States.

I mentioned that I had seen great military preparations through the

South, and was astonished at the alacrity with which the people sprang to arms. "Yes, sir," he remarked, and his tone of voice and manner of speech are rather remarkable for what are considered Yankee peculiarities. "In Eu-rope" (Mr. Seward also indulges in that pronunciation) "they laugh at us because of our fondness for military titles and displays. All your travellers in this country have commented on the number of generals, and colonels, and majors all over the States. But the fact is, we are a military people, and these signs of the fact were ignored. We are not less military because we have had no great standing armies. But perhaps we are the only people in the world where gentlemen go to a military academy who do not intend to follow the profession of arms."

In the course of our conversation, I asked him to have the goodness to direct that a sort of passport or protection should be given to me, as I might possibly fall in with some guerilla leader on my way northwards, in whose eyes I might not be entitled to safe conduct. Mr. Davis said, "I shall give such instructions to the Secretary of War as shall be necessary. But, sir, you are among civilised, intelligent people who understand your position, and appreciate your character. We do not seek the sympathy of England by unworthy means, for we respect ourselves, and we are glad to invite the scrutiny of men into our acts; as for our motives, we meet the eye of Heaven." I thought I could judge from his words that he had the highest idea of the French as soldiers, but that his feelings and associations were more identified with England, although he was quite aware of the difficulty of conquering the repugnance which exists to slavery.

Mr. Davis made no allusion to the authorities at Washington, but he asked me if I thought it was supposed in England there would be war between the two States. I answered, that I was under the impression the public thought there would be no actual hostilities. "And yet you see we are driven to take up arms for the defence of our rights and liberties."

As I saw an immense mass of papers on his table, I rose and made my bow, and Mr. Davis, seeing me to the door, gave me his hand and said, "As long as you may stay among us you shall receive every facility it is in our power to afford to you, and I shall always be glad to see you." Colonel Wigfall was outside, and took me to the room of the Secretary of War, Mr. [Leroy Pope] Walker, whom we found closeted with General Beauregard and two other officers in a room full of maps and plans. He is the kind of man generally represented in our types of a "Yankee"—tall, lean, straight-haired, angular, with fiery, impulsive eyes and manner—a ruminator of tobacco and a profuse spitter—a lawyer, I believe, certainly not a soldier; ardent, devoted to the cause, and confident to the last degree of its speedy success.

The news that two more States had joined the Confederacy, making ten in all, was enough to put them in good humour.[5] "Is it not too bad these Yankees will not let us go our own way, and keep their cursed Union to themselves? If they force us to it, we may be obliged to drive them beyond the Susquehanna." Beauregard was in excellent spirits, busy measuring off miles of country with his compass as if he were dividing empires.

From this room I proceeded to the office of Mr. [Judah P.] Benjamin, the Attorney-General of the Confederate States, the most brilliant perhaps of the whole of the famous Southern orators. He is a short, stout man, with a full face, olive-coloured, and most decidedly Jewish features, with the brightest large black eyes, one of which is somewhat diverse from the other, and a brisk, lively, agreeable manner, combined with much vivacity of speech and quickness of utterance. He is one of the first lawyers or advocates in the United States, and had a large practice at Washington, where his annual receipts from his profession were not less than £8000 to £10,000 a year. But his love of the card table rendered him a prey to older and cooler hands, who waited till the sponge was full at the end of the session, and then squeezed it to the last drop.

Mr. Benjamin is the most open, frank, and cordial of the Confederates whom I have yet met. In a few seconds he was telling me all about the course of Government with respect to privateers and letters of marque and reprisal, in order probably to ascertain what were our views in England on the subject. I observed it was likely the North would not respect their flag and would treat their privateers as pirates. "We have an easy remedy for that. For any man under our flag

[5]The legislatures of Arkansas and Tennessee passed secession ordinances on May 6, 1861. The Tennessee ordinance was submitted to public vote on June 8, but the legislative action was considered tantamount to secession.

whom the authorities of the United States dare to execute, we shall hang two of their people." "Suppose, Mr. Attorney-General, England, or any of the great powers which decreed the abolition of privateering, refuses to recognise your flag?" "We intend to claim, and do claim, the exercise of all the rights and privileges of an independent sovereign State, and any attempt to refuse us the full measure of those rights would be an act of hostility to our country." "But if England, for example, declared your privateers were pirates?" "As the United States never admitted the principle laid down at the Congress of Paris, neither have the Confederate States. If England thinks fit to declare privateers under our flag pirates, it would be nothing more or less than a declaration of war against us, and we must meet it as best we can."[6] In fact, Mr. Benjamin did not appear afraid of anything; but his confidence respecting Great Britain was based a good deal, no doubt, on his firm faith in cotton, and in England's utter subjection to her cotton interest and manufactures. "All this coyness about acknowledging a slave power will come right at last. We hear our commissioners have gone on to Paris, which looks as if they had met with no encouragement at London; but we are quite easy in our minds on this point at present."

As I was going downstairs, Mr. Browne called me into his room. He said that the Attorney-General and himself were in a state of perplexity as to the form in which letters of marque and reprisal should be made out. They had consulted all the books they could get but found no examples to suit their case, and he wished to know, as I was a barrister, whether I could aid him. I told him it was so much my regard to my own position as a neutral, as the *vafri inscitia juris* [ignorance of the law] which prevented me throwing any light on the subject. There are not only Yankee shipowners but English firms ready with sailors and steamers for the Confederate Government, and the owner of the *Camilla* might be tempted to part with his yacht by the offers made to him.

---

[6]By the Declaration of Paris, 1856, western European nations outlawed privateering; that is, the practice of one belligerent authorizing privately owned vessels to seize its enemy's commercial ships. The United States was not party to the Declaration; thus, neither it nor the Confederacy was bound by it. This conversation focuses on the Confederate right to engage in privateering and what action southerners might take if Britain treated privateers as pirates. The British solved the dilemma by closing her ports to both Union and Confederate privateers on June 1, 1861.

Being invited to attend a levée or reception held by Mrs. Davis, the President's wife, I returned to the hotel to prepare for the occasion. On my way I passed a company of volunteers, one hundred and twenty artillerymen, and three fieldpieces, on their way to the station for Virginia, followed by a crowd of "citizens" and Negroes of both sexes, cheering vociferously. The band was playing that excellent quick-step "Dixie." The men were stout, fine fellows, dressed in coarse grey tunics with yellow facings and French caps. They were armed with smoothbore muskets and their knapsacks were unfit for marching, being waterproof bags slung from the shoulders. The guns had no caissons, and the shoeing of the troops was certainly deficient in soling. The Zouave mania is quite as rampant here as it is in New York, and the smallest children are thrust into baggy red breeches and are sent out with flags and tin swords to impede the highways.

The modest villa in which the President lives is painted white— another "White House"—and stands in a small garden. The door was open. A coloured servant took in our names, and Mr. Browne presented me to Mrs. Davis, whom I could just make out in the *demi-jour* [half-light] of a moderately-sized parlour, surrounded by a few ladies and gentlemen, the former in bonnets, the latter in morning dress *à la midi* [in the southern fashion]. There was no affectation of state or ceremony in the reception. Mrs. Davis, whom some of her friends call "Queen Varina," is a comely, sprightly woman, verging on matronhood, of good figure and manners, well-dressed, ladylike, and clever, and she seemed a great favourite with those around her, though I did hear one of them say, "It must be very nice to be the President's wife, and be the first lady in the Confederate States." Mrs. Davis, whom the President C. S. married *en secondes noces* [in a second marriage], exercised considerable social influence in Washington, where I met many of her friends. She was just now inclined to be angry because the papers contained a report that a reward was offered in the North for the head of the arch rebel Jeff Davis. "They are quite capable, I believe," she said, "of such acts." There were not more than eighteen or twenty persons present, as each party came in and stayed only a few moments, and, after a time, I made my bow and retired, receiving from Mrs. Davis an invitation to come in the evening when I would find the President at home.

At sundown, amid great cheering, the guns in front of the State

Department fired ten rounds to announce that Tennessee and Arkansas had joined the Confederacy.

In the evening I dined with Mr. Benjamin and his brother-in-law,[7] a gentleman of New Orleans, Colonel Wigfall coming in at the end of the dinner. The New Orleans people of French descent, or "Creoles," as they call themselves, speak French in preference to English, and Mr. Benjamin's brother-in-law laboured considerably in trying to make himself understood in our vernacular. The conversation, Franco-English, [was] very pleasant, for Mr. Benjamin is agreeable and lively. He is certain that the English law authorities must advise the Government that the blockade of the Southern ports is illegal so long as the President claims them to be ports of the United States. "At present," he said, "their paper blockade does no harm; the season for shipping cotton is over; but in October next, when the Mississippi is floating cotton by the thousands of bales, and all our wharfs are full, it is inevitable that the Yankees must come to trouble with this attempt to coerce us."[8] Mr. Benjamin walked back to the hotel with me.

May 8th.   Early this morning, as usual, my faithful Wigfall comes in and sits by my bedside and passing his hands through his locks, pours out his ideas with wonderful lucidity and odd affection of logic all his own. "We are a peculiar people, sir! You don't understand us, and you can't understand us, because we are known to you only by Northern writers and Northern papers, who know nothing of us themselves, or misrepresent what they do know. We are an agricultural people; we are a primitive but a civilised people. We have no cities—we don't want them. We have no literature—we don't need any yet. We have no press—we are glad of it. We do not require a press because we go out and discuss all public questions from the

[7]Benjamin's brother-in-law was Jules de St. Martin. In 1833 Benjamin married Marie Nathalie de St. Martin, who lived in Paris for much of her married life. The separation of Benjamin and his wife does not seem to have affected the friendship between the two men.
[8]Benjamin considered Lincoln's blockade of southern ports illegal because blockade proclamations were issued only between nations at war, and throughout Lincoln insisted that the Civil War was an insurrection. He also thought it a "paper blockade," inasmuch as the North did not have the naval power in 1861 to enforce it effectively.

stump with our people. We have no commercial marine—no navy—
we don't want them. We are better without them. Your ships carry
our produce, and you can protect your own vessels. We want no
manufactures: we desire no trading, no mechanical or manufacturing
classes. As long as we have our rice, our sugar, our tobacco, and our
cotton, we can command wealth to purchase all we want from those
nations with which we are in amity, and to lay up money besides.
But with the Yankees we will never trade—never. Not one pound of
cotton shall ever go from the South to their accursed cities; not one
ounce of their steel or their manufactures shall ever cross our border."
And so on. What the Senator who is preparing a bill for drafting the
people into the army fears is, that the North will begin active operations before the South is ready for resistance. "Give us till November
to drill our men, and we shall be irresistible." He deprecates any
offensive movement and is opposed to an attack on Washington,
which many journals here advocate.

Mr. Walker sent me over a letter recommending me to all officers
of the Confederate States, and I received an invitation from the
President to dine with him tomorrow, which I was much chagrined
to be obliged to refuse. In fact, it is most important to complete my
Southern tour speedily, as all mail communication will soon be suspended from the South and the blockade effectually cuts off any
communication by sea. Rails torn up, bridges broken, telegraphs
down—trains searched—the war is begun. The North is pouring its
hosts to the battle, and it has met the paeans of the conquering
Charlestonians with a universal yell of indignation and an oath of
vengeance.

I expressed a belief in a letter, written a few days after my arrival
(March 27th), that the South would never go back into the Union.
The North think that they can coerce the South, and I am not prepared to say they are right or wrong; but I am convinced that the
South can only be forced back by such a conquest as that which laid
Poland prostrate at the feet of Russia. It may be that such a conquest
can be made by the North, but success must destroy the Union as it
has been constituted in times past. A strong Government must be the
logical consequence of victory, and the triumph of the South will be
attended by a similar result, for which, indeed, many Southerners are
very well disposed. To the people of the Confederate States there

would be no terror in such an issue, for it appears to me they are pining for a strong Government exceedingly. The North must accept it, whether they like it or not.

Neither party—if such a term can be applied to the rest of the United States and to those States which disclaim the authority of the Federal Government—was prepared for the aggressive or resisting power of the other. Already the Confederate States perceive that they cannot carry all before them with a rush, while the North have learnt that they must put forth all their strength to make good a tithe of their lately uttered threats. But the Montgomery Government are anxious to gain time and to prepare a regular army. The North, distracted by apprehension of vast disturbance in their complicated relations, are clamouring for instant action and speedy consummation. The counsels of moderate men, as they are called, have been utterly overruled.

In the evening I paid farewell visits and spent an hour with Mr. [Robert] Toombs, who is unquestionably one of the most original, quaint, and earnest of the Southern leaders, and whose eloquence and power as a debater are greatly esteemed by his country men. He is something of an Anglo-maniac, and an Anglo-phobist—a combination not unusual in America—that is, he is proud of being connected with and descended from respectable English families and admires our mixed constitution, whilst he is an enemy of what is called English policy, and is a strong pro-slavery champion. Wigfall and he are very uneasy about the scant supply of gunpowder in the Southern States and the difficulty of obtaining it.

In the evening had a little reunion in the bedroom as before—Mr. Wigfall, Mr. [Lawrence] Keitt, an eminent Southern politician, Col. Pickett, Mr. Browne, Mr. Benjamin, Mr. George Sanders, and others. The last named gentleman was dismissed or recalled from his post at Liverpool because he fraternised with Mazzini and other Red Republicans *à ce qu' on dit* [so they say]. Here he is a slavery man and a friend of an oligarchy. Your "Rights of Man" man is often most inconsistent with himself, and is generally found associated with the men of force and violence.

May 9th.   My faithful Wigfall was good enough to come in early, in order to show me some comments on my letters in the *New York*

Times. It appears the papers were angry because I said that New York was apathetic when I landed, and they try to prove it was wrong by showing there was a "glorious outburst of Union feeling" after the news of the fall of Sumter. But no! New York was then engaged in discussing States' Rights, and in reading articles to prove the new Government would be traitors if they endeavoured to reinforce the Federal forts, or were perusing leaders in favour of the Southern Government. New York must pay the penalty of its indifference and bear the consequence of listening to such counsellors.

Before my departure I had a little farewell levée—Mr. Toombs, Mr. Browne, Mr. Benjamin, Mr. Walker, Major Deas, Colonel Pickett, Major Calhoun, Captain [Roswell] Ripley, and others—who were exceedingly kind with letters of introduction and offers of service. Dined as usual on a composite dinner—Southern meat and poultry bad—at three o'clock, and at four, P.M., drove down to the steep banks of the Alabama River, where the castle-like hulk of the *Southern Republic* was waiting to receive us. I bade good-by to Montgomery without regret. The native people were not very attractive, and the city has nothing to make up for their deficiency, but of my friends there I must always retain pleasant memories and, indeed, I hope some day I shall be able to keep my promise to return to see more of the Confederate ministers and their chief.

The vessel was nothing more than a vast wooden house of three separate stories, floating on a pontoon which upheld the engine, with a dining hall or saloon on the second story surrounded by sleeping berths, and a nest of smaller rooms upstairs; on the metal roof was a "musical" instrument called a "calliope," played like a piano by keys, which acted on levers and valves, admitting steam into metal cups, where it produced the requisite notes—high, resonant, and not unpleasing at a moderate distance. It is 417 miles to Mobile, but at this season the steamer can maintain a good rate of speed as there is very little cotton or cargo to be taken on board at the landing, and the stream is full.

The river is about 200 yards broad and of the colour of chocolate and milk, with high, steep, wooded banks, rising so much above the surface of the stream, that a person on the upper deck of the towering *Southern Republic* cannot get a glimpse of the fields and country beyond. High banks and bluffs spring up to the height of 150 or even

200 feet above the river, the breadth of which is so uniform as give the Alabama the appearance of a canal, only relieved by sudden bends and rapid curves. The surface is covered with masses of drift wood, whole trees, and small islands of branches. Now and then a sharp, black, fang-like projection standing stiffly in the current gives warning of a snag, but the helmsman, who commands the whole course of the river from an elevated house amidships on the upper deck, can see these in time; and at night pine boughs are lighted in iron cressets at the bows to illuminate the water.

The value of land on the sides of this river is great, as it yields nine to eleven bales of cotton to the acre—worth £10 a bale at present prices.[9] The only evidences of this wealth to be seen by us consisted of the cotton sheds on the top of the banks, and slides of timber, with steps at each side down to the landings, so constructed that cotton bales could be shot down on board the vessel. These shoots and staircases are generally protected by a roof of plants, and lead to unknown regions inhabited by niggers and their masters, the latter all talking politics. They never will, never can be conquered—nothing on earth could induce them to go back into the Union. They will burn every bale of cotton, and fire every house, and lay waste every field and homestead before they will yield to the Yankees. And so they talk through the glimmering of bad cigars for hours.

Some of the landings were far more important than others. There were some, for example, where an iron railroad was worked down the bank by windlasses for hoisting up goods; others where the Negroes half-naked leaped ashore, and rushing to piles of firewood, tossed them on board to feed the engine which, all uncovered and open to the lower deck, lighted up the darkness by the glare from the stoke-holes, which cried for ever, "Give, give!" as the Negroes ceaselessly thrust the pine beams into their hungry maws. I could understand

---

[9]The average weight of a bale of cotton was 450 pounds; the average price in 1861, 11 cents a pound. Thus a bale of cotton was worth approximately $50, or roughly the equivalent of 10 English pounds. While Russell's calculation of the bale price is quite accurate, his estimate of the number of bales that could be raised on an acre is exaggerated, according to other accounts. Explaining "Cotton and its Cultivation" to readers of *Harper's Monthly Magazine* (February 1854), T. B. Thorpe, a minor southern literary figure, declared that 1000 pounds per acre, or approximately two bales, was considered a "great yield."

how easily a steamer can "burn up," and how hopeless escape would be under such circumstances. The whole framework of the vessel is of the lightest resinous pine, so raw that the turpentine oozes out through the paint; the hull is a mere shell. If the vessel once caught fire, all that could be done would be to turn her round and run her to the bank, in the hope of holding there long enough to enable the people to escape into the trees; but if she were not near a landing, many must be lost; as the bank is steep down, the vessel cannot be run aground; and in some places the trees are in eight and ten feet of water. A few minutes would suffice to set the vessel in a blaze from stem to stern; and if there were cotton on board, the bales would burn almost like powder. The scene at each landing was repeated, with few variations, ten times till we reached Selma, 110 miles distance, at 11:30 at night.

Selma, which is connected with the Tennessee and Mississippi rivers by railroad, is built upon a steep, lofty bluff, and the lights in the windows, and the lofty hotels above us, put me in mind of the old town of Edinburgh, seen from Princes Street. Besides us there was a hugh storied wharf, so that our passengers could step on shore from any deck they pleased.

May 10th. The cabin of one of these steamers, in the month of May, is not favourable to sleep. The wooden beams of the engines reek and scream "consumedly," and the great engines themselves throb as if they would break through their thin, pulse covers of pine —and the whistle sounds, and the calliope shrieks out "Dixie" incessantly. So, when I was up and dressed, breakfast was over, and I had an opportunity to seeing the slaves on board, male and female, acting as stewards and stewardesses, at their morning meal, which they took with much good spirits and decorum. They were nicely dressed— clean and neat.

The river, the scenery, and the scenes were just the same as yesterday—high banks, cotton-slides, wooding stations, cane-brakes—and a very miserable Negro population, if the specimens of women and children at the landings fairly represented the mass of the slaves. They were in strong contrast to the comfortable, well-dressed domestic slaves on board, and it can well be imagined there is a wide difference between the classes, and that those condemned to work in the open fields must suffer exceedingly.

Tonight, on the lower deck, amid wood faggots and barrels, a dance of Negroes was arranged by an enthusiast, who desired to show how "happy they were." That is the favourite theme of Southerners.

May 11th. At early dawn the steamer went its way through a broad bay of snags bordered with driftwood, and with steam-trumpet and calliope announced its arrival at the quay of Mobile, which presented a fringe of tall warehouses and shops alongside, over which were names indicating Scotch, Irish, English, many Spanish, German, Italian, and French owners. The quays which usually, as we were told, are lined with stately hulls and a forest of masts, were deserted; although the port was not actually blockaded, there were squadrons of the United States ships at Pensacola on the east, and at New Orleans on the west.

The hotel, a fine building of the American stamp, was the seat of a Vigilance Committee, and as we put down our names in the book they were minutely inspected by some gentlemen who came out of the parlour. It was fortunate they did not find traces of Lincolnism about us, as it appeared by the papers that they were busy deporting "Abolitionists" after certain preliminary processes supposed to "Give them a rise, and open their eyes to a sense of their situation." The citizens were busy in drilling, marching, and drum-beating, and the Confederate flag few from every spire and steeple. The day was so hot that it was little more inviting to go out in the sun than it would be in the dog days at Malaga,[10] to which, by-the-bye, Mobile bears some "kinder sorter" resemblance, but, nevertheless, I sallied forth, and had a drive on a shell road by the head of the bay, where there were pretty villarettes in charming groves of magnolia, orange trees, and live oaks. Wide streets of similar houses spring out to meet the country through sandy roads.

Many Mobilians called, and among them the mayor, Mr. Forsyth, in whom I recognised the most remarkable of the Southern Commissioners I had met at Washington. Mr. [James] Magee, the acting

[10]A city in southern Spain.

British Consul, was also good enough to wait upon me with offers of any assistance in his power. I hear he has most difficult questions to deal with, arising out of the claims of distressed British subjects, and disputed nationality. In the evening the Consul and Dr. [Josiah C.] Nott, a savant and physician of Mobile, well known to ethnologists for his work on the *Types of Mankind*, written conjointly with the Mr. [George R.] Gliddon, dined with me, and I learned from them that, notwithstanding the intimate commercial relations between Mobile and the great Northern cities, the people here are of the most ultra-secessionist doctrines. The wealth and manhood of the city will be devoted to repel the "Lincolnite mercenaries" to the last.

After dinner we walked through the city, which abounds in oyster saloons, drinking houses, lager beer and wine shops, and gambling and dancing places. The market was well worthy of a visit—something like St. John's at Liverpool on a Saturday night, crowded with Negroes, mulattoes, quadroons, and mestizos of all sort, Spanish, Italian, and French, speaking their own tongues, or a quaint lingua franca, and dressed in very striking and pretty costumes. The fruit and vegetable stalls displayed very fine produce, and some staples, remarkable for novelty, ugliness, and goodness. After our stroll we went into one of the great oyster saloons and in a room upstairs had opportunity of tasting those great bivalvians in the form of natural fish puddings, fried in batter, roasted, stewed, devilled, broiled, and in many other ways, *plus* raw. I am bound to observe that the Mobile people ate them as if there was no blockade, and as though oysters were a specific for political indigestions and civil wars; a fierce Marseillais are they—living in the most foreign looking city I have yet seen in the States. My private room in the hotel was large, well-lighted with gas, and exceedingly well furnished in the German fashion, with French pendule and mirrors. The charge for a private room varies from £1 to £1, 5s, a day; the bed room and board are charged separately, from 10s. 6d. to 12s. 6d. a day, but meals served in the private room are all charged extra, and heavily too. Exclusiveness is an aristocratic taste which must be paid for.

May 12th.   Mr. Forsyth had been good enough to invite me to an excursion down the Bay of Mobile, to the forts built by Uncle Sam and his French engineers to sink his Britishers—now turned by

"C.S.A." against the hated Stars and Stripes. The mayor and the principal merchants and many politicians—and are not all men politicians in America?—formed the party. If any judgment of men's acts can be formed from their words, the Mobilites, who are the representatives of the third greatest port of the United States, will perish ere they submit to the Yankees and people of New York. I have now been in North Carolina, South Carolina, Georgia, Alabama, and in none of these great States have I found the least indication of the Union sentiment, or of the attachment for the Union which Mr. Seward always assumes to exist in the South. If there were any considerable amount of it, I was in a position as a neutral to have been aware of its existence.

Those who might have at one time opposed secession, have now bowed their heads to the majesty of the majority. General Scott, who was a short time ago written of in the usual inflated style, to which respectable military mediocrity and success are entitled in the States, is now reviled by the Southern papers as an infamous hoary traitor and the like. If an officer prefers his allegiance to the United States flag, and remains in the Federal service after his State has gone out, his property is liable to confiscation by the State authorities, and his family and kindred are exposed to the gravest suspicion, and must prove their loyalty by extra zeal in the cause of secession.

Our merry company comprised naval and military officers in the service of the Confederate States, journalists, politicians, professional men, merchants, and not one of them had a word but of hate and execration for the North. The British and German settlers are quite as vehement as the natives in upholding States' Rights, and among the most ardent upholders of slavery are the Irish proprietors and mercantile classes.

The Bay of Mobile, which is about thirty miles long with a breadth varying from three to seven miles, is formed by the outfall of the Alabama and of the Tombigbee River, and is shallow and dangerous, full of banks and trees, embedded in the sands. The shores are low wooded and are dotted here and there with pretty villas; but present no attractive scenery.

The sea breeze somewhat alleviated the fierceness of the sun, which was, however, too hot to be quite agreeable. Our steamer, crowded to the sponsons, made little way against the tide; but at length, after nearly four hours' sail, we hauled up alongside a jetty at Fort Gaines, which is on the right hand or western exit of harbour, and would command, were it finished, the light draft channel; it is now merely a shell of masonry, but Colonel [William] Hardee, who has charge of the defences of Mobile, told me that they would finish it speedily.

The Colonel is an agreeable, delicate-looking man, scarcely of middle age, and is well known in the States as the author of *The Tactics*, which is, however, merely a translation of the French manual of arms. He does not appear to be possessed of any great energy or capacity, but is, no doubt, a respectable officer.

Upon landing we found a small body of men on guard in the fort. A few cannon of moderate calibre were mounted on the sandhills and on the beach. We entered the unfinished work and were received with a salute. The men felt difficulty in combining discipline with citizenship. They were "bored" with their sandhill, and one of them asked me when I "thought them damned Yankees were coming." He wanted to touch off a few pills he knew would be good for their complaint. I must say I could sympathise with the feelings of the young officer who said he would sooner have a day with the "Lincolnites" than a week with the mosquitoes for which this locality is famous.

From Fort Gaines the steamer ran across to Fort Morgan, about three miles distant, passing in its way seven vessels, mostly British, at anchor, where hundreds may be seen, I am told, during the cotton season. This work has a formidable sea face, and may give great trouble to Uncle Sam when he wants to visit his loving subjects in Mobile in his gunboats. It is the work of [Simon] Bernard, I presume, and like most of his designs has a weak long base towards the land; but it is provided with a wet ditch and drawbridge, with demilunes covering the curtains, and has a regular bastioned trace. It has one row of casemates, armed with 32- and 42-pounders. The barbette guns are 8-inch and 10-inch guns; the external works at the salients are armed with howitzers and fieldpieces, and as we crossed the draw bridge, a salute was fired from a field battery, on a flanking bastion, in our honour.

Inside the work was crammed with men, some of whom slept in the casemates—others in tents in the parade grounds and enceinte of the fort. They were Alabama Volunteers, and sturdy a lot of fellows as ever shouldered musket; dressed in homespun coarse grey suits, with blue and yellow worsted facings and stripes—to European eyes not very respectful to their officers, but very obedient, I am told, and very peremptorily ordered about as I heard.

There were 700 or 800 men in the work, and an undue proportion of officers, all of whom were introduced to the strangers in turn. The officers were a very gentlemanly, nice-looking set of young fellows, and several of them had just come over from Europe to take up arms for their State. I forget the name of the officer in command, though I cannot forget his courtesy, nor an excellent lunch he gave us in his casemate after a hot walk round the parapets, and some practice with solid shot from the barbette guns, which did not tend to make me think much of the greatly-be-praised Columbiads.

One of the officers named [Dabney] Maury, a relative of [Matthew] "deep-sea Maury,"[11] struck me as an ingenious and clever officer; the utmost harmony, kindliness, and devotion to the cause prevailed among the garrison, from the chief down to the youngest ensign. In its present state the fort would suffer exceedingly from a heavy bombardment—the magazines would be in danger and the traverses are inadequate. All the barracks and wooden buildings should be destroyed if they wish to avoid the fate of Sumter.

On our cruise homeward, in the enjoyment of a cold dinner, we had the inevitable discussion of the Northern and Southern contest. Mr. Forsyth, the editor and proprietor of the *Mobile Register,* is impassioned for the cause, though he was not at one time considered a pure Southerner. There is difference of opinion relative to an attack on Washington. General St. George [Cocke],[12] commanding the Army of Virginia on the Potomac, declares there is no intention of attacking it, or any place outside the limits of that free and sovereign State. But then the conduct of the Federal Government in Maryland is considered by the more fiery Southerners to justify the expulsion of "Lin-

[11]Dabney Herndon Maury, a Confederate general who saw service chiefly in the Mississippi region, was the nephew of Matthew Fontaine Maury, known as "deep-sea" Maury because he instituted the system of deep-sea sounding and suggested the laying of transoceanic cables.

[12]Cocke's name is spelled "Cooke" in the 1863 London imprint, but the reference is clearly to the Philip St. George Cocke who commanded Virginia Volunteers along the Potomac River from April to October 1861. Cocke is easily confused with Philip St. George Cooke, also a Virginian but a general in the Union army. In 1861 Cooke was also in the Washington area, serving as a brigade commander in McDowell's army.

coln and his Myrmidons," "the Border Ruffians and Cassius M. Clay," from the capital. Butler has seized on the Relay House, on the junction of the Baltimore and Ohio Railroad with the rail from Washington, and has displayed a good deal of vigour since his arrival at Annapolis.[13] He is a Democrat, and a celebrated criminal lawyer in Massachusetts. Troops are pouring into New York, and are preparing to attack Alexandria, on the Virginia side, below Washington and the Navy Yard, where a large Confederate flag is flying, which can be seen from the President's windows in the White House.

There is a secret soreness even here at the small effect produced in England compared with what they anticipated by the attack on Sumter; but hopes are excited that Mr. [William H.] Gregory, who was travelling through the States some time ago, will have a strong party to support his forthcoming motion for a recognition of the South.[14] The next conflict which takes place will be more bloody than that at Sumter. The gladiators are approaching—Washington, Annapolis, Pennsylvania are military departments, each with a chief and staff, to which is now added that of Ohio, under Major G[eorge] B. McClellan, Major General of Ohio Volunteers in Cincinnati. The authorities on each side are busy administering oaths of allegiance.

The harbour of Charleston is reported to be under blockade by the *Niagara* steam frigate, and a force of United States troops at St. Louis, Missouri, under Captain [Nathaniel] Lyon, has attacked and dispersed a body of state militia under one Brigadier General [Daniel M.] Frost, to the intense indignation of all Mobile. The argument is, that Missouri gave up the St. Louis Arsenal to the United States Government, and could take it back if she pleased, and was certainly competent to prevent the United States troops stirring beyond the arsenal.[15]

[13]The seizure of the Relay House occurred on May 5, 1861.

[14]Gregory was the leader of the so-called "southern lobby" in the British House of Commons. In May 1861, he arranged a meeting between Confederate envoys and Lord John Russell, Britain's Foreign Minister, and introduced a resolution in Parliament to recognize the Confederacy. Gregory withdrew the resolution a month later because of lack of support.

[15]The fighting in St. Louis on May 10, 1861, also included a riot. Lyon's force of some 7,000 men overwhelmed the prosecessionist Missourians. After they surrendered, Lyon turned them over to pro-Union German-American troops who marched the southerners through the city. A shot or two rang out, a riot ensued, and twenty-eight people lay dead when it was over.

May 13th.   I was busy making arrangements to get to Pensacola and Fort Pickens all day. The land journey was represented as being most tedious and exceedingly comfortless in all respects, through a waste of sand in which we ran the chance of being smothered or lost. And then I had set my mind on seeing Fort Pickens as well as Pensacola, and it would be difficult, to say the least of it, to get across from an enemy's camp to the Federal fortress and then return again. The United States squadron blockaded the port of Pensacola, but I thought it likely they would permit me to run in to visit Fort Pickens, and that the Federals would allow me to sail thence across to General [Braxton] Bragg, as they might be assured I would not communicate any information of what I had seen in my character as neutral to any but the journal in Europe, which I represented, and in the interests of which I was bound to see and report all that I could as to the state of both parties. It was, at all events, worth while to make the attempt, and after a long search I heard of a schooner which was ready for the voyage at a reasonable rate, all things considered.

Mr. Forsyth asked if I had any objection to take with me three gentlemen of Mobile who were anxious to be of the party, as they wanted to see their friends at Pensacola, where it was believed a "fight" was to come off immediately. But there was a difficulty. I told Mr. Forsyth that I could not possibly assent to any persons coming with me who were not neutrals. There was a suggestion that I should say these gentlemen were my friends, but as I had only seen two of them on board the steamer yesterday, I could not accede to that idea. At last it was agreed that his friends, being in no way employed by or connected with the Confederate Government, should have a place in the little schooner which we had picked out at the quayside and hired for the occasion, and go on the voyage with the plain understanding that they were to accept all the consequences of being citizens of Mobile.

Later paid my respects to Mrs. [Margaret] Forsyth, whom I found anxiously waiting for news from her young son who had gone off to join the Confederate army. She told me that nearly all the ladies in Mobile are engaged in making cartridges and in preparing lint or clothing for the army. Not the smallest fear is entertained of the swarming black population.

May 14th.   Down to our yacht, the *Diana*, which is to be ready this afternoon, and saw her cleared out a little—a broad-beamed, flat-floored schooner, some fifty tons burthen, with a centre-board, badly caulked, and dirty enough—unfamiliar with paint. The skipper was a long-legged, ungainly young fellow, with long hair and an inexpressive face, just relieved by the twinkle of a very "Yankee" eye; but that was all of the hated creature about him, for a more earnest seceder I never heard.

His crew consisted of three rough, mechanical sort of men and a Negro cook. Having freighted the vessel with a small stock of stores, a British flag, kindly lent by the acting Consul, Mr. Magee, and a tablecloth to serve as a flag of truce, our party weighed from the quay of Mobile at five o'clock in the evening, with the manifest approbation of the small crowd who had assembled to see us off, the rumour having spread through the town that we were bound to see the great fight. The breeze was favourable and steady; at nine o'clock, P.M., the lights of Fort Morgan were on our port beam, and for some time we were expecting to see the flash of a gun, as the skipper confidently declared they would never allow us to pass unchallenged.

The darkness of the night might possibly have favoured us or the sentries were remiss; at all events, we were soon creeping through the "Swash," which is a narrow channel over the bar, through which our skipper worked us by means of a sounding pole.

As the *Diana* flew along the grim shore, we lay listlessly on the deck admiring the excessive brightness of the stars, or watching the trailing fire of her wake. Hour after hour passed watching the play of large fish and the surf on the beach; one by one the cigar-lights died out; and muffling ourselves upon the deck or creeping into the little cabin, the party slumbered. I was awoke by the Captain talking to one of his hands close to me, and on looking up saw that he was staring through a wonderful black tube, which he denominated his "tallowscope," at the shore.

Looking in the direction, I observed the glare of a fire in the wood, which on examination through an opera glass resolved itself into a steady central light with some small specks around it. "Wa'll," said the Captain, "I guess it is just some of them d---d Yankees as is landed from their tarnation boats, and is 'connoitering' for a road to Mobile." There was an old iron cannonade on board, and it struck me as a curious exemplification of the recklessness of our American cousins, when the skipper said, "Let us put a bag of bullets in the ould gun, and touch it off at them"; which he no doubt would have done, seconded by one of our party, who drew his revolver to contribute to the broadside, but that I represented to them it was just as likely to be a party out from the camp at Pensacola, and that, anyhow, I strongly objected to any belligerent act whilst I was on board. It was very probably, indeed, the watchfire of a Confederate patrol, for the gentry of the country have formed themselves into a body of regular cavalry for such service; but the skipper declared that our chaps knew better than to be showing their lights in that way, when we were within ten miles of the entrance of Pensacola.

[May 15th.]   With the first rays of the sun, Fort McRae, Fort Pickens, and the masts of the squadron were visible ahead, rising above the blended horizon of land and sea. We drew upon them rapidly and soon could make out the rival flags—the Stars and Bars and Stars and Stripes—flouting defiance at each other.

On the land side on our left is Fort McRae, and on the end of the sandbank, called Santa Rosa Island, directly opposite, rises the outline of the much-talked-of Fort Pickens. Through the glass the blockading squadron is seen to consist of a sailing frigate, a sloop, and three steamers; and as we are scrutinising them, a small schooner glides from under the shelter of the guardship and makes towards us like a hawk on a sparrow. Hand over hand she comes, a great swaggering ensign at her peak, and a gun all ready at her bow; and rounding up alongside us a boat manned by four men is lowered, an officer jumps in, and is soon under our counter. The officer, a bluff, sailor-like looking fellow, in a uniform a little the worse for wear, and wearing his beard as officers of the United States Navy generally do, fixed his eye on the skipper—who did not seem quite at his ease and had, indeed, confessed to us that he had been warned off by the *Oriental,* as the tender was named, only a short time before—and said, "Hallo, sir, I think I have seen you before: what schooner is this?" "The *Diana* of Mobile." "I thought so." Stepping on deck, he said, "Gentlemen, I am Mr. [George W.] Brown, Master in the United States Navy, in charge of the boarding schooner *Oriental.* " We each gave our names, whereupon Mr. Brown said, "I have no doubt it will be all right; be good enough to let me have your papers. And now, sir, make sail, and lie-to under the quarter of that steamer there, the *Powhatan*." The Captain did not look at all happy when the officer called his attention to the indorsement on his papers; nor did the Mobile party seem very comfortable when he remarked, "I suppose, gentlemen, you are quite well aware there is a strict blockade of this port?"

In half an hour the schooner lay under the guns of the *Powhatan*, which is a stumpy, thick-set, powerful steamer of the old paddle-wheel kind, something like the *Leopard*. We proceeded alongside in the cutter's boat, and were ushered into the cabin, where the officer commanding, Lieutenant David Porter, received us, begged us to be seated, and then inquired into the object of our visit, which he communicated to the flagship by signal, in order to get instructions as to our disposal. Nothing could exceed his courtesy; and I was most favourably impressed by himself, his officers, and crew. He took me over the ship, which is armed with 1-inch Dahlgrens and an 11-inch pivot gun, with rifled fieldpieces and howitzers on the sponsons. Her boarding nettings were triced up, bows and weak portions padded with dead wood and old sails and everything ready for action.

Lieutenant Porter has been in and out of the harbour examining the enemy's works at all hours of the night, and he has marked off on the chart, as he showed me, the bearings of the various spots where he can sweep or enfilade their works. The crew, all things considered, were very clean and their personnel exceedingly fine.

Front View of Fort Pickens *(From* Harper's Pictorial History of the Civil War *(New York: Harper & Bros., 1868), Vol. 1, p. 71. Courtesy of the New York Public Library)*

We were not the only prize that was made by the *Oriental* this morning. A ragged little schooner lay at the other side of the *Powhatan*, the master of which stood rubbing his knuckles into his eyes, and uttering dolorous expressions in broken English and Italian, for he was a noble Roman of Civita Vecchia.[16] Lieutenant Porter let me into the secret. These small traders at Mobile, pretending great zeal for the Confederate cause, load their vessels with fruit, vegetables, and things of which they know the squadron is much in want, as well as the garrison of the Confederate forts. They set out with the most valiant intention of running the blockade, and are duly captured by the squadron, the officers of which are only too glad to pay fair prices for the cargoes. They return to Mobile, keep their money in their pockets, and declare they have been plundered by the Yankees. If they get in, they demand still higher prices from the Confederates and lay claim to the most exalted patriotism.

By signal from the flagship *Sabine,* we were ordered to repair on board to see the senior officer, Captain [Henry A.] Adams; and for the first time since I trod the deck of the old *Leander* in Balaklava harbour, I stood on board a 50-gun sailing frigate. Captain Adams, a grey-haired veteran of very gentle manners and great urbanity, received us in his cabin and listened by my explanation of the cause of my visit with interest. About myself there was no difficulty; but he very justly observed he did not think it would be right to let the gentlemen from Mobile examine Fort Pickens and then go among the Confederate camps. I am bound to say these gentlemen scarcely seemed to desire or anticipate such a favour.

Major [Israel] Vogdes, an engineer officer from the fort, who happened to be on board, volunteered to take a letter to Colonel Harvey Brown, requesting permission to visit it; and I finally arranged with Captain Adams that the *Diana* was to be permitted to pass the blockade into Pensacola harbour, and thence to return to Mobile, my visit to Pickens depending on the pleasure of the Commandant of the place. "I fear, Mr. Russell," said Captain Adams, "in giving you this permission, I expose myself to misrepresentation and unfounded attacks. Gentlemen of the press in our country care little about private character and are, I fear, rather unscrupulous in what they say;

---

[16]A coastal city in west-central Italy, just to the north of Rome.

but I rely upon your character that no improper use shall be made of this permission. You must hoist a flag of truce, as General Bragg, who commands over there, has sent me word he considers our blockade a declaration of war and will fire upon any vessel which approaches him from our fleet."

In the course of conversation, whilst treating me to such man-of-war luxuries as the friendly officer had at his disposal, he gave me an illustration of the miseries of this cruel conflict—of the unspeakable desolation of homes, of the bitterness of feeling engendered in families. A Pennsylvanian by birth, he married long ago a lady of Louisiana, where he resided on his plantation till his ship was commissioned. He was absent on foreign service when the feud began and received orders at sea, on the South American station, to repair direct to blockade Pensacola. He has just heard that one of his sons is enlisted in the Confederate army, and that two others have joined the forces in Virginia; and as he said sadly, "God knows, when I open my broadside, but that I may be killing my own children." But that was not all. One of the Mobile gentlemen brought him a letter from his daughter, in which she informs him that she has been elected *vivandière* [17] to a New Orleans regiment, with which she intends to push on to Washington, and get a lock of old Abe Lincoln's hair; and the letter concluded with the charitable wish that her father might starve to death if he persisted in his wicked blockade; but not the less determined was the gallant old sailor to do his duty.

With thanks for his kindness and courtesy, I parted from Captain Adams, feeling more than ever the terrible and earnest nature of the impending conflict. May the kindly good old man be shielded on the day of battle!

The boat which took us from the *Powhatan* to the *Diana* was in charge of a young officer related to Captain Porter, who amused me by the spirit with which he bandied remarks about the war with the Mobile men, who had now recovered their equanimity, and were indulging in what is called chaff about the blockade. "Well," he said, "you were the first to begin it; let us see whether you won't be the first to leave it off. I guess our Northern ice will pretty soon put out your Southern fire."

[17] A woman accompanying the troops and selling them wines, refreshments, and supplies.

As we got abreast of Fort Pickens, I ordered tablecloth No. 1 to be hoisted to the peak; and through the glass I saw that our appearance attracted no ordinary attention from the garrison of Pickens close at hand on our right, and the more distant Confederates on Fort McRae and the sandhills on our left. The latter work is weak and badly built, quite under the command of Pickens, but is supported by the old Spanish fort of Barrancas upon high ground further inland, and by numerous batteries at the water line and partly concealed amidst the woods which fringe the shore as far as the navy yard of Warrington, near Pensacola. The wind was light, but the tide bore us onwards toward the Confederate works. Arms glanced in the blazing sun where regiments were engaged at drill, clouds of dust rose from the sandy roads, horsemen riding along the beach, groups of men in uniform, gave a martial appearance to the place in unison with the black muzzles of the guns which peeped from the white sand batteries from the entrance of the harbour to the navy yard now close at hand. As at Sumter, Major Anderson permitted the Carolinians to erect the batteries he might have so readily destroyed in the commencement, so the Federal officers here have allowed General Bragg to work away at his leisure, mounting cannon after cannon, throwing up earthworks, and strengthening his batteries till he has assumed so formidable an attitude, that I doubt very much whether the fort and the fleet combined can silence his fire.

At last the Captain let go his anchor off the end of a wooden jetty, which was crowded with ammunition, shot, shell, casks of provisions, and commissariat stores. A small steamer was engaged in adding to the collection, and numerous light craft gave evidence that all trade had not ceased. Indeed, inside Santa Rosa Island, which runs for forty-five miles from Pickens eastward parallel to the shore, there is a considerable coasting traffic carried on for the benefit of the Confederates.

The skipper went ashore with my letters to General Bragg and speedily returned with an orderly, who brought permission for the *Diana* to come alongside the wharf. The Mobile gentlemen were soon on shore, eager to seek their friends; in a few seconds the officer of the quartermaster-general's department on duty came on board to conduct me to the officers' quarters, whilst waiting for my reply from General Bragg.

The navy yard is surrounded by a high wall, the gates closely guarded by sentries; the houses, gardens, workshops, factories, forges, slips, and building sheds are complete of their kind and cover upwards of three hundred acres; and with the forts which protect the entrance, cost the United States Government no less than six millions sterling. Inside these was the greatest activity and and life—Zouave, Chasseurs, and all kind of military eccentricities were drilling, parading, exercising, sitting in the shade, loading tumbrils, playing cards, or sleeping on the grass. Tents were pitched under the trees and on the little lawns and grass-covered quadrangles. The houses, each numbered and marked with the name of the functionary to whose use it was assigned, were models of neatness, with gardens in front, filled with glorious tropical flowers. They were painted green and white, provided with porticoes, Venetian blinds, verandahs, and colonnades, to protect the inmates as much as possible from the blazing sun, which in the dog days is worthy of Calcutta. The old *Fulton* is the only ship on the stocks. From the naval arsenal quantities of shot and shell are constantly pouring to the batteries. Piles of cannon balls dot the grounds, but the only ordnance I saw were two old mortars placed as ornaments in the main avenue, one dated 1776.

The quartermaster conducted me through shady walks into one of the houses, then into a long room, and presented me *en masse* to a body of officers, mostly belonging to a Zouave regiment from New Orleans, who were seated at a very comfortable dinner, with abundance of champagne, claret, beer, and ice. They were all young, full of life and spirits, except three or four graver and older men, who were Europeans. From these officers I learned that Mr. Jefferson Davis, his wife, Mr. Wigfall, and Mr. [Stephen] Mallory, Secretary to the Navy, had come down from Montgomery and had been visiting the works all day.

After dinner an aide-de-camp from General Bragg entered with a request that I would accompany him to the commanding officer's quarter. As the sand outside the navy yard was deep, and rendered walking very disagreeable, the young officer stopped a cart, into which we got and were proceeding on our way, when a tall, elderly man, in a blue frock coat with a gold star on the shoulder, trousers with a gold stripe and gilt buttons, rode past, followed by an orderly, who looked more like a dragoon than anything I have yet seen in the

States. "There's General Bragg," quoth the aide, and I was duly presented to the General, who reined up by the wagon. He sent his orderly off at once for a light cart drawn by a pair of mules, in which I completed my journey, and was safely decarted at the door of a substantial house surrounded by trees of lime, oak, and sycamore.

General Bragg received me at the steps and took me to his private room, where we remained for a long time in conversation. He had retired from the United States Army after the Mexican War to his plantation in Louisiana; but suddenly the Northern States declared their intention of using force on free and sovereign States which were exercising their constitutional rights to secede from the Federal Union.

Neither he nor his family were responsible for the system of slavery. His ancestors found it established by law and flourishing, and had left his property, consisting of slaves, which was granted to him by the laws and Constitution of the United States. Slaves were necessary for the actual cultivation of the soil in the South; Europeans and Yankees who settled there speedily became convinced of that; and if a Northern population were settled in Louisiana tomorrow, they would discover that they must till the land by the labour of the black race, and that the only mode of making the black race work was to hold them in a condition of involuntary servitude. "Only the other day, Colonel Harvey Brown, at Pickens, over the way, carried off a number of Negroes from Tortugas, and put them to work at Santa Rosa. Why? Because his white soldiers were not able for it." No. The North was bent on subjugating the South, and as long as he had a drop of blood in his body, he would resist such an infamous attempt.

Before supper General Bragg opened his maps and pointed out to me in detail the position of all his works, the line of fire of each gun, and the particular object to be expected from its effects. "I know every inch of Pickens," he said, "for I happened to be stationed there as soon as I left West Point, and I don't think there is a stone in it that I am not as well acquainted with as Harvey Brown."

His staff, consisting of four intelligent young men, two of them lately belonging to the United States Army, supped with us, and after a very agreeable evening, horses were ordered round to the door and I returned to the navy yard. As I rode home with my honest orderly beside instead of behind me, for he was of a conversational turn, I was much perplexed in my mind, endeavouring to determine which was right and which was wrong in this quarrel. Here was the General's orderly beside me, an intelligent middle-aged man, who had come to do battle with as much sincerity as ever actuated old John Brown or any New England puritan to make war against slavery. "I have left my old woman and the children to the care of the niggers; I have turned up all my cotton land and planted it with corn, and I don't intend to go back alive till I've seen the back of the last Yankee in our Southern States." "And are wife and children alone with the Negroes?" "Yes, sir. There's only one white man on the plantation, an overseer sort of chap." "Are not you afraid of the slaves rising?" "They're ignorant poor creatures, to be sure, but as yet they're faithful. Anyway, I put my trust in God, and I know He'll watch over the house while I'm away fighting for this good cause!" This man came from Mississippi and had twenty-five slaves, which represented a money value of at least £5000. He was beyond the age of enthusiasm, and was actuated, no doubt, by strong principles, to him unquestionable and sacred.

May 16th. Lieutenant [Towson] Ellis, General Bragg's aide-de-camp, came on board at an early hour, in order to take me round the works, and I was soon on the back of the General's charger, safely ensconced between the raised pummel and cantle of the great brass-bound saddle, with emblazoned saddlecloth and mighty stirrups of brass, fit for the fattest marshall that ever led an army of France to victory; all my efforts to touch with my toe the wonderful supports which, in consonance with the American idea, dangled far beneath, were ineffectual.

From headquarters we started on our little tour of inspection of the batteries. Certainly, anything more calculated to shake confidence in American journalism could not be seen; for I had been led to believe that the works were of the most formidable description, mounting hundreds of guns. Where hundreds was written, tens would have been nearer the truth.

I visited ten out of the thirteen batteries which General Bragg has erected against Fort Pickens. I saw but five heavy siege guns in the whole of the works among the fifty or fifty-five pieces with which they were armed. There may be about eighty altogether on the lines, which describe an arc of 135 degrees for about three miles round Pickens, at an average distance of a mile and one-third. I was rather interested with Fort Barrancas, built by the Spaniards long ago—an old work on the old plan, weakly armed, but possessing a tolerable command from the face of fire.

The working parties, as they were called—volunteers from Mississippi and Alabama, great long bearded fellows in flannel shirts and slouched hats, uniformless in all save brightly burnished arms and resolute purpose—were lying about among the works or contributing languidly to their completion.

Considerable improvements were in the course of execution; but the officers were not always agreed as to the work to be done. Captain A., at the wheel-barrows: "Now then, you men, wheel up these sandbags, and range them just at this corner." Major B.: "My good Captain A., what do you want the bags there for? Did I not tell you, these merlons were not to be finished till we had completed the parapet on the front?" Captain A.: "Well, Major, as you did, and your order made me think you knew darned little about your business; and so I am going to do a little engineering of my own."

Altogether, I was quite satisfied General Bragg was perfectly correct in refusing to open his fire on Fort Pickens and on the fleet, which ought certainly to have knocked his works about his ears in spite of his advantages of position, and of some well placed mortar batteries among the brushwood, at distances from Pickens of 2500 and 2800 yards. The magazines of the batteries I visited did not contain ammunition for more than one day's ordinary firing. The shot were badly cast, with projecting flanges from the mould, which would be very injurious to soft metal guns in firing. As to men, as in guns, the Southern papers had lied consumedly. I could not say how many were in Pensacola itself, for I did not visit the camp; at the outside guess of the numbers there were 2000. I saw, however, all the camps here, and I doubt exceedingly if General Bragg—who at this time is represented to have any number from 30,000 to 50,000 men under his command—has 8000 troops to support his batteries, or 10,000, including Pensacola, all told.

On my return to headquarters I found General Bragg in his room,

engaged writing an official letter in reply to my request to be permitted to visit Fort Pickens, in which he gave me full permission to do
as I pleased. Not only this, but he had prepared a number of letters
of introduction to the military authorities and to his personal friends
at New Orleans, requesting them to give me every facility and
friendly assistance in their power. He asked me my opinion about the
batteries and their armament, which I freely gave him *quantum valeat*
[for what it was worth]. "Well," he said, "I think your conclusions
are pretty just; but, nevertheless, some fine day I shall be forced to
try the mettle of our friends on the opposite side." All I could say
was, "May God defend the right." "A good saying, to which I say,
Amen. And drink with you to it."

There was a room outside, full of generals and colonels, to whom
I was duly introduced, but the time for departure had come and I
bade good-by to the General and rode down to the wharf.

The schooner was all ready for sea, but the Mobile gentlemen had
gone off to Pensacola, and as I did not desire to invite them to visit
Fort Pickens—where, indeed, they would have most likely met with
a refusal—I resolved to sail without them and to return to the navy
yard in the evening in order to take them back on our homeward
voyage. "Now then, Captain, cast loose; we are going to Fort Pickens." The worthy seaman had by this time become utterly at sea and
did not appear to know whether he belonged to the Confederate
States, Abraham Lincoln, or the British navy. But this order roused
him a little and looking at me with all his eyes, he exclaimed. "Why,
you don't mean to say you are going to make me bring the *Diana*
alongside that darned Yankee fort!" Our tablecloth, somewhat macu-
lated with gravy, was hoisted once more to the peak and, after some
formalities between the guardians of the jetty and ourselves, the
schooner canted round in the tideway, and with a fine light breeze
ran down towards the Stars and Stripes.

What magical power there is in the colours of a piece of bunting!
Hard must it be for this race, so arrogant, so great, to see stripe and
star torn from the fair standard with which they would fain have
shadowed all the kingdoms of the world; but their great continent is
large enough for many nations.

In five minutes we were out of "sheark" depth and alongside the jetty, where Major Vogdes, Mr. Brown, of the *Oriental,* and an officer, introduced as Captain [William Farquhar] Barry of the United States artillery, were waiting to receive us. Major Vogdes said that Colonel Brown would most gladly permit me to go over the fort but that he could not receive any of the other gentlemen of the party; they were permitted to wander about at their discretion. Some friends whom they picked up amongst the officers took them on a ride along the island, which is merely a sandbank covered with coarse vegetation, a few trees, and pools of brackish water.

If I were selecting a summer habitation I should certainly not choose Fort Pickens. It is, like all other American works I have seen, strong on the sea faces and weak toward the land. The outer gate was closed but at a talismanic knock from Captain Barry, the wicket was thrown open by the guard and we passed through a vaulted gallery into the parade ground, which was full of men engaged in strengthening the place and digging deep pits in the centre as shell traps. The men were United States Regulars, not comparable in physique to the Southern volunteers, but infinitely superior in cleanliness and soldierly smartness. The officer on duty led me to one of the angles of the fort and turned in to a covered way which had been ingeniously contrived by tilting up gun platforms and beams of wood at an angle against the wall and piling earth and sand banks against them for several feet in thickness. The casemates, which otherwise would have been exposed to a plunging fire in the rear, were thus effectually protected.

Fort Pickens is an oblique and somewhat narrow parallelogram, with one obtuse angle facing the sea and the other toward the land. The bastion at the acute angle towards Barrancas is the weakest part of the work, and men were engaged in throwing up an extempore glacis to cover the wall and the casemates from fire. The guns were of what is considered small calibre in these days, 32- and 42-pounders, with four or five heavy columbiads. An immense amount of work had been done within the last three weeks, but as yet the preparations are by no means complete. From the walls, which are made of a hard baked brick, nine feet in thickness, there is a good view of the enemy's position.

As I was looking at the works from the wall, Captain Vogdes made a sly remark now and then, blinking his eyes and looking closely at my face to see if he could extract any information. Probably no person has ever been permitted to visit two hostile camps within sight of each other save myself. I was neither spy, herald, nor ambassador; and both sides trusted to me fully on the understanding that I would not make use of any information here but that it might be communicated to the world at the other side of the Atlantic.

As it was approaching evening and I had seen everything in the fort, the hospital, casemates, magazines, bakehouses, tasted the rations, and drank the whiskey, I set out for the schooner accompanied by Colonel Brown and Captain Barry and other officers, and picking up my friends at the bakehouse outside.

Having bidden our acquaintances good-by, we got on board the *Diana*, which steered toward Warrington Navy Yard, to take the rest of the party on board. The sentries along the beach and on the batteries grounded arms and stared with surprise as the *Diana*, with her tablecloth flying, crossed over from Pickens and ran slowly along the Confederate works.

It was almost dark as the *Diana* shot out seawards between Pickens and McRae; and for some anxious minutes we were doubtful which would be the first to take a shot at us. Our tablecloth still fluttered; but the colour might be invisible. A lantern was hoisted astern by my order as soon as the schooner was clear of the forts, and with a cool sea breeze we glided out into the night, the black form of the *Powhatan* being just visible, the rest of the squadron lost in the darkness.

[May 17th.] Having been fourteen hours beating some twenty-seven miles, I was landed at last at a wharf in the suburbs of the town about five o'clock in the evening. On my way to the Battle House I met seven distinct companies marching through the streets to drill and the air was filled with sounds of bugling and drumming. In the evening a number of gentlemen called upon me to inquire what I thought of Fort Pickens and Pensacola, and I had some difficulty in parrying their very [pointed] questions, but at last adopted a formula which appeared to please them—I assured my friends I thought it would be an exceedingly tough business whenever the bombardment took place.

May 18th. An exceedingly hot day, which gives bad promise of comfort for the Federal soldiers who are coming, as the Washington Government asserts, to put down rebellion in these quarters. The mosquitoes are advancing in numbers and force. The day I first came I asked the waiter if they were numerous. "I wish they were a hundred times as many," said he. On inquiring if he had any possible reason for such an extraordinary aspiration, he said, "because we would get rid of those darned black Republicans out of Fort Pickens all the sooner." The man seemed to infer they would not bite the Confederate soldiers.

I dined at Dr. Nott's, and met Judge Campbell, who has resigned his high post as one of the Judges of the Supreme Court of the United States, and explained his reasons for doing so in a letter, charging Mr. Seward with treachery, dissimulation, and falsehood. He seemed to me a great casuist rather than a profound lawyer and to delight in subtle distinctions and technical abstractions; but I had the advantage of hearing from him at great length the whole history of the Dred Scott case, and a recapitulation of the arguments used on both sides, the force of which, in his opinion, was irresistibly in favour of the decision of the Court. Mr. Forsyth, Colonel Hardee, and others were of the company.

To me it was very painful to hear a sweet ringing silvery voice, issuing from a very pretty mouth, "I'm so delighted to hear that the Yankees in Fortress Monroe have got typhus fever. I hope it may kill them all." This was said by one of the most charming young persons possible and uttered with unmistakable sincerity, just as if she had said, "I hear all the snakes in Virginia are dying of poison." I fear the young lady did not think very highly of me for refusing to sympathise with her wishes in that particular form. But all the ladies in Mobile belong to "The Yankee Emancipation Society." They spend their days sewing cartridges, carding lint, preparing bandages, and I'm not quite sure that they don't fill shells and fuses as well. Their zeal and energy will go far to sustain the South in the forthcoming struggle, and nowhere is the influence of women greater than in America.

As to Dr. Nott, his studies have induced him to take a purely materialist view of the question of slavery and, according to him, questions of moral and ethics, pertaining to its consideration, ought to be referred to the cubic capacity of the human cranium—the head that can take the largest charge of snipe shot will eventually dominate in some form or other over the head of inferior capacity.[18] Dr. Nott detests slavery, but he does not see what is to be done with the slaves and how the four millions of Negroes are to be prevented from becoming six, eight, or ten millions, if their growth is stimulated by high prices for Southern produce.

May 19th. The heat out of doors was so great that I felt little tempted to stir out, but at 2 o'clock Mr. Magee drove me to a pretty place, called Spring Hill, where a German merchant of the city has his country residence. I listened to the worthy German comparing the Fatherland to his adopted country, and now and then letting out the secret love of his heart for the old place. He, like all the better classes in the South, has the utmost dread of universal suffrage and would restrict the franchise largely tomorrow if he could.

May 20th. I left Mobile in the steamer *Florida* for New Orleans this morning at eight o'clock. She was crowded with passengers, in uniform. In my cabin was a notice of the rules and regulations of the steamer. No. 6 was as follows: "All slave servants must be cleared at the Custom House. Passengers having slaves will please report as soon as they come on board."

Our steamer proceeded up a kind of internal sea, formed by the shore on the right hand and on the left by a chain almost uninterrupted of reefs covered with sand, and exceedingly narrow, so that the surf of the ocean rollers at the other side could be seen through the foliage of the pine trees which line them. On our right the endless pines closed up the land view of the horizon; the beach was pierced by creeks without number, called bayous; and it was curious to watch the white sails of the little schooners gliding in and out among the trees along the green meadows that seemed to stretch as an impassa-

[18]Josiah Nott wrote a number of medical papers, many of them well received. In the 1850s he undertook studies attempting to relate mental capacity to the size of the human head, studies which led him to conclude that Negroes are less intelligent than those of Caucasian birth. Nott's theory was challenged by F. Tiedeman of the University of Heidelberg but accepted by Charles Darwin. Russell did not express his opinion of Nott's work but he seems to have been impressed with the man.

ble barrier to their exit. Immense troops of pelicans flapped over the sea, dropping incessantly on the fish which abound in the inner water; and long rows of the same birds stood digesting their plentiful meals on the white beach by the ocean foam.

There was some anxiety in the passengers' minds, as it was reported that the United States cruisers had been seen inside and that they even burned the batteries on Ship Island.[19] We saw nothing of a character more formidable than coasting craft and a return steamer from New Orleans.

The approach to New Orleans is indicated by large hamlets and scattered towns along the seashore, hid in the piney woods, which offer a retreat to the merchants and their families from the fervid heat of the unwholesome city in summer time. As seen from the sea, these sanitary settlements have a picturesque effect and an air of charming freshness and lightness. There are detached villas of every variety of architecture in which timber can be constructed, painted in the brightest hues—greens, and blues, and rose tints—each embowered in magnolias and rhododendrons. From every garden a very long and slender pier, terminated by a bathing-box, stretches into the shallow sea; and the general aspect of these houses, with the light domes and spires of churches rising above the lines of white railings set in the dark green of the pines, is light and novel. To each of these cities there is a jetty, at two of which we touched, and landed newspapers, received or discharged a few bales of goods, and were off again.

The livelong day my fellow passengers never ceased talking politics, except when they were eating and drinking, because the horrible chewing and spitting are not at all compatible with the maintenance of active discussion. The fiercest of them all was a thin, fiery-eyed woman who at dinner expressed a fervid desire for bits of "Old Abe" —his ear, his hair—but whether for the purpose of eating or as curious reliques, she did not enlighten the company.

At night the steamer entered a dismal canal through a swamp which is infamous as the most mosquito-haunted place along the infested shore; the mouths of the Mississippi themselves being quite

---

[19]Ship Island is located about ten miles southeast of present-day Gulfport, Mississippi.

innocent, compared to the entrance of Lake Pontchartrain. When I woke up at daylight I found the vessel lying alongside a wharf with a railway train alongside, which is to take us to the city of New Orleans, six miles distant.

A village of restaurants or "restaurats," as they are called here, and of bathing-boxes had grown up around the terminus; all of the names of the owners, the notices and signboards being French. Outside the settlement the railroad passes through a swamp through which the overflowings of the Mississippi creep in black currents. The spires of New Orleans rise above the underwood and semi-tropical vegetation of this swamp. Nearer to the city lies a marshy plain, in which flocks of cattle, up to the belly in soft earth, are floundering among the clumps of vegetation. The nearer approach to New Orleans by rail lies through a suburb of exceedingly broad lanes, lined on each side of rows of miserable, mean one-storied houses, inhabited, if I am to judge from the specimens I saw, by a miserable and sickly population.

A great number of the men and women had evident traces of Negro blood in their veins, and of the purer-blooded whites, many had the peculiar look of the fishy-fleshy population of the Levantine towns,[20] and all were pale and lean. The railway terminus is marked by a dirty, barrack-like shed in the city. Selecting one of the numerous tumble down hackney carriages which crowded the street outside the station, I directed the man to drive me to the house of Mr. [William] Mure, the British Consul, who had been kind enough to invite me as his guest for the period of my stay in New Orleans.

The streets are badly paved, as those of most of the American cities I have ever been in, but in other respects they are more worthy of a great city than are those of New York. There is an air thoroughly French about the people—cafes, restaurants, billiard-rooms abound, with oyster and lager beer saloons interspersed. The shops are all *magazins* [emporiums]; the people in the streets are speaking French, particularly the Negroes, who are going out shopping with their masters and mistresses, exceedingly well dressed, noisy, and not unhappy looking. The extent of the drive gave an imposing idea of the size of New Orleans—the richness of some of the shops, the

---

[20]The region of the lands of the eastern Mediterranean.

vehicles in the streets and the multitude of well-dressed people on the pavements, an impression of its wealth and the comfort of the inhabitants. The Confederate flag was flying from the public buildings and from many private houses. Military companies paraded through the streets and a large proportion of men were in uniform.

Whatever may be the number of the Unionists or of the non-secessionists, a pressure too potent to be resisted has been directed by the popular party against the friends of the Federal Government. The agent of Brown Brothers, of Liverpool and New York, has closed their office and is going away in consequence of the intimidation of the mob, or as the phrase is here, the "excitement of the citizens," on hearing of the subscription made by the firm to the New York fund after Sumter had been fired upon.[21] Their agent in Mobile has been compelled to adopt the same course. Other houses follow their example, but as most business transactions are over for the season, the mercantile community hope the contest will be ended before the next season, by the recognition of Southern independence.

The streets are full of Turcos, Zouaves, Chasseurs; walls are covered with placards of volunteer companies; there are Pickwick rifles, LaFayette, Beauregard, MacMahon guards, Irish, German, Italian and Spanish and native volunteers, among them the Meagher rifles, indignant with the gentleman from whom they took their name because of his adhesion to the North, are going to rebaptise themselves and to seek glory under one more auspicious.[22] In fact, New Orleans looks like a suburb of the camp at Châlons.[23] Tailors are busy night and day making uniforms. I went into a shop with the Consul for some shirts—the mistress and all her seamstresses were busy preparing flags as hard as the sewing machine could stitch them and could attend to no business for the present. The Irish population, finding

[21]Immediately following the surrender of Fort Sumter, merchants and financiers in New York City subscribed funds to support the Union cause. The English firm of Brown Brothers, with its main American branch in New York, pledged money to this fund.

[22]"Meagher Rifles" was named in honor of Thomas Francis Meagher, an Irish-American political leader in New York City. Commissioned a brigadier general, United States Volunteers, Meagher commanded Irish-American units during most of the war.

[23]Site of an important nineteenth-century military base on the Marne, in northeastern France.

themselves unable to migrate northwards, and being without work, have rushed to arms with enthusiasm to support Southern institutions.

May 22nd. The thermometer today marked 95° in the shade. It is not to be wondered at that New Orleans suffers from terrible epidemics. At the side of each street a filthy open sewer flows to and fro with the tide in the blazing sun.

I sat for some time listening to the opinions of the various merchants who came in to talk over the news and politics in general. There are some who maintain there will be no war after all; that the North will not fight, and that the friends of the Southern cause will recover their courage when this tyranny is over. No one imagines the South will ever go back to the Union voluntarily or that the North has power to thrust it back at the point of the bayonet.

The South had commenced preparation for the contest by sowing grain instead of planting cotton, to compensate for the loss of supplies from the North. The payment of debts to Northern creditors is declared to be illegal, and "stay laws" have been adopted in most of the seceding States, by which the ordinary laws for the recovery of debts in the States themselves are for the time suspended, which may lead one into the belief that the legislators themselves belong to the debtor instead of the creditor class.

May 23rd. I dined with Major [Henry J.] Ranney, the president on one of the railways,[24] with whom Mr. Ward was stopping. Among the company were Mr. [George] Eustis, son-in-law to Mr. [John] Slidell; Mr. [Isaac E.] Morse, the attorney-general of the State; Mr. [E. W.] Moise, a Jew supposed to have considerable influence with the Governor, and a vehement politician; and others. The table was excellent and the wines were worthy of the reputation which our host enjoys. One of the slave servants who waited at table, an intelligent yellow "boy," was pointed out to me as the son of General Andrew Jackson.

None of the Southern gentlemen have the smallest apprehension of a servile insurrection. They use the universal formula "our

[24]Henry Joseph Ranney was president of the New Canal and Shell Railroad Company.

Negroes are the happiest, most contented, and most comfortable people on the face of the earth." I admit I have been struck by well-clad and good-humoured Negroes in the streets, but they are in the minority; many look morose, ill-clad, and discontented. The patrols I know have been strengthened, and I heard a young lady the other night say, "I shall not be a bit afraid to go back to the plantation, though mamma says the Negroes are after mischief."

May 24th. A great budget of news today, which with the events of the week may be briefly enumerated. The fighting has actually commenced between the United States steamers off Fortress Monroe and the Confederate battery erected at Sewall's Point—both sides claim a certain success. The Confederates declare they riddled the steamer and that they killed and wounded a number of the sailors. The captain of the vessel says he desisted from want of ammunition, but believed he killed a number of the rebels, and knows he had no loss himself. Beriah Magoffin, Governor of the sovereign State of Kentucky, has warned off both Federal and Confederate soldiers from his territory. The Confederate Congress has passed an act authorising persons indebted to the United States, except Delaware, Maryland, Kentucky, Missouri, and the District of Columbia, to pay the amount of their debts to the Confederate treasury. The state convention of North Carolina has passed an ordinance of secession. Arkansas has sent its delegates to the Southern Congress. Several Southern vessels have been made prizes by the blockading squadron; but the event which causes the greatest excitement and indignation here, was the seizure, on Monday, by the United States marshals, in every large city throughout the Union, of the telegraphic dispatches of the last twelve months.

In the course of the day I went to the St. Charles Hotel, which is an enormous establishment of the American type, with a Southern character to it. A number of gentlemen were seated in the hall, and front of the office, with their legs up against the wall and on the backs of chairs, smoking, spitting, and reading the papers. Officers crowded the bar. The bustle and noise of the place would make it anything but an agreeable residence for one fond of quiet; but this hotel is famous for its difficulties.

At half-past four, I went down by train to the terminus on the lake where I had landed, and dined with Mr. Eustis. The dinner was worthy of the reputation of the French cook. The pleasures of the evening were enhanced by the most glorious sunset, which cast its last rays through a wilderness of laurel roses in full bloom which thronged the garden. At dusk the air was perfectly alive with fire flies and strange beetles. Flies and coleopteras buzzed through the open windows, and flopped among the glasses. At half-past nine, we returned home in cars drawn by horses along the rail.

May 25th. Virginia had indeed been invaded by the Federals. Alexandria has been seized. It is impossible to describe the excitement and rage of the people; they take, however, some consolation in the fact that Colonel [Ephriam] Ellsworth in command of a regiment of New York Zouaves, was shot by J[ames] T. Jackson, the landlord of an inn in the city, called the Marshal House. Ellsworth, on the arrival of his regiment in Alexandria, proceeded to take down the secession flag which had been long seen from the President's windows. He went out upon the roof, cut it from the staff, and was proceeding with it downstairs, when a man rushed out of a room, levelling a double-barreled gun, shot Colonel Ellsworth dead, and fired the other barrel at one of his men, who had struck at the piece when the murderer presented it at the Colonel. Almost instantaneously, the Zouave shot Jackson in the head and as he was falling dead thrust his sabre bayonet through his body. Strange to say, the people of New Orleans consider Jackson was completely right in shooting the Federal Colonel, and maintain that the Zouave who shot Jackson was guilty of murder. Their theory is that Ellsworth had come over with a horde of ruffianly abolitionists or, as the Richmond *Examiner* has it, "the band of thieves, robbers, and assassins, in the pay of Abraham Lincoln, commonly known as the United States Army," to violate the territory of a sovereign state in order to execute their bloody and brutal purposes, and that he was in the act of committing a robbery by taking a flag which did not belong to him when he met his righteous fate.

It is curious to observe how passion blinds man's reason in this quarrel. More curious still to see, by the light of this event, how differently the same occurrence is viewed by Northerners and Southerners respectively. Jackson is depicted in the Northern papers as a fiend and an assassin; even his face in death is declared to have worn a revolting expression of rage and hate. The Confederate flag which was the cause of the fatal affray is described by one writer as having been purified of its baseness, by contract with Ellsworth's blood. The invasion of Virginia is hailed on all sides of the North with the utmost enthusiasm. "Ellsworth is a martyr hero whose name is to be held sacred forever."

On the other hand, the Southern papers declare that the invasion of Virginia, is "an act of the Washington tyrants, which indicates their bloody and brutal purpose to exterminate the Southern people." As it seems to me, Colonel Ellsworth, however injudicious he may have been, was actually in the performance of his duty when taking down the flag of an enemy.

In the evening I visited Mr. Slidell, whom I found at home with his family, Mrs. [Mathilde] Slidell and her sister Madame [Caroline] Beauregard, wife of the general, two very charming young ladies, daughters of the house, and a parlour full of fair companions, engaged, as hard as they could, in carding lint with their fair hands. Among the company was Mr. Slidell's son,[25] who had just travelled from school at the North under a feigned name, in order to escape violence at the hands of the Union mobs which are said to be insulting and outraging every Southern man. The conversation, as in the case of most Creole domestic circles, was carried on in French. I rarely met a man whose features have a greater *finesse* and firmness of purpose than Mr. Slidell's; his keen grey eye is full of life, his thin, firmly set lips indicate resolution and passion. Mr. Slidell, though born in a Northern state, is perhaps one of the most determined disunionists in the Southern Confederacy; he is not a speaker of note, nor a ready stump orator, nor an able writer, but he is an excellent judge of mankind, adroit, persevering, and subtle, full of device, and fond of intrigue; one of those men, who, unknown almost to the outer world, organises and sustains a faction and exalts it into the position of a party—what is called here a "wire-puller." Mr. Slidell is to the South something greater than Mr. Thurlow Weed has been to his party in the North. He, like every one else, is convinced that recognition must come soon; but, under any circumstances, he is

[25]Alfred Slidell was an only son.

quite satisfied the government and independence of the Southern Confederacy are as completely established as those of any power in the World. Mr. Slidell and the members of his family possess *naïveté*, good sense, and agreeable manners; and the regrets I heard expressed in Washington society, at their absence, had every justification.

May 26th.   All disposable regiments are on the march to Virginia. It was bad policy for Mr. Jefferson Davis to menace Washington before he could seriously carry out his threats, because the North was excited by the speech of his Secretary of War to take extraordinary measures for the defence of their capital; and General Scott was enabled by their enthusiasm not only to provide for its defence, but to effect a lodgment at Alexandria, as a base of operation against the enemy.

When the Congress at Montgomery adjourned the other day, they resolved to meet on the 20th of July at Richmond, which thus becomes the capital of the Confederacy. The city is not much more than one hundred miles south of Washington, with which it was in communication by rail and river, and the selection must cause a collision between the two armies in front of the rival capitals. The seizure of the Norfolk Navy Yard by the Confederates rendered it necessary to reinforce Fortress Monroe, and for the present the Potomac and the Chesapeake are out of danger.

The military precautions taken by General Scott and the movements attributed to him to hold Baltimore and to maintain his communications between Washington and the North, afford evidence of judgment and military skill. The Northern papers are clamouring for an immediate advance of their raw levies to Richmond, which General Scott resists.

In one respect the South has shown greater sagacity than the North. Mr. Jefferson Davis, having seen service in the field and having been Secretary of War, perceived the dangers and inefficiency of irregular levies, and therefore induced the Montgomery Congress to pass a bill which binds volunteers to serve during the war, unless sooner discharged, and reserved to the President of the Southern Confederacy the appointment of staff and field officers, the right of veto to battalion officers elected by each company, and the power of organising companies of volunteers into squadrons, battalions, and regiments. Writing to the *Times* this date, I observed: "Although immense levies of men may be got together for purposes of local defence or aggressive operations, it will be very difficult to move these masses like regular armies. There is an utter want of field-trains, equipage, and commissariat, which cannot be made good in a day, a week, or a month. The absence of cavalry, and the utter deficiency of artillery, may prevent either side obtaining any decisive result in one engagement; but there can be no doubt large losses will be incurred whenever these masses of men are fairly opposed to each other in the open field.

May 27th. In every State there is only one voice audible. Here-after, indeed, State jealousies may work their own way; but if words mean anything, all the Southern people are determined to resist Mr. Lincoln's invasion as long as they have a man or a dollar. Still, there are certain hard facts which militate against the truth of their own assertions, "that they are united to a man, and prepared to fight to a man." Only 15,000 are under arms out of the 50,000 men in the State of Louisiana liable to military service.

"Charges of abolitionism" appear in the reports of police cases in the papers every morning; and persons found guilty not of expressing opinions against slavery, but of stating their belief that the Northern-ers will be successful, are sent to prison for six months. The accused are generally foreigners or belong to the lower orders, who have got no interest in the support of slavery.

Every night since I have been in New Orleans there have been one or two fires; tonight there were three—one a tremendous conflagra-tion. When I inquired to what they were attributable, a gentleman who sat near, bent over, and looking me straight in the face, said, in a low voice, "The slaves." The flues, perhaps, and the system of stoves may also bear some of the blame. There is great enthusiasm among the townspeople in consequence of the Washington artillery, a crack corps, furnished by the first people in New Orleans, being ordered off for Virginia.

May 28th. On dropping in at the Consulate today, I found the skippers of several English vessels who are anxious to clear out lest they be detained by the Federal cruisers. The United States steam frigates *Brooklyn* and *Niagara* have been for some days past blockading Pass à l'outre.[26]

I dined with a large party at the lake, who had invited me as their guest, among whom were Mr. Slidell, Governor [Paul] Hébert, and others. I observed in New York that every man had his own solution of the cause of the present difficulty and contradicted plumply his neighbour the moment he attempted to propound his own theory. Here I found every one agreed as to the righteousness of the quarrel, but all differed as to the best mode of action for the South to pursue. Nor was there any approach to unanimity as the evening waxed older. Incidentally we had wild tales of Southern life, some good songs, curiously intermingled with political discussions, and what the Northerners call hyphileutin' talk.

After dinner I went in company of some of my hosts to the Boston Club, which has, I need not say, no connection with the city of that name. More fires, the tocsin sounding, and so to bed.

May 29th.   Dined in the evening with Mr. Aristide Miltenberger, where I met His Excellency Mr. [Thomas] Moore, the Governor of Louisiana, his military secretary, and a small party.

It is a strange country indeed; one of the evils which afflicts the Louisianians, they say, is the preponderance and influence of South Carolinian Jews, and Jews generally, such as Moise, Mordecai, Josephs, and Judah Benjamin, and others. The subtlety and keenness of the Caucasian intellect give men a high place among a people who admire ability and dexterity, and are at the same time reckless of means and averse to labour. The Governor is supposed to be somewhat under the influence of the Hebrews, but he is a man quite competent to think and to act for himself—a plain, sincere ruler of a slave State, and an upholder of the patriarchal institute. After dinner we accompanied Madame [Catherine] Miltenberger (who affords in her own person a very complete refutation of the dogma that American women furnish no examples of the charms which surround their English sisters in the transit from the prime of life

---

[26]Pass à l'outre is one of the main channels at the mouth of the Mississippi leading from the river into the Gulf of Mexico. At the present time it is more commonly referred to as North Pass.

towards middle age), in a drive along the shell road to the lake and canal; the most remarkable object being a long wall lined with a glorious growth of orange trees; clouds of mosquitoes effectually interfered with an enjoyment of the drive.

May 30th. I dined with Madame and M. Miltenberger and drove out with them to visit the scene of our defeat in 1815, which lies at the distance of some miles down the river. The Americans are naturally very proud of their victory, which was gained at a most trifling loss of themselves, which they erroneously conceive to be a proof of their gallantry in resisting the assault. It is one of the events which have created a fixed idea in their minds that they are able to "whip the world."

On returning from my visit I went to the club, where I had a long conversation with Dr. [William] Rushton, who is strongly convinced of the impossibility of carrying on government, or conducting municipal affairs, until universal suffrage is put down. He gave many instances of the terrorism, violence, and assassinations which prevail during election times in New Orleans. M. Miltenberger, on the contrary, thinks matters are very well as they are, and declares all these stories are fanciful. Incendiarism rife again. All the club windows crowded with men looking at a tremendous fire which burned down three or four stores and houses.

May 31st. I went with Mr. Mure to visit the jail, a square, whitewashed building, with cracked walls and barred windows. This crowded and most noisome place was filled with felons of every description, as well as with poor wretches merely guilty of larceny. Hardened murderers, thieves, and assassins were here associated with boys in their teens who were undergoing imprisonment for some trifling robbery. It was not pleasant to rub elbows with miscreants who lunged past, almost smiling defiance, whilst the slim warder, in his straw hat, shirt sleeves, and drawers told you how such a fellow had murdered his mother, how another had killed a policeman, or a third had destroyed no less than three persons in a few moments. Here were seventy murderers, pirates, burglars, violators, and thieves, circulating among men who had been proved guilty of no offence, but were merely waiting for their trial.

A verandah ran along one side of the wall, above a row of small cells, containing truckle beds for the inmates. "That's a desperate chap, I can tell you," said the warder, pointing to a man who, naked to his shirt, was sitting on the floor, with heavy irons on his legs, engaged in playing cards with a fellow prisoner, and smoking with an air of supreme contentment. The prisoner turned at the words, and gave a kind of grunt and chuckle and then played his next card.

Passing from the yard, we proceeded upstairs to the first floor, where were the debtors' rooms. These were tolerably comfortable, in comparison to the wretched cells we had seen; but the poorer debtors were crowded together, three or four in a room. As far as I could ascertain, there is no insolvency law, but the debtor is free, after ninety days' imprisonment, if his board and lodging be paid for. "And what if they are not?" "Oh, well, in that case we keep them till all is paid, adding of course for every day they are kept."

My attention was attracted from this extraordinary room to an open gallery at the other side of the courtyard, in which were a number of women with dishevelled hair and torn clothing, some walking up and down restlessly, others screaming loudly, while some with indecent gestures were yelling to the wretched men opposite to them, as they were engaged in their miserable promenade.

Shame and horror to a Christian land! These women were maniacs! They are kept here until there is room for them at the State Lunatic Asylum. Night and day their terrible cries and ravings echo through the dreary, waking hours and the fitful slumbers of the wretched men so soon to die.

We next visited the women's gallery, where female criminals of all classes are huddled together indiscriminately. On opening the door, the stench from the open verandah in which the prisoners were sitting was so vile that I could not proceed further; but I saw enough to convince me that the poor, erring woman who was put in there for trifling offence, and placed in contact with the beings who were uttering such language as we heard, might indeed leave hope behind her.

The prisoners had no beds to sleep upon, not even a blanket, and are thrust in to lie as they please, five in each small cell. It may be imagined what the tropical heat produces under such conditions as these; but as the surgeon was out, I could obtain no information respecting the rates of sickness or mortality.

I next proceeded to a yard somewhat smaller than that appropriated to serious offenders, in which were confined prisoners condemned for short sentences, for such offences as drunkenness, assault, and the like. Among the prisoners were some English sailors, confined for assaults on their officers, or breach of articles; all of whom had complaints to make on the Consul, as to arbitrary arrests and unfounded charges. Mr. Mure told me that when the port is full he is constantly engaged inquiring into such cases; and I am sorry to learn that the men of our commercial marine occasion a good deal of trouble to the authorities.

I left the prison in no very charitable mood towards the people who sanctioned such a disgraceful institution, and proceeded to complete my tour of the city. The "levee," which is an enormous embankment to prevent the inundation of the river, is now nearly deserted except by the river steamers, and those which have been unable to run the blockade. As New Orleans is on an average three feet below the level of the river at high water, this work requires constant supervision; it is not less than fifteen feet broad, and rises five or six feet above the level of the adjacent street, and it is continued in an almost unbroken line for several hundred of miles up the course of the Mississippi. When the bank gives way, or a "crevasse," as it is technically called, occurs, the damage done to the plantations has sometimes to be calculated by millions of dollars; when the river is very low there is a new form of danger, in what is called the "caving in" of the bank, which, left without the support of the water pressure, slides into the bed of the giant river.

New Orleans is called the "Crescent City" in consequence of its being built on a curve of the river, which is here about the breadth of the Thames at Gravesend, and of great depth. Enormous cotton presses are erected near the banks, where the bales are compressed by machinery before storage on shipboard, at a heavy cost to the planter.

As the city of New Orleans is nearly 1700 miles south of New York, it is not surprising that it rejoices in a semi-tropical climate. The markets are excellent, each municipality, or grand division, being provided with its own. They swarm with specimens of the composite races which inhabit the city, from the thorough-bred, wooly-headed Negro, who is suspiciously like a native-born African, to the Creole who boasts that every drop of blood in his veins in purely French.

I was struck by the absence of any whites of the labouring classes, and when I inquired what had become of the men who work on the levee and at the cotton presses in competition with the Negroes, I was told they had been enlisted for the war.

June 1st. The respectable people of the city are menaced with two internal evils in consequence of the destitution caused by the stoppage of trade with the North and with Europe. The municipal authorities, for want of funds, threaten to close the city schools and to disband the police; at the same time employers refuse to pay their workmen on the ground of inability. The British Consulate was thronged today by Irish, English, and Scotch, entreating to be sent North or to Europe. The stories told by some of these poor fellows were most pitiable, and were vouched for by facts and papers; but Mr. Mure has no funds at his disposal to enable him to comply with their prayers. Nothing remains for them but to enlist. For the third or fourth time I heard cases of British subjects being forcibly carried off to fill the ranks of so-called volunteer companies and regiments. In some instances they have been knocked down, bound, and confined in barracks, till in despair they consented to serve. Those who have friends aware of their condition were relieved by the interference of the Consul; but there are many, no doubt, thus coerced and placed in involuntary servitude without his knowledge.

The great commercial community of New Orleans, which now feels the pressure of the blockade, depends upon the interference of the European Powers next October. They have among them men who refuse to pay their debts to Northern houses, but they deny that they intend to repudiate and promise to pay all who are not black Republicans when the war is over. Repudiation is a word out of favour, as they feel the character of the Southern States and of Mr. Jefferson Davis himself has been much injured in Europe by the breach of honesty and honour of which they have been guilty; but I am assured on all sides that every State will eventually redeem all its obligations. Meantime, money here is fast vanishing. Bills on New York are worth nothing, and bills on England are at 18 per cent discount from the par value of gold; but the people of this city will endure all this and much more to escape from the hated rule of the Yankees.

Through the present gloom come the rays of a glorious future, which shall see a grand slave confederacy enclosing the Gulf in its arms, and swelling to the shores of the Potomac and Chesapeake, with the entire control of the Mississippi and a monopoly of the great staples on which so much of the manufactures and commerce of England and France depend. They believe themselves, in fact, to be masters of the destiny of the world. Cotton is king—not alone king but czar; and coupled with the gratification and profit to be derived from this mighty agency, they look forward with intense satisfaction to the complete humiliation of their hated enemies in the New England States, to the destruction of their usurious rival New York, and to the impoverishment and ruin of the States which have excited their enmity by personal liberty bills, and have outraged and insulted them by harbouring abolitionists and an anti-slavery press.

It is remarkable that in New Orleans, as in New York, the opinion of the most wealthy and intelligent men in the community, so far as I can judge, regards universal suffrage as organised confiscation, legalised violence and corruption, a mortal disease in the body politic. The other night, as I sat in the club house, I heard a discussion in reference to the operations of the Thugs in this city, a band of native-born Americans who at election times were wont deliberately to shoot down Irish and German voters occupying positions as leaders. These Thugs were only supressed by an armed vigilance committee of which a physician who sat at table was one of the members.

Having made some purchases and paid all my visits, I returned to prepare for my voyage up the Mississippi and visits to several planters on its banks—my first being to Governor Roman.

Four

UP THE MISSISSIPPI

(June 2–June 20, 1861)

June 2nd. My good friend the Consul was up early to see me off; and we drove together to the steamer *J. C. Cotton*. The people were going to mass as we passed through the streets, and it was pitiable to see the children dressed out as Zouaves, with tin swords and all sorts of pseudo-military tomfoolery; streets crowded with military companies; bands playing on all sides.

Before we left the door a poor black sailor came up to entreat Mr. Mure's interference. The moment he arrived in New Orleans he had been seized by the police. On his stating that he was a free-born British subject, the authorities ordered him to be taken to Mr. Mure; he could not be allowed to go at liberty on account of his colour; the laws of the State forbade such dangerous experiments on the feelings of the slave population; and if the Consul did not provide for him, he would be arrested and kept in prison, if no worse fate befell him. The police came as far as the door with him and remained outside to arrest him if the Consul did not afford him protection and provide for him, so that he should not be seen at large in the streets of the city. Free coloured persons are liable to seizure by the police, and to imprisonment, and may be sold into servitude under certain circumstances.

On arriving at the steamer I found a considerable party of citizens assembled to see off their friends. The aspect of New Orleans from the river is marred by the very poor houses lining the quays on the levee. Wide streets open on long vistas bordered by the most paltry little domiciles; and the great conceptions of those who planned them, notwithstanding the prosperity of the city, have not been realised.

As we are now floating nine feet higher than the level of the streets, we could look down upon a sea of flat roofs and low wooden houses, painted white, pierced by the domes and spires of churches and public buildings. Grass was growing in many of the streets. At the other side of the river there is a smaller city of shingle-roofed houses, with a background of low timber.

The steamer stopped continually at various points along the levee, discharging commissariat stores, parcels, and passengers; and after a time glided up into the open country, which spread beneath us for several miles at each side of the banks, with a continuous background of forest. All this part of the river is called the Coast, and the country adjacent is remarkable for its fertility. The sugar plantations are bounded by lines drawn at right angles to the banks of the river, and extending through the forest. The villas of the proprietors are thickly planted in the midst of the green fields, with the usual porticoes, pillars, verandahs, and green blinds; and in the vicinity of each are rows of whitewashed huts, which are the slave quarters. These fields, level as a billiard table, are of the brightest green with crops of maize and sugar.

But few persons were visible; not a boat was to be seen; and in the course of sixty-two miles we met only two steamers.[1] The dead, uniform line of the levee compresses [the Mississippi River] at each side, and the turbid waters flow without let in a current of uniform breadth between the monotonous banks. The gables of the summit of one house resemble those of another; and but for the enormous

[1]The Mississippi River was used chiefly for moving agricultural produce, and traffic was heaviest during the harvest season. The lack of traffic in June was due more to its seasonal nature than to the blockade.

scale of river and banks, and the black faces of the few Negroes visible, a passenger might think he was on board a Dutch *trek-schuit*. [2] In fact, the Mississippi is a huge trench-like canal draining a continent.

At half-past three, P.M., the steamer ran alongside the levee at the right bank, and discharged me at "Cahabanooze," in the Indian tongue, or "The ducks' sleeping place," together with an English merchant of New Orleans, M. LaVille Beaufevre, son-in-law of Governor Roman, and his wife. The Governor was waiting to receive us on the levee, and led the way through a gate in the paling which separated his ground from the roadside, towards the house, a substantial, square, two-storied mansion, with a verandah all round it, embosomed amid venerable trees, and surrounded by magnolias. [3] By way of explaining the proximity of house to the river, M. Roman told me that a considerable portion of the garden in front had a short time ago been carried off by the Mississippi; nor is he at all sure the house itself will not share the same fate; I hope sincerely it may not. My quarters were in a detached house complete in itself, containing four bedrooms, library, and sitting room, close to the mansion and surrounded, like it, by fine trees.

After we had sat for some time in the shade of the finest group, M. Roman, or, as he is called the Governor—once a captain always a captain—asked me whether I would like to visit the slave quarters. I assented, and the Governor led the way to a high paling at the back of the house, inside which the scraping of fiddles was audible. As we passed the back of the mansion, some young women flitted past in snow-white dresses, crinolines, pink sashes, and gaudily coloured handkerchiefs on their heads, who were, the Governor told me, the domestic servants going off to a dance at the sugarhouse; he lets his slaves dance every Sunday. The American planters who are not Catholics, although they do not make the slaves work on Sunday except there is something to do, rarely grant them the indulgence of a dance; but a few permit them some hours of relaxation on each Saturday afternoon.

We entered, by a wicker gate, a square enclosure, lined with Negro

[2] A towing boat used on canals in Holland.
[3] André Roman's sugar plantation was located in Ascension Parish, midway between New Orleans and Baton Rouge.

huts, built of wood, something like those which came from Malta to the Crimea in the early part of the campaign. They were not furnished with windows—a wood slide or grating admits all the air a Negro desires. There is a partition dividing the hut into two departments, one of which is used as the sleeping room and contains a truckle bedstead and a mattress stuffed with cotton wool, or the hair-like fibres of dried Spanish moss. The wardrobes of the inmates hang from nails or pegs driven into the wall. The other room is furnished with a dresser on which are arranged a few articles of crockery and kitchen utensils. Sometimes there is a table in addition to the plain wooden chairs, more or less dilapidated, constituting the furniture—a hearth, in connection with a brick chimney outside the cottage, in which, hot as the day may be, some embers are sure to be found burning. The ground round the huts was covered with litter and dust, heaps of old shoes, fragments of clothing and feathers, amidst which pigs and poultry were recreating. Curs of low degree scampered in and out of the shade, or around two huge dogs, *chiens de garde* [watch-dogs], which are let loose at night to guard the precincts; belly deep, in a pool of stagnant water, thirty or forty mules were swinking in the sun and enjoying their day of rest.

The huts of the Negroes engaged in the house are separated from those of the slaves devoted to field labour out of doors by a wooden paling. I looked into several of the houses, but somehow or other felt a repugnance, I dare say unjustifiable, to examine the penetralia, although invited—indeed, urged, to do so by the Governor. It was not that I expected to come upon anything dreadful, but I could not divest myself of some regard for the feelings of the poor creatures, slaves though they were, who stood by, shy, curtsying, and silent, as I broke in upon their family circle, felt their beds, and turned over their clothing. What right had I to do so?

Swarms of flies, tin cooking utensils attracting them by remnants of molasses, crockery, broken and old, on the dressers, more or less old clothes on the wall, these varied over and over again, were found in all the huts, not a sign or ornament or decoration was visible; not the most tawdry print, image of Virgin or Saviour; not a prayerbook or printed volume. The slaves are not encouraged, or indeed permitted to read, and some communities of slaveowners punish heavily those attempting to instruct them.

All the slaves seemed respectful to their master. It struck me more and more, however, as I examined the expression of the faces of the slaves, that deep dejection is the prevailing, if not universal, characteristic of the race. Here there were abundant evidences that they were well treated; they had good clothing of its kind, food, and a master who wittingly could do them no injustice, as he is, I am sure, incapable of it. Still they all looked sad, and even the old woman who boasted that she had held her old owner in her arms when he was an infant did not smile cheerfully, as the nurse at home would have done, at the sight of her ancient charge.

Before leaving the enclosure I was taken to the hospital, which was in charge of an old Negress. The naked rooms contained several flock beds on rough stands and five patients, three of whom were women. They sat listlessly on the beds, looking out into space; no books to amuse them, no conversation—nothing but their own dull thought, if they had any. They were suffering from pneumonia and swellings of the glands of the neck; one man had fever. Their medical attendant visits them regularly, and each plantation has a practitioner who is engaged by the term of his services.

The scraping of the fiddles attracted us to the sugarhouse; some fifteen women and as many men were assembled, and four couples were dancing a kind of Irish jig to the music of the Negro musicians.

At this time of year there is no work done in the sugarhouse, but when the crushing and boiling are going on the labour is intensely trying, and the hands work in gangs night and day; and, if the heat of the fires be superadded to the temperature in September, it may be conceded that nothing but "involuntary servitude" could go through the toil and suffering required to produce sugar.

In the afternoon the Governor's son came in from the company which he commands; his men are of the best families in the country —planters and the like. We sauntered about the gardens, diminished, as I have said, by a freak of the river. The French Creoles love gardens; the Anglo-Saxons hereabout do not much affect them and cultivate their crops up to the very doorway.

In the evening several officers of M. Alfred Roman's company and neighbouring planters dropped in, and we sat out in the twilight, under the trees in the verandah, illuminated by the flashing fireflies, and talking politics. I was struck by the profound silence which reigned all around us, except a low rushing sound, like that made by the wind blowing over cornfields, which came from the mighty river before us. Nothing else was audible but the sound of our own voices and the distant bark of a dog. After the steamer which bore us had passed on, I do not believe a single boat floated up or down the stream, and but one solitary planter, in his gig or buggy, traversed the road which lay between the garden palings and the bank of the great river.

Our friends were all Creoles—that is, natives of Louisiana—of French or Spanish descent. They are kinder and better masters, according to universal repute, than native Americans or Scotch; but the New England Yankee is reputed to be the severest of all slaveowners. All these gentlemen to a man are resolute that England must get their cotton or perish. With their faithful Negroes to raise their corn, sugar, and cotton, whilst their young men are at the wars; with France and England to pour gold into their lap with which to purchase all they need in the contest, they believe they can beat all the power of the Northern world in arms. Illimitable fields, tilled by multitudinous Negroes, open on their sight, and they behold the empires of Europe, with their manufactures, their industry, and their wealth, prostrate at the base of their throne, crying out "Cotton! More cotton! That is all we ask!"

Mr. [E. J.] Forstall maintains the South can raise an enormous revenue by a small direct taxation; whilst the North, deprived of Southern resources, will refuse to pay taxes at all, and will accumulate enormous debts inevitably leading to its financial ruin. He, like every Southern man I have as yet met, expresses unbounded confidence in Mr. Jefferson Davis. I am asked invariably, as the second question from a stranger, "Have you seen our President, sir? don't you think him a very able man?" This unanimity in the estimate of his character, and universal confidence in the head of the State, will prove of incalculable value in a civil war.

June 3rd.   At five o'clock this morning, having been awakened an hour earlier by a wonderful chorus of riotous mockingbirds, my old Negro attendant brought in my bath of Mississippi water, which, Nile like, casts down a strong deposit, and becomes as clear, if not so sweet, after standing. *"Le seigneur vous attend"*; and already I saw, outside my window, the Governor waiting. Early as it was, the sun felt excessively hot, and I envied the Governor his slouched hat as we rode through the fields crisp with dew. In a few minutes our horses were traversing narrow alleys between the tall fields of maize which rose far above our heads. This corn, as it is called, is the principal food of the Negroes; and every planter lays down a sufficient quantity to afford him, on an average, a supply all the year round. Outside this spread vast fields, hedgeless, wall-less, and unfenced, where the green cane was just learning to wave its long shoots in the wind—a lake of bright green sugar sprouts, along the margin of which, in the distance, rose an unbroken boundary of forest, two miles in depth, up to the swampy morass all to be cleared and turned into arable land in process of time. From the river front to this forest, the fields of rich loam, unfathomable, and yielding from one to one and a half hogsheads of sugar per acre under cultivation, extend for a mile and a half in depth. In the midst of this expanse white dots were visible like Sowars[4] seen on the early march, in Indian fields, many a time and oft. Those are the gangs of hands at work—we will see what they are at presently. This little reminiscence of Indian life was further heightened by the Negroes who ran beside us to whisk flies from the horses and to open the gates in the plantation boundary. When the Indian corn is not good, peas are sowed, alternately, between the stalks and are considered to be of much benefit; and when the cane is bad, corn is sowed with it for the same object. Before we came up to the gangs we passed a cart on the road containing a large cask, a bucket full of molasses, a pail of hominy, or boiled Indian corn, and a quantity of tin pannikins. The cask contained water for the Negroes, and the other vessels held the materials for their breakfast; in addition to which they generally have each a dried fish. The food was ample and looked wholesome, such as any labouring man would be well content with. Passing along through maize on one side and cane at another, we arrived at last at a patch of ground where men and women were hoeing.

Three gangs of Negroes were at work: one gang of men, with twenty mules and ploughs, were engaged in running through the furrows between the canes, cutting up the weeds and clearing away

[4]Mounted native soldiers in India.

the grass which is the enemy of the growing shoot. Another gang consisted of forty men, who were hoeing out the grass in Indian corn. The third gang, of thirty-six women, were engaged in hoeing out cane. Those who are mothers leave their children in charge of certain old women, unfit for anything else, and are permitted to go home, at appointed periods in the day to give the infants the breast. The overseers have power to give ten lashes, but heavier punishment ought to be reported to the Governor; however, it is not likely a good overseer would be checked, in any way, by his master. The anxieties attending the cultivation of sugar are great and so much depends upon the judicious employment of labour, it is scarcely possible to exaggerate the importance of experience in directing it, and of the power to insist on its application.

We returned to the house in time for breakfast, for which our early cup of coffee and biscuit and the ride has been good preparation. Here was old France again. One might imagine a lord of the seventeenth century in his hall, but for the black faces of the servitors and the strange dishes of tropical origin. There was the old French abundance, and numerous dishes and efflorescence of napkins, and the long-necked bottles of Bordeaux, with a steady current of pleasant small talk.

After breakfast the Governor drove out by the ever-silent levee for some miles, passing estate after estate, where grove nodded to grove, each alley saw its brother. One could form no idea, from the small limited frontage of these plantations, that the proprietors were men of many thousands a year, because the estates extend on an average for three or four miles back to the forest. The absence of human beings on the road was a feature which impressed one more and more. But for the tall chimneys of the factories and the sugarhouses, one might believe that these villas had been erected by some pleasure loving people who had all fled from the river banks for fear of pestilence.

At night, there are regular patrols and watchmen who look after the levee and the Negroes. A number of dogs are also loosed, but I am assured that the creatures do not tear the Negroes; they are taught "merely" to catch and mumble them, to treat them as a well-broken retriever uses a wounded wild duck.

[June 4th.] The carriage is ready and the word farewell is spoken at last. Mr. Alfred Roman [is] my companion. As we jog along in an easy rolling carriage drawn by a pair of stout horses, a number of white people meet us coming from the Catholic chapel of the parish, where they had been attending the service for the repose of the soul of a lady much beloved in the neighbourhood. The black people must be supposed to have very happy souls, or to be utterly lost, for I have failed to find that any such services are ever considered necessary in their case although they may have been very good—or, where the service would be most desirable—very bad Catholics. The dead, leaden uniformity of the scenery forced one to converse in order to escape profound melancholy; the levee on the right hand, above which nothing was visible but the sky; on the left plantations with cypress fences, whitewashed and pointed wooden gates leading to the planters' houses, and rugged gardens surrounded with shrubs, through which could be seen the slave quarters. Men making eighty or ninety hogsheads of sugar in a year lived in most wretched tumble-down wooden houses not much larger than ox sheds.

As we drove on the storm gathered overhead, and the rain fell in torrents—the Mississippi flowed lifelessly by—not a boat on its broad surface.

At the ferry-house I was attended by one stout young slave who was to row me over. The Negro groped under the shed and pulled out a piece of wood like a large spatula, some four feet long, and a small round pole a little longer. "What are those?" quoth I. "Dem's oars, Massa," was my sable ferryman's brisk reply. "I'm very sure they are not; if they were spliced they might make an oar between them." "Golly, and dat's the trute, Massa." "Then go and get oars, will you?" While he was hunting about we entered the shed at the ferry for shelter from the rain. We found "a solitary woman sitting" smoking a pipe by the ashes on the hearth, blear-eyed, low-browed, and morose—young as she was. She never said a word nor moved as we came in, sat and smoked, and looked through her gummy eyes at chickens about the size of sparrows, and at a cat not larger than a rat which ran about on the dirty floor. A little girl, some four years of age, not overdressed—indeed, half-naked, "not to put too fine a point upon it"—crawled out from under the bed where she had hid on our approach. As she seemed incapable of appreciating the use of a small

piece of silver presented to her—having no precise ideas in coinage
or toffy—her parent took the obolus in charge, with unmistakable
decision; but still the lady would not stir a step or aid our guide who
now insisted on the "key ov de oar-house." The little thing sidled off
and hunted it out from the top of the bedstead, and when it was
found, and the boat was ready, I was not sorry to quit the company
of the silent woman in black. The boatman pushed off his skiff, in
shape a snuffer-dish, some ten feet long and a foot deep, into the
water—there was a good deal of rain in it. I got in too, and the
conscious waters immediately began vigorously spurting through the
cotton wadding wherewith the craft was caulked. Had we gone out
into the stream we should have had a swim for it, and they do say
that the Mississippi is the most dangerous river in the known world.
"Why! deuce take you" (I said at least that, in my wrath), "don't you
see the boat is leaky?" "See it now for true, Massa. Nobody able to
tell dat till Massa get in though." Another skiff proved to be more
staunch. I bade good-by to my friend Roman and sat down in my
boat, which was forced by the Negro against the stream close to the
bank, in order to get a good start across to the other side. The view
from my lonely position was curious, but not at all picturesque. The
world was bounded on both sides by a high bank, which constricted
the broad river, just as if one were sailing down an open sewer of
enormous length and breadth. Above the bank rose the tops of tall
trees and the chimneys of sugarhouses and that was all to be seen
save the sky.

A quarter of an hour brought us to the levee on the other side. I
ascended the bank, and across the road, directly in front appeared a
carriage gateway and wickets of wood, painted white, in a line of
dark palings of the same material, which extended up and down the
road far as the eye could see, and guarded widespread fields of maize
and sugar cane. An avenue lined with trees, with branches close set,
drooping and overarching a walk paved with red brick, led to the
house, the porch of which was visible at the extremity of the lawn,
with clustering flowers, rose-jassamine, and creepers clinging to the
pillars supporting the verandah. The view from the belvedere on the
roof was one of the most striking of its kind in the world.

If the English agriculturist could see six thousand acres of the
finest land in one field, unbroken by hedge or boundary, and covered

with the most magnificent crops of tasseling Indian corn and sprouting sugar cane, as level as a billiard table, he would surely doubt his senses. But there is literally such a sight. My host was not ostentatiously proud in telling me that, in the year 1857, he had purchased this estate for £300,000 and an adjacent property, of 8000 acres, for £150,000, and that he had left Belfast in early youth, poor and unfriended to seek his fortune and indeed scarcely knowing what fortune meant, in the New World. He is not yet fifty years of age, and his confidence in the great future of sugar induced him to embark this enormous fortune in an estate of which the blockade has stricken with paralysis.

I found Mr. Ward and a few merchants from New Orleans in possession of the bachelor's house. The service was performed by slaves, and the order and regularity of the attendants were worthy of a well-regulated English mansion. In Southern houses along the Coast, as the Mississippi above New Orleans is termed, beef and mutton are rarely met with, and the more seldom the better. Fish, also, is scarce, but turkeys, geese, poultry, and preparations of pig, excellent vegetables, and wine of the best quality, render the absence of the accustomed dishes little to be regretted.

The silence which struck me at Governor Roman's is not broken at Mr. [John] Burnside's, and when the last thrill of the mockingbird's song has died out through the grove, a stillness of Avernian profundity settles on hut, field, and river.

June 5th.   The smart Negro who waited on me this morning spoke English. I asked him if he knew how to read and write. "We must not do that, sir." "Where were you born?" "I was raised on the plantation, Massa, but I have been to New Orleans;" and then he added, with an air of pride, "I sp'ose, sir, Massa Burnside not take less than 1500 dollars for me." Downstairs to breakfast, the luxuries of which are fish, prawns, and red meat which has been sent for to Donaldsonville by boat rowed by an old Negro. Breakfast over, I walked down to the yard, where the horses were waiting, and proceeded to visit the saccharine principality. Mr. [H. M.] Seale, the overseer of this portion of the estate, was my guide, if not philosopher and friend.

The wealth of the land is inexhaustible. The cane is grown from stalks which are laid in pits during the winter till the ground has been ploughed, when each piece of cane is laid longitudinally on the ridge and covered with earth, and from each joint of the stalk springs forth a separate sprout when the crop begins to grow. At present the sugar cane is waiting for its full development, but the Negro labour around its stem has ceased; in the midst of this waste of plenty and wealth, where are the human beings who produce both? One must go far to discover them; they are buried in sugar and in maize, or hidden in Negro quarters. In truth, there is no trace of them, over all this expanse of land, unless one knows where to seek; no "ploughboy whistles o'er the lea;" no rustic stands to do his own work, but the gang is moved off in silence from point to point, like a *corps d'armée* of some despotic emperor manoeuvring in the battle field.

Admitting everything that can be said, I am more persuaded, from what I see, that the real foundation of slavery in the Southern States lies in the power of obtaining labour. Granting the heat and the malaria, it is not for a moment to be argued that planters could not find white men to do their work if they would pay them for the risk. A Negro, it is true, bears heat well, and can toil under the blazing sun of Louisiana, in the stifling air between the thick set sugar canes, but the Irishman who is employed in the stokehole of a steamer is exposed to a higher temperature and physical exertion even more arduous. The Irish labourer can, however, set a value on his work; the African slave can only determine the amount of work to be got from him by the exhaustion of his powers. More than that, the white man seems to be exempt from the inflammatory disease, pneumonia, and attacks of the mucous membrane and respiratory organs to which the blacks are subject; and if the statistics of Negro mortality were rigidly examined, I doubt that they would exhibit as large a proportion of mortality and sickness as would be found amongst gangs of white men under similar circumstances. But the slave is subjected to rigid control; he is deprived of stimulating drinks in which the free white labourer would indulge; and he is obliged to support life upon an anti-phlogistic diet,[5] which gives him, however, sufficient strength to execute his daily task.

It is in the supposed cheapness of slave labour and its profitable

[5] A diet that reduces inflammation or fever.

adaptation in the production of Southern crops, that the whole gist and essence of the question really lies. It is calculated that each fieldhand, as an able-bodied Negro is called, yields seven hogsheads of sugar a year, which, at the rate of fourpence a pound, at an average of a hogshead an acre, would produce to the planter £140 for every slave. This is wonderful interest on the planter's money; but he sometimes gets two hogsheads an acre and even as many as three hogsheads have been produced in good years on the best lands; in other words, two and a quarter tons of sugar and refuse stuff, called "bagasse," have been obtained from an acre of cane. Not one planter of the many I have asked has ever given an estimate of the annual cost of a slave's maintenance; the idea of calculating it never comes into their heads.

The first place I visited with the overseer was a new sugarhouse, which Negro carpenters and masons were engaged in erecting. It would have been amusing had not the subject been so grave, to hear the overseer's praises of the intelligence and skill of these workmen, and his boast that they did all the work of skilled labourers on the estate, and then to listen to him, in a few minutes, expatiating on the utter helplessness and ignorance of the black race, their incapacity to do any good, or even to take care of themselves.

Mr. Seale conducted me to a kind of forcing-house, where the young Negroes are kept in charge of certain old crones too old for work, whilst their parents are away in the cane and Indian corn. A host of children of both sexes were seated in the verandah of a large wooden shed, or playing around it, very happily and noisily. I was glad to see the boys and girls of nine, ten, and eleven years of age were at this season, at all events, exempted from the cruel fate which befalls poor children of their age in the mining and manufacturing districts of England. At the sight of the overseer the little ones came forward in tumultuous glee, babbling out "Massa Seale," and evidently pleased to see him.

The children were quite sufficiently clad, ran about round us, patted the horses, felt our legs, tried to climb up on the stirrup, and twinkled their black and ochrey eyes at Massa Seale. Some were exceedingly fair; and Mr. Seale, observing that my eye followed these, murmured something about the overseers before Mr. Burnside's time being rather a bad lot. He talked about their colour and complexion quite openly; nor did it seem to strike him that there was any particular turpitude in the white man who had left his offspring as slaves on the plantation.

A tall, well-built lad of some nine or ten years stood by me, looking curiously into my face. "What is your name?" said I. "George," he replied. "Do you know how to read or write?" He evidently did not understand the question. "Do you go to church or chapel?" A dubious shake of the head. "Did you ever hear of our Saviour?" At this point Mr. Seale interposed, and said, "I think we had better go on, as the sun is getting hot," and so we rode gently through the little ones; and when we had got some distance he said, rather apologetically, "We don't think it right to put these things into their heads so young, it only disturbs their minds, and leads them astray."

Now, in this one quarter there were no less than eighty children, some twelve and some even fourteen years of age. No education— no God—their whole life—food and play, to strengthen their muscles and fit them for the work of a slave. "And when they die?" "Well," said Mr. Seale, "they are buried in that field there by their own people, and some of them have a sort of prayers over them, I believe." The overseer, it is certain, had no fastidious notions about slavery; it was to him the right thing in the right place, and his *summum bonum* [major objective] was a high price for sugar, a good crop, and a healthy plantation. Nay, I am sure I would not wrong him if I said he could see no impropriety in running a good cargo of regular black slaves, who might clear a great backwood and swampy undergrowth, which was now exhausting the energies of his fieldhands, in the absence of Irish navvies.

June 6th. Breakfast is served. Then come the newspapers, which are perused eagerly with ejaculations, "Do you hear what they are doing now—infernal villains! that Lincoln must be mad!" and the like. At one o'clock, in spite of the sun, [we] rode out along the road by the Mississippi to Mr. Burnside's plantation called Orange Grove, from a few trees which still remain in front of the overseer's house. We visited an old Negro, called "Boatswain," who lived with his old wife in a wooden hut close by the margin of the Mississippi. His business is to go to Donaldsonville for letters, or meat, or ice for the house—a tough row for the withered old man. He is an African born and he just remembers being carried on board ship and taken to some big city before he came upon the plantation.

"Do you remember nothing of the country you came from, Boatswain?" "Yes, sir. Jist remember trees and sweet things my mother gave me, and much hot sand I put my feet in, and big leaves that we play with—all us little children—and plenty to eat, and big birds and shells." "Would you like to go back, Boatswain?" "What for, sir? no one know old Boatswain there. My old missus Sally inside." "Are you quite happy, Boatswain?" "I'm getting very old, massa. Massa Burnside very good to Boatswain, but who care for such dam old nigger? Golla Mighty gave me fourteen children, but he took them all away again from Sally and me. No budy care much for dam old nigger like me."

On Orange Grove Plantation, although the crops were fine, the Negroes unquestionably seemed less comfortable than those in the quarters of Houmas, separated from them by a mere nominal division. Then, again, there were more children with fair complexions to be seen peeping out of the huts; some of these were attributed to the former overseer, one Johnson by name, but Mr. [Benjamin] Gibbs, as if to vindicate his memory, told me confidentially [that Johnson] had paid a large sum of money to the former proprietor of the estate for one of his children and had carried it away with him when he left. "All the children on the estate," added he, "are healthy, and I can show my lot against Seale's over there, though I hear tell he had a great show of them out to you yesterday."

It is among these men that, at times, slavery assumes its harshest aspect and that the Negroes are exposed to the severest labour; but it is also true that the slaves have closer relations with the families of their owners, and live in more intimate connection with them than they do under the strict police of the large plantations.

At dinner in the evening Mr. Burnside entertained a number of planters in the neighborhood—Mr. Duncan Kenner, a medical gentleman named [Thomas] Cottman, and others—the last named gentleman is a Unionist and does not hesitate to defend his opinions.

June 7th. Extraordinary delusions prevail on both sides. The North believe that battalions of scalping Indian savages are actually stationed at Harpers Ferry. One of the most important movements has been made by Major General McClellan, who has marched a force into western Virginia from Cincinnati, has occupied a portion of the line of the Baltimore and Ohio Railway, which was threatened with destruction by the secessionists; and has already advanced as far as Grafton. Gen. [Irwin] McDowell has been appointed to the command of the Federal forces in Virginia. Every day regiments are pouring down from the North to Washington. General Butler, who is in command at Fortress Monroe, has determined to employ Negro fugitives, whom he has called "Contrabands," in the works about the fort, feeding them, and charging the cost of their keep against the worth of their services; and Mr. Cameron, the Secretary of War, has ordered him to refrain from surrendering such slaves to their masters, whilst he is to permit no interference by his soldiers with the relations of persons held to service under the laws of the States in which they are in.

Mr. Jefferson Davis has arrived at Richmond. At sea the Federal steamers have captured a number of Southern vessels; and some small retaliations have been made by the Confederate privateers. The largest mass of the Confederate troops have assembled at a place called Manassas Junction, on the railway from western Virginia to Alexandria.

The Northern papers are filled with an account of a battle at Philippi, and a great victory, in which no less than two of their men were wounded and two were reported missing as the whole casualties; but Napoleon scarcely expended so much ink over Austerlitz as is absorbed on this glory in the sensation headings of the New York papers.[6]

After breakfast I accompanied a party of Mr. Burnside's friends to visit the plantations of Governor Manning, close at hand. One plantation is like another as two peas. We had the same paths through

---

[6]Brigadier General Thomas A. Morris, under McClellan's command, surprised Confederates defending Philippi in western Virginia on June 3, 1861. Northern troops defeated the southerners so quickly that the importance of the skirmish was blown out of proportion by the northern press. To indicate the speed of the southern defeat, northerners referred to the battle as the "Philippi Races."

tasseling corn high above our heads, or through wastes of rising sugar cane; but the slave quarters at Governor Manning's were larger, better built, and more comfortable looking than any I have seen.

When I got back, Mr. Burnside was seated in his verandah, gazing with anxiety, but not with apprehension, on the marching columns of black clouds which were lighted up from time to time by heavy flashes and shaken by rolls of thunder. Day after day the planters have been looking for rain, tapping glasses, scrutinising aneroids, consulting Negro weather prophets, and now and then their expectations were excited by clouds moving down the river, only to be disappointed by their departure into space, or, worse, than all, their favouring more distant plantations with a shower that brought gold to many a coffer.

My good host is rather uneasy about his prospects this year, owing to the war; and no wonder. He reckoned on an income of £100,000 for his sugar alone; but if he cannot send it North it is impossible to estimate the diminution of his profits. I fancy, indeed, he more and more regrets that he embarked his capital in these great sugar swamps, and that he would gladly now invest it at a loss in the old country of which he is yet a subject, for he has never been naturalised in the United States. Nevertheless, he rejoices in the finest clarets and in wines of fabulous price, which are tended by an old white-headed Negro, who takes as much care of the fluid as if he was accustomed to drink it every day.

June 8th. According to promise, the inmates of Mr. Burnside's house proceeded to pay a visit today to the plantation of Mr. [Henry] McCall, who lives at the other side of the river some ten or twelve miles away.

The more one sees of a planter's life the greater is the conviction that its charms come from a particular turn of mind, which is separated by a wide interval from modern ideas in Europe. The planter is a denomadised Arab—he has fixed himself with horses and slaves in a fertile spot, where he guards his women with Oriental care, exercises patriarchal sway, and is at once fierce, tender, and hospitable. The inner life of his household is exceedingly charming, because one is astonished to find the graces and accomplishments of womanhood displayed in a scene which has a certain sort of savage rudeness about it after all, and where all kinds of incongruous accidents are visible in the service of the table, in the furniture of the house, in its decorations, menials, and surrounding scenery.

June 9th.   A thunderstorm, which lasted all the morning and afternoon till three o'clock. When it cleared I drove, in company with Mr. Burnside and his friends to dinner with Mr. Duncan Kenner, who lives some ten or twelve miles above Houmas. He is one of the sporting men of the South, well known on the Charleston racecourse, and keeps a large stable of racehorses and brood mares, under the management of an Englishman.

It is observable, however, that the Creoles do not exhibit any great enthusiasm for horse racing, but that they apply themselves rather to cultivate their plantations and to domestic duties; and it is even remarkable that they do not stand prominently forward in the State Legislature or aspire to high political influence and position, although their numbers and wealth would fairly entitle them to both.

June 10th.   At last *venit summa dies et ineluctabile tempus* [came the final day and the inevitable moment]. I had seen as much as might be of the best phase of the great institution—less than I could desire of a most exemplary, kind-hearted, clear-headed, honest man. In the calm of a glorious summer evening we crossed the Father of Waters, waving an adieu to the good friend who stood on the shore, and turning our backs on the home we had left behind us. It was dark when the boat reached Donaldsonville on the opposite "Coast."

As the steamer could not be up from New Orleans till dawn, it was a relief to saunter through Donaldsonville to see society, which consisted of several gentlemen and various Jews playing games unknown to Hoyle, in oaken barrooms flanked by billiard tables. Doctor Cottman, who had crossed the river to see patients suffering from an attack of euchre,[7] took us round to a little club, where I was introduced to a number of gentlemen, who expressed great pleasure at seeing me, shook hands violently, and walked away; and, finally, melted off into a cloud of mosquitoes by the river bank.

The *Acadia* was now alongside and in the early morning Donald-

[7]The card game.

sonville receded rapidly into trees and clouds. To bed and after a long sleep look out again on the scene.

[June 11th–13th.] Before noon the steamer hauled alongside a stationary hulk at Baton Rouge, which once "walked the waters" by the aid of machinery, but which was now used as a floating hotel, depôt, and storehouse—315 feet long, and fully 30 feet on the upper deck above the level of the river. The *Acadia* stopped, and I disembarked. Here were my quarters till the boat for Natchez should arrive.

Baton Rouge is the capital of the State of Louisiana, and the Statehouse thereof is a very quaint and very new example of bad taste. The Deaf and Dumb Asylum near it is in a much better style. It was my intention to have visited the State Prison and Penitentiary, but the day was too hot, and the distance too great, and so I dined at the oddest little Creole restaurant, with the funniest old hostess, and the strangest company in the world.

Precisely at seven o'clock on Wednesday morning the *Mary T.* came alongside, and soon afterward bore me on to Natchez, through scenery which became wilder and less cultivated as she got upwards. Of the 1500 steamers on the river, not a tithe are now in employment and the owners of these profitable flotillas are "in a bad way." It was late at night when the steamer arrived at Natchez, and next morning early I took shelter in another engineless steamer beside the bank of the river at Natchez-under-the-Hill, which was thought to be a hotel by its owners.

In the morning I asked for breakfast. "There is nothing for breakfast; go to Curry's on shore." Walk up hill to Curry's—a barroom occupied by a waiter and flies. "Can I have any breakfast?" "No, sir-ree"; this was "Jeff. Davis's fast day." My hunger was assuaged by Mr. [Levin] Marshall, who drove me to his comfortable mansion through a country like the wooded parts of Sussex, abounding in fine trees, and in the only lawns and park-like fields I have yet seen in America.

The gentleman in whose house I was stopping was not insensible to the dangers of the future and would, I think, like many others, not at all regret to find himself and property safe in England. His father, the very day of our arrival, had proceeded to Canada with his daughters but the Confederate authorities are now determined to confiscate

all property belonging to persons who endeavour to evade the re-
sponsibilities of patriotism. In such matters the pressure of the majority is irresistible and a sort of mob law supplants any remissness on
the part of the authorities. In the South, where the deeds of the land
of cypress and myrtle are exaggerated by passion, this power will be
exercised very rigorously. The very language of the people is full of
the excesses generally accepted as types of Americanism.

June 14th. Last night with my good host from his plantation to the
great two-storied steamer *General Quitman*, at Natchez. She was
crowded with planters, soldiers and their families, and as the lights
shone out of her windows, looked like a walled castle blazing from
double lines of embrasures.

Before noon we were in sight of Vicksburg, which is situated on
a high bank or bluff on the left bank of the river, about 400 miles
above New Orleans and some 120 miles from Natchez.

Mr. [T. C.] McMacken, the proprietor of the "Washington," declares himself to have been the pioneer of hotels in the Far West; but
he has now built himself this huge caravanserai, and rests from his
wanderings. We entered the dining saloon, and found the tables
closely packed with a numerous company of every condition in life,
from generals to planters down to soldiers in the uniform of privates.
At the end of the room there was a long table on which the joints
and dishes were brought hot from the kitchen to be carved by the
Negro waiters, male and female, and as each was brought in the
proprietor, standing in the centre of the room, shouted out with a
loud voice, "Now, then, here is a splendid goose! ladies and gentlemen, don't neglect the goose and apple-sauce! Here's a piece of beef
that I can recommend! upon my honour you will never regret taking
a slice of the beef. Oyster-pie! oyster-pie! never was better oyster-pie
seen in Vicksburg. Run about, boys, and take orders. Ladies and
gentlemen, just look at that turkey! who's for turkey?"—and so on,
wiping the perspiration from his forehead and combating with the
flies.

Altogether it was a semi-barbarous scene, but the host was active
and attentive. The little Negroes who ran about to take orders were
smart, but now and then came into violent collision, and were cuffed
incontinently. One mild-looking little fellow stood by my chair and

appeared so sad that I asked him, "Are you happy, my boy?" He looked quite frightened. "Why don't you answer me?" "I'se afeered, sir; I can't tell that to Massa." "Is not your master kind to you?" "Massa very kind man, sir; very good man when he is not angry with me," and his eyes filled with tears to the brim.

When dinner was over, the mayor and several gentlemen of the city were good enough to request that I would attend a meeting, at a room in the railway station, where some of the inhabitants of the town had assembled. Accordingly I went to the terminus and found a room filled with gentlemen. Large china bowls, blocks of ice, bottles of wine and spirits, and boxes of cigars were on the table, and all the materials for a symposium.

The company discussed recent events, some of which I learned for the first time. Dislike was expressed to the course of the authorities in demanding Negro labour for the fortification along the river, and uneasiness was expressed respecting a Negro plot in Arkansas; but the most interesting matter was Judge Taney's protest against the legality of the President's course in suspending the writ of *habeas corpus* in the case of Merryman. The lawyers who were present at this meeting were delighted with his argument, which insists that Congress alone can suspend the writ, and that the President cannot legally do so.[8]

The news of the defeat of an expedition from Fortress Monroe against a Confederate post at Great Bethel has caused great rejoicing.[9] The accounts show that there was the grossest mismanagement on the part of the Federal officers. The Northern papers particularly regret the loss of Major [Theodore] Winthrop, aide-de-camp to General Butler, a writer of promise. At 4 P.M. I bade the company farewell, and the train started for Jackson. The line runs through a poor clay

[8]U.S. military authorities arrested John Merryman, a Maryland secessionist, soon after Lincoln placed the state under martial law in 1861. When Roger B. Taney, Chief Justice of the U.S. Supreme Court, arrived in Baltimore to carry out his circuit court duties, he sought to have Merryman brought before him in order to determine the legality of his arrest. Military authorities ignored Taney's order and, in frustration, the chief justice wrote to Lincoln criticizing as illegal the president's suspension of the writ of habeas corpus.
[9]The Battle of Bethel, sometimes erroneously cited as the first land battle of the Civil War, took place on June 10, 1861.

country, cut up with gullys and watercourses made by violent rain.

At six o'clock the train stopped in the country at a railway crossing by the side of a large platform. On the right was a common, bounded by a few detached wooden houses, separated by palings from each other, and surrounded by rows of trees. In front of the station were two long wooden sheds, which as the signboard indicates, were exchanges or drinking saloons; and beyond these again were visible some rudimentary streets of straggling houses, above which rose three pretentious spires and domes, resolved into insignificance by nearer approach. This was Jackson.

Our host was at the station in his carriage, and drove us to his residence, which consisted of some detached houses shaded by trees in a small enclosure, and bounded by a kitchen garden.

In the evening I walked out with him to the adjacent city, which has no title to the name, except as being the State capital. It would be curious to inquire how many men there are in the city of Jackson exercising mechanical arts or engaged in small commerce, in skilled or manual labour, who are really Americans in the proper sense of the word. I was struck by the names over the doors of the shops, which were German, Irish, Italian, French, and by foreign tongues and accents in the streets; but, on the other hand, it is the native-born American who obtains the highest political stations and arrogates to himself the largest share of governmental emoluments.

Jackson proper consists of strings of wooden houses, with white porticoes and pillars a world too wide for their shrunk rooms, and various religious and other public edifices. There are of course a monster hotel and blazing barrooms—the former celebrated as the scene of many a serious difficulty, out of some of which the participators never escaped alive. The streets consist of rows of houses such as I have seen at Macon, Montgomery, and Baton Rouge; and as we walked towards the capitol or Statehouse there were many more invitations "to take a drink" addressed to my friend and me than we were able to comply with. Our steps were bent on the Statehouse, which is a pile of stone, with open colonnades, and an air of importance at a distance which a nearer examination of its dilapidated condition does not confirm. Mr. [John J.] Pettus, the Governor of the State of Mississippi, was in the capitol; and on sending in our cards, we were introduced to his room, which certainly was of more than republican simplicity. The apartment was surrounded with some common glass cases, containing papers and odd volumes of books; the furniture, a table or desk, and a few chairs and a ragged carpet; the glass in the windows cracked and broken; the walls and ceiling discoloured by mildew.

The Governor is a silent man, of abrupt speech, but easy of access; and, indeed, whilst we were speaking, strangers and soldiers walked in and out of his room, looked around them, and acted in all respects as if they were in a public house, except in ordering drinks. This grim, tall, angular man seemed to me such a development of public institutions in the South as Mr. Seward was in a higher phase in the North. For years he hunted deer and trapped in the forest of the Far West, and lived in a Natty Bumppo or David Crockett state of life; and he was not ashamed of the fact when taunted with it during his election contest, but very rightly made the most of his independence and his hard work.

The pecuniary honours of his position are not very great as the Governor of the enormous State of Mississippi. He has simply an income of £800 a year and a house provided for his use; he is not only quite contented with what he has but believes that the society in which he lives is the highest development of civilised life, notwithstanding the fact that there are more outrages on the person in his State, nay, more murders perpetrated in the very capital, than were known in the worst days of mediaeval Venice or Florence—indeed, as a citizen said to me, "Well, I think our average in Jackson is a murder a month"; but he used a milder name for the crime.

The Governor conversed on the aspect of affairs, and evinced that wonderful confidence in his own people which, whether it arises from ignorance of the power of the North, or a conviction of greater resources, is to me so remarkable. "Well, sir," said he, dropping a portentous plug of tobacco just outside the spittoon, with the air of a man who wished to show he could have hit the centre if he liked, "England is no doubt a great country, and has got fleets and the like of that, and may have a good deal to do in Eu-*rope;* but the sovereign State of Mississippi can do a great deal better without England than England can do without her." Having some slight recollection of Mississippi repudiation, in which Mr. Jefferson Davis was so actively engaged, I thought it possible that the Governor might be right;[10] and after a time his Excellency shook me by the hand, and I left, much wondering within myself what manner of men they must be in the State of Mississippi, when Mr. Pettus is their chosen Governor; and yet, after all, he is honest and fierce; and perhaps he is so far qualified as well as any other man to be Governor of the State. There are newspapers, electric telegraphs, and railways; there are many educated families, even much good society, I am told, in the State; but the larger masses of the people struck me as being in a condition not much elevated from that of the original backwoodsman. On my return to the doctor's house I found some letters which had been forwarded to me from New Orleans had gone astray, and was obliged, therefore, to make arrangements for my departure on the following evening.

June 16th.   When my work was over I walked out and sat in the shade with a gentleman whose talk turned upon the practises of the Mississippi duello. Without the smallest animus and in the most natural way in the world, he told tale after tale of blood, and recounted terrible tragedies enacted outside bars of hotels and in the public streets close beside us. There may, indeed, be security for property, but there is not for the life of its owner in difficulties, who may be shot by a stray bullet from a pistol as he walks up the street.

I learned many valuable facts. I was warned, for example, against the impolicy of trusting to small-bored pistols or to pocket six-shooters in case of a close fight, because suppose you hit your man mortally he may still run in upon you and rip you up with a bowie knife before he falls dead; whereas if you drive a good heavy bullet into him or make a hole in him with a "Derringer" ball, he gets faintish and drops at once. Many illustrations, too, were given of the value of practical lessons of this sort. One particularly struck me. If a gentleman with whom you are engaged in altercation moves his hand towards his breeches pocket, or behind his back, you must

---

[10]During his campaign for the Mississippi legislature in 1842, Davis had advocated allowing the state courts to decide the question of repudiating the state's debt. Davis was defeated and the legislature later repudiated the debt; still, Robert J. Walker, Polk's secretary of the treasury and a well-known figure in English financial circles, accused Davis of being a repudiator, and the charge was generally believed.

smash him or shoot him at once, for he is either going to draw his six-shooter, to pull out a bowie knife, or to shoot you through the lining of his pocket. The latter practice is considered rather ungentlemanly, but it has somewhat been more honored lately in the observance than in the breach. In fact, the savage practice of walking about with pistols, knives, and poniards, in barrooms and gambling saloons, with passions ungoverned because there is no law to punish the deeds to which they lead, affords facilities for crime which an uncivilised condition of society leaves too often without punishment.

Our host gave me an early dinner at which I met some of the citizens of Jackson, and at six o'clock [P.M.] I proceeded by train for Memphis. The carriages were, of course, full of soldiers or volunteers bound for a large camp at a place called Corinth, who made night hideous by their song and cries, stimulated by enormous draughts of whiskey and a proportionate consumption of tobacco, by teeth and by fire. The heat of the carriages added to the discomforts arising from these causes and from great quantities of biting insects in the sleeping places. The people have all the air and manners of settlers. Altogether the impression produced on my mind was by no means agreeable, and I felt as if I was indeed in the land of Lynch law and bowie knives and where the passions of men have not yet been subordinated to the influence of the tribunals of justice. Much of this feeling has no doubt been produced by the tales to which I have been listening around me—most of which have a smack of manslaughter about them.

June 17th. If it was any consolation to me that the very noisy and very turbulent warriors of last night were exceedingly sick, dejected, and crestfallen this morning, I had it to the full. Their cries for water were incessant to allay the internal fires caused by "40 rod" and "60 rod," as whiskey is called, which is supposed to kill people at those distances. Their officers had no control over them—and the only authority they seemed to respect was that of the "gentlemanly" conductor whom they were accustomed to fear individually, as he is a great man in America and has much authority and power to make himself disagreeable if he likes.

The victory at Big or Little Bethel has greatly elated these men, and they think they can walk over the Northern States. It was a relief to get out of the train for a few minutes at a station called Holly Springs [Mississippi], where the passengers breakfasted at a dirty table on most execrable coffee, corn bread, rancid butter, and very dubious meats, and the wild soldiers outside made the most of their time, as they had recovered from their temporary depression by this time, and got out on the tops of the carriages, over which they performed tumultuous dances to the music of their band and the great admiration of the surrounding Negrodom. Their demeanour is very unlike that of the unexcitable staid people of the North.

In order to conceal from the minds of the people that the government at Washington claims to be that of the United States, the press politicians and speakers divert their attention to the names of Lincoln, Seward, and other black Republicans, and class the whole of the North together as the Abolitionists. They call the Federal levies "Lincoln's mercenaries" and "abolition hordes," though their own troops are paid at the same rate of those of the United States.

The enthusiasm for the Southern cause among all the people is most remarkable, the sight of the flag waving from the carriage windows drew all the population of the hamlets and the workers in the field, black and white, to the side of the carriages to cheer for Jeff. Davis and the Southern Confederacy, and to wave whatever they could lay hold of in the air. The country seems very poorly cultivated, the fields full of stumps of trees, and the plantation houses very indifferent. At every station more "soldiers," as they are called, got in, till the smell and heat were suffocating.

These men were as fanciful in their names and dress as could be. In the train which preceded us there was a band of volunteers armed with rifled pistols and enormous bowie knives, who called themselves "The Toothpick Company." They carried along with them a coffin with a plate inscribed, "Abe Lincoln, died ————," and declared they were "bound" to bring his body back in it and that they did not intend to use muskets or rifles, but just go in with knife and six-shooter, and whip the Yankees straight away.

At the station of Grand Junction [Tennessee], north of Holly Springs, which latter is 210 miles north of Jackson, several hundreds of our warrior friends were turned out in order to take the train northeastward for Richmond, Virginia. The 1st Company, seventy rank and file, consisted of Irishmen armed with sporting rifles without bayonets. Five-sixths of the 2nd Company, who were armed with muskets, were of the same nationality. The 3rd Company were all Americans. The 4th Company were almost all Irish.

But these fellows were, nevertheless, the material for fighting and for marching after proper drill and with good officers, even though there was too large a proportion of old men and young lads in the ranks. To judge from their dress, these recruits came from the labouring and poorest classes of whites. The officers affected a French cut and bearing with indifferent success, and in the luggage vans there were three foolish young women with slop-dress imitation clothes of the Vivandière type, who with dishevelled hair, dirty faces, and dusty hats and jackets, looked sad, sorry, and absurd. Their notions of propriety did not justify them in adopting straps, boots, and trousers, and the rest of the tawdry ill-made costume looked very bad indeed.

The train, which still bore a large number of soldiers for the camp of Corinth, proceeded through dreary swamps, stunted forests, and clearings of the rudest kind at very long intervals.

On approaching Memphis the line ascends towards the bluff of the Mississippi, and farms of a better appearance come in sight on the side of the rail; but after all I do not envy the fate of the man who, surrounded by slaves and shut out from the world, has to pass his life in this dismal region, be the crops never so good.

It was 1:40 P.M. when the train arrived at Memphis. I was speedily on my way to the Gayoso House, so called after an old Spanish ruler of the district, which is situated in the street on the bluff which runs parallel with the course of the Mississippi. This resuscitated Egyptian city is a place of importance and extends for several miles along the high bank of the river, though it does not run very far back. The streets are at right angles to the principal throughfares, which are parallel to the stream; and I by no means expected to see the lofty stores, warehouses, rows of shops, and handsome buildings on the broad esplanade along the river, and the extent and size of the edifices public and private in this city, which is one of the developments of trade and commerce created by the Mississippi. Memphis contains nearly 30,000 inhabitants, but many of them are foreigners, and there is a nomad [drift] into and out of the place, which abounds in haunts for Bohemians, drinking and dancing saloons, and gaming rooms. And this strange kaleidoscope of Negroes and whites of the extreme of civilisation in its American development, and of the semi-savage degraded by his contact with the white; of enormous steamers on the river, which bears equally the dugout or canoe of the black fisherman; the rail, penetrating the inmost recesses of swamps, which on either side of it remain no doubt in the same state as they were centuries ago; the roll of heavily laden wagons through the streets; the rattle of omnibuses and all the phenomena of active commercial life before our eyes, included in the same scope of vision which takes in at the other side of the Mississippi lands scarcely yet settled, though the march of empire has gone thousands of miles beyond them, amuses but perplexes the traveller in this new land.

The evening was so exceedingly warm that I was glad to remain within the walls of my darkened bedroom. All the six hundred and odd guests whom the Gayoso House is said to accommodate were apparently in the passage at one time. At present it is the headquarters of General Gideon J. Pillow, who is charged with the defences of the Tennessee side of the river and commands a considerable body of troops around the city and in the works above. The house is consequently filled with men in uniform, belonging to the General's staff or the various regiments of Tennessee troops.

The Governors and the Legislatures of the States view with dislike every action on the part of Mr. Davis which tends to form the State troops into a national army. At first, indeed, the doctrine prevailed that troops could not be sent beyond the limits of the State in which they were raised—then it was argued that they ought not to be called upon to move outside their borders; and I have heard people in the South inveighing against the sloth and want of spirit of the Virginians who allowed their State to be invaded without resisting the enemy.

On hearing of my arrival, General Pillow sent his aide-de-camp to inform me that he was about starting in a steamer up the river to make an inspection of the works and garrison at Fort Randolph and at other points where batteries had been erected to command the stream, supported by large levies of Tennesseeans. The aide-de-camp conducted me to the General, whom I found in his bedroom, fitted up as an office, littered with plans and papers. Before the Mexican War, General Pillow was a flourishing solicitor, connected in business with President [James K.] Polk, and commanding so much influence that when the expedition was formed he received the nomination of brigadier general of volunteers. He served with distinction and was severely wounded at the Battle of Chapultepec and at the conclusion of the campaign he retired into civil life and was engaged directing the work of his plantation till this great rebellion summoned him once more to the field.

Of course there is, and must be, always an inclination to deride these volunteer officers on the part of regular soldiers; and I was informed by one of the officers in attendance on the General that he had made himself ludicrously celebrated in Mexico for having undertaken to throw up a battery which, when completed, was found to face the wrong way so that the guns were exposed to the enemy. General Pillow is a small, compact, clear-complexioned man, with short grey whiskers, cut in the English fashion, a quick eye, and a pompous manner of speech; and I had not been long in his company before I heard of Chapultepec and his wound, which causes him to limp a little in his walk and gives him inconvenience in the saddle. He wore a round black hat, plain blue frock coat, dark trousers, and brass spurs on his boots; but no sign of military rank. The General ordered carriages to the door, and we went to see the batteries on the bluff or front of the esplanade, which are intended to check any ship attempting to pass down the river from Cairo, where the Federals under General [Benjamin] Prentiss have entrenched themselves and are understood to mediate an expedition against the city. A parapet of cotton bales, covered with tarpaulin, has been erected close to the edge of the bank of earth which rises to heights varying from 60 to 150 feet almost perpendicularly from the waters of the Mississippi, with zigzag roads running down through it to the landing places. This parapet could offer no cover against vertical fire and is so placed that well-directed shell into the bank below it would tumble it all into the water. The zigzag roads are barricaded with weak planks, which would be shivered to pieces by boat guns; and the assaulting parties could easily mount through these covered ways to the rear of the parapet and up to the very centre of the esplanade.

The blockade of the river at this point is complete; not a boat is permitted to pass either up or down. At the extremity of the esplanade, on an angle of the bank, an earthen battery, mounted with six heavy guns, has been thrown up, which has a fine command of the river; and the General informed me he intends to mount sixteen guns in addition on a prolongation of the face of the same work.

The inspection over, we drove down a steep road to the water beneath, where the *Ingomar*, a large river steamer now chartered for the service of the State of Tennessee, was lying to receive us. The vessel was crowded with troops—all volunteers, of course—about to join those in camp. Great as were their numbers, the proportion of the officers was inordinately large, and the rank of the greater number preposterously high. It seemed to me as if I was introduced to a battalion of colonels, and that I was not permitted to pierce to any lower strata of military rank. I counted seventeen colonels and believe the number not then exhausted.

General [Charles] Clark of Mississippi, who had come over from the camp at Corinth, was on board, and I had the pleasure of making his acquaintance. He spoke with sense and firmness of the present troubles, and dealt with the political difficulties in a tone of moderation which bespoke of gentleman and a man of education and thought. He also had served in the Mexican War and had the air and manner of a soldier. With all his quietness of tone, there was not the smallest disposition to be traced in his words to retire from the present contest or to consent to a reunion with the United States under any circumstances whatever.

Our voyage as we steamed up the river afforded no novelty, nor any physical difference worthy of remark to contrast it with the lower portions of the stream, except that upon our right hand side, which is, in effect, the left bank, there are ranges of exceedingly high bluffs, some parallel with and others at right angles to the course of the stream. The river is of the same pea-soup colour with the same masses of leaves, decaying vegetation, stumps of trees, forming small floating islands, or giant cotton trees, pines, and balks of timber whirling down the current. I was furnished with a small berth to which I retired at midnight, just as the *Ingomar* was brought to at the Chickasaw Bluffs above which lies Camp Randolph.

June 18th.   On looking out of my cabin window this morning I found the steamer fast alongside a small wharf, above which rose, to the height of 150 feet, at an angle of 45 degrees, the rugged bluff already mentioned. The wharf was covered with commissariat stores and ammunition. Three heavy guns which some men were endeavouring to sling to rude bullock carts, in a manner defiant of all the laws of gravitation, seemed likely to go slap into the water at every moment; but of the many great strapping fellows who were lounging about, not one gave a hand to the working party. A dusty track wound up the hill to the brow and there disappeared; and at the height of fifty feet or so above the level of the river two earthworks had been rudely erected in an ineffective position. The volunteers who were lounging about the edge of the stream were dressed in different ways and had no uniform.

General Pillow proceeded on shore after breakfast, and we mounted the coarse cart-horse chargers which were in waiting at the jetty to receive us. Certainly, a more extraordinary maze could not be conceived even in the dreams of a sick engineer—a number of mad beavers might possibly construct such dams. They were so ingeniously made as to prevent the troops engaged in their defence from resisting the enemy's attacks or getting away from them when the assailants had got inside—most difficult and troublesome to defend, and still more difficult for the defenders to leave, the latter perhaps being their chief merit.

The General ordered some practice to be made with round shot down the river. An old forty-two-pound carronade was loaded with some difficulty and pointed at a tree about 1700 yards—which I was told, however, was not less than 2500 yards—distant. The General and his staff took their posts on the parapet to leeward, and I ventured to say, "I think, General, the smoke will prevent your seeing the shot." To which the General replied, "No, sir," in a tone which indicated, "I beg you to understand I have been wounded in Mexico, and know all about this kind of thing." "Fire," the string was pulled and out of the touch-hole popped a piece of metal with a little chirrup. "Darn these friction tubes! I prefer the linstock and match," quoth one of the staff, *sotto voce* [in an undertone], "but General Pillow will have us use friction tubes made at Memphis, that ar'nt worth a cuss." Tube No. 2, however, did explode, but where the ball went no one could say, as the smoke drifted right into our eyes.

The General then moved to the other side of the gun, which was fired a third time, the shot falling short in good line, but without any ricochet. Gun No. 3 was next fired. Off went the ball down the river, but off went the gun, too, and with a frantic leap it jumped, all wonderful, for the poor old-fashioned chamber carronade had been loaded with a charge and a solid shot heavy enough to make it burst with indignation. Most of us felt relieved when the firing was over, and for my own part, I would much rather have been close to the target than to the battery.

The volunteers were mostly engaged at drill in distinct companies, but by order of the General some 700 or 800 of them were formed into line for inspection. Many of these men were in their shirt sleeves, and the awkwardness with which they handled their arms showed that, however good they might be as shots, they were bad hands at manual platoon exercise; but such great strapping fellows, that, as I walked down the ranks there were few whose shoulders were not above the level of my head, excepting here and there a weedly old man or a growing lad. They were armed with old pattern percussion muskets, no two clad alike, many very badly shod, few with knap-sacks, but all provided with a tin water-flask and a blanket. These men have been only five weeks enrolled, and were called out by the State of Tennessee in anticipation of the vote of secession.

I could get no exact details as to the supply of food, but from the Quartermaster-General I heard that each man had from 3/4 lb. to 1 1/4 lb. of meat, and a sufficiency of bread, sugar, coffee, and rice daily; however, these military Olivers "asked for more." Neither whiskey nor tobacco was served out to them, which to such heavy consumers of both must prove one source of dissatisfaction. The officers were plain, farmerly planters, merchants, lawyers, and the like—energetic, determined men, but utterly ignorant of the most rudimentary parts of military science. It is this want to knowledge on the part of the officer which renders it so difficult to arrive at a tolerable condition of discipline among volunteers, as the privates are quite well aware they know as much of soldiering as the great major-ity of their officers.

Having gone down the lines of these motley companies, the Gen-eral addressed them in a harangue in which he expatiated on their patriotism, on their courage, and the atrocity of the enemy, in an odd farrago of military and political subjects. But the only matter which appeared to interest them much was the announcement that they would be released from work in another day or so, and that Negroes would be sent to perform all that was required. This announcement was received with the words, "Bully for us!" and "That's good." And when General Pillow wound up a florid peroration by assuring them, "When the hour of danger comes I will be with you," the effect was by no means equal to his expectations. The men did not seem to care much whether General Pillow was with them or not at that eventful moment; and, indeed, all dusty as he was in his plain clothes he did not look very imposing or give one an idea that he would contribute much to the means of resistance. However, one of the officers called out, "Boys, three cheers for General Pillow."

What they may do in the North I know not, but certainly the Southern soldiers cannot cheer, and what passes muster for that jubilant sound is a shrill ringing scream with a touch of the Indian war-whoop in it. As these cries ended a stentorian voice shouted out, "Who cares for General Pillow?" No one answered; whence I inferred the General would not be very popular until the niggers were actually at work in the trenches.

We returned to the steamer, headed upstream, and proceeded onward for more than an hour to another landing, protected by a battery, where we disembarked, the General being received by a guard dressed in uniform, who turned out with some appearance of soldierly smartness. On my remarking the difference to the General, he told me the corps encamped at this point was composed of gentleman planters and farmers. They had all clad themselves and consisted of some of the best families in the State of Tennessee.

In the afternoon we returned to Memphis. Here I was obliged to cut short my Southern tour, though I would willingly have stayed, to have seen the most remarkable social and political changes in the world has probably ever witnessed. The necessity of my position obliged me to return northwards—unless I could write, there was no use in my being on the spot at all. By this time the Federal fleets have succeeded in closing the ports, if not effectually, so far as to render the carriage of letters precarious and the route must be at best devious and uncertain.

Mr. Jefferson Davis was, I was assured, prepared to give me every facility at Richmond to enable me to know and to see all that was most interesting in the military and political action of the new Confederacy; but of what use could this knowledge be if I could not communicate it to the journal I served?

Much, therefore, as I desired to go to Richmond, where I was urged to repair by many considerations and by the earnest appeals of those around me, I felt it would be impossible, notwithstanding the interest attached to the proceedings there, to perform my duties in a place cut off from all communication with the outer world; and so I decided to proceed to Chicago, and thence to Washington, where the Federals had assembled a large army with the purpose of marching upon Richmond, in obedience to the cry of nearly every journal of influence in the Northern cities.

My resolution was mainly formed in consequence of the intelligence which was communicated to me at Memphis, and I told General Pillow that I would continue my journey to Cairo in order to get within the Federal lines. As the river was blockaded, the only means of doing so was to proceed by rail to Columbus [Kentucky], and thence to take a steamer to the Federal position; and so, whilst the General was continuing his inspection, I rode to the telegraph office in one of the camps to order my luggage to be prepared for departure as soon as I arrived, and thence went on board the steamer, where I sat down in the cabin to write my last dispatch from Dixie.

So far I had certainly no reason to agree with Mr. Seward in thinking this rebellion was the result of a localised energetic action on the part of a fierce minority in the seceding States, and that there was in each a large, if inert, mass opposed to secession which would rally round the Stars and Stripes the instant they were displayed in their sight. On the contrary, I met everywhere with but one feeling, with exceptions which proved its unanimity and its force. To a man the people went with their States, and had but one battle cry, "States' Rights, and death to those who make war against them!"

Day after day I had seen this feeling intensified by the accounts which came from the North of a fixed determination to maintain the war; and day after day, I am bound to add, the impression on my mind was strengthened that "States' Rights" meant protection to slavery, extension of slave territory, and free trade in slave produce with the outer world; nor was it any argument against the conclusion that the popular passion gave vent to the most vehement outcries against Yankees, abolitionists, German mercenaries, and modern invasion. I was fully satisfied in my mind also that the population of the South, who had taken up arms, were so convinced of the right-eousness of their cause, and so competent to vindicate it that they would fight with the utmost energy and valour in its defence and successful establishment.

The saloon in which I was sitting afforded abundant evidence of the vigour with which the South are entering upon the contest. Men of every variety and condition of life had taken up arms against the cursed Yankee and the black Republican—there was not a man there who would not have given his life for the rare pleasure of striking Mr. Lincoln's head off his shoulders, and yet to a cold European the scene was almost ludicrous.

The general result of my intercourse with Americans is to produce the notion that they consider Great Britain in a state of corruption and decay, and eagerly seek to exalt France at her expense. Their language is the sole link between England and the United States and it only binds the England of 1770 to the American of 1860.

There is scarcely an American on either side of Mason and Dixon's line who does not religiously believe that the colonies, alone and single-handed, encountered the whole undivided force of Great Brit-ain in the revolution and defeated it. Their delusions are increased and solidified by the extraordinary text books of so-called history, and by the feasts, and festivals and celebrations of their everyday political life, in all of which we pass through imaginary Caudine Forks;[11] and they entertain towards the old country at best very much the feeling which a high-spirited young man would feel to-wards the guardian who, when he had come of age and was free from all control, sought to restrain the passions of his early life.

June 19th. I had to rise at three o'clock, A.M., to reach the train, which started before five. The omnibus which took us to the station was literally nave [up to the wheels' hubs] in the dust; and of all the bad roads and dusty streets I have yet seen in the New World, where both prevail North and South, those of Memphis are the worst.

By the time I had arrived at the station my clothes were covered

[11]A mountain pass in southern Italy, where the Romans were surrounded and forced to surrender their army to local tribesmen in 321 B.C.

with a fine alluvial deposit in a state of powder; the platform was crowded with volunteers moving off for the wars, and I was obliged to take my place in a carriage full of Confederate officers and soldiers who had a large supply of whiskey, which at that early hour they were consuming as a prophylactic against the influence of the morning dews, which hereabouts are of such a deadly character that, to be quite safe from their influence, it appears to be necessary, judging from the examples of my companions, to get as nearly drunk as possible. Whiskey, by-the-by, is also a sovereign specific against the bites of rattlesnakes. All the dews of the Mississippi and the rattlesnakes of the prairie might have spent their force or venom in vain on my companions before we had got as far as Union City.

I was evidently regarded with considerable suspicion by my fellow passengers when they heard I was going to Cairo, until the conductor obligingly informed them who I was, whereupon I was much entreated to fortify myself against the dews and rattlesnakes and received many offers of service and kindness.

Whatever may be the normal comforts of American railway cars, they are certainly most unpleasant conveyances when the war spirit is abroad, and the heat of the day, which was excessive, did not contribute to diminish the annoyance of foul air—the odour of whiskey, tobacco, and the like, combined with innumerable flies.

The portion of Tennessee through which the rail runs is exceedingly uninteresting and looks unhealthy, the clearings occur at long intervals in the forest and the unwholesome population, who came out of their low shanties, situated amidst blackened stumps of trees or fields of Indian corn, did not seem prosperous or comfortable. The twists and curves of the rail through cane brakes and swamps exceeded in that respect any line I have ever travelled on; but the vertical irregularities of the rail were still greater and the engine bounded as if it were at sea.

The great attraction of this train lay in a vast supply of stores with which several large vans were closely packed, and for fully two hours the train was delayed, whilst hampers of wine, spirits, vegetables, fruit, meat, groceries, and all the various articles acceptable to soldiers living under canvas were disgorged on the platform and carried away by the expectant military.

At Columbus the steamer was waiting to convey us up to Cairo, and I congratulated myself on the good fortune of arriving in time for the last opportunity that will be afforded to proceeding north-ward by this route. General Pillow on the one hand, and General Prentiss on the other, have resolved to blockade the Mississippi, and as the facilities for Confederates going up to Columbus and obtaining information of what is happening in the Federal camps cannot readily be checked, the general in command of the port to which I am bound has intimated that the steamers must cease running. It was late in the day when we entered once more on the Father of Waters, which is here just as broad, as muddy, as deep, and as wooded as it is at Baton Rouge or Vicksburg.

In about two hours or so the captain pointed out to me a tall building and some sheds which seemed to arise out of a wide reach in the river; "that's Cairey," said he, "where the Unionists have their camp," and very soon the Stars and Stripes were visible, waving from a lofty staff, at the angle of low land formed by the junction of the Mississippi and Ohio.

As the steamer approached the desolate embankment which seemed the only barrier between the low land on which the so-called city was built, and the waters of the great river rising above it, it certainly became impossible to believe that sane men, even as speculators, could have fixed upon such a spot as the possible site of a great city—an emporium of trade and commerce. A more desolate, woebegone looking place, now that all trade and commerce had ceased, cannot be conceived; but as the southern terminus of the Central Illinois Railway, it displayed a very different scene before the war broke out.

With the exception of the large hotel, which rises far above the levee of the river, the public edifices are represented by a church and spire, and the rest of the town by a line of shanties and small houses, the rooms and upper stories of which are just visible above the embankment. The stream, firmed by the united efforts of the Missis-sippi and the Ohio, did not appear to gain much breadth, and each of the confluents looked as large as its produce with the other. Three steamers lay alongside the wooden wharves projecting from the em-bankment, which was also lined by some flatboats. Sentries paraded the gangways as the steamer made fast along the shore, but no inquiry was directed to any of the passengers, and I walked up the levee and proceeded straight to the hotel, which put me very much in mind of an effort made by speculating proprietors to create a watering place on some lifeless beach. In the hall there were a number of officers in United States uniforms, and the lower part of the hotel was, apparently, occupied as a military bureau; finally, I was shoved into a small dungeon with a window opening out on the angle formed by the two rivers, which was lined with sheds and huts and terminated by a battery.

I was introduced to General Prentiss, an agreeable person, without anything about him to indicate the soldier. Soon after nightfall I retired to my room and battled with mosquitoes till I sank into sleep and exhaustion and abandoned myself to their mercies; perhaps, after all, there were not more than a hundred or so, and their united efforts could not absorb as much blood as would be taken out by one leech, but then their horrible acrimony which leaves a wreck behind in the place where they have banqueted, inspires the utmost indignation and appears to be an indefensible prolongation of the outrage of the original bite.

June 20th.   When I awoke this morning and sat down to consider what I had seen within the last two months and to arrive at some general results from the retrospect, I own that after much thought my mind was reduced to a hazy analysis of the abstract principles of right and wrong, in which it failed to come to any definite conclusion.

On the whole, the impression left upon my mind by what I had seen in slave States is unfavorable to the institution of slavery, both as regards its effects on the slave and its influence on the master. I have reason to believe that the more deeply the institution is probed, the more clearly will its unsoundness and its radical evils be discerned. The constant appeals made to the physical comforts of the slaves, and their supposed contentment, have little or no effect on any person who acts up to a higher standard of human happiness than that which is applied to swine or the beast of the fields, "See how fat my pigs are."

Slavery is a curse, with its time of accomplishment not quite at hand—it is a cancer, the ravages of which are covered by fair outward show, and by the apparent health of the sufferer.

Never did a people enter on a war so utterly destitute of any reason for waging it, or of the means of bringing it to a successful termination against internal enemies.

After breakfast I went down about the works which fortify the bank of mud, in the shape of a V, formed by the two rivers—a *flèche* [arrow] with a ditch, scarp, and counter-scarp. Some heavy pieces cover the end of the spit at the other side of the Mississippi, at Bird's Point. On the side of Missouri there is a field entrenchment held by a regiment of Germans, Poles, and Hungarians, about 100 strong, with two field batteries. The sacred soil of Kentucky, on the other side of the Ohio, is tabooed by Beriah Magoffin, but it is not possible for the belligerents to stand so close face to face without occupying either Columbus or Hickman [Kentucky]. The thermometer was at 100° soon after breakfast and it was not wonderful to find that the men in Camp Defiance, which is the name of the cantonment on the mud between the levees of the Ohio and Mississippi, were suffering from diarrhoea and fever.

In the evening there was a review of three regiments, forming a brigade of some 2800 men, who went through their drill, advancing in columns of company, moving *en échelon* [in formation], changing front, deploying into line on the centre company, very creditable. It was curious to see what a start ran through the men during the parade when a gun was fired from the battery close at hand, and how their heads turned towards the river; but the steamer which had appeared round the bend hoisted the private signs by which she was known as a friend and tranquility was restored.

I am not sure that most of these troops desire anything but a long residence at a tolerably comfortable station, with plenty of pay and no marching.

Five

RETURN TO WASHINGTON
(June 21–July 7, 1861)

June 21st.   During my short sojourn in this country I have never yet met any person who could show me where the sovereignty of the Union resides. General Prentiss, however, and his Illinois Volunteers are quite ready to fight for it.

In the afternoon the General drove me round the camps in company with Mr. [Elihu] Washburne, Member of Congress from Illinois, his staff, and a party of officers, among whom was Mr. [Richard J.] Oglesby, colonel of a regiment of State volunteers, who struck me by his shrewdness, simple honesty, and zeal. He told me that he had begun life in the utmost obscurity, but that somehow or other he got into a lawyer's office and there, by hard drudgery, by mother wit, and industry, notwithstanding a defective education, he had raised himself not only to independence but to such a position that 1000 men had gathered at his call and selected one who had never led a company in his life to be their colonel; in fact, he is an excellent orator of the western school and made good, homely, telling speeches to his men.

At each station the officers came out of their tents, shook hands all round, and gave an unfailing invitation to get down and take a drink, and the guns on the General's approach fired salutes, as though it was a time of profoundest peace. Powder was certainly more plentiful than in the Confederate camps, where salutes are not permitted unless by special orders or great occasions.

The General remained for some time in the camp of the Chicago Light Artillery, which was commanded by a fine young Scotchman who told me that the privates of his company represented a million and a half of dollars in property. Their guns, horses, carriages, and accoutrements were all in the most creditable order, and there was an air about the men and about their camp which showed they did not belong to the same class as the better-disciplined Hungarians close at hand.

Whilst we were seated a number of privates came forward and sang the "Star-Spangled Banner" and a patriotic song to the air of "God Save the Queen," and the rest of the artillerymen, and a number of stragglers from the other camps, assembled and then formed lines behind the singers. When the chorus was over there arose a great shout for Washburne, and the honorable Congressman was fain to come forward and make a speech in which he assured his hearers of a very speedy victory and the advent of liberty all over the land. Then "General Prentiss" was called for; and as citizen soldiers command their generals on such occasions, he too was obliged to speak and to tell his audience "the world had never seen any men more devoted, gallant, or patriotic than themselves." "Oglesby" was next summoned, and the tall, portly, good-humoured old man stepped to the front, and with excellent tact and good sense dished up in the Buncombe style, told them the time for making speeches had passed, indeed it had lasted too long; and although it was said there was very little fighting when there was much talking, he believed too much talking was likely to lead to a great deal more fighting than anyone desired.

Colonel, General, and all addressed the soldiers as "gentlemen," and their auditory did not on their part refrain from expressing their sentiments in the most unmistakable manner. "Bully for you, General!" "Bravo, Washburne!" "That's so, Colonel!" and the like, interrupted the harangues and when the oratorical exercises were over the men crowded round the staff, cheered and hurrahed, and tossed up their caps in the greatest delight.

With the exception of the foreign officers, and some of the staff, there are very few of the colonels, majors, captains, or lieutenants who know anything of their business. The men do not care for them and never think of saluting them. A regiment of Germans was sent across from Bird's Point this evening for plundering and robbing the houses in the district in which they were quartered.

Fine as the men are, incomparably better armed, clad—and doubtless better fed—than the Southern troops, they will scarcely meet them man to man in the field with any chance of success. Among the officers are barroom keepers, grocers' apprentices, and such like—often inferior socially, and in every other respect, to the men whom they are supposed to command. General Prentiss has seen service, I believe, in Mexico; but he appears to me to be rather an ardent politician, embittered against slaveholders of the South, than a judicious or skilful military leader.

June 22nd. The heat drove me in among the flies of the crowded hotel, where Brigadier Prentiss is planning one of those absurd expeditions against a secessionist camp at Commerce, in the State of Missouri, about two hours steaming up the river, and some twelve or fourteen miles inland. Cairo abounds in secessionists and spies, and it is needful to take great precautions lest the expedition be known; but, after all, stores must be got ready, and put on board the steamers, and preparations must be made which cannot be concealed from the world. At dusk 700 men, supported by a six-pounder fieldpiece, were put on board the *City of Alton,* on which they clustered like bees in a swarm, and as the huge engine laboured up and down against the stream and the boat swayed from side to side, I felt a considerable desire to see General Prentiss chucked into the stream for his utter recklessness in cramming on board one huge tinderbox, all fire and touchwood, so many human beings, who, in event of an explosion, or a shot in the boiler, or of a heavy musketry fire on the banks, would have been converted into a great slaughterhouse. One small boat hung from her stern, and although there were plenty of river flats and numerous steamers, even the horses belonging to the fieldpiece were crammed in among the men along the deck.

At night there was a kind of *émeute* [riot] in camp. The day, as I have said, was excessively hot, and on returning to their tents and huts from evening parade, the men found the contractor who supplies them with water had not filled the barrels; so they forced the sentries, broke barracks after hours, mobbed their officers, and streamed up to the hotel, which they surrounded, calling out, "Water, water," in chorus. The General came out and got up on a rail: "Gentlemen," said he, "it is not my fault you are without water. It's your officers who are to blame; not me." ("Groans for the Quartermaster," from the men.) "If it is the fault of the contractor, I'll see that he is punished. I'll take steps at once to see that the matter is remedied. And now, gentlemen, I hope you'll go back to your quarters"; and the gentlemen took it into their heads very good-humouredly to obey the suggestion, fell in, and marched back two deep to their huts.

As the General was smoking his cigar before going to bed, I asked him why the officers had not more control over the men. "Well," said he, "the officers are to blame for all this. The truth is, the term for which these volunteers enlisted is drawing to a close, and they have not as yet enrolled themselves in the United States Army. They are merely volunteer regiments of the State of Illinois. If they are displeased with anything, therefore, they might refuse to enter the service or take fresh engagements; and the officers would find themselves suddenly left without any men; they therefore curry favour with the privates, many of them, too, having an eye to the votes of the men when the elections of officers in the new regiments are to take place."

In reference to the discipline maintained in the camp, I must admit the proper precautions are used to prevent spies entering the lines. The sentries are posted closely and permit no one to go in without a pass in the day and a countersign at night.

June 23rd. The latest information which I received today is of a nature to hasten my departure for Washington; it can no longer be doubted that a battle between the two armies assembled in the neighborhood of the capital is imminent. The vague hope which from time to time I have entertained of being able to visit Richmond before I finally take up my quarters with the only army from which I can communicate regularly with Europe has now vanished.

At four o'clock in the evening I started by train on the famous Central Illinois line from Cairo to Chicago.

The carriages were tolerably well filled with soldiers, and in addition to them there were a few unfortunate women, undergoing deportation to some more moral neighbourhood. Neither the look, language, nor manners of my fellow passengers inspired me with an exalted notion of the intelligence, comfort, and respectability of the people which are so much vaunted by Mr. Seward and American journals, and which, though truly attributed, no doubt, to the people of the New England States, cannot be affirmed with equal justice to belong to all the other components of the Union.

As the Southerners say, their Negroes are the happiest people on earth, so the Northerners boast, "We are the most enlightened nation in the world."

Leaving the shanties, which face the levees, and some poor wooden houses with a short vista of cross streets partially flooded at right angles to them, the rail suddenly plunges into an unmistakable swamp, where a forest of dead trees wave their ghostly, leafless arms over their buried trunks, like plumes over a hearse—a cheerless, miserable place, sacred to the ague and fever.

When we left this swamp and forest and came out after a run of many miles on the clear lands which abut the prairie, large fields of corn lay around us, which bore a peculiarly blighted and harassed look. Night was falling as the train rattled out into the wild, flat sea of waving grass, dotted by patch-like Indian corn enclosures; but halts at such places as Jonesboro and Cobden enabled us to see that these settlements in Illinois were neither very flourishing nor very civilised.

There were no physical signs to mark the transition from the land of the secessionist to Union-loving soil. Until the troops were quartered there, Cairo was for secession, and southern Illinois is supposed to be deeply tainted with disaffection to Mr. Lincoln.

One of my friends argues that as slavery is at the base of secession, it follows that States or portions of States will be disposed to join the Confederates or the Federalists just as the climate may be favourable or adverse to the growth of slave produce. Thus in the mountainous parts of the border States of Kentucky and Tennessee, in the north-western part of Virginia, vulgarly called the panhandle, and in the pine woods of North Carolina, where white men can work at the rosin and naval store manufactories, there is a decided feeling in favour of the Union.

[June 24th.] Next morning, just at dawn, I woke up and got out on the platform of the carriage, which is the favourite resort of smokers and their antithetics, those who love pure fresh air, notwithstanding the printed caution, "It is dangerous to stand on the platform"; and under the eye of early morn saw spread around a flat sea-like expanse not yet warmed into colour and life by the sun. The line was no longer guarded from daring secessionists by soldiers' outposts, and small camps had disappeared. The train sped through the centre of the great verdant circle as a ship through the sea, leaving the rigid iron wake behind it tapering to a point at the horizon, and as the light spread over it the surface of the crisping corn waved in broad undulations beneath the breeze from east to west. This is the prairie indeed. Hereabouts it is covered with the finest crops, some already cut and stacked. Looking around one could see church spires rising in the distance from the white patches of houses, and by degrees the tracks across the fertile waste became apparent, and then carts and horses were seen toiling through the rich soil.

A large species of partridge or grouse appeared very abundant, and rose in flocks from the long grass at the side of the rail or from the rich carpet of flowers on the margin of the corn fields. They sat on the fence almost unmoved by the rushing engine, and literally swarmed along the line. These are called "prairie chickens" by the people, and afford excellent sport.

At the little stations which occur at every few miles—there are some forty of them, at each of which the train stops, in 365 miles between Cairo and Chicago—the Union flag floated in the air. These little communities which we passed were but the growth of a few years, and as we approached the northern portion of the line we could see, as it were, the village swelling into the town, and the town spreading out to the dimensions of the city.

The scene now began to change as we approached Chicago, the prairie subsided into swampy land, and thick belts of trees fringed the horizon; on our right glimpses of the sea could be caught through openings in the wood—the inland sea on which stands the Queen of the Lakes. Michigan looks broad and blue as the Mediterranean. Large farmhouses stud the country, and houses which must be the retreat of merchants and citizens of means; and when the train, leaving the land altogether, dashes out on a pier and causeway built along the borders of the land, we see lines of noble houses, a fine boulevard, a forest of masts, huge isolated piles of masonry, the famed grain elevators by which so many have been hoisted to fortune, churches and public edifices, and the apparatus of a great city; and just at nine o'clock the train gives its last steam shout and comes to a standstill in the spacious station of the Central Illinois Company, and in half-an-hour more I am in comfortable quarters at the Richmond House, where I find letters waiting for me, by which it appears that the necessity for my being in Washington in all haste no longer exists. The wary general who commands is aware that the advance to Richmond for which so many journals are clamouring, would be attended with serious risk at present, and the politicians must be content to wait a little longer.

[June 25th–June 30th.]   I shall here briefly recapitulate what has occurred since the last mention of political events.

In the first place the South has been developing every day greater energy in widening the breach between it and the North, and preparing to fill it with dead; and the North, so far as I can judge, has been busy in raising up the Union as a nationality, and making out the crime of treason from the act of secession. The South has been using conscription in Virginia and is entering upon the conflict with unsurpassable determination. The North is availing itself of its greater resources and its foreign vagabondage and destitution to swell the ranks of its volunteers, and boasts of its enormous armies, as if it supposed conscripts well led do not fight better than volunteers badly officered. Virginia has been invaded on three points, one below and two above Washington, and passports are now issued on both sides.

The career open to the Southern privateers is effectually closed by the Duke of Newcastle's notification that the British Government will not permit the cruisers of either side to bring their prizes into or condemn them in English ports; but, strange to say, the Northerners feel indignant against Great Britain for an act which deprives their enemy of an enormous advantage, and which must reduce their privateering to the mere work of plunder and destruction on the high seas. In the same way the North affects to consider the declaration of neutrality, and the concession of limited belligerent rights to the seceding States, as deeply injurious and insulting; whereas our course has, in fact, removed the greatest difficulty from the part of the Washington Cabinet, and saved us from inconsistencies and serious risks in our course of action.[1]

Secession was an accomplished fact months before Mr. Lincoln came into office, but we heard no talk of rebels and pirates till Sumter had fallen, and the North was perfectly quiescent—not only that— the people of wealth in New York were calmly considering the results of secession as an accomplished fact, and seeking to make the best of it; nay, more, when I arrived in Washington some members of the Cabinet were perfectly ready to let the South go.

I am not going to reiterate what every Crispinus from the old country has said again and again concerning [Chicago]—not one word of statistics, of corn elevators, of shipping, or of the piles of buildings raised from the foundation by ingenious applications of screws. Nor am I going to enlarge on the splendid future of that which has so much present prosperity, or on the benefits of mankind opened up by the Illinois Central Railway. It is enough to say that by the borders of this lake there has sprung up in thirty years a wonderful city of fine streets, luxurious hotels, handsome shops, magnificent stores, great warehouses, extensive quays, capacious docks; and that as long as corn holds its own, and the mouths of Europe are open, and her hands full, Chicago will acquire greater importance, size, and wealth with every year. The only drawback, perhaps, to the comfort of the money-making inhabitants, and of the stranger within the gates, is to be found in the clouds of dust and in the unpaved streets and thoroughfares, which give anguish to horse and man.

I spent three days here writing my letters and repairing the wear

[1]On May 13, 1861, Great Britain declared her neutrality in the Civil War and extended belligerent status and rights to the Confederate States. She closed her ports to both Union and Confederate privateers on June 1.

and tear of my Southern expedition; and although it was hot enough, the breeze from the lake carried health and vigour to the frame, enervated by the sun of Louisiana and Mississippi.

Nearly one half of the various companies enrolled in this district are Germans, and are the descendants of German parents, and speak only the language of the old country; two-thirds of the remainder are Irish, or of immediate Irish descent; but it is said that a grand reserve of Americans born lies behind this *avant garde,* who will come into the battle should there ever be need for their services.

I was invited before I left to visit the camp of a Colonel [John B.] Turchin, who was described to me as a Russian officer of great ability and experience in European warfare, in command of a regiment consisting of Poles, Hungarians, and Germans who were about to start for the seat of war; but I was only able to walk through his tents, where I was astonished at the amalgam of nations that constituted his battalion; though, on inspection, I am bound to say there proved to be an American element in the ranks which did not appear to have coalesced with the bulk of the rude and, I fear, predatory Cossacks of the Union. Many young men of good position have gone to the wars, although there was no complaint, as in Southern cities, that merchant's offices have been deserted, and great establishments left destitute of clerks and working hands. In warlike operations, however, Chicago, with its communication open to the sea, its access to the head waters of the Mississippi, its intercourse with the marts of commerce and of manufacture, may be considered to possess greater belligerent power and strength than the great city of New Orleans; and there is much greater probability of Chicago sending its contingent to attack the Crescent City than there is of the latter being able to dispatch a soldier within five hundred miles of its streets.

At eight o'clock on the morning of the 27th I left Chicago for Niagara, [where] news was brought to me that General Scott had ordered, or been forced to order, the advance of the Federal troops encamped in front of Washington, under the command of McDowell, against the Confederates, commanded by Beauregard, who was described as occupying the most formidable position, covered with entrenchments and batteries in front of a ridge of hills, through which the railway passes to Richmond.

The New York papers represent the Federal army to be of some grand indefinite strength, varying from 60,000 to 120,000 men, full of fight, admirably equipped, well disciplined, and provided with an overwhelming force of artillery. General Scott, I am very well assured, did not feel such confidence in the result of an invasion of Virginia, that he would hurry raw levies and a rabble of regiments to undertake a most arduous military operation.

The day I was introduced to the General he was seated at a table in the unpretending room which served as his boudoir in the still humbler house where he held his headquarters. On the table before him were some plans and maps of the harbour defences of the Southern ports. I inferred he was about to organise a force for the occupation of positions along the coast. But when I mentioned my impression to one of his officers, he said, "Oh, no, the General advised that long ago; but he is now convinced we are too late. All he can hope now is to be allowed time to prepare a force for the field, but there are hopes that some compromise will yet take place."

The probabilities of this compromise have vanished: few entertain them now. They have been hanging secessionists in Illinois, and the courthouse itself has been made the scene of Lynch law murder in Ogle County.[2] Petitions, prepared by citizens of New York to the President, for a general convention to consider a compromise have been seized. The Confederates have raised batteries along the Virginian shore of the Potomac. General [Nathaniel] Banks, at Baltimore, has deposed the police authorities *"proprio motu"* [in his own way], in spite of the protest of the board.[3] Engagements have occurred between the Federal steamers and the Confederate batteries on the Potomac. On all points, wherever the Federal pickets have advanced in Virginia, they have encountered opposition and have been obliged to halt or to retire.

[2]In the aftermath of Fort Sumter, feelings between Unionists and prosoutherners in northern Illinois became especially tense. Men in various localities were beaten for speaking out for the North or South. The high point of this antagonism came on June 19, 1861, in Lane, Ogle County, when a mob hanged T. D. Burke, a Confederate sympathizer suspected of arson.
[3]Banks arrested George B. Kane, Baltimore's prosouthern chief of police, and replaced him with Colonel John Kenly of his own staff. In retaliation, the city police board put the entire force on "furlough" until further notice. Kenly simply commissioned a new police force from the ranks of the city's unemployed.

[July 1st.]   In the evening I left Niagara on my way to New York.

July 2nd.   At early dawn this morning, looking out of the sleeping car, I saw through the mist a broad, placid river on the right and on the left high wooded banks running sharply into the stream, against the base of which the rails were laid. West Point, which is celebrated for its picturesque scenery as much as for its military school, could not be seen through the fog, and I regretted time did not allow me to stop and pay a visit to the academy.

At about 9 A.M. the train reached New York, and the first thing which struck me was the changed aspect of the streets. Instead of peaceful citizens, men in military uniforms thronged the pathways, and such multitudes of United States flags floated from the windows and roofs of the houses as to convey the impression that it was a great holiday festival. The appearance of New York when I first saw it was very different. For one day, indeed, after my arrival, there were men in uniform to be seen in the streets, but they disappeared after St. Patrick had been duly honoured. Now, fully a third of the people carried arms, and were dressed in some kind of martial garb.

There has been indeed a change in New York. I was desirous of learning how far the tone of conversation "in the city" had altered, and soon after breakfast I went down Broadway to Pine Street and Wall Street. Wall Street and Pine Street are bent on battle. As long as there was a chance that the struggle might not take place, the merchants of New York were silent, fearful of offending their Southern friends and connections, but inflicting infinite damage of their own government and misleading both sides. Their sentiments, sympathies, and business bound them with the South; and, indeed, till "the glorious uprising" the South believed New York was with them, as might be credited from the tone of some organs in the press, and I remember hearing it said by Southerners in Washington, that it was very likely New York would go out of the Union! When the merchants, however, saw that the South was determined to quit the Union, they resolved to avert the permanent loss of the great profits derived from their connection with the South by some present sacrifices. They rushed to the platforms, and the oath was taken to trample secession under foot, and to quench the fire of the Southern heart forever.

The change in manner, in tone, in argument, is most remarkable. I met men today who last March argued coolly and philosophically about the right of secession. They are now furious at the idea of such wickedness. "We must maintain our glorious Union, sir." "We must have a country." "We cannot allow two nations to grow up on this Continent, sir." "We must possess the entire control of the Mississippi." These "musts," and "can'ts," and "won'ts," are the angry utterances of a spirited people who have had their will so long that they at last believe it is omnipotent. Assuredly, they will not have it over the South without a tremendous and long-sustained contest, in which they must put forth every exertion, and use all the resources of superior means they so abundantly possess.

It is absurd to assert, as do the New York people, to give some semblance of reason to their sudden outburst, that it was caused by the insult to the flag at Sumter. Some of the gentlemen who are now so patriotic and Unionistic were last March prepared to maintain that if the President attempted to reinforce Sumter or Pickens, he would be responsible for the destruction of the Union. Many journals in New York and out of it held the same doctrine.

One word to these gentlemen. I am pretty well satisfied that if they had always spoke, written, and acted as they do now, the people of Charleston would not have attacked Sumter so readily. The abrupt outburst of the North and the demonstration at New York filled the South, first with astonishment, and then with something like fear, which was rapidly fanned into anger by the press and the politicians, as well as by the pride inherent in slaveholders.

I wonder what Mr. Seward will say when I get back to Washington. Before I left, he was of the opinion—at all events, he stated— that all the States would come back, at the rate of one a month. The nature of the process was not stated; but we are told there are 250,000 Federal troops now under arms, prepared to try a new one.

July 3rd.   Up early, breakfasted at five, A.M., on my way to Washington.

Nearly four months since I went by this road to Washington. The change which has since occurred is beyond belief. Men were then speaking of place under Government, of compromises between North and South, and of peace; now they only talk of war and battle.

Ever since I came out of the South, and could see the newspapers, I have been struck by the easiness of the American people, by their excessive credulity. Whether they wish it or not, they are certainly deceived. Not a day has passed without the announcement that the Federal troops were moving, and that "a great battle was expected" by somebody unknown, at some place or other.

I could not help observing the arrogant tone with which writers of stupendous ignorance on military matters write of the operations which they think the generals should undertake. They demand that an army, which has neither adequate transport, artillery, or cavalry, shall be pushed forward to Richmond to crush out secession, and at the same time their columns teem with accounts from the army which prove that it is not only ill disciplined, but that it is ill provided. A general outcry has been raised against the War Department and the contractors, and it is openly stated that Mr. Cameron, the Secretary, has not clean hands.

The country between Washington and Philadelphia is destitute of natural beauties but it affords abundant evidence that it is inhabited by a prosperous, comfortable, middle-class community. From every village church, and from many houses, the Union flag was displayed. Four months ago not one was to be seen. When we were crossing in the steam ferryboat at Philadelphia I saw some volunteers looking up and smiling at a hatchet which was over the cabin door, and it was not till I saw it had the words "States' Rights Fire Axe" painted along the handle I could account for the attraction. It would fare ill with any vessel in Southern waters which displayed an axe to the citizens inscribed with "Down with States' Rights" on it. There is certainly less vehemence and bitterness among the Northerners; but it might be erroneous to suppose there was less determination.

Below Philadelphia, from Havre-de-Grâce [Maryland] all the way to Baltimore, and thence on to Washington, the stations on the rail were guarded by soldiers, as though an enemy were expected to destroy the bridges and to tear up the rails. Wooden bridges and causeways, carried over piles and embankments, are necessary in consequence of the nature of the country; and at each of these a small camp was formed for the soldiers who have to guard the approaches. Sentinels are posted, pickets thrown out, and in the open field by the wayside troops are to be seen moving, as though a battle was close at hand. In one word, we are in the State of Maryland. By these means alone are communications maintained between the North and the capital. As we approach Baltimore the number of sentinels and camps increase, and earthworks have been thrown up on the high grounds commanding the city. The display of Federal flags from the public buildings and some shipping in the river was so limited as to contrast strongly with those symbols of Union sentiment in the Northern cities.

It is about forty miles from Baltimore to Washington and at every quarter of a mile for the whole distance a picket of soldiers guarded the rails. Camps appeared on both sides, larger and more closely packed together; and the rays of the setting sun fell on countless lines of tents as we approached the unfinished dome of the Capitol.

To me all this was a wonderful sight. As I drove up Pennsylvania Avenue I could scarce credit that the busy thoroughfare—all red, white, and blue with flags, filled with dust from galloping chargers and commissariat carts; the sidewalks thronged with people, of whom a large proportion carried sword or bayonet; shops full of life and activity—was the same as that through which I had driven the first morning of my arrival. Washington now, indeed, is the capital of the United States, but it is no longer the scene of beneficent legislation and of peaceful government. It is the representative of armed force engaged in war—menaced whilst in the very act of raising its arm by the enemy it seeks to strike.

To avoid the tumult of Willard's, I requested a friend to hire apartments and drove to a house in Pennsylvania Avenue, close to the War Department, where he had succeeded in engaging a sitting room about twelve feet square and a bedroom to correspond, in a very small mansion, next door to a spirit merchant's.

July 4th. "Independence Day." Fortunate to escape this great national festival in the large cities of the Union where it is celebrated with many days before and after of surplus rejoicing, by fireworks and an incessant fusillade in the streets, I was, nevertheless, subjected to the small ebullition of the Washington juveniles to bell-ringing and discharges of cannon and musketry. On this day Congress meets. Never before has any legislative body assembled under circumstances so grave. By their action they will decide whether the Union can ever be restored, and will determine whether the States of the North are to commence an invasion for the purpose of sub-

Pennsylvania Avenue, Washington *(From* Battles and Leaders of the Civil War *(New York: The Century Co., 1887), Vol. 1, p. 158. Courtesy of the New York Public Library)*

jecting by force of arms, and depriving of their freedom, the States of the South.

Mr. [Henry] Wilson gave me to understand that some military movements of the utmost importance might be expected in a few days and that General McDowell would positively attack the rebels in front of Washington. The Confederates occupy the whole of northern Virginia, commencing from the peninsula above Fortress Monroe on the right, or east, and extending along the Potomac, to the extreme verge of the State, by the Baltimore and Ohio Railway. This immense line, however, is broken by great intervals, and the army with which McDowell will have to deal may be considered as detached, covering the approaches to Richmond, whilst its left flank is protected by a corps of observation stationed near Winchester, under General [Thomas J.] Jackson. A Federal corps is being prepared to watch the corps and engage it, whilst McDowell advances on the main body. To the right of this again, or further west, another body of Federals, under General McClellan, is operating in the valleys of the Shenandoah and in western Virginia; but I did not hear of any of these things from Mr. Wilson, who was, I am sure, in perfect ignorance of the plans, in a military sense, of the general. I sat at Mr. Sumner's desk and wrote the final paragraphs of a letter describing my impressions of the South in a place but little disposed to give a favourable colour to them.

When the Senate had adjourned, I drove to the State Department and saw Mr. Seward, who looked much more worn and haggard than when I saw him last, three months ago. He congratulated me on my safe return from the South in time to witness some stirring events. "Well, Mr. Secretary, I am quite sure that if all the South are of the same mind as those I met in my travels, there will be many battles before they submit to the Federal Government. I heard that I must procure a passport in order to travel through the States and go into the camps in front of Washington."

"Yes, sir; you must send your passport here from Lord Lyons with his signature. It will be no good till I have signed it and then it must be sent to General Scott, as commander-in-chief of the United States Army, who will subscribe it, after which it will be available for all legitmate purposes. You are not in any way impaired in your liberty by the process."

It was not my place to remark that such doctrines were exactly identical with all that despotic governments in Europe have advanced as the ground of action in cases of revolt, or with a view to the maintenance of their strong Governments. "The Executive," said he, "has declared in the inaugural that the rights of the Federal Government shall be fully vindicated. We are dealing with an insurrection within our own country, of our own people. We do not hesitate to resist it to the uttermost. If any European Power provokes a war, we shall not shrink from it. A contest between Great Britain and the United States would wrap the world in fire, and at the end it would not be the United States which would have to lament the results of the conflict."

I could not but admire the confidence—may I say the coolness?— of the statesman who sat in his modest little room within the sound of the evening's guns, in a capital menaced by their forces who spoke so fearlessly of war with a power which could have blotted out the paper blockade of the Southern forts and coast in a few hours, and, in conjunction with the Southern armies, have repeated the occupation and destruction of the capital.

The President sent for Mr. Seward whilst I was in the State Department, and I walked up Pennsylvania Avenue. Directly opposite my lodgings are the headquarters of General [Joseph] Mansfield, commanding the district, which are marked by a guard at the door and a couple of six pounder guns pointing down the street. I called upon the General but he was busy examining certain inhabitants of Alexandria and of Washington itself, who had been brought before him on the charge of being secessionists, and I left my card, and proceeded to General Scott's headquarters. The General received me in a small room and expressed his gratification at my return, but I saw he was so busy with reports, dispatches, and maps, that I did not trespass on his time.

All the population of Washington had turned out in their best to listen to the military bands, the music of which was rendered nearly inaudible by the constant discharge of fireworks. The camp of the 12th New York presented a very pretty and animated scene. The men liberated from duty were enjoying themselves out and inside their tents, and the sutlers' booths were driving a roaring trade. I was introduced to Colonel [Daniel] Butterfield, commanding the regiment, who was a merchant of New York; but notwithstanding the training of the counting house, he looked very much like a soldier and had got his regiment very fairly in hand. The Colonel had prepared a number of statistical tables in which the nationality, height, weight, breadth of chest, age, and other particulars respecting the men under his command were entered. I looked over the book, and as far as I could judge, but two out of twelve of the soldiers were native-born Americans, the rest being Irish, German, English, and European-born generally. According to the commanding officer they were in the highest state of discipline and obedience. He had given them leave to go out as they pleased for the day, but at tattoo only 14 men out of 1000 were absent, and some of those had been accounted for by reports that they were incapable of locomotion owing to the hospitality of the citizens.

When I returned to my lodgings, the coloured boy whom I had hired at Niagara was absent, and I was told he had not come in since the night before. "These free coloured boys," said my landlord, "are a bad set; now they are worse than ever; the officers of the army are taking them all away from us; it's just the life they like; they get little work, have good pay; but what they like most is robbing and plundering the farmers' houses over in Virginia; what with Germans, Irish, and free niggers, Lord help the poor Virginians, I say; but they'll give them a turn yet."

The sounds in Washington tonight might have led one to believe the city was carried by storm. Constant explosion of firearms, fireworks, shouting, and cries in the streets, which combined with the heat and the abominable odours of the undrained houses and mosquitoes to drive sleep far away.

July 5th. In the forenoon Mr. John Bigelow, whose acquaintance I made, found me out and proffered his services; which, as the whilom editor of the [New York] *Evening Post* and as a leading Republican, he was in a position to render valuable and most effective. Mr. Bigelow was of opinion that the army would move at once; "but," said I, "where is the transport—where the cavalry and guns?" "Oh," replied he, "I suppose we have got everything that is required. I know nothing of these things, but I am told cavalry are no use in the wooded country towards Richmond." I have not yet been able to go through the camps, but I doubt very much whether the material or commissariat of the grand army of the North is at all adequate to a campaign.

The Congress met today to hear the President's Message read. Somehow or other there is not such anxiety and eagerness to hear what Mr. Lincoln has to say as one could expect on such a momentous occasion. The President has, it is said, written much of it in his own fashion, which has been revised and altered by his ministers; but he has written it again and repeated himself, and after many struggles a good deal of pure Lincolnism goes down to Congress.

At a little after half-past eleven I went down to the Capitol. Pennsylvania Avenue was thronged as before but on approaching Capitol Hill, the crowd rather thinned away, as though they shunned, or had no curiosity to hear the President's Message. One would have thought that, where every one who could get in was at liberty to attend the galleries in both Houses, there would have been an immense pressure from the inhabitants and strangers in the city as well as from the citizen soldiers, of which such multitudes were in the street; but when I looked up from the floor of the Senate, I was astonished to see that the galleries were not more than three parts filled.

The Capitol would be best described by a series of photographs. Like the Great Republic itself, it is unfinished. It resembles it in another respect: it looks best at a distance; and, again, it is incongruous in its parts. The passages are so dark that artificial light is often required to enable one to find his way. The offices and bureaux of the committees are better than the chambers of the Senate and the House of Representatives. All the encaustics and the white marble and stone staircases suffer from tobacco juice, though there is a liberal display of spittoons at every corner. The official messenger, doorkeepers, and porters wear no distinctive badge or dress. No policemen are on duty, as in our Houses of Parliament; no soldiery, *gendarmerie* [armed guard], or *sergent-de-ville* [constable] in the precincts; the crowd wanders about the passages as it pleases, and shows utmost propriety, never going where it ought not to intrude. There is a special gallery set apart for women; the reporters are commodiously placed in an ample gallery, above the Speaker's chair; the diplomatic circles have their gallery facing the reporters, and they are placed so low down in the somewhat depressed chamber that every word can be heard from speakers in the remotest parts of the house very distinctly.

Senators Sumner and Wilson introduced me to a chair and made me acquainted with a number of Senators before the business of the day began. Mr. Sumner, as the Chairman of the Committee on Foreign Relations, is supposed to be viewed with some jealousy by Mr. Seward, on account of the disposition attributed to him to interfere in diplomatic questions; but if he does so, we shall have no reason to complain, as the Senator is most desirous of keeping the peace between the two countries and of mollifying any little acerbities and irritations which may at present exist between them. Senator Wilson is a man who has risen from what would be considered in any country but a republic the lowest ranks of the people. He apprenticed himself to a poor shoemaker when he was twenty-two years of age, and when he was twenty-four years old he began to go to school and devoted all his earnings to the improvement of education. He got on by degrees, till he set up as a master shoemaker and manufacturer, became a "major general" of the State militia; finally was made

Senator of the United States, and is now "Chairman of the Committee of the Senate on Military Affairs."

It was a hot day, but there was no excuse for the slop coats and light-coloured clothing and felt wide-awakes worn by so many Senators in such a place. They gave the meeting the aspect of a gathering of bakers or millers; nor did the constant use of the spittoons beside their desks, their reading the newspapers and writing letters during the dispatch of business, or the hurrying to and fro of the pages of the House between the seats do anything but derogate from the dignity of the assemblage, and, according to European notions, violate the respect due to a Senate Chamber.

The House of Representatives exaggerates all the peculiarities I have observed in the Senate, but the debates are not regarded with so much interest as those of the Upper House; indeed, they are of far less importance. Strong minded statesmen and officers—Presidents or Ministers—do not care much for the House of Representatives, so long as they are sure of the Senate.

After the lapse of an hour, Mr. Hay, the President's secretary, made his appearance of the floor, and sent in the Message to the Clerk of the Senate, Mr. [John] Forney, who proceeded to read it to the House. It was listened to in silence, scarcely broken except when some Senator murmured "Good, that is so;" but in fact the general purport of it was already known to the supporters of the Ministry, and not a sound came from the galleries. Soon after Mr. Forney had finished, the galleries were cleared and I returned up Pennsylvania Avenue, in which the crowds of soldiers around barrooms, oyster shops, and restaurants, and groups of men in officers' uniform, and the clattering of disorderly mounted cavaliers in the dust, increased my apprehension that discipline was very little regarded, and that the army over the Potomac had not a very strong hand to keep it within bounds.

After dinner I made a round of visits, and heard the diplomatists speaking of the Message; few, if any of them, in its favour. With the exception perhaps of Baron [Frederick C. J.] Gerolt, the Prussian Minister, there is not one member of the Legations who justifies the attempt of the Northern States to assert the supremacy of the Federal Government by the force of arms.

July 6th. I breakfasted with Mr. Bigelow this morning, to meet General McDowell who commands the army of the Potomac, now so soon to move. He came in without an aide-de-camp, and on foot, from his quarters in the city. He is a man about forty years of age, square and powerfully built but with rather a stout and clumsy figure and limbs, a good head covered with close-cut thick dark hair, small light blue eyes, short nose, large cheeks and jaw, relieved by an iron grey tuft somewhat of the French type, and affecting in dress the style of our gallant allies. His manner is frank, simple, and agreeable, and he did not hesitate to speak with great openness of the difficulties he had to contend with and the imperfection of all the arrangements of the army.

As an officer of the Regular Army he has a thorough contempt for what he calls "political generals"—the men who use their influence with President and Congress to obtain military rank, which in time of war places them before the public in the front of events and gives them an appearance of leading in the greatest of all political movements. Nor is General McDowell enamoured of volunteers, for he served in Mexico and has from what he saw there formed rather an unfavourable opinion of their capabilities in the field. He is inclined,

Brigadier-General Irwin McDowell *(Library of Congress)*

however, to hold the Southern troops in too little respect, and he told me that the volunteers from the slave States, who entered the field full of exultation and boastings, did not make good their words and that they suffered especially from sickness and disease, in consequence of their disorderly habits and dissipation. His regard for old associations was evinced in many questions he asked me about Beauregard, with whom he had been a student at West Point, where the Confederate commander was noted for his studious and reserved habits and his excellence in feats of strength and athletic exercises.

As proof of the low standard established in his army, he mentioned that some officers of considerable rank were more than suspected of selling rations, and of illicit connections with sutlers for purposes of pecuniary advantage. The General walked back with me as far as my lodgings, and I observed that not one of the many soldiers he passed in the streets saluted him, though his rank was indicated by his velvet collar and cuffs and a gold star on the shoulder strap.

I dined at lodgings next door to mine. Beneath us was a wine and spirit store, and crowds of officers and men flocked indiscriminately to make their purchases with a good deal of tumult, which increased as the night came on. Later still, there was a great disturbance in the city. A body of New York Zouaves wrecked some houses of bad repute, in one of which a private of the regiment was murdered early this morning. The cavalry patrols were called out and charged the rioters who were dispersed with difficulty after resistance in which men on both sides were wounded. There is no police, no provost guard. Soldiers wander about the streets and beg for money to get whiskey. My coloured gentleman has been led away by the Saturnalia and has taken to gambling in the camps, which are surrounded by hordes of rascally followers and sutlers' servants, and I find myself on the eve of a campaign, without servant, horse, equipment, or means of transport.

July 7th.   Mr. Bigelow invited me to breakfast to meet Senator [Preston] King, Mr. Olmsted, Mr. Thurlow Weed, a Senator from Missouri, a West Point professor, and others. It was indicative of the serious difficulties which embarrass the action of the Government to hear Mr. Wilson, the Chairman of the Military Committee of the Senate, inveigh against the officers of the Regular Army, and attack

West Point itself. Whilst the New York papers were lauding General Scott and his plans to the skies, the Washington politicians were speaking of him as obstructive, obstinate, and prejudiced—unfit for the times and the occasion.

General Scott refused to accept cavalry and artillery at the beginning of the levy and said that they were not required; now he was calling for both arms most urgently. The officers of the Regular Army had followed suit. Although they were urgently pressed by the politicians to occupy Harpers Ferry and Manassas, they refused to do either, and the result is that the enemy have obtained invaluable supplies from the first place and are now assembled in force in a most formidable position at the second. Everything as yet accomplished has been done by political generals—not by the officers of the Regular Army. Butler and Banks saved Baltimore in spite of General Scott. There was an attempt made to cry up Lyon in Missouri; but in fact it was Frank Blair, the brother of the Postmaster-General, who had been the soul and body of all the actions in the State. The first step taken by McClellan in western Virginia was atrocious—he talked of slaves in a public document as property. Butler, at Monroe, had dealt with them in a very different spirit and had used them for State purposes under the name of contraband. One man alone displayed powers of administrative ability, and that was Quartermaster [Montgomery] Meigs; and unquestionably from all I heard, the praise was well bestowed. It is plain enough that the political leaders fear the consequences of delay and that they are urging the military authorities to action, which the latter have too much professional knowledge to take with their present means. These Northern men know nothing of the South, and with them it is *omni ignotum pro minimo* [all show and little substance]. The West Point professor listened to them with a quiet smile and exchanged glances with me now and then, as much as to say, "Did you ever hear such fools in your life?"

But the conviction of ultimate success is not less strong here than it is in the South. The differences between these gentleman and the Southerners is that in the South the leaders of the people, soldiers and civilians, are all actually under arms, and are ready to make good their words by exposing their bodies in battle.

Six

BULL RUN

(July 8–July 26, 1861)

July 8th. I hired a horse at a livery stable and rode out to Arlington Heights, at the other side of the Potomac, where the Federal army is encamped. The road to the Long Bridge passes by a four-sided shaft of blocks of white marble, contributed, with appropriate mottoes, by the various States, as a fitting monument to Washington. It is not yet completed and the materials lie in the field. Further on is the red, and rather fantastic, pile of the Smithsonian Institute, and then the road makes a dip to the bridge. Through the green forest leaves gleams the white canvas of the tents, and on the highest ridge westward rises an imposing structure with a portico and colonnade in front, facing the river, which is called Arlington House, and belong by descent through Mr. [George] Custis, from the wife of George Washington, to General Lee of the Confederate army. It is now occupied by General McDowell as his headquarters, and a large United States flag floats from the roof, which shames even the ample proportions of the many Stars and Stripes rising up from the camps in the trees.

The road to Arlington House passed through some of the finest woods I have yet seen in America, but the axe was already busy amongst them and the trunks of giant oaks were prostrate on the ground. The tents of the General and his small staff were pitched on the little plateau in which stood the house, and from it a very striking and picturesque view of the city, with the White House, the Treasury, the Post Office, Patent Office, and Capitol was visible, and a wide spread of country, studded with tents also as far as the eye could reach, towards Maryland. There were only four small tents for the whole of the headquarters of the grand army of the Potomac, and in front of one we found General McDowell, seated in a chair examining some plans and maps.

I went over some of the camps with the General. The artillery is the most efficient looking arm of the service, but the horses are too light, and the number of the different calibres quite destructive to continuous efficiency in action. Altogether I was not favourably impressed with what I saw, for I had been led by reiterated statements to believe to some extent the extravagant stories of the papers, and expected to find upwards of 100,000 men in the highest state of efficiency, whereas there were not more than a third of the number, and those in a very incomplete, ill-disciplined state. Some of these regiments were called out under the President's proclamation for three months only and will soon have served their full time, and as it is very likely they will go home, General Scott is urged not to lose their service but to get into Richmond before they are disbanded.

It would scarcely be credited, were I not told it by General McDowell, that there is no such thing procurable as a decent map of Virginia. He knows little or nothing of the country before him, more than the general direction of the main roads, which are bad at the best; and he can obtain no information, inasmuch as the enemy are in full force all along his front, and he has not a cavalry officer capable of conducting a reconnaissance, which would be difficult enough in the best hands, owing to the dense woods which rise up in front of his lines, screening the enemy completely. The Confederates have thrown up very heavy batteries at Manassas, about thirty miles away, where the railway from the west crosses the line to Richmond, and I do not think General McDowell much likes the look of them, but the cry for action is so strong the President cannot resist it.

In the course of my ride I heard occasional dropping shots in the camp. To my looks of inquiry, an engineer officer said quietly. "They are volunteers shooting themselves." The number of accidents from the carelessness of the men is astonishing; in every day's paper there is an account of deaths and wounds caused by the discharge of firearms in the tents.

The most absurd rumors were flying about the staff, one of whom declared very positively that there was going to be a compromise, and that Jeff Davis had made an overture for peace. The papers are filled with accounts of an action in Missouri, at a place called Carthage, between the Federals commanded by Colonel [Franz] Sigel, consisting for the most part of Germans, and the Confederates under General [Mosby] Parsons, in which the former were obliged to retreat, although it is admitted the State troops were miserably armed and had most ineffective artillery, whilst their opponents had every advantage in both respects and were commanded by officers of European experience.[1]

July 9th. Every preparation is being made to put the army on a war footing, to provide them with shoes, ammunition wagons, and horses.

I had the honour of dining with General Scott, who has moved to new quarters near the War Department, and met General [John C.] Frémont, who is designated, according to rumour, to take command of an important district in the West and to clear the right bank of the Mississippi and the course of the Missouri. "The Pathfinder" is a strong Republican and abolitionist, whom the Germans delight to honour—a man with a dreamy, deep blue eye, a gentlemanly address, pleasant features, and an active frame, but without the smallest external indication of extraordinary vigour, intelligence, or ability; if he has military genius, it must come by intuition, for assuredly he has no professional acquirements or experience. Two or three members of Congress, and the General's staff, and Mr. Bigelow, completed the company. The General has become visibly weaker since I first saw

---

[1]The fighting around Carthage, Missouri, occurred on July 5, 1861. Sigel's force consisted of some 1,100 men; Confederate troop strength was close to 4,000 men, many of whom were not armed. Nevertheless, the Confederates forced a Union retreat from the area.

him. He walks down to his office, close at hand, with difficulty; returns a short time before dinner and reposes; and when he has dismissed his guests at an early hour or even before he does so, stretches himself on his bed, and then before midnight rouses himself to look at dispatches or to transact any necessary business. In case of an action, it is his intention to proceed to the field in a light carriage, which is always ready for the purpose, with horses and driver; nor is he unprepared with precedents of great military commanders who have successfully conducted engagements under similar circumstances.

Although the discussion of military questions and of politics was eschewed, incidental allusions were made to matters going on around us, and I thought I could perceive that the General regarded the situation with much more apprehension than the politicians and that his influence extended itself to the views of his staff. The General is annoyed and distressed by the plundering propensities of the Federal troops, who have been committing terrible depredations on the people of Virginia. It is not to be supposed, however, that the Germans, who have entered upon this campaign as mercenaries, will desist from so profitable and interesting a pursuit as the detection of secesh sentiment, chickens, watches, horses, and dollars. I mentioned that I had seen some farm houses completely sacked close to the aqueduct. The General merely said, "It is deplorable!" and raised up his hands as if in disgust.

July 10th. Today was spent in a lengthy excursion along the front of the camp in Virginia, round by the Chain Bridge which crosses the Potomac about four miles from Washington.

The Government have been coerced, as they say, by the safety of the Republic, to destroy the liberty of the press, which is guaranteed by the Constitution, and this is not the first instance in which the Constitution of the United States will be made *nominis umbra* [less inviolable]. The telegraph, according to General Scott's order, confirmed by the Minister of War, Simon Cameron, is to convey no dispatches respecting military movements not permitted by the General; and today the newspaper correspondents have agreed to yield obedience to the order, reserving to themselves a certain freedom of detail in writing their dispatches, and relying on the Government to publish the official accounts of all battles very speedily. They will break this agreement if they can, and the Government will not observe their part of the bargain. The freedom of the press, as I take it, does not include the right to publish news hostile to the cause of the country in which it is published; neither can it involve any obligation on the part of the Government to publish dispatches which may be injurious to the party they represent.

The most important event today is the passage of the Loan Bill, which authorises Mr. Chase to borrow a sum of £50,000,000. I just got into the House in time to hear Mr. [Clement] Vallandigham, who is an ultra-Democrat, and very nearly a secessionist, conclude a well-delivered argumentative address. He is a tall, slight man, of a bilious temperament, with light flashing eyes, dark hair and complexion, and considerable oratorical power. "Deem me ef I wouldn't just ride that Vallandiggaim on a reay-al," quoth a citizen to his friend, as the speaker sat down amid a few feeble expressions of assent. Mr. Chase has also obtained the consent of the Lower House to his bill for closing the Southern ports by the decree of the President, but I hear some more substantial measures are in contemplation for that purpose. Whilst the House is finding the money, the Government are preparing to spend it, and they have obtained the approval of the Senate to the enrollment of half a million of men, and the expenditure of one hundred millions of dollars to carry on the war.

July 12th.   There are rumours that the Federals, under Brigadier McClellan, who have advanced into western Virginia, have gained some successes; but so far it seems to have no larger dimensions than the onward raid of one clan against another in the Highlands. McClellan is, however, considered a very steady and respectable professional soldier. A friend of his told me today one of the more serious complaints the Central Illinois Company had against him was that, during the Italian war,[2] he seemed to forget their business; and that he was busied with maps stretched out on the floor, whereupon he, superincumbent, penned out the points of battle and strategy when he ought to have been attending to passenger trains and traffic.

[2] The Franco-Austrian War, 1859, fought in northern Italy between France and Italy on one side and Austria on the other.

That which was flat blasphemy in a railway office may be amazingly approved in the field.

July 13th. I have had a long day's ride through the camps of the various regiments across the Potomac, and at this side of it, which the weather did not render very agreeable to myself or the poor hack that I had hired for the day, till my American quartermaine gets me a decent mount. I wished to see with my own eyes what is the real condition of the army which the North have sent down to the Potomac to undertake such a vast task as the conquest of the South. The Northern papers describe it as a magnificent force, complete in all respects, well disciplined, well clad, provided with fine artillery, and with every requirement to make it effective for all military operations in the field.

In one word, then, they are grossly and utterly ignorant of what an army is or should be. In the first place, there are not, I should think, 30,000 men of all sorts available for the campaign. The papers estimate it at any number from 50,000 to 100,000, giving the preference to 75,000. In the next place, their artillery is miserably deficient; they have not, I should think, more than five complete batteries, or six batteries, including scratch guns, and these are of different calibres, badly horsed, miserably equipped, and provided with the worst set of gunners and drivers which I ever beheld. They have no cavalry, only a few scarecrow-men, who would dissolve partnership with their steeds at the first serious combined movement, mounted in high saddles, on wretched mouthless screws, and some few regulars from the frontiers, who may be good for Indians, but who would go over like ninepins at a charge from Punjaubee irregulars. Their transport is tolerably good, but inadequate; they have no carriage for reserve ammunition; the commissariat drivers are civilians under little or no control; the officers are unsoldierly-looking men; the camps are dirty to excess; the men are dressed in all sorts of uniforms; and from what I hear, I doubt if any of these regiments have ever performed a brigade evolution together, or if any of the officers know what it is to deploy a brigade from column into line. They are mostly three months' men whose time is nearly up. They were rejoicing today over the fact that it was so, and that they had kept the enemy from Washington "without a fight." And it is with this rabblement that the North propose not only to subdue the South but according to some of their papers, to humiliate Great Britain and conquer Canada afterwards.

Major General McClellan—I beg his pardon for styling him Brigadier—has really been successful. By a very well-conducted and rather rapid march, he was enabled to bring superior forces to bear on some raw levies under General Garnett (who came over with me in the steamer), which fled after a few shots and were utterly routed when their gallant commander fell in an abortive attempt to rally them by the banks of the Cheat River.[3] In this "great battle" McClellan's loss is less than 30 killed and wounded, and the Confederates' loss is less than 100. But the dispersion of such guerilla bands has the most useful effect among the people of the district; and McClellan has done good service, especially as his little victory will lead to the discomfiture of all the secessionists in the valley of the Kanawha, and in the valley of western Virginia. I left Washington this afternoon with the Sanitary Commissioners for Baltimore, in order to visit the Federal camps at Fortress Monroe, to which we proceeded down the Chesapeake the same night.

July 14th.   At six o'clock this morning the steamer arrived at the wharf under the walls of Fortress Monroe, which presented a very different appearance from the quiet of its aspect when first I saw it some months ago. Camps spread around it, the parapets lined with sentries, guns looking out towards the land, lighters and steamers alongside the wharf, a strong guard at the end of the pier, passes to be scrutinised and permits to be given. I landed with the members of the Sanitary Commission and repaired to a very large pile of buildings, called "The Hygeia Hotel," for once on a time Fortress Monroe was looked upon as the resort of the sickly who required bracing air and an abundance of oysters; it is now occupied by the wounded in the several actions and skirmishes which have taken place, particularly at Bethel; and it is so densely crowded that we had difficulty in procuring the use of some small dirty rooms to dress in. As the business of the Commission was principally directed to ascer-

---

[3]The skirmish, fought in the Cheat River Valley on July 13, 1861, is known as the Battle of Corrick's (also spelled Carrick's) Ford.

tain the state of the hospitals, they considered it necessary in the first instance to visit General Butler, the commander of the post, who has been recommending himself to the Federal Government by his activity ever since he came down to Baltimore, and the whole body marched to the fort, crossing the drawbridge after some parley with the guard, and received permission, on the production of passes, to enter the court.

The interior of the work covers a space of about seven or eight acres, as far as I could judge, and is laid out with some degree of taste; rows of fine trees border the walks through the grass plots; the officers' quarters, neat and snug, are surrounded with little patches of flowers and covered with creepers. All order and neatness, however, were fast disappearing beneath the tramp of mailed feet, for at least 1200 men had pitched their tents inside the place. We sent in our names to the General, who lives in a detached house close to the sea face of the fort, and sat down on a bench under the shade of some trees to avoid the excessive heat of the sun until the commander of the place could receive the Commissioners. He was evidently in no great hurry to do so. In about half an hour an aide-de-camp came out to say that the General was getting up and that he would see us after breakfast. Some of the Commissioners, from purely sanitary considerations, would have been much better pleased to have seen him at breakfast, as they had only partaken of a very light meal on board the steamer at five o'clock in the morning; but we were interested meantime by the morning parade of a portion of the garrison, consisting of 300 regulars, a Massachusetts volunteer battalion, and the 2nd New York Regiment.

It was quite refreshing to the eye to see the cleanliness of the regulars—their white gloves and belts, and polished buttons, contrasted with the slovenly aspect of the volunteers; but, as far as the material went, the volunteers had by far the best of the comparison. The civilians who were with me did not pay much attention to the regulars and evidently preferred the volunteers, although they could not be insensible to the magnificent drum-major who led the band of the regulars. Presently General Butler came out of his quarters and walked down the lines, followed by a few officers. He is a stout, middle-aged man, strongly built, with coarse limbs, his features indicative of great shrewdness and craft, his forehead high, the elevation being in some degree due perhaps to the want of hair; with a strong obliquity of vision, which may perhaps have been caused by an injury, as the eyelid hangs with a peculiar droop over the organ.

The General, whose manner is quick, decided, and abrupt, but not at all rude or unpleasant, at once acceded to the wishes of the Sanitary Commissioners and expressed his desire to make my stay at the fort as agreeable and useful as he could. "You can first visit the hospitals in company with these gentlemen and then come over with me to our camp where I will show you everything that is to be seen. I have ordered a steamer to be in readiness to take you to Newport News." He speaks rapidly and either affects or possesses great decision. The Commissioners accordingly proceeded to make the most of their time in visiting the Hygeia Hotel, being accompanied by the medical officers of the garrison.

The rooms, but a short time ago occupied by the fair ladies of Virginia, when they came down to enjoy the sea breezes, were now crowded with Federal soldiers, many of them suffering from the loss of limb or serious wounds, others from the worst form of camp disease. At last we came into a room in which two soldiers were sitting up, the first we had seen, reading the newspapers. One of them had his hand shattered by a bullet, the other was suffering from a gunshot wound through the body. "Where were you hit?" I inquired of the first. "Well," he said, "I guess my rifle went off when I was cleaning it in camp." "Were you wounded at Bethel?" I asked of the second. "No, sir," he replied, "I got this wound from a comrade who discharged his piece by accident in one of the tents as I was standing outside."

The Americans were fighting for the combined excellences and strength of the States of New England, and of the rest of the Federal power over the Confederates, for they could not in their heart of hearts believe the old Union could be restored by force of arms. The newspapers and illustrated periodicals which they read were the pabulum that fed the flames of patriotism incessantly. Such capacity for enormous lying, both in creation and absorption, the world never heard. Sufficient for the hour is the falsehood.

There were lady nurses in attendance on the patients; who followed—let us believe, as I do, out of some higher motive than the mere desire of human praise—the example of Miss [Florence] Nightingale. I loitered behind in the rooms, asking many questions respecting the nationality of the men, in which the members of the Sanitary Commission took no interest, and I was just turning into one near the corner of the passage when I was stopped by a loud smack. A young Scotchman was dividing his attention between a basin of soup and a demure young lady from Philadelphia who was feeding him with a spoon, his only arm being engaged in holding her round the waist, in order to prevent her being tired, I presume. Miss Rachel, or Deborah, had a pair of very pretty blue eyes, but they flashed very angrily from under her trim little cap at the unwilling intruder, and then she said, in severest tones, "Will you take your medicine, or not?" Sandy smiled and pretended to be very penitent.

When we returned with the doctors from our inspection, we walked round the parapets of the fortress, why so called I know not, because it is merely a fort. The guns and mortars are old fashioned and heavy, with the exception of some new-fashioned and very heavy Columbiads, which are cast-iron 8-, 10-, and 12-inch guns, in which I have no faith whatever. The armament is not sufficiently powerful to prevent its interior being searched out by the long range fire of ships with rifle guns, or mortar boats; but it would require closer and harder work to breach the masses of brick and masonry which constitute the parapets and casemates. The guns, carriages, rammers, shot, were dirty, rusty, and neglected; but General Butler told me he was busy polishing up things about the fortress as fast as he could.

At the end of our promenade round the ramparts, Lieutenant [George] Butler, the General's nephew and aide-de-camp, came to tell us the boat was ready, and we met His Excellency in the courtyard, whence we walked down to the wharf. On our way, General Butler called my attention to an enormous heap of hollow iron lying on the sand, which was the Union gun that is intended to throw a shot of some 351 lbs. weight or more, to astonish the Confederates at Sewall's Point opposite, when it is mounted. This gun, if I mistake not, was made after the design of Captain [Thomas J.] Rodman of the United States artillery, who in a series of remarkable papers, the publication of which has cost the country a large sum of money, has given us the result of long continued investigation and experiments on the best method of cooling masses of iron for ordnance purposes and of making powder for heavy shot. The piece must weigh about 20 tons, but a similar gun, mounted on an artificial island, called the Rip Raps, in the Channel opposite the fortress, is said to be worked with facility. The Confederates have raised some of the vessels sunk by the United States officers when the navy yard at Gosport was destroyed, and as some of these are to be converted into rams, the Federal are preparing their heaviest ordnance to try the effect of crushing weights at low velocities against their sides, should they attempt to play any pranks among the transport vessels. The General said: "It is not by these great masses of iron this contest is to be decided; we must bring sharp points of steel, directed by superior intelligence." Hitherto General Butler's attempts at Big Bethel have not been crowned with success in employing such means, but it must be admitted that, according to his own statement, his lieutenants were guilty of carelessness and neglect of ordinary military precautions in the conduct of the expedition he ordered.

When the General, Commissioners, and staff had embarked, the steamer moved across the broad estuary to Newport News. On arriving at the low shore we landed at a wooden jetty and proceeded to visit the camp of the Federals. The day was excessively hot and many of the soldiers were laying down in the shade of arbours formed of branches from the neighbouring pine wood, but most of them got up when they heard the General was coming round. A sentry walked up and down at the end of the street, and as the General came up to him he called out "Halt." The man stood still. "I just want to show you, sir, what scoundrels our Government has to deal with. This man belongs to a regiment which has had new clothing recently served out to it. Look what it is made of." So saying the General stuck his forefinger into the breast of the man's coat and with a rapid scratch of his nail tore open the cloth as if it was of blotting paper. "Shoddy, sir. Nothing but shoddy. I wish I had these contractors in the trenches here, and if hard work would not make honest men of them, they'd have enough of it to be examples for the rest of their fellows." A vivacious prying man, this Butler, full of bustling life, self-esteem, revelling in the exercise of power.

There was nothing to complain of in the camp except the swarms of flies, the very bad smells, and perhaps the shabby clothing of the men. The tents were good enough. The rations were ample, but

nevertheless there was a want of order, discipline, and quiet in the
lines which did not augur well for the internal economy of the regiments.

From the fort the General proceeded to the house of one of the
officers near the jetty, formerly the residence of a Virginian farmer,
who had now gone to Secessia, where we were most hospitably
treated at an excellent lunch served by the slaves of the former
proprietor.

In the afternoon the boat returned to Fortress Monroe and the
General invited me to dinner, where I had the pleasure of meeting
Mrs. [Sarah] Butler, his staff, and a couple of regimental officers from
the neighbouring camp. As it was still early, General Butler proposed
a ride to visit the interesting village of Hampton, which lies some six
or seven miles outside the fort and forms his advance post. In the
precincts of the fort outside, a population of contraband Negroes has
been collected, whom the General employs in various works about
the place, military and civil. The General was proud of them, and
they seemed proud of themselves, saluting him with a ludicrous
mixture of awe and familiarity as he rode past. "How do, Massa
Butler? How do, General?" accompanied by absurd bows and
scrapes. "Just to think," said the General, "that every one of these
fellows represents some 1000 dollars at least out of the pockets of the
chivalry yonder." "Nasty, idle, dirty beasts," says one of the staff,
sotto voce [in an aside]; "I wish to Heaven they were all at the bottom
of the Chesapeake. The General insists on it that they do work, but
they are far more trouble than they are worth."

The principal object of our visit was the fortified trench which has
been raised outside the town towards the Confederate lines. Having
inspected the works, the General returned and we made a tour of the
camps of the force intended to defend Hampton. I was by no means
sorry when he pulled up outside the pretty villa, standing in a garden,
which was occupied by Colonel Max Weber, of the German Turner
Regiment. The Colonel insisted on our partaking of the hospitalities
of his little mess and produced some bottles of sparkling hock and
a block of ice, by no means unwelcome after our fatiguing ride. His
Major, whose name I have unfortunately forgotten and who spoke
English better than his chief, had served in some capacity or other in
the Crimea and made many inquiries after the officers of the Guards

whom he had known there. I took the opportunity of asking him in what state the troops were. "The whole thing is a robbery," he exclaimed; "this war is for the contractors; the men do not get a third of what the Government pay for them; as for discipline, my God! it exists not. We Germans are well enough, of course; we know our affair; but as for the Americans, what would you? They make colonels out of doctors and lawyers, and captains out of fellows who are not fit to brush a soldier's shoe." "But the men get their pay?" "Yes, that is so. At the end of two months, they get it, and by that time it is due to sutlers, who charge them 100 per cent."

It is easy to believe these old soldiers do not put much confidence in General Butler, though they admit his energy. "Look you; one good officer with 5000 steady troops, such as we have in Europe, shall come down any night and walk over us all into Fortress Monroe whenever he pleased, if he knew how these troops were placed."

The shades of evening were now falling, and as I had been up before 5 o'clock in the morning, I was not sorry when General Butler said, "Now we will go home to tea, or you will detain the steamer." At the tea-table there were no additions to the General's family; he therefore spoke without any reserve. Going over the map he explained his views in reference to future operations and showed cause, with more military acumen than I would have expected from a gentleman of the long robe, why he believed Fortress Monroe was the true base of operations against Richmond. I have been convinced for some time, that if a sufficient force could be left to cover Washington, the Federals should move against Richmond from the Peninsula, where they could form their depots at leisure and advance, protected by their gunboats, on a very short line which offers far greater facilities and advantage than the inland route from Alexandria to Richmond, which, difficult in itself from the nature of the country, is exposed to the action of a hostile population and, above all, to the danger of constant attacks by the enemies' cavalry, tending more or less to destroy all communication with the base of the Federal operations.

The threat of seizing Washington led to a concentration of the Union troops in front of it, which caused in turn the collection of the Confederates on the lines below to defend Richmond. It is plain that if the Federals can cover Washington, and at the same time assemble a force at Monroe strong enough to march on Richmond, as they desire, the Confederates will be placed in an exceedingly hazardous position, scarcely possible to escape from; and there is no reason why the North, with their overwhelming preponderance, should not do so, unless they be carried away by the fatal spirit of brag and bluster which comes from their press to overrate their own strength and to despise their enemy's.

At 10 o'clock the Quartermaster came to say that a screw steamer called the *Elizabeth* was getting up steam for my reception, and I bade good-by to the General, stepped on board the little vessel, and with the aid of the Negro cook, steward, butler, boots, and servant, roused out the captain from a small wooden trench which he claimed at his berth, turned into it, and fell asleep just as the first difficult convulsions of the screw aroused the steamer from her coma and forced her languidly against the tide in the direction of Baltimore.

July 15th.   I need not speak much of the events of last night, which were not unimportant, perhaps, to some of the insects which played a leading part in them. The heat was literally overpowering; for in addition to the hot night there was the full power of most irritable boilers close at hand to aggravate the natural *désagrément* [unpleasantness] of the situation. About an hour after dawn, when I turned out on deck, there was nothing visible but a warm grey mist; but a knotty old pilot on deck told me we were only going six knots an hour against tide and wind, and that we were likely to make less way as the day wore on. In fact, instead of being near Baltimore, we were much nearer Fortress Monroe. Need I repeat the horrors of this day? Stewed, boiled, baked, and grilled on board this miserable *Elizabeth!* The captain was a shy, silent man, much given to short naps in my temporary berth, and the mate was so wild, he might have swam off with perfect propriety to the woods on either side of us, and taken to a tree as an aborigen or chimpanzee. Two men of more retiring habits, the Negro, a black boy, and a very fat Negress who officiated as cook, filled up the "balance" of the crew.

I could not write, for the vibration of the deck of the little craft gave a St. Vitus dance to pen and pencil; reading was out of the question from the heat and flies; and below stairs the fat cook banished repose by vapours from her dreadful cauldrons, where, Medea-like, she was boiling some death broth. Our breakfast was of the simplest and—may I add?—the least enticing; and if the dinner could have been worse it was so; though it was rendered attractive by hunger and by the kindness of the sailors who shared it with me.

I decided very quickly that as Annapolis lay somewhere ahead on our left and was much nearer than Baltimore, it would be best to run for it while there was daylight. The captain demurred. He had been ordered to take his vessel to Baltimore, and General Butler might come down on him for not doing so; but I proposed to sign a letter stating he had gone to Annapolis at my request, and the steamer was put a point or two to westward. By-and-by the houses of a considerable town, crowned by steeples, and a large Corinthian-looking building, came in view. Annapolis looks very well from the river side. The approach is guarded by some very poor earthworks and one small fort. A dismantled sloop of war lay off the sea wall, banking up a green lawn covered with trees, in front of an old-fashioned pile of buildings, which formerly, I think, and very recently indeed, was occupied by the cadets of the United States Naval School.

About seven o'clock the steamer hove alongside a wooden pier which was quite deserted. Only some ten or twelve sailing boats, yachts, and schooners lay at anchor in the placid waters of the port which was once the capital of Maryland, and for which the early Republicans prophesied a great future. But Baltimore has eclipsed Annapolis into utter obscurity. I walked to the only hotel in the place and found that the train for the junction with Washington had started, and that the next train left at some impossible hour in the morning. It is an old Rip Van Winkle sort of place. Quaint-looking boarders came down to the tea table and talked secession, and when I was detected, as must very soon be the case, owing to the hotel book, I was treated to some ill-favoured glances, as my recent letters have been denounced in the strongest way for their supposed hostility to States' Rights and the Domestic Institution. The spirit of the people has, however, been broken by the Federal occupation, and by the decision with which Butler acted when he came down here with the troops to open communications with Washington after the Baltimoreans had attacked the soldiery on their way through the city from the north.

July 16th. I baffled many curious and civil citizens by breakfasting in my room, where I remained writing till late in the day. In the afternoon I walked to the Statehouse. The hall door was open, but the rooms were closed; and I remained in the hall, which is graced by two indifferent huge statues of Law and Justice holding gas lamps, and by an old rusty cannon dug out of the river, and supposed to have belonged to the original British colonists. After half hour I was warned by my watch that it was time to get ready for the train, which started at 4:15 P.M. At the junction with the Washington line from Baltimore there is a strong guard thrown out from the camp near at hand. The officers, who had a mess in a little wayside inn on the line, invited me to rest till the train came up, and from them I heard that an advance had been actually ordered, and that if the "rebels" stood there would soon be a tall fight close to Washington. They were very cheery, hospitable fellows, and enjoyed their new mode of life amazingly. The men of the regiment to which they belonged were Germans, almost to a man. When the train came in, I found it was full of soldiers, and I learned that three more heavy trains were to follow, in addition to four which had already passed laden with troops.

On arriving at the Washington platform, the first person I saw was General McDowell alone, looking anxiously into the carriages. He asked where I came from and when he heard from Annapolis, inquired eagerly if I had seen two batteries of artillery—Barry's and another—which he had ordered up and was waiting for, but which had "gone astray." I was surprised to find the General engaged in such duty, and took leave to say so. "Well, it is quite true, Mr. Russell; but I am obliged to look after them myself, as I have so small a staff, and they are all engaged out with my headquarters. You are aware I have advanced? No! Well, you have just come in time, and I shall be happy, indeed, to take you with me. I have made arrangements for the correspondents of our papers to take the field under certain regulations, and I have suggested to them they should wear a white uniform, to indicate the purity of their character." The General could hear nothing of his guns; his carriage was waiting, and I accepted his offer of a seat to my lodgings. Although he spoke confidently, he did not seem in good spirits. There was the greatest difficulty in finding out anything about the enemy. Beauregard was said to have advanced to Fairfax Court House, but he could not get any certain knowledge of the fact. "Can you not order a reconnaissance?" "Wait till you see the country. But even if it were as flat as Flanders, I have not an officer on whom I could depend for the work. They would fall into some trap, or bring on a great engagement when I did not seek it or desire it." I think he was not so much disposed to undervalue the Confederates as before, for he said they had selected a very strong position, and had made a regular *levée en masse* [rising up] of the people of Virginia, as a proof of the energy and determination with which they were entering on the campaign.

On arriving at my lodgings, I sent to the livery stables to inquire after horses. None fit for the saddle to be had at any price. The sutlers, the cavalry, the mounted officers, had been purchasing up all the droves of horses which came to the markets. McDowell had barely extra mounts for his own use. And yet horses must be had; and, even provided with them, I must take the field without tent or servant, canteen or food—a waif to fortune.

July 17th. I went up to General Scott's quarters and saw some of his staff—young men, some of whom knew nothing of soldiers, not even the enforcing of drill—and found them reflecting, doubtless, the shades which cross the mind of the old chief who was now seeking repose. McDowell is to advance tomorrow from Fairfax Court House, and will march some eight or ten miles to Centreville, directly in front of which at a place called Manassas, stands the army of the Southern enemy. I look around me for a staff and look in vain. There are a few plodding old pedants with map and rules and compasses who sit in small rooms and write memoranda; and there are some ignorant and not very active young men, who loiter about the headquarter halls, and strut up the street with brass spurs on their heels and kepis raked over their eyes as though they were soldiers, but I see no system, no order, no knowledge, no dash!

The worst-served English general has always a young fellow or two about him who can fly across country, draw a rough sketch map, ride like a foxhunter, and find something out about the enemy and their position, understand and convey orders, and obey them. I look about for the types of these in vain. McDowell can find out nothing about the enemy; he has not a trustworthy map of the country; no knowledge of their position, force, or numbers. All the people, he

says, are against the Government. Fairfax Court House was abandoned as he approached, the enemy in their retreat being followed
by the inhabitants. "Where were the Confederate entrenchments?"
"Only in the imagination of those New York newspapers; when they
want to fill up a column they write a full account of the enemy's
fortifications. No one can contradict them at the time, and it's a good
joke when it's found out to be a lie." Colonel Cullum went over the
maps with me at General Scott's and spoke with some greater confidence of McDowell's prospects of success. There is a considerable
force of Confederates at a place called Winchester, which is connected with Manassas by rail, and this force could be thrown on the
right of the Federals as they advanced, but that another corps, under
[Robert] Patterson, is in observation with orders to engage them if
they attempt to move eastwards.

The batteries for which General McDowell was looking last night
have arrived, and were sent on this morning. One is under Barry, of
the United States Regular Artillery, whom I met at Fort Pickens. The
other is a volunteer battery. The onward movement of the army has
been productive of a great improvement in the streets of Washington,
which are no longer crowded with turbulent and disorderly volunteers or by soldiers disgracing the name, who accost you in the
by-ways for money. There are comparatively few today; small
shoals, which have escaped the meshes of the net, are endeavouring
to make the most of their time before they cross the river to face the
enemy.

Still horse hunting, but in vain. Nothing to sell except at unheard-
of rates. I saw many officers driving over the Long Bridge with large
stores of provisions, either unable to procure horses or satisfied that
a wagon was the chariot of Mars. It is not fair to ridicule either
officers or men of this army, and if they were not so inflated by a
pestilent vanity, no one would dream of doing so; but the excessive
bragging and boasting in which the volunteers and the press indulge
really provoke criticism and tax patience and forbearance overmuch.
Even the regular officers talk proudly of the patriotism of the army,
and challenge the world to show such another, although in their
hearts, and more, with their lips, they own they do not depend on
them.

In the evening I received a message to say that the advance of the
army would take place tomorrow as soon as General McDowell had

satisfied himself by a reconnaissance that he could carry out his plan of turning the right of the enemy by passing Occaguan Creek. Along Pennsylvania Avenue, along the various shops, hotels, and drinking bars, groups of people were collected, listening to the most exaggerated accounts of desperate fighting and of the utter demoralisation of the rebels. I was rather amused by hearing the florid accounts which were given in the hall of Willard's by various inebriated officers, who were drawing upon their imagination for their facts, knowing, as I did, that the entrenchments at Fairfax had been abandoned without a shot on the advance of the Federal troops. The New York papers came in with glowing descriptions of the magnificent march of the grand army of the Potomac, which was stated to consist of upwards of 70,000 men; whereas I knew not half that number were actually on the field. Multitudes of people believe General Winfield Scott, who was now fast asleep in his modest bed in Pennsylvania Avenue, is about to take the field in person. The horse dealers are still utterly impracticable. A citizen who owned a dark bay, spavined and ringboned, asked me one thousand dollars for the right of possession. I ventured to suggest that it was not worth the money. "Well," said he, "take it or leave it. If you want to see this fight a thousand dollars is cheap. I guess there were chaps paid more than that to see Jenny Lind on her first night; and this battle is not going to be repeated, I can tell you. The price of horses will rise when the chaps out there have had themselves pretty well used up with bowie-knives and six-shooters."

July 18th.   After breakfast. Leaving headquarters, I went across to General Mansfield's and was going upstairs, when the General himself, a white-headed, grey-bearded, and rather soldierly-looking man, dashed out of his room in some excitement, and exclaimed, "Mr. Russell, I fear there is bad news from the front." "Are they fighting, General?" "Yes, sir. That fellow [Daniel] Tyler has been engaged, and we are whipped."[4] Again I went off to the horse dealer; but this time the price of the steed had been raised to £220; "for,"

[4]While moving his army toward Manassas, General McDowell sent Tyler on a reconnaissance toward Blackburn's Ford, where Tyler's men encountered Confederate troops commanded by James Longstreet and suffered losses of 19 killed, 38 wounded, and 26 missing in action.

says he, "I don't want my animals to be ripped up by them cannon and them musketry, and those who wish to be guilty of such cruelty must pay for it." At the War Office, at the Department of State, at the Senate, and at the White House, messengers and orderlies running in and out, military aides, and civilians with anxious faces betokened the activity and perturbation which reigned within. I met Senator Sumner radiant with joy. "We have obtained a great success; the rebels are falling back in all directions. General Scott says we ought to be in Richmond by Saturday night." Soon afterwards a United States officer, who had visited me in company with General Meigs, riding rapidly past, called out, "You have heard we are whipped; these confounded volunteers have run away." I drove to the Capitol, where people said one could actually see smoke of the cannon, but on arriving there it was evident that the fire from some burning houses and from wood cut down for cooking purposes had been mistaken for tokens of the fight.

It was strange to stand outside the walls of the Senate whilst legislators were debating inside respecting the best means of punishing the rebels and traitors, and to think that amidst the dim horizon of woods which bounded the west towards the plains of Manassas, the army of the United States was then contending, at least with doubtful fortune, against the forces of the desperate and hopeless outlaws whose fate these United States Senators pretended to hold in the hollow of their hands. Nor was it unworthy of note that many of the tradespeople along Pennsylvania Avenue, and the ladies whom one saw sauntering in the streets, were exchanging significant nods and smiles and rubbing their hands with satisfaction. I entered one shop where the proprietor and his wife ran forward to meet me. "Have you heard the news? Beauregard has knocked them into a cocked hat." "Believe me," said the good lady, "it is the finger of the Almighty is in it. Didn't he curse the niggers, and why should he take their part now with these Yankee abolitionists against true white men?" "But how do you know this?" said I. "Why, it's all true enough, depend upon it, no matter how we know it. We've got our underground railway as well as the abolitionists."

On my way to dinner at the legation I met the President crossing Pennsylvania Avenue, striding like a crane in the bulrush swamp along the great blocks of marble, dressed in an oddly cut suit of grey, with a felt hat on the back of his head, wiping his face with a red pocket handkerchief. He was evidently in a hurry, on his way to the White House, where I believe a telegraph has been established in communication with McDowell's headquarters.

The calm of the Legation contrasts wonderfully in troubled times with the excitement and storm of the world outside. There is no minister of the European Powers in Washington who watches with so much interest the march of events as Lord Lyons and who feels as much sympathy perhaps in the Federal Government as the constituted Executive of the country to which he is accredited; but in virtue of his position he knows little or nothing officially of what passes around him and may be regarded as a medium for the communication of dispatches to Mr. Seward, and for the discharge of a great deal of the most causeless and unmeaning vituperation from the conductors of the New York press against England.

On my return to [the] lodgings I received a note from the headquarters of the Federals, stating that the serious action between the two armies would probably be postponed for some days. McDowell's original idea was to avoid forcing the enemy's position directly in front, which was defended by movable batteries commanding the fords over a stream called "Bull's Run." He therefore proposed to make a demonstration on some point near the centre of their line, and at the same time throw the mass of his force below their extreme right so as to turn it and get possession of the Manassas Railway in their rear: a movement which would separate him, by-the-bye, from his own communications and enable any general worth his salt to make a magnificent counter by marching on Washington, only 27 miles away, which he could take with the greatest ease and leave the enemy in the rear to march 120 miles to Richmond, if they dared, or to make a hasty retreat upon the higher Potomac and to cross into the hostile country of Maryland.

McDowell, however, has found the country on his left densely wooded and difficult. It is as new to him as it was to Braddock when he cut his weary way through forest and swamp in this very district to reach, hundreds of miles away, the scene of his fatal repulse at Fort DeQuesne.[5] And so, having moved his whole army, McDowell finds

[5]In 1756, during the French and Indian War, General Edward Braddock marched an army through western Virginia and Pennsylvania in an attempt to drive the French out of their fort at the Forks of the Ohio.

himself obliged to form a new plan of attack, and, prudently fearful
of pushing his underdone and overpraised levies into a river in face
of an enemy, is endeavouring to ascertain with what chance of success he can attack and turn their left.

Whilst he was engaged in a reconnaissance today, General Tyler
did one of those things which must be expected from ambitious
officers without any fear of punishment, in countries where military
discipline is scarcely known. Ordered to reconnoitre the position of
the enemy on the left front, when the army moved from Fairfax to
Centreville this morning, General Tyler thrust forward some 3000 or
4000 men of his divisions down to the very banks of "Bull's Run,"
which was said to be thickly wooded, and there brought up his men
under a heavy fire of artillery and musketry, from which they retired
in confusion.

I went to Willard's, where the news of the battle, as it was called,
was eagerly discussed. One little man in front of the cigar stand
declared it was all an affair of cavalry. "But how could that be among
the piney woods and with a river in front, major?" "Our boys, sir,
left their horses, crossed the water at a run, and went right away
through them with their swords and six-shooters." "I tell you what
it is, Mr. Russell," said a man who followed me out of the crowd and
placed his hand on my shoulder, "they were whipped like curs, and
they ran like curs, and I know it." "How?" "Well, I'd rather be
excused telling you."

July 19th.   I rose early this morning in order to prepare for contin-
gencies. Yesterday was so hot that officers and men on the field
suffered from something like sunstroke. To unaccustomed frames
today the heat felt unsupportable. A troop of regular cavalry, riding
through the street at an early hour, were so exhausted, horse and
man, that a runaway cab could have bowled them over like nine pins.

For hours I went horse hunting; but Rothschild himself, even the
hunting Baron, could not have got a steed. In Pennsylvania Avenue
the people were standing in the shade under the ailanthus trees,
speculating on the news brought by dusty orderlies, or on the ideas
of passing Congressmen. A party of captured Confederates, on their
march to General Mansfield's quarters, created intense interest, and
I followed them to the house and went up to see the General, whilst

the prisoners sat down on the pavement and steps outside. From an expression he let fall, I inferred he did not very well know what to do with his prisoners. "Rebels taken in arms in Europe are generally hung or blown away from guns, I believe; but we are more merciful." General Mansfield evidently wished to be spared the embarrassment of dealing with prisoners.

After dinner I paid a visit to a family whose daughters—bright-eyed, pretty, and clever—were seated out on the doorsteps amid the lightning flashes, one of them, at least, dreaming with open eyes of a young artillery officer then sleeping among his guns, probably in front of Fairfax Court House.

July 20th.   The great battle which is to arrest rebellion, or to make it a power in the land, is no longer distant or doubtful. McDowell has completed his reconnaissance of the country in front of the enemy, and General Scott anticipates that he will be in possession of Manassas tomorrow night. All the statements of officers concur in describing the Confederates as strongly entrenched along the line of Bull's Run covering the railroad. In the main thoroughfares of the city there is still a scattered army of idle soldiers moving through the civil crowd, though how they come here no one knows. The officers clustering round the hotels and running in and out of the barrooms and eating-houses are still more numerous. When I inquired at the headquarters who these were, the answer was that the majority were skulkers, but that there was no power at such a moment to send them back to their regiments or punish them. In fact, deducting the reserves, the rear guards, and the scanty garrisons at the earthworks, McDowell will not have 25,000 men to undertake his seven days' march through a hostile country to the Confederate capital; and yet, strange to say, in the pride and passion of the politicians no doubt is permitted to rise for a moment respecting his complete success.

I was desirous of seeing what impression was produced upon the Congress of the United States by the crisis which was approaching and drove down to the Senate at noon. There was no appearance of popular enthusiasm, excitement, or emotion among the people in the passages. They drank their iced water, ate cakes or lozenges, chewed and chatted, or dashed at their acquaintances amongst the members, as though nothing more important than a railway bill or a postal

concession was being debated inside. I entered the Senate and found
the house engaged in not listening to Mr. [Milton S.] Latham, the
Senator from California, who was delivering an elaborate lecture on
the aspect of political affairs from a Republican point of view. The
Senators were, as usual, engaged in reading newspapers, writing letters, or in whispered conversation, whilst the Senator received his
applause from the people in the galleries, who were scarcely restrained from stamping their feet at the most highly flown passages.
Whilst I was listening to what is by courtesy called the debate, a
messenger from Centreville sent in a letter to me, stating that General
McDowell would advance early in the morning and expected to
engage the enemy before noon. At the same moment a Senator who
had received a dispatch left his seat and read it to a brother legislator,
and the news it contained was speedily diffused from one seat to
another, and groups formed on the edge of the floor eagerly discussing the welcome intelligence.

The President's hammer again and again called them to order; and
from out of this knot, Senator Sumner, his face lighted with pleasure,
came to tell me the good news. "McDowell has carried Bull's Run
without firing a shot. Seven regiments attacked it at the point of the
bayonet and the enemy immediately fled. General Scott only gives
McDowell till midday tomorrow to be in possession of Manassas."
Soon afterwards, Mr. Hay, the President's secretary, appeared on the
floor to communicate a message to the Senate. I asked him if the news
was true. "All I can tell you," said he, "is that the President has heard
nothing at all about it, and that General Scott, from whom we have
just received a communication, is equally ignorant of the reported
success."

Some Senators and many Congressmen have already gone to join
McDowell's army or to follow in its wake, in the hope of seeing the
Lord deliver the Philistines into his hands. Every carriage, gig, wagon,
and hack has been engaged by people going out to see the fight. The
price is enhanced by mysterious communications respecting the horrible slaughter in the skirmishes at Bull's Run. The French cooks and
hotel keepers, by some occult process of reasoning, have arrived at
the conclusion that they must treble the prices of their wines and of
the hampers of provisions which the Washington people are ordering
to comfort themselves at their bloody derby. "There was not less

than 18,000 men, sir, killed and destroyed. I don't care what General Scott says to the contrary, he was not there. I saw a reliable gentleman, ten minutes ago, as cum straight from the place, and he swore there was a string of wagons three miles long with the wounded. While these Yankees lie so, I should not be surprised to hear they said they did not lose 1000 men in that big fight the day before yesterday."

General [Joseph E.] Johnston, who has been for some days with a considerable force in an entrenched position at Winchester in the valley of the Shenandoah, had occupied General Scott's attention, in consequence of the facility which he possessed to move into Maryland by Harpers Ferry, or to fall on the Federals by the Manassas Gap Railway, which was available by a long march from the town he occupied. General Patterson, with a Federal corps of equal strength, had accordingly been dispatched to attack him, or at all events, to prevent his leaving Winchester without an action; but the news tonight is that Patterson, who was an officer of some reputation, has allowed Johnston to evacuate Winchester and has not pursued him, so that it is impossible to predict where the latter will appear.

Having failed utterly in my attempts to get a horse, I was obliged to negotiate with a livery stable keeper who had a hooded gig, or tilbury, left on his hands, to which he proposed to add a splinter-bar and pole so as to make it available for two horses, on condition that I paid him the assessed value of the vehicle and horses in case they were destroyed by the enemy. Of what particular value my executors might have regarded the guarantee in question, the worthy man did not inquire, nor did he stipulate for any value to be put on the driver; but it struck me that, if these were in any way seriously damaged, the occupants of the vehicle were not likely to escape. The driver, indeed, seemed by no means willing to undertake the job, and again and again it was proposed to me that I should drive, but I persistently refused.

On completing my bargain with the stable keeper, I went over to the Legation, and found Lord Lyons in the garden. I went to request that he would permit Mr. [Frederick] Warre, one of the *attachés,* to accompany me as he had expressed a desire to that effect. His Lordship hesitated at first but finally he consented on the distinct assurance that I was to be back the following night and would not, under any event, proceed onwards with General McDowell's army till after I had returned to Washington.

I returned to my lodgings and got to bed after midnight. My mind had been so much occupied with the coming event that I slept uneasily, and once or twice started up, fancying I was called. The moon shone in through the mosquito curtains of my bed, and just ere daybreak I was aroused by some noise in the adjoining room and looking out, in a half dreamy state, imagined I saw General McDowell standing at the table, on which a candle was burning low, so distinctly that I woke up with the words, "General, is that you?" Nor did I convince myself it was a dream till I had walked into the room.

July 21st.   Punctual to time, our carriage appeared at the door, with a spare horse, followed by the black quadruped on which the Negro boy sat with difficulty, in consequence of its high spirits and excessively hard mouth. I swallowed a cup of tea and a morsel of bread, put the remainder of the tea into a bottle, got a flask of light Bordeaux, a bottle of water, a paper of sandwiches, and having replenished my small flask with brandy, stowed them all away in the bottom of the gig; but my friend, who is not accustomed to rise very early in the morning, did not make his appearance, and I was obliged to send several times to the Legation to quicken his movements. When I had just resolved to leave him behind, he appeared in person, quite unprovided with *viaticum* [provisions], so that my slender store had now to meet the demands of two instead of one. We are off at last. The *amicus* [friend] and self find contracted space behind the driver. The Negro boy, grinning half with pain and "the balance" with pleasure, as the Americans say, held his rampant charger, which made continual efforts to leap into the gig, and thus through the deserted city we proceeded towards the Long Bridge, where a sentry examined our papers, and said with a grin, "You'll find plenty of Congressmen on before you." And then our driver whipped his horses through the embankment of Fort Runyon and dashed off along a country road, much cut up with gun and cart wheels, towards the main turnpike.

The promise of a lovely day, given by the early dawn, was likely to be realised to the fullest, and the placid beauty of the scenery as we drove through the woods below Arlington, and beheld the white buildings shining in the early sunlight, and the Potomac, like a broad silver riband dividing the picture, breathed of peace. The silence close to the city was unbroken. From the time we passed the guard beyond the Long Bridge, for several miles we did not meet a human being, except a few soldiers in the neighbourhood of the deserted camps, and when we passed beyond the range of tents we drove for nearly two hours through a densely wooded, undulating country; the houses, close to the roadside, shut up and deserted, window high in the crops of Indian corn, fast ripening for the sickle; alternate field and forest, the latter generally still holding possession of the hollows, and, except when the road, deep and filled with loose stones, passed over the summit of the ridges, the eye caught on either side little but fir trees and maize, and the deserted wooden houses, standing amidst the slave quarters.

As we got further into the country the traces of the debatable land between the two armies vanished, and Negroes looked out from their quarters, or sickly looking women and children were summoned forth by the rattle of the wheels to see who was hurrying to the war. Now and then a white man looked out, with an ugly scowl on his face, but the country seemed drained of the adult male population, and such of the inhabitants as we saw were neither as comfortably dressed nor as healthy looking as the shambling slaves who shuffled about the plantations. The road was so cut up by gun wheels, ammunition, and commissariat wagons, that our horses made but slow way against the continual draft upon the collar; but at last the driver, who had known the country in happier times, announced that we had entered the high road for Fairfax Court House. Unfortunately my watch had gone down, but I guessed it was then a little before nine o'clock. In a few minutes afterwards I thought I heard, through the eternal clatter and jingle of the old gig, a sound which made me call the driver to stop. He pulled up and we listened. In a minute or so, the well-known boom of a gun, followed by two or three in rapid succession, but at a considerable distance, reached my ear. "Did you hear that?" The driver heard nothing, nor did my companion, but the black boy on the lead horse, with eyes starting out of his head, cried, "I hear them, massa; I hear them, sure enough, like de gun in de navy yard"; and as he spoke the thudding noise, like taps with a gentle hand upon a muffled drum, were repeated, which were heard both by Mr. Warre and the driver. "They are at it! We shall be late! Drive

on as fast as you can!" We rattled on still faster, and presently came
up to a farm house, where a man and woman and some Negroes
beside them, were standing out by the hedge row above us, looking
up the road in the direction of a cloud of dust, which we could see
rising above the tops of the trees. We halted for a moment. "How
long have the guns been going, sir?" "Well, ever since early this
morning," said he; "they've been having a fight. And I do really
believe some of our poor Union chaps have had enough of it already.
For here's some of them darned secessionists marching down to go
into Alexandry." The driver did not seem altogether content with
this explanation of the dust in front of us and presently, when a turn
of the road brought to view a body of armed men, stretching to an
interminable distance, with bayonets glittering in the sunlight
through the clouds of dust, seemed inclined to halt or turn back
again. A nearer approach satisfied me they were friends, and as soon
as we came up with the head of the column I saw that they could not
be engaged in the performance of any military duty. The men were
marching without any resemblance or order, in twos and threes or
larger troops. Some without arms, carrying great bundles on their
backs; others with their coats hung from their firelocks; many foot
sore. They were all talking, and in haste; many plodding along laughing, so I concluded that they could not belong to a defeated army, and
imagined McDowell was effecting some flank movement. "Where are
you going to, may I ask?"

"If this is the road to Alexandria, we are going there."

"There is an action going on in front, is there not?"

"Well, so we believe, but we have not been fighting."

Although they were in such good spirits, they were not communi-
cative, and we resumed our journey, impeded by the straggling
troops and by the country cars containing their baggage and chairs,
and tables and domestic furniture, which had never belonged to
regiment in the field. Still they came pouring on. I ordered the driver
to stop at a rivulet, where a number of men were seated in the shade,
drinking the water and bathing their hands and feet. On getting out
I asked an officer, "May I beg to know, sir, where your regiment is
going to?" "Well, I reckon, sir, we are going home to Pennsylvania."
"This is the 4th Pennsylvania Regiment, is it not, sir?" "It is so, sir;
that's the fact." "I should think there is severe fighting going on

behind you, judging from the firing (for every moment the sound of the cannon had been growing more distinct and more heavy)?" "Well, I reckon, sir, there is." I paused for a moment, not knowing what to say, and yet anxious for an explanation; and the epauletted gentleman, after a few seconds' awkward hesitation, added, "We are going home because, as you see, the men's time's up, sir. We have had three months of this sort of work, and that's quite enough of it." The men who were listening to the conversation expressed their assent to the noble and patriotic utterances of the centurion, and, making him a low bow, we resumed our journey.

It must have been about eleven o'clock when we came to the first traces of the Confederate camp in front of Fairfax Court House, where they had cut a few trenches and levelled the trees across the road so as to form a rude abattis; but the works were of a most superficial character and would scarcely have given cover either to the guns, for which embrasures were left at the flanks to sweep the road or to the infantry intended to defend them.

The Confederate force stationed here must have consisted, to a considerable extent, of cavalry. The bowers of branches which they had made to shelter their tents, camp tables, empty boxes, and packing-cases, in the *débris* one usually sees around an encampment, showed they had not been destitute of creature comforts.

Some time before noon the driver, urged continually by adjurations to get on, whipped his horses into Fairfax Court House, a village which derives its name from a large brick building, in which the sessions of the county are held. Some thirty or forty houses, for the most part detached, with gardens or small strips of land about them, form a main street. The inhabitants who remained had by no means an agreeable expression of countenance and did not seem on very good terms with the Federal soldiers, who were lounging up and down the streets or standing in the shade of the trees and doorways. I asked the sergeant of the picket in the street how long the firing had been going on. He replied that it had commenced at half-past seven or eight and had been increasing ever since. "Some of them will lose their eyes and back teeth," he added, "before it is over." The driver, pulling up at a roadside inn in the town, here made the startling announcement that both he and his horses must have something to eat, and although we would have been happy to join him, seeing that we had no breakfast, we could not afford the time, and were not displeased when a thin-faced, shrewish woman in black came out into the verandah and said she could not let us have anything unless we liked to wait till the regular dinner hour of the house, which was at one o'clock. The horses got a bucket of water, which they needed in that broiling sun; and the cannonade, which by this time had increased into a respectable tumult that gave evidence of well-sustained action, added vigour to the driver's arm, and in a mile or two more we dashed into a village of burnt houses, the charred brick chimney stacks standing amidst the blackened embers being all that remained of what once was Germantown. The firing of this village was severely censured by General McDowell, who probably does not appreciate the value of such agencies employed "by our glorious Union army to develop loyal sentiments among the people of Virginia."

The driver, passing through the town, drove straight on, but after some time I fancied the sound of the guns seemed dying away towards our left. In an hour more we had gained the high road to Centreville, on which were many buggies, commissariat carts, and wagons full of civilians, and a brisk canter brought us in sight of a rising ground over which the road led directly through a few houses on each side and dipped out of sight, the slopes of the hill being covered with men, carts, and horses, and the summit crested with spectators with their backs turned towards us and gazing on the valley beyond. "There's Centreville," says the driver, and on our poor panting horses were forced, passing directly through the Confederate bivouacs, commissariat parks, folds of oxen, and two German regiments, with a battery of artillery, halting on the rising ground by the roadside. The heat was intense. Our driver complained of hunger and thirst, to which neither I nor my companion were insensible; and so pulling up on the top of the hill, I sent the boy down to the village which we had passed, to see if he could find shelter for the horses and a morsel for our breakfastless selves.

It was a strange scene before us. From the hill a densely wooded country, dotted at intervals with green fields and cleared lands, spread five or six miles in front, bounded by a line of blue and purple ridges, terminating abruptly in escarpments towards the left front, and swelling gradually towards the right into the lower spines of an offshoot from the Blue Ridge Mountains. On our left the view was circumscribed by a forest which clothed the side of the ridge on which we stood and covered its shoulder far down into the plain. A gap in the nearest chain of the hills in our front was pointed out by the bystanders as the Pass of Manassas, by which the railway from the west is carried into the plain, and still nearer at hand, before us, is the junction of that rail with the line from Alexandria, and with the railway leading southwards to Richmond. The intervening space was not a dead level; undulating lines of forest marked the course of the streams which intersected it, and gave, by their variety of colour and shading, an additional charm to the landscape which, enclosed in a framework of blue and purple hills, softened into violet in the extreme distance, presented one of the most agreeable displays of simple pastoral woodland scenery that could be conceived.

But the sounds which came upon the breeze, and the fights which met our eyes, were in terrible variance with the tranquil character of the landscape. The woods far and near echoed to the roar of cannon, and then frayed lines of blue smoke marked the spots whence came the muttering sound of rolling musketry; the white puffs of smoke burst high above the tree tops, and the gunners' rings from shell and howitzer marked the fire of the artillery.

Clouds of dust shifted and moved through the forest; and through the wavering mists of light blue smoke, and the thicker masses which rose commingling from the feet of men and the mouths of cannon, I could see the gleam of arms and the twinkling of bayonets.

On the hill beside me there was a crowd of civilians on horseback, and in all sorts of vehicles, with a few of the fairer, if not gentler sex. A few officers and some soldiers, who had struggled from the regiments in reserve, moved about among the spectators and pretended to explain the movements of the troops below, of which they were profoundly ignorant.

The cannonade and musketry had been exaggerated by the distance and by the rolling echoes of the hills; and sweeping the position narrowly with my glass from point to point, I failed to discover any traces of close encounter or very severe fighting. The spectators were all excited, and a lady with an opera glass who was near me was quite beside herself when an unusually heavy discharge roused the current of her blood—"That is splendid. Oh, my! Is not that first-rate? I guess we will be in Richmond this time tomorrow." These, mingled with coarser exclamations, burst from the politicians who had come out to see the triumph of the Union arms. I was particularly irritated by constant applications for the loan of my glass. One broken-down looking soldier observing my flask, asked me for a drink, and took a startling pull which left but little between the bottom and utter vacuity.

From the line of the smoke it appeared to me that the action was in an oblique line from our left, extending farther outwards towards the right, bisected by a road from Centreville, which descended the hill close at hand and ran right across the undulating plain, its course being marked by the white covers of the baggage and commissariat wagons as far as a turn of the road, where the trees closed in upon them. Beyond the right of the curling smoke clouds of dust appeared from time to time in the distance, as if bodies of cavalry were moving over a sandy plain.

Notwithstanding all the exultation and boastings of the people at Centreville, I was well convinced no advance of any importance or any great success had been achieved, because the ammunition and baggage wagons had never moved, nor had the reserves received any orders to follow in the line of the army.

The clouds of dust on the right were quite inexplicable. As we were looking, my philosophic companion asked me in perfect seriousness, "Are we really seeing a battle now? Are they supposed to be fighting where all that smoke is going on? This is rather interesting, you know."

An English gentleman, who came up flushed and heated from the plain, told us that the Federals had been advancing steadily in spite of a stubborn resistance and had behaved most gallantly.

Loud cheers suddenly burst from the spectators as a man dressed in the uniform of an officer, whom I had seen riding violently across the plain in an open space below, galloped along the front, waving his cap and shouting at the top of his voice. He was brought up by the press of people round his horse close to where I stood. "We've whipped them on all points," he cried. "We have taken all their batteries. They are retreating as fast as they can, and we are after them." Such cheers as rent the welkin! The Congressmen shook hands with each other, and cried out, "Bully for us. Bravo, didn't I tell you so." The Germans uttered their martial cheers and the Irish hurrahed wildly. At this moment my horse was brought up the hill, and I mounted and turned towards the road to the front, whilst Mr. Warre proceeded straight down the hill.

By the time I reached the lane, which was in a few minutes, the string of commissariat wagons was moving onward pretty briskly, and I was detained until my friends appeared at the roadside. I told Mr. Warre I was going forward to the front as fast as I could, but that I would come back under any circumstances about an hour before dusk and would go straight to the spot where we had put up the gig by the roadside, in order to return to Washington. Then getting into the fields, I pressed my horse, which was quite recovered from his twenty-seven mile's ride and full of spirit and mettle, as fast as I could, making detours here and there to get through the ox fences and by the small streams which cut up the country. The firing did not increase but rather diminished in volume, though it now sounded close at hand.

I had ridden between three and a half and four miles, as well as I could judge, when I was obliged to turn for the third and fourth time into the road by a considerable stream, which was spanned by a bridge, towards which I was threading my way, when my attention was attracted by loud shouts in advance, and I perceived several wagons coming from the direction of the battlefield, the drivers of which were endeavouring to force their horses past the ammunition carts going in the contrary direction near the bridge; a thick cloud of dust rose behind them, and running by the side of the wagons, were a number of men in uniform whom I supposed to be the guard. My first impression was that the wagons were returning for fresh supplies of ammunition. But every moment the crowd increased, drivers and men cried out with the most vehement gestures, "Turn back! Turn back! We are whipped." They seized the heads of the horses and swore at the opposing drivers. Emerging from the crowd a breathless man in the uniform of an officer with an empty scabbard dangling by his side, was cut off by getting between my horse and a cart for a moment. "What is the matter, sir? What is all this about?" "Why it means we are pretty badly whipped, that's the truth," he gasped, and continued.

By this time the confusion had been communicating itself through the line of wagons towards the rear, and the drivers endeavoured to turn round their vehicles in the narrow road, which caused the usual amount of imprecations from the men and plunging and kicking from the horses.

The crowd from the front continually increased, the heat, the uproar, and the dust were beyond description, and these were augmented when some cavalry soldiers, flourishing their sabres and preceded by an officer, who cried out, "Make way there—make way there for the General," attempted to force a covered wagon in which was seated a man with a bloody handkerchief round his head, through the press.

I had succeeded in getting across the bridge with great difficulty before the wagon came up, and I saw the crowd on the road was still gathering thicker and thicker. Again I asked an officer, who was on foot, with his sword under his arm, "What is all this for?" "We are whipped, sir. We are all in retreat. You are all to go back." "Can you tell me where I can find General McDowell?" "No! nor can any one else."

A few shells could be heard bursting not very far off but there was nothing to account for such an extraordinary scene. A third officer, however, confirmed the report that the whole army was in retreat, and that the Federals were beaten on all points, but there was nothing in this disorder to indicate a general rout. All these things took place in a few seconds. I got up out of the road into a cornfield, through which men were hastily walking or running, their faces streaming with perspiration, and generally without arms, and worked my way for about half a mile or so, as well as I could judge, against an increasing stream of fugitives, the ground being strewed with coats, blankets, firelocks, cooking tins, caps, belts, bayonets—asking in vain where General McDowell was.

Again I was compelled by the condition of the fields to come into the road; and having passed a piece of wood and a regiment which seemed to be moving back in column of march in tolerably good order, I turned once more into an opening close to a white house, not far from the lane, beyond which there was a belt of forest. Two fieldpieces unlimbered near the house, with panting horses in the rear, were pointed towards the front, and along the road beside them there swept a tolerably steady column of men mingled with field ambulances and light baggage carts, back to Centreville. I had just stretched out my hand to get a cigar light from a German gunner, when the dropping shots which had been sounding through the woods in front of us suddenly swelled into an animated fire. In a few seconds a crowd of men rushed out of the wood down towards the guns, and the artillerymen near me seized the trail of a piece and were wheeling it round to fire, when an officer or sergeant called out. "Stop! stop! They are our own men;" and in two or three minutes the whole battalion came sweeping past the guns at the double, and in the utmost disorder. Some of the artillerymen dragged the horses out of the tumbrils; and for a moment the confusion was so great I could not understand what had taken place; but a soldier whom I stopped, said, "We are pursued by their cavalry; they have cut us all to pieces."

It could not be doubted that something serious was taking place; and at that moment a shell burst in front of the house, scattering the soldiers near it, which was followed by another that bounded along the road; and in a few minutes more out came another regiment from the wood, almost as broken as the first. The scene on the road had now assumed an aspect which has not a parallel in any description I have ever read. Infantry soldiers on mules and draught horses, with the harness clinging to their heels, as much frightened as their riders; Negro servants on their masters' chargers; ambulances crowded with unwounded soldiers; wagons swarming with men who threw out the contents in the road to make room, grinding through a shouting, screaming mass of men on foot, who were literally yelling with rage at every halt, and shrieking out. "Here are the cavalry! Will you get on?" This portion of the force was evidently in discord.

There was nothing left for it but to go with the current one could not stem. I turned round my horse from the deserted guns and endeavoured to find out what had occurred as I rode quietly back on the skirts of the crowd. I talked with those on all sides of me. Some uttered prodigious nonsense, describing batteries tier over tier, and ambuscades, and blood running knee deep. Others described how their boys had carried whole lines of entrenchments but were beaten back for want of reinforcements. The names of many regiments were mentioned as being utterly destroyed. Cavalry and bayonet charges and masked batteries played prominent parts in all the narrations. Some of the officers seemed to feel the disgrace of defeat; but the strangest thing was the general indifference with which the event seemed to be regarded by those who collected their senses as soon as they got out of fire, and who said they were just going as far as Centreville, and would have a big fight tomorrow.

By this time I was unwillingly approaching Centreville in the midst of heat, dust, confusions, imprecations inconceivable. On arriving at the place where a small rivulet crossed the road, the throng increased still more. The ground over which I had passed going out was now covered with arms, clothing of all kinds, accoutrements thrown off and left to be trampled in the dust under the hoofs of men and horses. The runaways ran alongside the wagons, striving to force themselves in among the occupants, who resisted tooth and nail. The drivers spurred, and whipped, and urged the horses to the utmost of their bent. I felt an inclination to laugh, which was overcome by disgust, and by that vague sense of something extraordinary taking place which is experienced when a man sees a number of people acting as if driven by some unknown terror. As I rode in the crowd, with men clinging to the stirrup leathers, or holding on by anything they could lay hands on, so that I had some apprehension of being pulled off, I spoke to the men and asked them over and over again not to be in such a hurry. "There's no enemy to pursue you. All the cavalry in the world could not get at you." But I might as well have talked to the stones.

For my own part, I wanted to get out of the ruck as fast as I could, for the heat and dust were very distressing, particularly to a half-starved man. Many of the fugitives were in the last stages of exhaustion, and some actually sank down by the fences, at the risk of being trampled to death. Above the roar of the flight, which was like the rush of a great river, the guns burst forth from time to time.

It never occurred to me that this was a grand *débâcle*. All along I believed the mass of the army was not broken, and that all I saw around was the result of confusion created in a crude organisation by a forced retreat; and knowing the reserves were at Centreville and beyond, I said to myself, "Let us see how this will be when we get to the hill." Trotting along briskly through the fields, I arrived at the foot of the slope on which Centreville stands, and met a German regiment just deploying into line very well and steadily—the men in the rear companies laughing, smoking and singing, and jesting with the fugitives, who were filing past; but no thought of stopping the wagons, as the orders repeated from mouth to mouth were that they were to fall back beyond Centreville.

The air of the men was good. The officers cheerful, and one big German with a great pipe in his bearded mouth, with spectacles on nose, amused himself by pricking the horses with his sabre point, as he passed, to the sore discomfiture of the riders. Behind the regiment came a battery of brass fieldpieces, and another regiment in column of march was following the guns. They were going to form line at the end of the slope, and no fairer position could well be offered for a defensive attitude, although it might be turned. But it was getting too late for the enemy wherever they were to attempt such an extensive operation. Several times I had been asked by officers and men, "Where do you think we will halt? Where are the rest of the army?" I always replied "Centreville," and I had heard hundreds of the fugitives say they were going to Centreville.

I rode up the road, turned into the little street which carried the road on the right hand side to Fairfax Court House and the hill, and went straight to the place where I had left the buggy in a lane on the left of the road beside a small house and shed, expecting to find Mr. Warre ready for a start, as I had faithfully promised Lord Lyons he should be back that night in Washington. The buggy was not there. I pulled open the door of the shed in which the horses had been sheltered out of the sun. They were gone. "Oh," said I, to myself, "of course! What a stupid fellow I am. Warre has had the horses put in and taken the gig to the top of the hill, in order to see the last of it before we go." And so I rode over to the ridge, but arriving there could see no sign of our vehicle far or near. There were two carriages of some kind or other still remaining on the hill, and a few spectators, civilians and military, gazing on the scene below, which was softened in the golden rays of the declining sun. The smoke wreaths had ceased to curl over the green sheets of billowy forest as sea foam crisping in a gentle breeze breaks the lines of the ocean. But far and near yellow and dun-coloured piles of dust seamed the landscape, leaving behind them long trailing clouds of lighter vapours which were dotted now and then by white puff balls from the bursting of shell. On the right these clouds were very heavy and seemed to approach rapidly, and it occurred to me they might be caused by an advance of the much spoken of and little seen cavalry; and remembering the cross road from Germantown, it seemed a very fine and very feasible operation for the Confederates to cut right in on the line of retreat and communication, in which case the fate of the army and of Washington could not be dubious. There were now few civilians on the hill and these were thinning away. Some were gesticulating and explaining to one another the causes of the retreat, looking very hot and red. The confusion among the last portion of the carriages and fugitives on the road, which I had outstripped, had been renewed again, and the crowd there presented a remarkable and ludicrous aspect through the glass; but there were two strong battalions in good order near the foot of the hill, a battery on the slope, another on the top, and a portion of a regiment in and about the houses of the village.

A farewell look at the scene presented no new features. Still the clouds of dust moved onwards denser and higher; flashes of arms lighted them up at times; the fields were dotted by fugitives, among whom many mounted men were marked by their greater speed, and the little flocks of dust rising from the horses' feet.

I put up my glass, and turning from the hill, with difficulty forced my way through the crowd of vehicles which were making their way towards the main road in the direction of the lane, hoping that by some lucky accident I might find the gig in waiting for me. But I sought in vain; a sick soldier who was on a stretcher in front of the house near the corner of the land, leaning on his elbow and looking at the stream of men and carriages, asked me if I could tell him what they were in such a hurry for, and I said they were merely getting back to their bivouacs. A man dressed in civilian's clothes grinned as I spoke. "I think they'll go farther than that," said he; and then added, "If you're looking for the wagon you came in, it's pretty well back to Washington by this time. I think I saw you down there with a nigger and two men. Yes. They're all off, gone more than an hour and a-half ago, I think, and a stout man—I thought was you at first—along with them."

Nothing was left for it but to brace up the girths for a ride to the capital, for which, hungry and fagged as I was, I felt very little inclination. I was trotting quietly down the hill road beyond Centreville, when suddenly the guns on the other side, or from a battery very near, opened fire, and a fresh outburst of artillery sounded through the woods. In an instant the mass of vehicles and retreating soldiers, teamsters, and civilians, as if agonised by an electric shock, quivered throughout the tortuous line. With dreadful shouts and cursings, the drivers lashed their maddened horses, and, leaping from the carts, left them to their fate and ran on foot. Artillerymen and foot soldiers, and Negroes mounted on gun horses, with the chain traces and loose trappings trailing in the dust, spurred and flogged their steeds down the road or by the side paths. The firing continued and seemed to approach the hill, and at every report the agitated body of horsemen and wagons was seized, as it were, with a fresh convulsion.

Once more the dreaded cry, "The cavalry! cavalry are coming!" rang through the crowd, and looking back to Centreville I perceived coming down the hill, between me and the sky, a number of mounted men, who might at a hasty glance be taken for horsemen in the act of sabreing the fugitives. In reality they were soldiers and civilians with, I regret to say, some officers among them, who were whipping and striking their horses with sticks or whatever else they could lay hands on. I called out to the men who were frantic with terror beside me, "They are not cavalry at all; they're your own men"—but they did not heed me. A fellow who was shouting out, "Run! run!" as loud as he could beside me, seemed to take delight in creating alarm and as he was perfectly collected as far as I could judge, I said, "What on earth are you running for? What are you afraid of?" He was in the roadside below me, and at once turning on me, and exclaiming, "I'm not afraid of you," presented his piece and pulled the trigger so instantaneously, that had it gone off I could not have swerved from the ball. As the scoundrel deliberately drew up to examine the nipple, I judged it best not to give him another chance and spurred on through the crowd. The only conclusion I came to was that he was mad or drunken.

I galloped on for a short distance to head the ruck, for I could not tell whether this body of infantry intended moving back towards Centreville or were coming down the road; but the mounted men galloping furiously past me, with a cry of "Cavalry! cavalry!" on their lips, swept on faster than I did, augmenting the alarm and excitement. I came up with two officers who were riding more leisurely; and touching my hat, said, "I venture to suggest that these men should be stopped, sir. If not, they will alarm the whole of the post and pickets on to Washington. They will fly next and the consequences will be most disastrous." One of the two, looking at me for a moment, nodded his head without saying a word, spurred his horse to full speed, and dashed on in front along the road. Following more leisurely I observed the fugitives in front were suddenly checked in their speed; and as I turned my horse into the wood by the roadside to get on so as to prevent the chance of another blockup, I passed several private vehicles, in one of which Mr. Raymond of the *New York Times* was seated with some friends, looking by no means happy.

And I continued through the wood till I got a clear space in front on the road, along which a regiment of infantry was advancing towards me. They halted ere I came up, and with levelled firelocks arrested the men on horses and the carts and wagons galloping towards them, and blocked up the road to stop their progress. As I tried to edge by on the right of the column by the left of the road, a soldier presented his firelock at my head from the higher ground on which he stood, for the road had a deep trench cut on the side by which I was endeavouring to pass, and sung out, "Halt! Stop—or I fire!" The officers in front were waving their swords and shouting out, "Don't let a soul pass! Keep back! keep back!" Bowing to the officer who was near me, I said, "I beg to assure you, sir, I am not running away. I am a civilian and a British subject. I have done my best as I came along to stop this disgraceful rout. I am in no hurry; I merely want to get back to Washington tonight. I have been telling them all along there was no cavalry near us." The officer to whom I was speaking, young and somewhat excited kept repeating, "Keep back, sir! keep back! you must keep back." Again I said to him, "I assure you I am not with this crowd; my pulse is as cool as your own." But as he paid no attention to what I said, I suddenly bethought me of General Scott's letter, and addressing another officer, said, "I am a civilian going to Washington; will you be kind enough to look at this pass, specially given to me by General Scott." The officer looked at it and handed it to a mounted man, either adjutant or colonel, who, having examined it, returned it to me, saying, "Oh, yes! certainly. Pass that man!" And with a cry of "Pass that man!" along the line, I rode down the trench very leisurely and got out on the road, which was now clear, though some fugitives had stolen through the woods on the flanks of the column and were in front of me.

Arrived at the little inn where I had halted in the morning, I perceived the sharp-faced woman in black standing in the verandah with an elderly man, a taller and younger one dressed in black, a little girl, and a woman who stood in the passage of the door. I asked if I could get anything to eat. "Not a morsel; there's not a bit left in the house, but you can get something perhaps, if you like to stay till supper time."

Having received full directions from the people at the inn for the road to the Long Bridge, which I was most anxious to reach instead of going to Alexandria or to Gerogetown, I excused myself by saying I must press on to Washington, and galloped on for a mile, until I got into the cover of a wood, where I dismounted to examine the horse's hoofs and shift the saddle for a moment, wipe the sweat off his back, and make him and myself as comfortable as could be for our ride into Washington, which was still seventeen or eighteen miles before me.

The sun had set, but the rising moon was adding every moment to the lightness of the road as I mounted once more and set out at a long trot for the capital. The houses by the roadside were all closed up and in darkness, I knocked in vain at several for a drink of water, but was answered only by the angry barkings of the watch dogs from the slave quarters. It was a peculiarity of the road that the people, and soldiers I met, at points several miles apart, always insisted that I was twelve miles from Washington.

All by the sides of the old camps the men were standing, lining the road, and I was obliged to evade many a grasp at my bridle by shouting out, "Don't stop me; I've important news, it's all well!" and still the good horse, refreshed by the cool night air, went clattering on, till from the top of the road beyond Arlington I caught a sight of the lights of Washington and the white buildings of the Capitol, and of the Executive Mansion, glittering like snow in the moonlight. At the entrance to the Long Bridge the sentry challenged, and asked for the countersign. "I have not got it, but I've a pass from General Scott." An officer advanced from the guard, and on reading the pass permitted me to go on without difficulty. He said, "I have been obliged to let a good many go over tonight before you, Congressmen and others. I suppose you did not expect to be coming back so soon.

I fear it's a bad business." "Oh, not so bad after all; I expected to have been back tonight before nine o'clock, and crossed over this morning without the countersign." "Well, I guess," said he, "we don't do such quick fighting as that in this country."

As I crossed the Long Bridge there was scarce a sound to dispute the possession of its echoes with my horse's hoofs. The poor beast had carried me nobly and well, and I made up my mind to buy him, as I had no doubt he would answer perfectly to carry me back in a day or two to McDowell's army by the time he has organised for a new attack upon the enemy's position. Little did I conceive the greatness of the defeat, the magnitude of the disasters which it has entailed upon the United States. Had I sat down that night to write my letter, quite ignorant at the time of the great calamity which had befallen his army, in all probability I would have stated that McDowell had received a severe repulse, and had fallen back upon Centreville, that a disgraceful panic and confusion had attended the retreat of a portion of his army, but that the appearance of the reserves would probably prevent the enemy taking any advantage of the disorder. I should have led the world at home to believe, as, in fact, I believed myself, that McDowell's retrograde movement would be arrested at some point between Centreville and Fairfax Court House.

The letter that I was to write occupied my mind whilst I was crossing the Long Bridge, gazing at the lights reflected in the Potomac from the city. The night had become overcast, and heavy clouds rising up rapidly obscured the moon, forming a most phantastic mass of shapes in the sky.

At the Washington end of the bridge I was challenged again by the men of a whole regiment, who, with piled arms, were halted on the *chaussée* [road], smoking, laughing, and singing. "Stranger, have you been to the fight?" "I have been only a little beyond Centreville." But that was quite enough. Soldiers, civilians, and women, who seemed to be out unusually late, crowded round the horse, and again I told my stereotyped story of the unsuccessful attempt to carry the Confederate position, and the retreat to Centreville to await better luck next time.

As I passed Willard's Hotel a little further on, a clock—I think the only public clock which strikes the hours in Washington—tolled out the hour, and I supposed, from what the sentry told me, though I did not count the strikes, that it was eleven o'clock. All the rooms in the hotel were a blaze of light. The pavement before the door was crowded and some mounted men and the clattering of sabres on the pavement led me to infer that the escort of the wounded officer had arrived before me. I passed on to the livery stables, where every one was alive and stirring.

I walked to my lodgings and just as I turned the key in the door a flash of light made me pause for a moment, in expectation of the report of a gun; for I could not help thinking it quite possible that, somehow or another, the Confederate cavalry would try to beat up the lines, but no sound followed. It must have been lightning. I walked upstairs and saw a most welcome supper ready on the table. I would not have exchanged that repast and have waited half an hour for any banquet. Then, having pulled off my boots, bathed my head, trimmed candles, and lighted a pipe, I sat down to write, [but] my eyes closed, and my pen slipped, and with my head on the blotted paper, I fell fast asleep.

July 22nd. I awoke from a deep sleep this morning, about six o'clock. The rain was falling in torrents and beat with a dull, thudding sound on the [ledge] outside my window; but louder than all, came a strange sound, as if of the thread of men, a confused tramp and splashing, and a murmuring of voices. I got up and ran to the front room, the windows of which looked on the street and there, to my intense surprise, I saw a steady stream of men covered with mud, soaked through with rain, who were pouring irregularly, without any semblance of order up Pennsylvania Avenue towards the Capitol. A dense stream of vapour rose from the multitude; but looking closely at the men, I perceived they belonged to different regiments, New Yorkers, Michiganders, Rhode Islanders, Massachusetters, Minnesotans, mingled pellmell together. Many of them were without knapsacks, crossbelts, and firelocks. Some had neither greatcoats nor shoes, others were covered with blankets. Hastily putting on my clothes, I ran down stairs and asked an "officer" who was passing by, a pale young man who looked exhausted to death and who had lost his sword for the empty sheath dangled at his side, where the men were coming from. "Where from? Well, sir, I guess we're all coming out of Verginny as far as we can, and pretty well whipped too."

"What! the whole army, sir?" "That's more than I know. I know I'm going home. I've had enough of fighting to last my lifetime."

The news seemed incredible. But there before my eyes were the jaded, dispirited, broken remnants of regiments passing onwards, where and for what I knew not, and it was evident enough that the mass of the grand army of the Potomac was placing that river between it and the enemy as rapidly as possible.

Whilst the rain fell, the tramp of feet went steadily on. As I lifted my eyes now and then from the paper, I saw the beaten, footsore, spongy-looking soldiers, officers, and all the debris of the army filing through mud and rain, and forming in crowds in front of the spirit stores. Underneath my room is the magazine of Jost, *négociant en vins* [wine merchant], and he drives a roaring trade this morning, interrupted occasionally by loud disputes as to the score. When the lad came in with my breakfast he seemed a degree or two lighter in colour than usual. "What's the matter with you?" "I 'spects, massa, the seceshers soon be in here. I'm a free nigger; I must go, sar, afore de come cotch me."

The rain has abated a little, and the pavements are densely packed with men in uniform, some with, others without arms, on whom the shopkeepers are looking with evident alarm. They seem to be in possession of all the spirit houses. Now and then shots are heard down the street or in the distance, and cries and shouting, as if a scuffle or a difficulty were occurring. Willard's is turned into a barrack for officers, and presents such a scene in the hall as could only be witnessed in a city occupied by a demoralised army. There is no provost guard, no patrol, no authority visible in the streets. General Scott is quite overwhelmed by the affair and is unable to stir. General McDowell has not yet arrived. The Secretary of War knows not what to do, Mr. Lincoln is equally helpless, and Mr. Seward, who retains some calmness, is, notwithstanding his military rank and militia experience, without resource or expedient. There are a good many troops hanging on about the camps and forts on the other side of the river, it is said; but they are thoroughly disorganised and will run away if the enemy comes in sight without a shot, and then the capital must fall at once. Why Beauregard does not come I know not nor can I well guess. I have been expecting every hour since noon to hear his cannon.

Towards dark the rain moderated and the noise in the streets waxed louder; all kinds of rumours respecting the advance of the enemy, the annihilation of Federal regiments, the tremendous losses on both sides, charges of cavalry, stormings of great entrenchments and stupendous masked batteries, and elaborate reports of unparalleled feats of personal valour, were circulated under the genial influence of excitement, and by the quantities of alcohol necessary to keep out the influence of the external moisture. I did not hear one expression of confidence or see one cheerful face in all that vast crowd which but a few days before constituted an army, and was nothing better than a semi-armed mob. I could see no cannon returning, and to my inquiries after them, I got generally the answer, "I suppose the seceshers have got hold of them."

Whilst I was at table, several gentlemen who have *entrée* called on me, who confirmed my impressions respecting the magnitude of the disaster that is so rapidly developing its proportions. They agree in describing the army as disorganised. Washington is rendered almost untenable in consequence of the conduct of the army, which was not only to have defended it but to have captured the rival capital. Some of my visitors declared it was dangerous to move abroad in the streets. Many think the contest is now over; but the gentlemen of Washington have Southern sympathies, and I, on the contrary, am persuaded this prick in the great Northern balloon will let out a quantity of poisonous gas, and rouse the people to a sense of the nature of the conflict on which they have entered. The inmates of the White House are in a state of the utmost trepidation, and Mr. Lincoln, who sat in the telegraph operator's room with General Scott and Mr. Seward listening to the dispatches as they arrived from the scene of action, left it in despair when the fatal words tripped from the needle and the defeat was clearly revealed to him.

Once, indeed, if not twice, my attention was aroused by sounds like distant cannon and the outburst of musketry, but on reflection I was satisfied the Confederate general would never be rash enough to attack the place by night, and that after all the rain which had fallen, he in all probability would give horses and men a day's rest, marching them through the night, so as to appear before the city in the course of tomorrow.

July 23rd. The morning was far advanced when I awoke, and hearing the roll of wagons in the street, I at first imagined the Federals were actually about to abandon Washington itself; but on going to the window I perceived it arose from an irregular train of commissariat carts, country wagons, ambulances, and sutlers' vans in the centre of the street, the paths being crowded as before with soldiers, or rather with men in uniform, many of whom seemed as if they had been rolling in the mud. Poor General Mansfield was running back and forwards between his quarters and the War Department, and in the afternoon some efforts were made to restore order, by appointing rendezvous to which the fragments of regiments should repair, and by organising mounted patrols to clear the streets. In the middle of the day I went out through the streets and walked down to the Long Bridge with the intention of crossing, but it was literally blocked up from end to end with a mass of wagons and ambulances full of wounded men, whose cries of pain echoed above the shouts of the drivers, so that I abandoned the attempt to get across, which, indeed would not have been easy with any comfort, owing to the depth of mud in the roads. Today the aspect of Washington is more unseemly and disgraceful, if that were possible, than yesterday afternoon.

As I returned toward my lodgings a scene of greater disorder and violence than usual attracted my attention. A body of Confederate prisoners, marching two and two, were with difficulty saved by their guard from the murderous assaults of a hooting rabble, composed of civilians and men dressed like soldiers, who hurled all kinds of missiles they could lay their hands upon over the heads of the guard at their victims, spattering them with mud and filthy language. It was very gratifying to see the way in which the dastardly mob dispersed at the appearance of a squad of mounted men, who charged them boldly, and escorted the prisoners to General Mansfield.

Soon afterwards a report flew about that a crowd of soldiers were hanging a secessionist. A Senator rushed to General McDowell, and told him that he had seen the man swinging with his own eyes. Off went the General, *ventre à terre* [at full speed], and was considerably relieved by finding that they were hanging merely a dummy or effigy of Jeff. Davis, not having succeeded in getting the original yesterday.

Poor McDowell has been swiftly punished for his defeat, or rather for the unhappy termination to his advance. As soon as the disaster

The Long Bridge, Washington *(From* Battles and Leaders of the Civil War *(New York: The Century Co., 1887), Vol. 1, p. 167. Courtesy of the New York Public Library)*

was ascertained beyond doubt, the President telegraphed to General McClellan to come and take command of his army. It is a commentary full of instruction on the military system of the Americans that they have not a soldier who has ever handled a brigade in the field fit for the service in the North.

The new commander-in-chief is a brevet-major who has been in civil employ on a railway for several years. He went once, with two other West Point officers commissioned by Mr. Jefferson Davis, then Secretary of War, to examine and report on the operations in the Crimea, and I used to see him and his companions poking about the ruins of the deserted trenches and batteries, mounted on horses furnished by the courtesy of British officers, just as they lived in English quarters when they were snubbed and refused an audience by the Duke of Malakhoff in the French camp. Major McClellan forgot the affront, did not even mention it, and showed his Christian spirit by praising the allies and damning John Bull with very faint applause,

seasoned with lofty censure. He was very young, however, at the
time, and is so well spoken of that his appointment will be popular;
but all that he has done to gain such reputation and to earn the
confidence of the government is to have had some skirmishes with
bands of Confederates in western Virginia, in which the leader, Garnett, was killed, his "forces" routed, and finally, to the number of a
thousand, obliged to surrender as prisoners of war. That success,
however, at such a time is quite enough to elevate any man to the
highest command. McClellan is about thirty-six years of age, was
educated at West Point, where he was junior to McDowell, and a
class fellow of Beauregard.

I dined with Mr. [Henri] Mercier, the French Minister. Ever since
I first met M. Mercier he has expressed his conviction that the North
never can succeed in conquering the South, or even restoring the
Union, and that an attempt to do either by armed force must end in
disaster. He is the more confirmed in his opinions by the result of
Sunday's battle, but the inactivity of the Confederates give rise to the
belief that they suffered seriously in the affair.

It had been rumoured that the Confederates were advancing, and
the President and the Foreign Minister set out in a carriage to see with
their own eyes the state of the troops. What they beheld filled them
with despair. The plateau was covered with the men of different
regiments, driven by the patrols out of the city, or arrested in their
flight at the bridges. In Fort Corcoran the men were in utter disorder,
threatening to murder the officer of regulars who was essaying to get
them into some state of efficiency to meet the advancing enemy. He
had menaced one of the officers of the 69th with death for flat
disobedience to orders; the men had taken the part of their captain;
and the President drove into the work just in time to witness the
confusion. The soldiers with loud cries demanded that the officer
should be punished, and the President asked him why he had used
such violent language towards his subordinate. "I told him, Mr. President, that if he refused to obey my orders I would shoot him on the
spot; and I here repeat it, sir, that if I remain in command here, and
he or any other man refuses to obey my orders, I'll shoot him on the
spot."

The firmness of Sherman's language and demeanour in presence of the Chief of State overawed the mutineers, and they proceeded to put the work in some kind of order to resist the enemy.[6]

Mr. Seward was deeply impressed by the scene, and retired with the President to consult as to the best course to pursue, in some dejection, but they were rather comforted by the telegrams from all parts of the North, which proved that though disappointed and surprised, the people were not disheartened or ready to relinquish the contest.

July 24th. I rode out before breakfast across the Long Bridge over to Arlington House. General McDowell was seated at a table under a tree in front of his tent and got out his plans and maps to explain the scheme of battle.

Cast down from his high estate, placed as a subordinate on his junior, covered with obloquy and abuse, the American General displayed a calm self-possession and perfect amiability which could only proceed from a philosophic temperament and a consciousness that he would outlive the calumnies of his countrymen. He accused nobody; but it was not difficult to perceive he had been sacrificed to the vanity, self-seeking, and disobedience of some of his officers, and to radical vices in the composition of his army.

When McDowell found he could not turn the enemy's right as he intended, because the country by the Occoquan [River] was unfit for the movements of artillery or even infantry, he reconnoitered the ground towards their left and formed the project of turning it by a movement which would bring the weight of his columns on their extreme left, and at the same time overlap it, whilst a strong demonstration was made on the ford at Bull's Run, where General Tyler brought on the serious skirmish of the 18th. In order to carry out his plan, he had to debouch his columns from a narrow point at Centreville, and march them round by various roads to points on the upper part of the Run, where it was fordable in all directions, intending to turn the enemy's batteries on the lower roads and bridges. But al-

[6]This is apparently a second-hand account; Russell heard of William T. Sherman's ability as a commander and recorded the incident. At the time of this statement, Sherman commanded the 3d Brigade, First Division of McDowell's army. Russell did not meet Sherman until August 26, 1861, a fact he notes in that day's entry.

though he started them at an early hour, the troops moved so slowly
the Confederates became aware of their design and were enabled to
concentrate considerable masses of troops on their left.

The Federals were not only slow, but disorderly. The regiments in
advance stopped at streams to drink and fill their canteens, delaying
the regiments in the rear. They wasted their provisions so that many
of them were without food at noon, when they were exhausted by
the heat of the sun and by the stifling vapours of their own dense
columns. When they at last came into action some divisions were not
in their places, so that the line of battle was broken; and those which
were in their proper position were exposed, without support, to the
enemy's fire. A delusion of masked batteries pressed on their brain.
To this was soon added a hallucination about cavalry, which might
have been cured had the Federals possessed a few steady squadrons
to manoeuvre on their flanks and in the intervals of their line. Nevertheless, they advanced and encountered the enemy's fire with some
spirit; but the Confederates were enabled to move up fresh battalions
and to a certain extent to establish an equality between the numbers
of their own troops and the assailants, whilst they had the advantage
of better cover and ground. An apparition of a disorderly crowd of
horsemen in front of the much-boasting Fire Zouaves of New York
threw them into confusion and flight, and a battery which they ought
to have protected was taken. Another battery was captured by the
mistake of an officer who allowed a Confederate regiment to approach the guns, thinking they were Federal troops, till their first
volley destroyed both horses and gunners. At the critical moment,
General Johnston, who had escaped from the feeble observation and
untenacious grip of General Patterson and his time-expired volunteers, and had been hurrying down his troops from Winchester by
train, threw his fresh battalions on the flank and rear of the Federal
right.[7] When the General ordered a retreat, rendered necessary by the
failure of the attack—disorder spread, which increased—the retreat

[7]Russell is reporting the Union version for its defeat: the timely arrival of Johnston's
troops from the Shenandoah Valley. Actually Johnston and most of his army had
arrived at Bull Run the day before the battle, on July 20. Credit instead should be given
to "Stonewall" Jackson and Kirby Smith, who encouraged Confederate soldiers to
stand firm during the early hours of fighting when a Union victory seemed possible.

became a flight which degenerated—if a flight can degenerate—into a panic, the moment the Confederates pressed them with a few cavalry and horse artillery. The efforts of the generals to restore order and confidence were futile. Fortunately a weak reserve was posted at Centreville, and these were formed in line on the slope of the hill, whilst McDowell and his officers exerted themselves with indifferent success to arrest the mass of the army and make them draw up behind the reserve, telling the men a bold front was their sole chance of safety. At midnight it became evident the *morale* of the army was destroyed and nothing was left but a speedy retrograde movement, with the few regiments and guns which were in a condition approaching to efficiency, upon the defensive works of Washington.

Notwithstanding the reverse of fortune, McDowell did not appear willing to admit his estimate of the Southern troops was erroneous, or to say, "Change armies, and I'll fight the battle over again." He still held Mississippians, Alabamians, Louisianians, very cheap, and did not see or would not confess, the full extent of the calamity which had fallen so heavily on him personally. The fact of the evening's inactivity was conclusive in his mind that they had a dearly bought success, and he looked forward, though in a subordinate capacity, to a speedy and glorious revenge.

July 25th. The unfortunate General Patterson, who could not keep Johnston from getting away from Winchester, is to be dismissed the service—honourably, of course—that is, he is to be punished because his men would insist on going home in face of the enemy as soon as their three months were up, and that time happened to arrive just as it would be desirable to operate against the Confederates. The latter have lost their chance. The Senate, the House of Representatives, the Cabinet, the President, are all at their ease once more and feel secure in Washington. Up to this moment the Confederates could have taken it with very little trouble. Maryland could have been roused to arms, and Baltimore would have declared for them. The triumph of the non-aggressionists, at the head of whom is Mr. Davis, in resisting the demands of the party which urges an actual invasion of the North as the best way of obtaining peace, may prove to be very disastrous.

July 26th. General Meigs and I had a long conversation with General McDowell, who bears his supercession with admirable fortitude and complains of nothing, except of the failure of his officers to obey orders, and the hard fate which condemned him to lead an army of volunteers. The communications received from the Northern States have restored the spirits of all Union men, and not a few declare they are glad of the reverse as the North will now be obliged to put forth all its strength.

Seven

AFTERMATH

(JULY 27, 1861–APRIL 9, 1862)

July 27th.   So ill today from heat, bad smells in the house, and fatigue, that I sent for a great, fine Virginian practitioner, who ordered me powders to be taken in "mint juleps." Now mint juleps are made of whiskey, sugar, ice, very little water, and sprigs of fresh mint, to be sucked up after the manner of sherry cobblers, if so it be pleased, with a straw.

"A powder every two hours, with a mint julep. Why, that's six a day, Doctor. Won't that be—eh?—won't that be rather intoxicating?"

"Well, sir, that depends on the constitution. You'll find they will do you no harm, even if the worst takes place."

Day after day, till the month was over and August had come, I passed in a state of powder and julep, which the Virginian doctor declared saved my life. The first time I stirred out the change which had taken place in the streets was at once apparent; no drunken rabblement of armed men, no begging soldiers—instead of these were patrols in the streets, guards at the corners, and a rigid system of passes. The North begin to perceive their magnificent armies are mythical, but knowing they have the elements of making one, they are setting about the manufacture. Numbers of tapsters and serving men, and *canaille* [rabble] from the cities, who now disgrace swords and shoulder straps, are to be dismissed. Round the corner, with a kind of staff at his heels and an escort, comes Major General George B. McClellan, the young Napoleon (of western Virginia), the conqueror of Garnett, the captor of Pegram,[1] the commander-in-chief, under the President, of the army of the United States. He is a very squarely built, thick-throated, broad-chested man, under the middle height, with slightly bowed legs, a tendency to *embonpoint* [stoutness]. His head, covered with a closely cut crop of dark auburn hair, is well set on his shoulders. His features are regular and prepossessing—the brow small, contracted, and furrowed; the eyes deep and anxious looking. A short, thick, reddish moustache conceals his mouth; the rest of his face is clean shaven. He has made his father-in-law, Major [Randolph] Marcy, chief of his staff, and is a good deal influenced by his opinions, which are entitled to some weight, as Major Marcy is a soldier and has seen frontier wars, and is a great traveller. The task of licking this army into shape is of Herculean magnitude. Every one, however, is willing to do as he bids: the President confides in him, and "Georges" him; the press fawn upon him, the people trust him; he is "the little corporal" of unfought fields—*omnis ignotus pro mirifico* [a hero before the fact]—here. He looks like a stout little captain of dragoons, but for his American seat and saddle. The latter is adapted to a man who cannot ride: if a squadron so mounted were to attempt to fence or ditch, half of them would be ruptured or spilled. The seat is a marvel to any European. But McClellan is nevertheless "the man on horseback" just now, and the Americans must ride in his saddle or in anything he likes.[2]

In the evening of my first day's release from juleps the President held a reception or levée, and I went to the White House about nine o'clock, when the rooms were at their fullest. The company were

---

[1]On July 10, 1861, McClellan defeated Confederate Colonel John Pegram at Rich Mountain in western Virginia.

[2]The American saddle differed from its English counterpart in that the seat was deeper and the cantle raised higher. Further, the back jockey and skirt were more exposed and the stirrup straps sported a leather flap.

General George B.
McClellan *(Library of
Congress)*

arriving on foot, or crammed in hackney coaches, and did not affect
any neatness of attire or evening dress. The doors were open; anyone
could walk in who chose. Private soldiers, in hodden grey and hob-
nailed shoes, stood timorously chewing on the threshold of the state
apartment, alarmed at the lights and gilding, or haply, by the mar-
about feathers and flurry of a few ladies who were in ball costume,
till, assured by fellow citizens there was nothing to fear, they plunged
into the dreadful revelry.

The President, in a suit of black, stood near the door of one of the
rooms near the hall and shook hands with every one of the crowd,
who was then "passed" on by his secretary if the President didn't
wish to speak to him. Mr. Lincoln has recovered his spirits and
seemed in good humour. Mrs. Lincoln, who did the honours in another room surrounded by a few ladies, did not appear to be quite
so contented. All the ministers are present except Mr. Seward, who
has gone to his own state [New York] to ascertain the frame of mind
of the people and to judge for himself of the sentiments they entertain respecting the war. After walking up and down the hot and
crowded rooms for an hour and seeing and speaking to all the celebri-
ties, I withdrew. Colonel [Israel] Richardson in his official report
states Colonel [Dixon] Miles lost the battle of Bull Run by being
drunk and disorderly at a critical moment. Colonel Miles, who com-

manded a division of three brigades, writes to say he was not in any such state and has demanded a court of inquiry.[3] In a Philadelphia paper it is stated McDowell was helplessly drunk during the action and sat up all the night before drinking, smoking, and playing cards. McDowell never drinks, and never has drunk, wine, spirits, malt, tea, or coffee, or smoked or used tobacco in any form, nor does he play cards; and that remark does not apply to many other Federal officers.

Fresh volunteers are pouring in by the tens of thousands to take their places from all parts of the Union, and in three days after the battle, 80,000 men were accepted. Strange people. The regiments which have returned to New York after disgraceful conduct at Bull Run, with the stigmata of cowardice impressed by their commanding officers on the colours and souls of their corps, are actually welcomed with the utmost enthusiasm and receive popular ovation! It becomes obvious every day that McClellan does not intend to advance till he has got some semblance of an army: that will be a long time to come; but he can get a good deal of fighting out of them in a few months.

August 2nd.   Prince Napoleon [Jerome Bonaparte] has arrived.

August 3rd.   McClellan orders regular parades and drills in every regiment and insist on all orders being given by bugle note. I had a long ride through the camps and saw some improvement in the look of the men. Coming home by Georgetown, met the Prince driving with M. Mercier to pay a visit to the President. I am sure that the politicians are not quite well pleased with this arrival, because they do not understand it and cannot imagine a man would come so far without a purpose. The drunken soldiers now resort to quiet lanes and courts in the suburbs. Georgetown was full of them. It is a much more respectable and old-world looking place than the vulgar, empty, overgrown, mushroom neighbour, Washington. An officer who had fallen in his men to go on duty was walking down the line this evening when his eye rested on the neck of a bottle sticking out of a man's coat. "Thunder," quoth he, "James, what have you got there?" "Well, I guess, Captain, it's a drop of real good Bourbon."

[3]A Court of Inquiry decided that evidence was insufficient to convict Miles of drunkenness. Ill at the time of the battle, Miles was taking medication which may have impaired his reasoning.

"Then let us have a drink," said the captain; and thereupon proceeded to take a long pull and a strong pull, till the man cried out, "That is not fair, Captain. You won't leave me a drop"—a remonstrance which had a proper effect and the captain marched down his company to the bridge.

The Confederates on the right bank of the Potomac have now established a close blockade of the river. Lieutenant [Henry] Wise, of the Navy Department, admitted the fact, but said that the United States gunboats would soon sweep the rebels from the shore.

August 4th. I received a message from General McClellan that he was about to ride along the lines of the army across the river and would be happy if I accompanied him; but as I had many letters to write for the next mail, I was unwillingly obliged to abandon the chance of seeing the army under such favourable circumstances. There are daily arrivals at Washington of military adventurers from all parts of the world, some of them with many extraordinary certificates and qualifications; but as Mr. Seward says, "It is best to detain them with the hope of employment on the Northern side, lest some really good man should get among the rebels." Garibaldians, Hungarians, Poles, officers of Turkish and other contingents, the executory devises and remainders of European revolutions and wars, surround the State Department and infest unsuspecting politicians with illegible testimonials in unknown tongues.

August 5th. The roads from the station are crowded with troops coming from the North as fast as the railway can carry them. It is evident, as the war fever spreads, that such politicians as Mr. [John J.] Crittenden, who resist the extreme violence of the Republican party, will be stricken down. The Confiscation Bill for the emancipation of slaves and the absorption of property belonging to rebels has, indeed, been boldly resisted in the House of Representatives, but it passed with some trifling amendments.[4]

General McClellan invited the newspaper correspondents in

---

[4]This bill was the first of two confiscation acts passed by Congress. It freed all slaves employed or used by Confederates in arms against the United States. The Second Confiscation Act, 1862, provided that all slaves of southerners who supported the rebellion were free and also provided for the confiscation of other forms of property.

Washington to meet him today, and with their assent drew up a treaty of peace and amity, which is a curiosity in its way. In the first place, the editors are to abstain from printing anything which can give aid or comfort to the enemy, and their correspondents are to observe equal caution; in return for which complaisance, Government is to be asked to give the press opportunities for obtaining and transmitting intelligence suitable for publication, particularly touching engagements with the enemy. The Confederate privateer *Sumter* has forced the blockade at New Orleans and has already been heard of destroying a number of Union vessels.[5]

August 6th.   Prince Napoleon, anxious to visit the battlefield at Bull Run, has, to Mr. Seward's discomfiture, applied for passes, and arrangements are being made to escort him as far as the Confederate lines. This is a recognition of the Confederates as a belligerent power, which is by no means agreeable to the authorities.

August 7th.   In the evening I went to Mr. Seward's, who gave a reception in honour of Prince Napoleon. The Minister's rooms were crowded and intensely hot. Lord Lyons and most of the diplomatic circle were present. The Prince, to whom I was presented by Mr. Seward, asked me particularly about the roads from Alexandria to Fairfax Court House and from there to Centreville and Manassas. I told him I had not got quite as far as the latter place, at which he laughed. He inquired with much interest about General Beauregard, whether he spoke good French, if he seemed a man of capacity, or was the creation of an accident and of circumstances. His manner is perfectly easy but he gave no encouragement to bores, nor did he court popularity by unusual affability, and he moved off long before the guests were tired of looking at him.

August 8th.   I had arranged to go with Mr. Olmsted to visit the hospitals, but the heat was so intolerable, we abandoned the idea till the afternoon, when we drove across the Long Bridge and proceeded

[5]The C.S.S. *Sumter* escaped from New Orleans on June 30, 1861. After a brief but successful career raiding northern commercial shipping, *Sumter* was seized by the U.S. Consul at Tangier, Morocco, in February 1862.

to Alexandria. The town, which is now fully occupied by military, has an air which tells the tale of a hostile occupation. In a large building, which had once been a school, the wounded of Bull Run were lying, not uncomfortably packed, nor unskilfully cared for, and the arrangements were, taken together, creditable to the skill and humanity of the surgeons.

In Washington the only news tonight is that a small privateer from Charleston, mistaking the *St. Lawrence* for a merchant vessel, fired into her and was at once sent to Mr. Davy Jones by a rattling broadside. Congress having adjourned, there is but little to render Washington less uninteresting than it must be in its normal state.

[August 11th–16th.] I rode out this morning very early, and was rewarded by a breath of cold, fresh air, and by the sight of some very disorderly regiments just turning out to parade in the camps; but I was not particularly gratified by being mistaken for Prince Napoleon by some Irish recruits, who shouted out, "Bonaparte forever," and gradually subsided into requests for "something to drink your Royal Highness's health with." As I returned, I saw on the steps of General Mansfield's quarters, a tall, soldierly looking young man and I recognised him as one who had called upon me a few days before, renewing our slight acquaintance.

On returning from my ride next morning, I took up the Baltimore paper and saw a paragraph announcing the death of an English officer at the station; it was the poor fellow whom I saw sitting at General Mansfield's steps yesterday. Finding the Legation were anxious to see due care taken of the poor fellow's remains, I left for Baltimore at a quarter to three o'clock, and proceeded to inquire into the circumstances connected with his death. He had been struck down at the station by some cerebral attack, brought on by the heat and excitement; had been carried to the police station and placed upon a bench, from which he had fallen with his head downwards, and was found in that position, with life quite extinct. My astonishment may be conceived when I learned that the man had been buried the same morning, and so my mission was over, and I could only report what had occurred to Washington.

I remained in Baltimore a few days, and had an opportunity of knowing the feelings of some of the leading men in the place. There is a peculiar stamp about the Baltimore men which distinguishes them from most Americans—a style of dress, frankness of manner, and a general appearance assimilating them closely to the upper classes of Englishmen. They are fond of sport and travel, exclusive and high-spirited, and the iron rule of the Yankee is the more intolerable because they dare not resent it and are unable to shake it off.

I returned to Washington on the 15th August. Nothing changed; skirmishes along the front; McClellan reviewing. The loss of General Lyon, who was killed in an action at Wilson's Creek, Springfield, Missouri, is severely felt. He was one of the very few officers who combined military skill and personal bravery with political sagacity and moral firmness. The President has issued his proclamation for a day of fast and prayer, which is a sign that the Yankees are in a bad way, as they would never think of praying or fasting if their cause was prospering.

The pecuniary difficulties of the Government have been alleviated by the bankers of New York, Philadelphia, and Boston, who have agreed to lend them fifty millions of dollars, on condition that they receive the Treasury notes which Mr. Chase is about to issue.

Mr. Seward, with whom I dined and spent the evening on 16th August, has been much reassured and comforted by the demonstrations of readiness on the part of the people to continue the contest and of confidence in the cause among the moneyed men of the great cities. "All we want is time to develop our strength. We have been blamed for not making greater use of our navy and extending it at once. It was our first duty to provide for the safety of our capital. Besides a man will generally pay little attention to agencies he does not understand. None of us knew anything about a navy. I doubt if the President ever saw anything more formidable than a river steamboat, and I don't think Mr. Welles, the Secretary of the Navy, knew the stem from the stern of a ship. Of the whole Cabinet, I am the only member who ever was *fairly* at sea or crossed the Atlantic. Some of us never even saw it. No wonder we did not understand the necessity for creating a navy at once. Soon, however, our Government will be able to dispose of a respectable marine, and when our army is ready to move, co-operating with the fleet, the days of the rebellion are numbered."

"When will that be, Mr. Secretary?"

"Soon; very soon, I hope. We can, however, bear delays. The rebels will be ruined by it."

[August 17th–August 20th.] On the 17th August I returned to Baltimore on my way to Doughoregan Manor, the seat of Colonel [Charles] Carroll, in Maryland, where I had been invited to spend a few days by his son-in-law, an English gentleman of my acquaintance. Leaving Baltimore at 5:40 P.M., in company of Mr. Tucker Carroll, I proceeded by train to Ellicott's Mills, a station fourteen miles on the Ohio and Baltimore Railroad, from which our host's residence is distant more than an hour's drive. The country through which the line passes is picturesque and undulating, with hills and valleys and brawling streams, spreading in woodland and glade, ravine, and high uplands on either side, haunted by cotton factories, poisoning the air and water; but it has been a formidable district for the [railroad] engineers to get through, and the line abounds in those triumphs of engineering which are generally the ruin of shareholders.

All these lines are now in the hands of the military. At the Washington terminus there is a guard placed to see that no unauthorised person or unwilling volunteer is going north; the line is watched by patrols and sentries; troops are encamped along its course. The factory chimneys are smokeless; half the pleasant villas which cover the hills or dot the openings in the forest have a deserted look and closed windows. And so these great works, the Carrollton viaduct, the Thomas viaduct, and the high embankments are great cuttings in the ravine by the river side, over which the line passes, have almost a depressing effect, as if the people for whose use they were intended had all become extinct. At Ellicott's Mills, which is a considerable manufacturing town, more soldiers and Union flags. The people are Unionists, but the neighbouring gentry and country people are seceshers.

This is the case wherever there is a manufacturing population in Maryland, because the workmen are generally foreigners, or have come from the Northern States, and feel little sympathy with States' Rights doctrines, and the tendencies of the landed gentry to a conservative action on the slave question. There was no good will in the eyes of the mechanicals as they stared at our vehicle; for the political bias of Colonel Carroll was well known, as well as the general sentiments of his family. It was dark when we reached the manor, which is approached by an avenue of fine trees. The house is old-fashioned, and has received additions from time to time. But for the black faces of the domestics, one might easily fancy he was in some old country house in Ireland. The family have adhered to their ancient faith. The founder of the Carrolls in Maryland came over with the Catholic colonists led by Lord Baltimore, or by his brother, Leonard Calvert, and the colonel possesses some interesting deeds of grant and conveyance of the vast estates, which have been diminished by large sales year after year, but still spread over a considerable part of several counties in the State.

On the day after my arrival the rain fell in torrents. The weather is as uncertain as that of our own isle. The torrid heats at Washington, the other day, were succeeded by bitter cold days; now there is a dense mist, chilly and cheerless, seeming as a sort of strainer for the even downpour that falls through it continuously. The family after breakfast slipped round to the little chapel which forms the extremity of one wing of the house. The coloured people on the estate were already trooping across the lawn and up the avenue from the slave quarters, decently dressed for the most part, having due allowance for the extraordinary choice of colours in their gowns, bonnets, and ribbons, and for the unhappy imitations, on the part of the men, of the attire of their masters. They walked demurely and quietly past the house, and presently the priest, dressed like a French *curé*, trotted up, and service began. The Negro houses were of much better and more substantial character than those one sees in the South, though not remarkable for cleanliness and good order. Truth to say, they were palaces compared to the huts of Irish labourers, such as might be found, perhaps, on the estates of the colonel's kinsmen at home. The Negroes are far more independent than they are in the South. They are less civil, less obliging, and, [since] they do not come cringing to shake hands as the field hands on a Louisianian plantation, less servile. They inhabit the small village of brick and wood houses, across the road at the end of the avenue and in sight of the house. The usual swarms of little children, poultry, pigs, enlivened by goats, embarrassed the steps of the visitor, and the old people, or those who were not finely dressed enough for mass, peered out at the strangers from the glassless windows.

A little knot of friends and relations joined Colonel Carroll at dinner. There are few families in this part of Maryland which have not representatives in the army across the Potomac; and if Beauregard could but make his appearance, the women alone would give him welcome such as no conqueror ever received in liberated city.

Next day the rain fell incessantly. In the afternoon I was driven over a part of the estate in a close carriage, through the windows of which, however, I caught glimpses of a beautiful country, wooded gloriously, and soft, sylvan, and well-cultivated. The weather was too unfavourable to admit of a close inspection of the fields; but I visited one or two tobacco houses, where the fragrant Maryland was lying in masses on the ground, or hanging from the rafters, or filled the heavy hogsheads with compressed smoke.

Next day I took the train, at Ellicott's Mills, and went to Harpers Ferry. There is no one spot, in the history of this extraordinary war, which can be well more conspicuous. Had it nothing more to recommend it than the scenery, it might well command a visit from the tourist; but as the scene of old John Brown's raid upon the Federal arsenal, of that first passage of arms between the abolitionist and the slave conservatives, which has developed this great contest; above all, as the spot where important military demonstrations have been made on both sides, and will necessarily occur hereafter, this place, which probably derives its name from some wretched old boatman, will be renowned forever in the annals of the civil war of 1861.

Harpers Ferry lies in a gorge formed by a rush of the Potomac through the mountain ridges, which it cuts at right angles to its course at its junction with the river Shenandoah. So trenchant and abrupt is the division that little land is on the divided ridge to build upon. The precipitous hills on both sides are covered with forest, which has been cleared in patches here and there on the Maryland shore, to permit the erection of batteries. On the Virginia side there lies a mass of blackened and ruined buildings, from which a street lined with good houses stretches up the hill. Just above the junction of the Shenandoah with the Potomac, an elevated bridge or viaduct 300 yards long leaps from hill side to hill side. The arches had been broken—the rails which ran along the top torn up, and there is now a deep gulf fixed between the shores of Maryland and Virginia. The rail to Winchester from this point has been destroyed, and the line along the Potomac has also been ruined.

Harpers Ferry at present, for all practical purposes, may be considered as Confederate property. A few Union inhabitants remain in their houses, but many of the Government workmen and most of the inhabitants have gone off south. For strategical purposes its possession would be most important to a force desiring to operate on Maryland from Virginia. The Blue Ridge range running up the Shenandoah divides the country so as to permit a force debouching from Harpers Ferry to advance up the valley of the Shenandoah on the right, or to move to the left between the Blue Ridge and the Catoctin Mountains toward the Manassas Railway at its discretion.

On the journey from Harpers Ferry, the concentration of masses of troops along the road and the march of heavy artillery trains caused me to think a renewal of the offensive movement against Richmond was immediate, but at Washington I heard that all McClellan wanted or hoped for at present was to make Maryland safe and to gain time for the formation of his army. The Confederates appear to be moving towards their left, and McClellan is very uneasy lest they should make a vigorous attack before he is prepared to receive them.

In the evening the New York papers came in with the extracts from the London papers containing my account of the battle of Bull's Run. Utterly forgetting their own versions of the engagement, the New York editors now find it convenient to divert attention from the bitter truth that was in them, to the letter of the foreign newspaper correspondent. At the outset I had foreseen this would be the case and deliberately accepted the issue; but when I found the Northern journals far exceeding in severity anything I could have said and indulging in general invective against whole classes of American soldiery, officers, and statesmen, I was foolish enough to expect a little justice, not to say a word of the smallest generosity.

August 21st. The echoes of Bull Run are coming back with a vengeance. This day month the miserable fragments of a beaten, washed out, demoralised army, were flooding in disorder and dismay the streets of the capital from which they had issued forth to repel the tide of invasion. This day month and all the editors and journalists in the States, weeping, wailing, and gnashing their teeth, infused extra gall into their ink, and poured out invective, abuse, and obloquy on their defeated general and their broken hosts. The President and his ministers, stunned by the tremendous calamity, sat listening in fear and trembling for the sound of the enemy's cannon. The veteran soldier, on whom the boasted hopes of the nation rested, heartsick and beaten down, had neither counsel to give nor action to offer. At any moment the Confederate columns might be expected in Pennsylvania Avenue to receive the welcome of their friends and the submission of their helpless and disheartened enemies.

All this is forgotten. [New York editors] deny that they uttered cries of distress and appeals for help. Not only that, but they turn and rend those whose writing has been dug up after thirty days, and comes back as a rebuke to their pride. The storm has been gathering ever since, and I am no doubt to experience the truth of DeTocqueville's remark, "that a stranger who injures American vanity, no matter how justly, may make up his mind to be a martyr."

August 22nd.   A general officer said to me: "Of course you will never remain, when once all the press are down upon you. I would not take a million dollars to be in your place." "But is what I've written untrue?" "God bless you! do you know in this country if you can get enough of people to start a lie about any man, he would be ruined, if the Evangelists came forward to swear the story was false. There are thousands of people who this moment believe that McDowell, who never tasted anything stronger than a watermelon in all his life, was helplessly drunk at Bull's Run. Mind what I say; they'll run you into a mud hole as sure as you live." I was not much impressed with the danger of my position further than that I knew there would be a certain amount of risk from the rowdyism and vanity of what even the Americans admit to be the lower orders, for which I had been prepared from the moment I had dispatched my letter; but I confess I was not by any means disposed to think that the leaders of public opinion would seek the small gratification of revenge, and the petty popularity of pandering to the passion of the mob by creating a popular outcry against me.

August 23rd.   The torrent is swollen today by anonymous letters threatening me with bowie knife and revolver, or simply abusive, frantic with hate, and full of obscure warnings. Some bear the Washington postmark, others came from New York, the greater number—for I have had nine—are from Philadelphia. Perhaps they may come from the members of that "gallant" 4th Pennsylvania Regiment.

August 24th. Today there is an account in the papers of a brute shooting a Negro boy dead, because he asked him for a chew of tobacco. Will he be hanged? Not the smallest chance of it. The idea of hanging a white man for killing a nigger!

Before dinner I walked down to the Washington Navy Yard. Captain Dahlgren was sorely perplexed with an intoxicated Senator, whose name it is not necessary to mention, and who seemed to think he paid me a great compliment by expressing his repeated desire "to have a good look at" me. "I guess you're quite notorious now. You'll excuse me because I've dined, now—and so you are the Mr. &c., &c., &c." The Senator informed me that he was "none of your d—d blackfaced Republicans. He didn't care a d— about niggers—his business was to do good to his fellow white men, to hold our glorious Union together, and let the niggers take care of themselves."

I was glad when a diversion was effected by the arrival of Mr. Fox, Assistant Secretary of the Navy, and Mr. Blair, Postmaster-General, to consult with the Captain, who is greatly looked up to by all the members of the Cabinet—in fact he is rather inconvenienced by the perpetual visits of the President, who is animated by a most extraordinary curiosity about naval matters and machinery and is attracted by the novelty of the whole department, so that he is continually running down "to have a talk with Dahlgren" when he is not engaged in "a chat with George." In the evening a few of the gentlemen connected with the Foreign Legations came in, and had a great international reunion and discussion till a late hour. There is a good deal of agreeable banter reserved for myself, as to the exact form of death which I am most likely to meet. I was seriously advised by a friend not to stir out unarmed. I also received a letter from London, advising me to apply to Lord Lyons for protection, but that could only be extended to me within the walls of the Legation.

August 25th. I visited the Navy Department, which is a small red-brick building two storeys high, very plain and even humble. My business was to pave the way for a passage on board a steamer, in case of any naval expedition starting before the army was ready to move, but all difficulties were at once removed by the promptitude and courtesy of Mr. Fox, the Assistant Secretary, who promised to give an order for a passage whenever I required it.

On my return late, there was a letter on my table requesting me to visit General McClellan, but [the day] was then too far advanced to avail myself of the invitation which was only delivered after I left my lodgings.

August 26th. General [Stewart] Van Vliet called from General McClellan to say that the commander-in-chief would be happy to go round the camps with me when he next made an inspection and would send round an orderly and charger in time to get ready before he started. These little excursions are not the most agreeable affairs in the world, for McClellan delights in working down staff and escort, dashing from the Chain Bridge to Alexandria, and visiting all the posts, riding as hard as he can, and not returning till past midnight, so that if one has a regard for his cuticle, or his mail days, he will not rashly venture on such excursions. Today he is to inspect McDowell's division.

I set out accordingly over the Long Bridge, which is now very strictly guarded. On exhibiting my pass to the sentry at the entrance, he called across to the sergeant and spoke to him aside showing him the pass at the same time. "Are you Russell, of the London *Times?*" said the sergeant. I replied, "If you look at the pass, you will see who I am." He turned it over, examined it most narrowly and at last, with an expression of infinite dissatisfaction and anger upon his face, handed it back, saying to the sentry, "I suppose you must let him go."

The troops of McDowell's division were already drawn up on a rugged plain, close to the river's margin, in happier days the scene of the city races. Presently General McDowell and one of his aides cantered over, and whilst waiting for General McClellan, he talked of the fierce outburst directed against me in the press. "I must confess," he said laughingly, "I am much rejoiced to find you are as much abused as I have been. I hope you mind it as little as I did. Bull's Run was an unfortunate affair for both of us, for had I won it, you would have had to describe the pursuit of the flying enemy, and then you would have been the most popular writer in America, and I would have been lauded as the greatest of generals. See what measure has been meted to us now. I'm accused of drunkenness and gambling, and you, Mr. Russell—well!—I really do hope you are not so black as you are painted." Presently a cloud of dust on the road announced the arrival of the President, who came upon the ground in an open carriage with Mr. Seward by his side, accompanied by General McClellan and his staff in undress uniform, and an escort of the very dirtiest and most unsoldierly dragoons, with filthy accoutrements and ungroomed horses, I ever saw. The troops dressed into line and presented arms, whilst the band struck up the "Star Spangled Banner," as the Americans have got no air which corresponds with our National Anthem.

General McDowell seems on most excellent terms with the present commander-in-chief, as he is with the President. Immediately after Bull's Run, when the President first saw McDowell, he said to him, "I have not lost a particle of confidence in you," to which the General replied, "I don't see why you should, Mr. President." But there was a curious commentary, either on the sincerity of Mr. Lincoln or in his utter subservience to mob opinion, in the fact that he who can overrule Congress and act pretty much as he pleases in time of war, had, without opportunity for explanation or demand for it, at once displaced the man in whom he still retained the fullest confidence, degraded him to command of a division of the army of which he had been general-in-chief, and placed a junior officer over his head.

After some ordinary movements, the march past took place, which satisfied me that the new levies were very superior to the three months' men, though far, indeed, from being soldiers. Finer material could not be found in physique. With the exception of an assemblage of miserable scarecrows in rags and tatters, swept up in New York, no division of the ordinary line in any army could show a greater number of tall, robust men in the prime of life.

I returned from the field to Arlington House, having been invited to share the General's camp dinner. At the General's tent we found General [William T.] Sherman, General [Erasmus D.] Keyes, [James] Wadworth, and some others. Dinner was spread on a table covered by the flap of the tent and consisted of good plain fare, and a dessert of prodigious watermelons. I was exceedingly gratified to hear every officer present declare in the presence of the General who had commanded the army, and who himself said no words could exaggerate the disorder of the route, that my narrative of Bull's Run was not only true but moderate.

General Sherman, whom I met for the first time, said, "Mr. Russell, I can indorse every word that you wrote; your statements about the battle, which you say you did not witness, are equally correct. All the stories about charging batteries and attacks with the bayonet are simply falsehoods, so far as my command is concerned, though some of the troops did fight well. As to cavalry charges, I wish we had had a few cavalry to have tried one; those Black Horse fellows seemed as if their horses ran away with them." General Keyes said, "I don't think you made it half bad enough. I could not get the men to stand after they had received the first severe check. The enemy swept the open with a tremendous musketry fire. Some of our men and portions of regiments behaved admirably—we drove them easily at first; the cavalry did very little indeed; but when they did come on I could not get the infantry to stand, and after a harmless volley they broke." These officers were brigadiers in Tyler's division.

I returned to Washington at dusk over the Aqueduct Bridge.

August 27th.   Having a sincere regard and liking for many of the Southerners whom I have met, I cannot say their cause, or its origin, or its aim, recommends itself to my sympathies; and yet I am accused of aiding it by every means in my power because I do not re-echo the arrogant and empty boasting and insolent outburst of the people in the North, who threaten, as the first fruits of their success, to invade the territories subject to the British crown and to outrage and humiliate our flag.

August 29th.   It is hard to bear such a fate as befalls an unpopular man in the United States, because in no other country, as DeTocqueville (p. 222, Spencer's American edition, New York, 1858) remarks, is the press so powerful when it is unanimous.

The teeming anonymous letters I receive are filled with threats of assassination, tarring, feathering, and the like; and one of the most conspicuous of literary *sbirri* [henchmen] is in perfect rapture at the notion of a new "sensation" heading, for which he is working as hard as he can. I have no intention to add to the number of his castigations.

In the afternoon I drove to the waste grounds beyond the Capitol, in company with Mr. Olmsted, to see the 18th Massachusetts Regiment, who had just marched in and were pitching their tents very probably for the first time. They arrived from their State with camp equipments, wagons, horses, harness, commissariat stores complete, and were clad in the blue uniform of the United States; for the volunteer fancies in greys and greens are dying out. The men were uncommonly stout young fellows, with an odd slouching, lounging air about some of them, however, which I could not quite understand till I heard one sing out, "Hallo, sergeant, where am I to sling my hammock in this tent?" Many of them, in fact, are fishermen and sailors from Cape Cod, New Haven, and similar maritime places.

August 31st. A month during which I have been exposed to more calumny, falsehood, not to speak of danger. Scowling faces on every side—women turning up their pretty little noses—people turning round in the streets, or stopping to stare in front of me—the proprietors of the shops where I am known pointing me out to others; the words uttered, in various tones, "So, that's Bull-Run Russell!"—for, oddly enough, the Americans seem to think that a disgrace to their arms becomes diminished by fixing the name of the scene as a *sobriquet* on one who described it.

I dined with Lieutenant Wise, and met Captain Dahlgren, Captain [Andrew H.] Foote, U.S.N., and Colonel Fletcher Webster, son of the great American statesman, now commanding a regiment of volunteers. The naval captains were excellent specimens of the accomplished and able men who belong to the United States Navy. Foote, who is designated to the command of the flotilla which is to clear the Mississippi downwards will, I am certain, do good service—a calm, energetic, skilful officer. It will run hard against the Confederates when they get such men at work on the rivers and coasts, for they seem to understand their business thoroughly, and all they are not quite sure of is the readiness of the land forces to co-operate with their expeditionary movements. Incidentally I learned from the conversation—and it is a curious illustration of the power of the President—that it was he who ordered the attack on Charleston harbour, or, to speak with more accuracy, the movement of the armed squadron to relieve Sumter by force, if necessary; but, at all events, the action of the Confederates prevented the attempt.

September 1st. Took a ride early this morning over the Long Bridge. As I was passing out of the earthwork called a fort on the hill, a dirty German soldier called out from the parapet, "Pull-Run Russell! you shall never write Pulls' Runs again," and at the same time cocked his piece and levelled it at me. I immediately rode round into the fort, the fellow still presenting his firelock, and asked him what he meant, at the same time calling for the sergeant of the guard, who came at once, and, at my request, arrested the man, who recovered arms, and said, "It was a choake—I vant to freeken Pull-Run Russell." However, as his rifle was capped and loaded and on full cock, with his finger on the trigger, I did not quite see the fun of it, and I accordingly had the man marched to the tent of the officer, who promised to investigate the case and made a formal report of it to the brigadier. On reflection I resolved that it was best to let the matter drop; the joke might spread, and it was quite unpleasant enough as it was to bear the insolent looks and scowling faces of the guards at the post, to whom I was obliged to exhibit my pass whenever I went out to ride.

On my return I heard of the complete success of the Hatteras expedition, which shelled out and destroyed some sand batteries guarding the entrance to the great inland sea and navigation called Pamlico Sound in North Carolina, furnishing access to coasters for many miles into the Confederate States, and most useful to them in forwarding supplies and keeping up communications throughout.[6] The force was commanded by General Butler, who has come to Washington with the news, and has already made his speech to the mob outside Willard's. I called down to see him, but he had gone over to call on the President. The people were jubilant, one might have supposed Hatteras was the key to Richmond or Charleston, from the way they spoke of this unparalleled exploit.

September 2nd. It would seem as if the North were perfectly destitute of common sense. Here they are as rampant because they have succeeded with an overwhelming fleet in shelling out the defenders of some poor unfinished earthworks, on a spit of sand on the

[6]The capture of forts Hatteras and Clark by a joint army-navy expedition occurred on August 27–28, 1861.

coast of North Carolina, as if they had already crushed the Southern rebellion. They affect to consider this achievement a counterpoise to Bull Run, but it no more adds to their chances of crushing the Confederacy than shooting off the end of an elephant's tail contributes to the hunter's capture of the animal.

Going out for my usual ride today, I saw General Scott, between two aides-de-camp, slowly pacing homewards from the War Office. He is still commander-in-chief of the army, and affects to direct movements and to control the disposition of the troops, but a power greater than his increases steadily at General McClellan's headquarters. For my own part I confess that General McClellan does not appear to me a man of action, or, at least, a man who intends to act as speedily as the crisis demands. He should be out with his army across the Potomac, living among his generals, studying the composition of his army, investigating its defects, and, above all, showing himself to the men as soon afterwards as possible, if he cannot be with them at the time, in the small affairs which constantly occur along the front, and never permitting them to receive a blow without taking care that they give at least two in return. General Scott, *jam fracta membra labore* [the delegation of duties among his staff notwithstanding], would do all the work of departments and superintendence admirably well; but, as Montesquieu taught long ago, faction and intrigue are the cancers which peculiarly eat into the body politic of republics, and McClellan fears, no doubt, that his absence from the capital, even though he went but across the river, would animate his enemies to undermine and supplant him.

I have heard several people say lately, "I wish old Scott would go away," by which they mean that they would be happy to strike him down when his back was turned, but feared his personal influence with the President and his Cabinet. Hard is the fate of those who serve republics. The officers who met the old man in the street today passed him by without a salute or mark of recognition, although he wore his uniform coat with yellow lapels and yellow sash; and one of the group which came out of the restaurant close to the General's house, exclaimed, almost in his hearing, "Old fuss-and-feathers don't look first-rate today."

In the evening I went with a Scotch gentleman, who was formerly acquainted with General McClellan when he was superintendent of the Central Illinois Railway, to his headquarters. We found General McClellan, just returned from a long ride, and seated in his shirt sleeves on the side of his camp-bed. Telegraph wires ran all about the house, and dispatches were repeatedly brought in from the generals in the front. Sometimes McClellan laid down his cigar and went off to study a large map of the position which was fixed to the wall close to the head of his bed, but more frequently the contents of the dispatches caused him to smile or to utter some exclamation, which gave one an idea that he did not attach much importance to the news and had no great faith in the reports received from his subordinate officers, who are always under the impression that the enemy are coming on in force.

General McClellan took the situation of affairs in a very easy and philosophical spirit. According to his own map and showing, the enemy not only overlapped his lines from the batteries by which they blockaded the Potomac on the right, but have established themselves in a kind of salient angle on his front, at a place called Munson's Hill, where their flag waved from entrenchments within sight of the Capitol. However, from an observation he made, I imagined that the General would make an effort to recover his lost ground; and he promised to send an orderly round and let me know; so, before I retired, I gave orders to my groom to have "Walker" in readiness.

September 3rd. Notwithstanding the extreme heat, I went out early this morning to the Chain Bridge, from which the reconnaissance hinted at last night would necessarily start. This bridge is about four and a half or five miles above Washington and crosses the river at a picturesque spot almost deserving the name of a gorge, with high banks on both sides. The road from the city passes through a squalid settlement of European squatters, who in habitation, dress, appearance, and possibly civilisation are quite as bad as any Negroes on any Southern plantation I have visited. The camps of a division lie just beyond and a gawky sentry from New England, with whom I had some conversation, amused me by saying that the Colonel "was a darned deal more affeerd of the Irish squatters taking off his poultry at night than he was of the secessioners; anyways, he put out more sentries to guard them than he has to look after the others."

From the Chain Bridge I went some distance towards Falls Church until I was stopped by a picket, the officer of which refused to recognise General Scott's pass. "I guess the General's a dead man, sir." "Is he not commander-in-chief of the United States Army?" "Well, I believe that's a fact, sir; but you had better argue that point with McClellan. He is our boy, and I do believe he'd like to let the London *Times* know how we Green Mountain boys can fight, if they don't know already." On my way back by the upper road I passed a farmer's house which was occupied by some Federal officers, and there, seated in the verandah, with his legs cocked over the railing, was Mr. Lincoln, in a felt hat, and a loose grey shooting coat and long vest, "letting off," as the papers say, one of his jokes, to judge by his attitude and the laughter of the officers around him, utterly indifferent to the Confederate flag floating from Munson's Hill.

Just before midnight a considerable movement of troops took place through the streets, and I was about starting off to ascertain the cause, when I received information that General McClellan was only sending off two brigades and four batteries to the Chain Bridge to strengthen his right, which was menaced by the enemy.

September 4th. I rode over to the Chain Bridge again this morning at seven o'clock on the chance of there being a big fight, as the Americans say; but there was only some slight skirmishing going on; dropping shots now and then. I went down to the Long Bridge and was stopped by the sentry, so I produced General Scott's pass, which I kept always as a *dernier ressort* [last resort], but the officer on duty here also refused it, as passes were suspended. I returned and referred the matter to Colonel Cullum, who consulted General Scott, and informed me that the pass must be considered as perfectly valid, not having been revoked by the General, who, as Lieutenant General commanding the United States Army, was senior to every other officer and could only have his pass revoked by the President himself. I, therefore, procured a letter from Colonel Cullum stating, in writing, what he said in words, and with that and the pass went to General McClellan's headquarters. I sent up my papers, and Major [Edward M.] Hudson of his staff came down after a short time and said, that "General McClellan thought it would be much better if General Scott had given me a new special pass, but as General Scott had thought fit to take the present course on his own responsibility, General

McClellan could not interfere in the matter," whence it may be inferred there is no very pleasant feeling between headquarters of the army of the Potomac and headquarters of the army of the United States.

I went on to the Navy Yard, where a lookout man, who can command the whole of the country to Munson's Hill, is stationed, and I heard from Captain Dahlgren that there was no fighting whatever. However, people were so positive as to hearing cannonades and volleys of musketry that we went out to the reservoir hill at Georgetown, and gazing over the debatable land of Virginia—which, by the way, is very beautiful in the summer sunsets—became thoroughly satisfied of the delusion.

September 5th. Raining all day. McClellan abandoned his intention of inspecting the lines and I remained in, writing.

The event of the day was the appearance of the President in the Avenue in a suit of black and a parcel in his hand, walking umbrellaless in the rain. Mrs. Lincoln has returned,[7] and the worthy "Executive" will no longer be obliged to go "browsing round," as he says, among his friends at dinner time. He is working away at money matters with energy, but has been much disturbed in his course of studies by General Frémont's sudden outburst in the West, which proclaims emancipation, and draws out the arrow which the President intended to discharge from his own bow.[8]

September 6th. At 3:30 P.M. General McClellan sent over an orderly to say he was going across the river and would be glad of my company; but I was just finishing my letters for England and had to excuse myself for the moment; and when I was ready, the General and staff had gone *ventre à terre* [at full speed] into Virginia.

A new Major General—[Henry W.] Halleck—has been picked up in California, and is highly praised by General Scott and by Colonel Cullum, with whom I had a long talk about the generals on both

[7]Mary Lincoln spent the greater part of August 1861 at Long Branch, an ocean resort in New Jersey.
[8]Frémont issued a proclamation on August 30, 1861, freeing the slaves of Confederates in Missouri. Lincoln countermanded the order and several months later removed Frémont as commander in the West.

sides. Halleck is a West Point officer and has published some works on military science which are highly esteemed in the States. Before California became a State, he was secretary to the governor or officer commanding the territory, and eventually left the service and became a lawyer in the district, where he has amassed a large fortune. He is a man of great ability, very calm, practical, earnest, and cold, devoted to the Union—a soldier and something more. Lee is considered the ablest man on the [Confederate][9] side, but he is slow and timid. "Joe" Johnston is their best strategist. Beauregard is nobody and nothing —so think they at headquarters. All of them together are not equal to Halleck, who is to be employed in the West.

As I was anxious to explain to General McClellan the reason of my inability to go out with him, I called at his quarters about eleven o'clock, and found he had just returned from the ride. He received me in his shirt, in his bedroom at the top of the house, introduced me to General [Ambrose] Burnside—a soldierly, intelligent-looking man, with a very lofty forehead, and uncommonly bright dark eyes; and we had some conversation about matters of ordinary interest. The General told me he had received "sure information that Beauregard had packed up all his baggage, struck his tents, and is evidently preparing for a movement, so you may be wanted at a moment's notice." General Burnside returned to my rooms and we sat up discoursing of Bull's Run, in which his brigade was the first engaged in front. He spoke like a man of sense and a soldier of the action, and stood up for the conduct of some regiments, though he could not palliate the final disorder.

September 8th.   Rode over to Arlington House. Went round by Aqueduct Bridge, Georgetown, and out across Chain Bridge to Brigadier [William Farrar] Smith's headquarters, which are established in a comfortable house belonging to a secessionist farmer. The General belongs to the Regular Army, and, if one can judge from externals, is a good officer. General Smith, like most officers, is a Democrat and strong anti-abolitionist. As we were riding about it got out among the men that I was present, and I was regarded with no small curiosity, staring, and some angry looks. The men do not know what to make

[9]The 1863 London imprint reads "Federal side"—an obvious error.

of it when they see their officers in the company of one whom they are reading about in the papers as the most &c., &c., the world ever saw.

Going home, I met Mr. and Mrs. Lincoln in their new open carriage. The President was not so good-humoured, nor Mrs. Lincoln so affable, in their return to my salutation as usual. My unpopularity is certainly spreading upwards and downwards at the same time, and all because I could not turn the battle of Bull's Run into a Federal victory, because I would not pander to the vanity of the people, and, least of all, because I will not bow my knee to the degraded creatures who have made the very name of a free press odious to honourable men. They have written far severer things of their army than I have ever done. They have slandered their soldiers and their officers as I have never done.

September 9th. Lord A. V. Tempest and another British subject, who applied to Mr. Seward today for leave to go South, were curtly refused. The Foreign Secretary is not very pleased with us all just now, and there has been some little uneasiness between him and Lord Lyons. The real cause, perhaps, of Mr. Seward's annoyance is to be found in the exaggerated statements of the American papers respecting British reinforcements for Canada which, in truth, are the ordinary reliefs.[10] These small questions in the present condition of affairs cause irritation; but if the United States were not distracted by civil war, they would be seized eagerly as pretexts to excite the popular mind against Great Britain.

September 10th. A party of American officers passed the evening where I dined—all, of course, Federals, but holding very different views. A Massachusetts Colonel asserted that slavery was at the root of every evil which afflicted the Republic; that it was not necessary

---

[10]This is Russell's interpretation; however, Britain may well have been increasing troop strength in Canada because of worsening British-American relations. Anti-Canadian feeling was growing in northern states along the border because Canadian authorities refused to sell the Americans arms. Earlier, in May 1861, Seward had threatened to seize the *Peerless,* a Canadian steamship docked at Toronto but rumored to have been sold to the Confederacy. The rumor proved false; still, Seward's bluntness in dealing with the affair undoubtedly caused concern in London.

in the South or anywhere else and that the South maintained the institution for political as well as private ends. A Virginian Captain, on the contrary, declared that slavery was in itself good; that it could not be dangerous, as it was essentially conservative, and desired nothing better than to be left alone; but that the Northern fanatics, jealous of the superior political influence and ability of Southern statesmen, and sordid protectionists who wished to bind the South to take their goods exclusively, perpetrated all the mischief. An officer of the District of Columbia assigned all the misfortunes of the country to universal suffrage, to foreign immigration, and to these alone.

September 11th. Just as I was sitting down to my desk for the remainder of the day, a sound caught my ear which, repeated again and again, could not be mistaken. I perceived the glass vibrate to the distant discharge of cannon, which evidently did not proceed from a review or a salute. The sound was so close that in a few moments I was driving off towards the Chain Bridge, taking the upper road, as that by the canal has become a sea of mud filled with deep holes.

People were standing in high excitement watching the faint puffs of smoke which rose at intervals above the tree tops, and at every report a murmur—exclamations of "There, do you hear that?"—ran through the crowd. Captain [Orlando M.] Poe came along with dispatches from General McClellan and gave me a correct account of the affair.

All this noise and firing and excitement, I found, simply arose out of a reconnaissance made towards Lewinsville by Smith and a part of his brigade; but, fortunately for the reconnoitering party, the impatience of their enemies led them to open fire too soon. The Federals got their guns into position also, and covered their retreat, whilst reinforcements poured out of camp to their assistance, "and I doubt not," said Poe, "but that they will have an encounter of a tremendous scalping match in all the papers tomorrow, although we have only six or seven men killed and twelve wounded." Thus time passes away in expectation of some onward movement.

It is now quite plain McClellan has no intention of making a general defensive movement against Richmond. He is aware his army is not equal to the task—commissariat deficient, artillery wanting, no cavalry; above all, ill-officered, incoherent battalions. He hopes, no doubt, by constant reviewing and inspection, and by weeding out the preposterous fellows who render epaulettes ridiculous, to create an infantry which shall be able for a short campaign in the fine autumn weather, but I am quite satisfied he does not intend to move now and possibly will not do so till next year. I have arranged therefore to pay a short visit to the West, penetrating as far as I can, without leaving telegraphs and railways behind, so that if an advance takes place, I shall be back in time at Washington to assist at the earliest battle. These Federal armies do not move like the crops of the French Republic, or Crawford's Light Division.

In truth, Washington life is becoming exceedingly monotonous and uninteresting. The pleasant little evening parties or *tertulias* [informal gatherings], which once relieved the dullness of this dullest of capitals, take place no longer. But for the hospitability of Lord Lyons to the English residents, the place would be nearly insufferable.

September 12th. The day passed quietly in spite of rumours of another battle; the band played in the President's garden, and citizens and citizenesses strolled about the grounds as if secession had been annihilated. The President made a fitful appearance, in a grey shooting suit, with a number of dispatches in his hand, and walked off towards the State Department quite unnoticed by the crowd. I am sure not half a dozen persons saluted him—not one of the men I saw even touched his hat.

September 16th. McClellan takes no note of time even by its loss, which is all the more strange because he sets great store upon it in his report on the conduct of the war in the Crimea. However, he knows an army cannot be made in two months, and that the larger it is, the more time there is required to harmonize its components. The news from the Far West indicated a probability of some important operation taking place,[11] although my first love—the army of the

[11]Confederate General Sterling Price began a successful nine-day siege of Lexington, Missouri, on September 12, 1861. Union forces valiantly defended the city, but Frémont's failure to send reinforcements left them with no recourse but surrender.

Potomac—must be returned to. Anyway, there is the great Western Prairie to be seen and the people who have been pouring from their plains so many thousands upon the Southern States to assert the liberties of those coloured races whom they will not permit to cross their borders as freemen. Mr. Lincoln, Mr. Blair, and other abolition-ists, are actuated by similar sentiments, and seek to emancipate the slave and remove from him the protection of his master, in order that they may drive him from the continent altogether or force him to seek refuge in emigration.

[Editor's note: from September 18 to October 3 Russell was away from Washington, as intended, hunting quail.]

October 3rd.   In Washington once more. The fact is McClellan was not prepared to move and therefore not disposed to hazard a general engagement, which he might have brought on had the enemy been in force; perhaps he knew they were not, but found it conve-nient nevertheless to act as though he believed they had established themselves strongly in his front, as half the world will give him credit for knowing more than the civilian strategists who have already got into disgrace for urging McDowell on to Richmond. The Federal armies are not handled easily. They are luxurious in the matter of baggage, and canteens, and private stores; and this is just the sort of war in which the general who moves lightly and rapidly, striking blows unexpectedly and deranging communications, will obtain great results.

Although Beauregard's name is constantly mentioned, I fancy that, crafty and reticent as he is, the operations in front of us have been directed by an officer of larger capacity. As yet McClellan has certainly done nothing in the field to show he is like Napoleon. The value of his labours in camp has yet to be tested. I dined at the Legation and afterwards there was a meeting at my rooms, where I heard of all that had passed during my absence.

October 4th.   The next expedition of which I have been hearing for some time past is about to sail to Port Royal, under the command of General Burnside, in order to reduce the works erected at the entrance of [Port Royal] Sound, to secure a base of operations against Charleston, and to cut in upon the communication between that place and Savannah. Alas, for poor Trescot! his plantations, his secluded home! What will the good lady think of the Yankee invasion, which surely must succeed, as the naval force will be overwhelming? I visited the division of General Egbert Vielé, encamped near the Navy Yard, which is bound to Annapolis, as a part of General Burnside's expedition. When first I saw him, the General was an emeritus captain attached to the 7th New York Militia; now he is a Brigadier General, if not something more, commanding a corps of nearly 5000 men, with pay and allowances to match. His good lady wife, who accompanied him in the Mexican campaign—whereof came a book, lively and light, as a lady's should be—was about to accompany her husband in his assault on the Carolinians, and prepared for action by opening a small broadside on my unhappy self, whom she regarded as enemy of our glorious Union, and therefore an ally of the Evil Powers on both sides of the grave.[12] The women, North and South, are equally pitiless to their enemies and it was but the other day, a man with whom I was on very good terms in Washington, made an apology for not asking me to his house because his wife was a strong Union woman.

A gentleman who had been dining with Mr. Seward tonight told me the Minister had complained that I had not been near him for nearly two months; the fact was, however, that I had called twice immediately after the appearance in America of my letter dated July 22nd, and had met Mr. Seward afterwards, when his manner was, or appeared to me to be, cold and distant, and I have therefore abstained from intruding myself upon his notice.

October 5th.   A day of heat extreme. Tumbled in upon me an old familiar face, heated, wild-eyed, and excited, who had been in the South, where he was acting as correspondent to a London newspaper, and on his return to Washington had obtained a pass from General Scott. According to his own story, he had been expressing his opinion pretty freely in favour of the Southern cause in barrooms of Pennsylvania Avenue. That morning early he had been waited upon by an

---

[12]Mrs. Tersa Griffin Vielé was, in fact, reputed for her candor and forthright speech, something Russell may not have known before meeting her. Her book, *Following the Drum: A Glimpse of a Frontier Wife,* was published in 1858.

officer, who requested his attendance at the Provost Marshal's office; arrived there, a functionary, after a few queries, asked him to give up General Scott's pass, and when Mr. D——refused to do so, proceeded to execute a terrible sort of process verbal on a large sheet of foolscape, the initiatory flourishes and prolegomens of which so intimidated Mr. D—— that he gave up his pass and was permitted to depart in order that he might start for England by the next steamer.[13]

October 6th.   A day of wandering around, and visiting, and listening to rumours all unfounded. I have applied for permission to accompany the Burnside expedition but I am advised not to leave Washington, as McClellan will certainly advance as soon as the diversion has been made down South.

October 8th.   A review of the artillery at this side of the river took place today, which has been described in very inflated language by the American papers, the writers of which pronounce the sight to have been of unequalled splendour; whereas the appearance of horses and men was very far from respectable in all matters relating to grooming, cleanliness, and neatness. General Barry has done wonders in simplifying the force and reducing the number of calibres, which varied according to the fancy of each State, or men of each officer who raised a battery; but there are still field guns of three inches and of three inches and a half, Napoleon guns, rifled 10 lb. Parrots, ordinary 9-pounders, a variety of howitzers, 20 lb. Parrot rifled guns, and a variety of different projectiles in the caissons. As the men rode past, the eye was distressed by discrepancies in dress. Many wore red or white worsted comforters round their necks, few had straps to their trousers;[14] some had new coats, others old; some wore boots, others shoes; not one had clean spurs, bits, curb-chains, or buttons. The officers cannot get the men to do what the latter regard as works of supererogation.

---

[13]The reporter was Samuel Phillips Day of the London *Herald.* Day returned to England, where he published *Down South,* an extreme pro-southern tract which helped, for a time, to strengthen the Confederate cause in Great Britain.

[14]Trouser straps were a common part of men's apparel in the mid-nineteenth century; they were attached to each pant leg and worn under the foot or sometimes under the instep of the shoe.

Whilst I was standing in the crowd I heard a woman say, "I doubt if that Russell is riding about here. I should just like to see him to give him a piece of my mind. They say he's honest, but I call him a poor pre-jewdiced Britisher. This sight'll give him fits." I was quite delighted at my incognito. If the caricatures were at all like me, I should have what the Americans call a bad time of it.

On the return of the batteries a shell exploded in a caisson just in front of the President's house, and miraculous to state, did not fire the other projectiles. Had it done so the destruction of life in the crowded street—blocked up with artillery, men, and horses, and crowds of men, women, and children—would have been truly frightful. Such accidents are not uncommon—a wagon blew up the other day "out West," and killed and wounded several people, and though the accidents in camp from firearms are not so numerous as they were, there are still enough to present a heavy casualty list.

October 9th. A cold, gloomy day. I am laid up with the fever and ague, which visit the banks of the Potomac in autumn. It annoyed me the more because General McClellan is making a reconnaissance today towards Lewinsville, with 10,000 men.

Calling on the General the other night at his usual time of return, I was told by the orderly, who was closing the door, "The General's gone to bed tired, and can see no one. He sent the same message to the President, who came inquiring after him ten minutes ago."

This poor President! He is to be pitied; surrounded by such scenes, and trying with all his might to understand strategy, naval warfare, big guns, the movements of troops, military maps, reconnaissances, occupations, interior and exterior lines, and all the technical details of the art of slaying. He runs from one house to another, armed with plans, papers, reports, recommendations, sometimes good humoured, never angry, occasionally dejected, and always a little fussy. The other night, as I was sitting in the parlour at headquarters, with an English friend who had come to see his old acquaintance the General, walked in a tall man with a navvy's cap, and an ill-made shooting suit, from the pockets of which protruded paper and bundles. "Well," said he to Brigadier Van Vliet, who rose to receive him, "is George in?"

"Yes, sir. He's come back, but is lying down, very much fatigued. I'll send up, sir, and inform him you wish to see him."

"Oh, no; I can wait. I think I'll take supper with him. Well, and what are you now—I forgot your name—are you a major, or a colonel, or a general?"

"Whatever you like to make me, sir."

Seeing that General McClellan would be occupied, I walked out with my friend who asked when I got into the street why I stood up when that tall fellow came into the room. "Because it was the President." "The President of what?" "Of the United States." "Oh! come, now you're humbugging me. Let me have another look at him." He came back more incredulous than ever, but when I assured him I was quite serious, he exclaimed, "I give up the United States after this."

But for all that, there have been many more courtly presidents who, in a similar crisis, would have displayed less capacity, honesty, and plain dealing than Abraham Lincoln.

October 10th.   I got hold of McClellan's report on the Crimean War, which does not evince any capacity beyond the reports of our itinerant artillery officers. I like the man, but I do not think he is equal to his occasion or his place. There is one little piece of policy which shows he is looking ahead—either to gain the good will of the army or for some larger object. All his present purpose is to make himself known to the men personally, to familiarize them with his appearance, to gain the acquaintance of the officers; and with this object he spends nearly every day in the camps, riding out at nine o'clock, not returning till long after nightfall, examining the various regiments as he goes along, and having incessant inspections and reviews. He is the first general who could attempt to do all this without incurring censure and suspicion. Unfortunate McDowell could not inspect his small army without receiving a hint that he must not assume such airs, as they were more becoming a military despot than a simple lieutenant of the great democracy.

October 11th.   Mr. Mure, who has arrived here in wretched health from New Orleans, tells me that I am more detested in New Orleans than I am in New York. The charges against me were disposed of by Mr. Mure, who says that what I wrote of in New Orleans was true and has shown it to be so in his correspondence with the Governor, but, over and beyond that, I am disliked, because I do not praise the peculiar institution. He amused me by adding that the mayor of Jackson, with whom I sojourned, had published "a card," denying point blank that he had ever breathed a word to indicate that the good citizens around him were not famous for the love of law, order, and life, and a scrupulous regard to personal liberty. I can easily fancy Jackson is not a place where a mayor suspected by the citizens would be exempted from difficulties now and then; and if this disclaimer does my friend any good, he is very heartily welcome to it and more.

October 16th.   Day follows day and resembles its predecessor. McClellan is still reviewing, and the North are still waiting for victories and paying money, and the orators are still wrangling over the best way of cooking the hares which they have not yet caught. I visited General McDowell today at his tent in Arlington, and found him in a state of divine calm with his wife and *parvus Iulus* [small son]. A public man in the United States is very much like a great firework —he commences with some small scintillations which attract the eye of the public, and then he blazes up and flares out in blue, purple, and orange fires, to the intense admiration of the multitude, and dying out suddenly is thought of no more, his place being taken by a fresh Roman candle or Catherine wheel which is thought to be far finer than those which have just dazzled the eyes of the fickle spectators. Human nature is thus severely taxed.

October 18th.   Today Lord Lyons drove out with Mr. Seward to inspect the Federal camps, which are now in such order as to be worthy of a visit. It is reported in all the papers that I am going to England, but I have not the smallest intention of giving my enemies here such a treat at present. As Monsieur de Beaumont of the French Legation said, "I presume you are going to remain in Washington for the rest of your life, because I see it stated in the New York journals that you are leaving us in a day or two."

October 22nd.   Rain falling in torrents. As I write in come reports of a battle last night,[15] some forty miles up the [Potomac] river, which by signs and tokens I am led to believe was unfavourable to

---

[15]Battle of Ball's Bluff, October 21, 1861.

the Federals. They crossed the river intending to move upon Leesburg —were attacked by overwhelming forces and repulsed, but maintained themselves on the right bank till General Banks reinforced them and enabled them to hold their own. McClellan has gone or is going at once to the scene of action. It was three o'clock before I heard the news. Late at night the White House was placed in deep grief by the intelligence that in addition to other losses, Brigadier and Senator [Edward] Baker of [Oregon] was killed.[16] The President was inconsolable and walked up and down in his room for hours lamenting the loss of his friend. Mrs. Lincoln's grief was equally poignant. Before bedtime I told the German landlord to tell my servant I wanted my horse round at seven o'clock.

October 23rd. The roads were in a frightful state outside Washington—literally nothing but canals, in which earth and water were mixed together for depths varying from six inches to three feet above the surface; but late as it was, I pushed on, and had got as far as the turn of the road to Rockville, near the great falls some twelve miles beyond Washington, when I met an officer with a couple of orderlies, hurrying back from General Banks's headquarters, who told me the whole affair was over, and that I could not possibly get to the scene of action on one horse till next morning, even supposing that I pressed on all through the night, the roads being utterly villainous, and the country at night as black as ink; and so I returned to Washington.

October 24th. Colonel and Senator Baker was honoured by a ceremonial which was intended to be a public funeral. The procession down Pennsylvania Avenue was a tawdry, shabby string of hack carriages, men in light coats and white hats following the hearse, and three regiments of foot soldiers, of which one was simply an uncleanly, unwholesome-looking rabble. The President, in his carriage, and many of the Ministers and Senators, attended also and passed through unsympathetic lines of people on the kerbstones, not one of whom raised his hat to the bier as it passed or to the President. As the band turned into Pennsylvania Avenue, two officers in uniform

[16]The 1863 London imprint reads "Senator Baker of California. . . ."

came riding up in the contrary direction; they were smoking cigars; one of them let his fall on the ground, the other smoked lustily as the hearse passed, and reining up his horse continued to puff his weed under the nose of the President, Ministers, and Senators, with the air of a man who was doing a very soldierly, correct sort of thing.

October 26th. More reviews. Today rather a pretty sight—12 regiments, 16 guns, and a few squads of men with swords and pistols on horseback, called cavalry, comprising Fitz-John Porter's division. McClellan seemed to my eyes crestfallen and moody today.

McClellan has fallen very much in my opinion since the Leesburg disaster. He went to the spot, and with a little promptitude and ability could have turned the check into a successful advance, in the blaze of which the earlier repulse would have been forgotten. It is whispered that General [Charles P.] Stone, who ordered the movement, is guilty of treason—a common crime of unlucky generals—at all events he is to be displaced and will be put under surveillance.[17]

October 31st. Nothing doing, except that General Scott has at last sent in [his] resignation. McClellan is now indeed master of the situation.

November 1st. Again stagnation; not the smallest intention of moving; General Scott's resignation, of which I was aware long ago, is publicly known, and he is about to go to Europe and end his days probably in France. McClellan takes his place, minus the large salary.

November 2nd. A tremendous gale of wind and rain blew all day and caused much uneasiness, at the Navy Department and elsewhere, for the safety of the Burnside expedition. The secessionists are delighted, and those who can, say, *Afflavit Deus et hostes dissipantur* [God speaks and the enemy are scattered]. There is a project to send secret

---

[17]Stone, commander of Union forces at Ball's Bluff, was suspected of treason because of his defeat. He was arrested and held in prison for 189 days, but formal charges were never brought against him. Even so, Stone received only minor commands and was always closely watched by his superiors. Unable to take the pressure of suspicion any longer, he resigned from the service in 1864.

non-official commissioners to Europe, to counteract the machinations of the Confederates.

November 3rd.   For some reason or another a certain set of papers have lately taken to flatter Mrs. Lincoln in the most noisome manner, whilst others deal in dark insinuations against her loyalty, Union principles, and honesty. The poor lady is loyal as steel to her family and to Lincoln the first, but she is accessible to the influence of flattery, and has permitted her society to be infested by men who would not be received in any respectable private house in New York.

The ladies in Washington delight to hear or to invest small scandals connected with the White House; thus it is reported that the Scotch gardener left by Mr. Buchanan has been made a lieutenant in the United States Army, and had been specially detached to do duty at the White House, where he superintends the cooking. Another person connected with the establishment was made Commissioner of Public Buildings, but was dismissed because he would not put down the expense of a certain state dinner to the public account, and charge it under the head of "Improvement to the Grounds." But many more better tales than these go round, and it is not surprising if a woman is now and then put under close arrest, or sent off to Fort McHenry for too much *esprit* and inventiveness.[18]

November 4th.   General Frémont will certainly be recalled. There is not the smallest incident to note.

November 5th.   Small banquets, very simple and tolerable social, are the order of the day as winter closes around us; the country has become too deep in mud for pleasant excursions and at times the weather is raw and cold. General McDowell maintains there will be no difficulty in advancing during bad weather, because the men are so expert in felling trees they can make corduroy roads wherever they

---

[18]Russell did not name the ladies imprisoned; however, in the fall of 1861, Pinkerton detectives arrested Augusta Morris and Rose O'Neal Greenhow as Confederate spies. Both women were temporarily confined in Fort McHenry and eventually deported to the South.

like. I own the arguments surprised but did not convince me and I think the General will find out his mistake when the time comes.

November 6th. There is an uneasy feeling respecting the intentions of France, founded on the notion that the Emperor is not very friendly to the Federalists and would be little disposed to expose his subjects to privation and suffering from the scarcity of cotton and tobacco if, by intervention, he could avert such misfortunes. The inactivity of McClellan, which is not understood by the people, has created an undercurrent of unpopularity, to which his enemies are giving every possible strength, and some people are beginning to think the youthful Napoleon is only a Brummagem Bonaparte.

November 11th. The United States have now, according to the returns, 60,000 infantry, 600 pieces of artillery, 61,000 cavalry in the field, and yet they are not only unable to crush the Confederates but they cannot conquer the secession ladies in their capital. The Southern people here trust in a breakdown in the North before the screw can be turned to the utmost; and assert that the South does not want corn, wheat, leather, or food. Georgia makes cloth enough for all— the only deficiency will be the metal and *matériel* of war. When the North comes to discuss the question whether the war is to be against slavery or for the Union, leaving slavery to take care of itself, they think a split will be inevitable. Then the pressure of taxes will force on a solution, for the State taxes already amount to 2 to 3 per cent., and the people will not bear the addition. The North has set out with the principle of paying for everything, the South with the principle of paying for nothing; but this will be reversed in time. All the diplomatists, with one exception, are of the opinion the Union is broken forever, and the independence of the South virtually established.

November 12th. An eruption of dirty little boys in the streets shouting out, "Glorious Union victory! Charleston taken!" The story is that Burnside has landed and reduced the forts defending Port Royal. I met Mr. Fox, Assistant Secretary to the Navy, and Mr. Hay, secretary to Mr. Lincoln, in the Avenue. The former showed me

Burnside's dispatches from Beaufort, announcing reduction of the skirts of Port Royal. I had a long conversation with Mr. Chase, who is still sanguine that the war must speedily terminate. The success at Beaufort has made him radiant, and he told me that the Federal General Nelson—who is no other than the enormous blustering, boasting lieutenant in the navy whom I met at Washington on my first arrival—had gained an immense victory in Kentucky, killing and capturing a whole army and its generals.[19]

A strong Government will be the end of the struggle, but before they come to it there must be a complete change of administration and internal economy. Indeed, the Secretary of the Treasury candidly admitted that the expenses of the war were enormous and could not go at the present rate very long. The men are paid too highly; every one is paid too much. The scale is adopted to a small army not very popular in a country where labour is very well paid, and competition is necessary to obtain recruits at all. He has never disguised his belief the South might have been left to go at first, with a certainty of their return to the Union.

November 13th.   Dining with Mr. Seward, I heard the sentiment of dislike towards England is increasing because English subjects have assisted the South by smuggling and running the blockade. "It is strange," said Mr. Seward, "that this great free and civilised Union should be supported by Germans, whilst the English are the great smugglers who support our enemies in their rebellion." The British public have a right to their sympathies too, and the Government can scarcely help it if private individuals aid the South on their own responsibility. Mr. Seward feels keenly the attacks in the *New York Tribune* on him for arbitrary arrests, and representations have been made to Mr. Greeley privately on the subject; nor is he indifferent to similar English criticisms.

General McDowell asserts there is no nation in the world whose censure or praise the people of the United States care about except

---

[19]This account is exaggerated. General William Nelson occupied Prestonburg, Kentucky, on November 5, 1861, but did not capture a large Confederate force.

England, and with respect to her there is a morbid sensitiveness which can neither be explained nor justified.

November 14th. I dined with Mr. Seward—Mr. Raymond of New York, and two or three gentlemen being the only guests. Mr. Lincoln came in whilst we were playing a rubber and told some excellent west country stories. "Here, Mr. President, we have got the two *Times*—of New York and of London—if they would only do what is right and what we want, all will go well." "Yes," said Mr. Lincoln, "if the bad Times would go where we want them, good Times would be sure to follow."

Talking over Bull's Run, Mr. Seward remarked "that civilians sometimes displayed more courage than soldiers, but perhaps the courage was unprofessional. When we were cut off from Baltimore and the United States troops at Annapolis were separated by a country swarming with malcontents, not a soldier could be found to undertake the journey and communicate with them. At last a civilian volunteered and executed the business. So, after Bull's Run, there was only one officer, General Sherman, who was doing anything to get the troops into order when the President and myself drove over to see what we could do on that terrible Tuesday evening."

November 16th. A cold, raw day. As I was writing, a small friend of mine, who appears like a stormy petrel in moments of great storm, fluttered into my room, and having chirped out something about a "Jolly row"—"Seizure of Mason and Slidell"—"British flag insulted," and the like, vanished. Somewhat later, going down 17th Street, I met the French Minister, M. Mercier, wrapped in his cloak, coming from the British Legation. "Vous avez entendu quelque chose de nouveau?" "Mais non, excellence." And then, indeed, I learned there was no doubt about the fact that Captain [Charles] Wilkes, of the U.S. steamer *San Jacinto,* had forcibly boarded the *Trent,* a British mail steamer, off the Bahamas, and had taken Messrs. [James M.] Mason, Slidell, Eustis, and McClernand from on board by armed force, in defiance of the protests of the captain and naval officer in charge of the mails. This was indeed grave intelligence, and the

French Minister considered the act a flagrant outrage, which would not for a moment be justified.[20]

I went to the Legation, and found the young diplomatists in the "Chancellerie" as demure and innocent as if nothing had happened, though perhaps they were a trifle more lively than usual. An hour later, and the whole affair was published in full in the evening papers. Extraordinary exultation prevailed in the hotels and barrooms. The State Department has made of course no communication respecting the matter. All the English are satisfied that Mason and his friends must be put on board an English mail packet from the *San Jacinto* under a salute.

An officer of the United States Navy—whose name I shall not mention here—came in to see the buccaneers, as the knot of English bachelors of Washington are termed, and talked over the matter. "Of course," he said, "we shall apologise and give up poor Wilkes to vengeance by dismissing him, but under no circumstances shall we ever give up Mason and Slidell. No, sir; not a man dare propose such a humiliation to our flag." He says that Wilkes acted on his own responsibility, and that the San Jacinto was coming home from the African station when she encountered the *Trent.* Wilkes knew the rebel emissaries were on board, and thought he would cut a dash and get up a little sensation, being a bold and daring sort of a fellow with a quarrelsome disposition and a great love of notoriety, but an excellent officer.

November 17th.   The papers contain joyous articles on the *Trent* affair, and some have got up an immense amount of learning at a

[20]Russell must have misunderstood M. Mercier. Those men removed from the *Trent* included Mason, John Slidell, George Eustis (Slidell's son-in-law and secretary), and J. F. McFarland, Mason's secretary. John McClernand was a Union general who served mainly on the western front. Jefferson Davis had chosen Mason and Slidell to represent the Confederacy to Britain and France, respectively. The men and their secretaries escaped from the South on a blockade runner and boarded the *Trent* at Havana. Hearing that the southern commissioners were on the British ship, Wilkes stopped it one day out of port, removed the commissioners and their secretaries, and let the *Trent* proceed to England. Wilkes did not act illegally in stopping the *Trent,* but he violated international law in removing the Confederates. Instead, he should have brought the entire ship into port for adjudication, letting the courts decide whether or not Mason and Slidell were "contraband" and therefore subject to seizure.

short notice; but I am glad to say we had no discussion in camp. All the Foreign Ministers, without exception, have called on Lord Lyons —Russia, France, Italy, Prussia, Denmark. All are of accord.

November 18th.   There is a storm of exultation sweeping over the land. Wilkes is the hero of the hour. I saw Mr. F. Seward at the State Department at ten o'clock; but at the British Legation the orders are not to speak of the transaction, so at the State Department a judicious reticence is equally observed. The lawyers are busy furnishing arguments to the newspapers. The officers who held their tongues at first, astonished at the audacity of the act, are delighted to find any arguments in its favour.

McClellan, I understand, advised the immediate surrender of the prisoners; but the authorities, supported by the sudden outburst of public approval, refused to take that step. I saw Lord Lyons, who appeared very much impressed by the magnitude of the crisis. Thence I visited the Navy Department, where Captain Dahlgren and Lieutenant Wise discussed the affair. It is obvious that no Power could permit political offenders sailing as passengers in a mailboat under its flag, from one neutral port to another, to be taken by a belligerent, though the recognition of such a right would be, perhaps, more advantageous to England than to any other Power. But notwithstanding these discussions, our naval friends dined and spent the evening with us, in company of some other officers.

November 19th.   I rarely sat down to write under a sense of greater responsibility, for it is just possible my letter may contain the first account of the seizure of the Southern Commissioners which will reach England; and, having heard all opinions and looked at authorities, as far as I could, it appears to me that the conduct of the American officer, now sustained by his Government, is without excuse.

November 20th.   Today a grand review, the most remarkable feature of which was the able disposition made by General McDowell to march seventy infantry regiments, seventeen batteries, and seven cavalry regiments, into a very contracted space, from the adjoining camps. Of the display itself I wrote a long account, which is not worth repeating here. Among the 55,000 men present there were at least 20,000 Germans, and 12,000 Irish.

November 22nd.   All the American papers have agreed that the *Trent* business is quite according to law, custom, and international comity, and that England can do nothing. They cry out so loudly in this one key there is reason to suspect they have some inward doubts.

On looking over my diary I can see nothing but memoranda relating to quiet rides, visits to camps, conversations with this one or that other, a fresh outburst of anonymous threatening letters, as if I have anything to do with the *Trent* affair, and notes of small social reunions at our own rooms and the Washington houses which were open to us.

November 25th.   The tide of success runs strongly in favour of the North at present, although they generally get the worst of it in the small affairs in the front of Washington. The entrance to Savannah had been occupied, and by degrees the fleets are biting into the Confederate lines along the coast, and establishing positions which will afford bases of operation to the Federals hereafter. The President and Cabinet seem in better spirits.

December 2nd.   Congress opened today. The Senate did nothing. In the House of Representatives some buncombe resolutions were passed about Captain Wilkes, who has become a hero—"a great interpreter of international law," and also recommending that Messrs. Mason and Slidell be confined in felon's cells in retaliation for Colonel [Michael] Corcoran's treatment by the Confederates.[21]

December 3rd.   Drove down to the Capitol, and was introduced to the floor of the Senate by Senator Wilson, and arrived just as Mr. Forney commenced reading the President's Message, which was listened to with considerable interest.

I dined with Mr. Cameron, Secretary of War, where I met Mr. Forney, secretary of the Senate. He told me he once worked as a

[21]Corcoran was captured at Bull Run and held in a Confederate prison for a year because he refused to sign a parole agreement.

printer in the city of Washington, at ten dollars a week, and twenty cents an hour for extra work at the case on Sundays. Since that time he has worked onwards and upwards and amassed a large fortune by contracts for railways and similar great undertakings. He says the press rules America and that no one can face it and live; which is about the worst account of the chances of an honest longevity I can well conceive. His memory is exact, and his anecdotes, albeit he has never seen any but Americans, or stirred out of the States, very agreeable. Once there lived at Washington a publican's daughter, named Mary O'Neil, beautiful, bold and witty. She captivated a member of Congress, who failed to make her less than his wife; and by degrees Mrs. Eaton—who may now be seen in the streets of Washington, an old woman, still bright-eyed and, alas! bright-cheeked, retaining traces of her great beauty—became a leading personage in the State, and ruled the imperious, rugged, old Andrew Jackson so completely, that he broke up his Cabinet and dismissed his ministers on her account.[22] In the days of her power she had done some trifling service to Mr. Cameron, and he has just repaid it by conferring some military appointment on her grandchild.

The dinner, which was preceded by deputations, was finished by one which came from the Far West, and was introduced by Mr. Hannibal Hamlin, the Vice-President; Mr. Owen Lovejoy, Mr. [John A.] Bingham, and other ultra-abolitionist members of Congress; and then speeches were made, and healths were drunk, and toasts were pledged, till it was time for me to drive to a ball given by the officers of the 5th United States Cavalry, which was exceedingly pretty, and admirably arranged in wooden huts, specially erected and decorated for the occasion. A huge bonfire in the centre of the camp, surrounded by soldiers, by the carriage drivers, and by Negro servants, afforded the most striking play of colour and variety of light and shade I ever beheld.

[22]Russell has his facts garbled. The lady in question was Margaret (Peggy) O'Neale Timberlake Eaton. She married John Eaton, Jackson's secretary of war, in 1829, three months after the death of her first husband. The marriage caused a scandal because the usual mourning period for a spouse was one year. Wives of other cabinet members, wives of foreign diplomats, and even Emily Donelson, Jackson's niece and official hostess, refused to extend the usual courtesies to Mrs. Eaton. The scandal led to the resignation of Jackson's first cabinet.

December 6th. Mr. [G. W.] Riggs says the paper currency scheme will produce money and make every man richer. He is a banker and ought to know; but to my ignorant eye it seems likely to prove most destructive, and I confess, that whatever be the result of this war, I have no desire for the ruin of so many happy communities as have sprung up in the United States. Had it been possible for human beings to employ popular constitutions without intrigue and miserable self-seeking, and to be superior to faction and party passion, the condition of parts of the United States must cause regret that an exemption from the usual laws which regulate human nature was not made in America; but the strength of the United States—directed by violent passions, by party interest, and by selfish intrigues—was becoming dangerous to the peace of other nations, and therefore there is an utter want of sympathy with them in their time of trouble.

December 11th. The unanimity of the people of the South is forced on the conviction of the statesmen and people of the North by the very success of their expeditions in secession. They find the planters at Beaufort and elsewhere burning their cotton and crops, villages and towns deserted at their approach, hatred in every eye, and curses on women's tongues. They meet this by a corresponding change in their own programme. The war which was made to develop and maintain Union sentiment in the South, and to enable the people to rise against a desperate faction which had enthralled them, is now to be made a crusade against slaveholders and a war of subjugation —if need be, of extermination—against the whole of the Southern States. The Democrats will, of course, resist this barbarous and hopeless policy. There is a deputation of Irish Democrats here now to effect a general exchange of prisoners, which is an operation calculated to give a legitimate character to the war, and is *pro tanto* [as far as it goes] a recognition of the Confederacy as a belligerent power.

December 12th. In spite of drills and parades, McClellan has not got an army yet. A good officer, who served as brigade major in our service, told me the men were little short of mutinous, with all their fine talk, though they could fight well. Sometimes they refuse to mount guard, or to go on duty not to their tastes; officers refuse to serve under others to whom they have a dislike; men offer similar personal objections to officers. McClellan is enforcing discipline and really intends to execute a most villainous deserter this time.

December 15th. The first echo of the *San Jacinto's* guns in England reverberated in the United States, and produced a profound sensation. The people had made up their minds John Bull would acquiesce in the seizure, and not say a word about it; or they affected to think so; and the cry of anger which has resounded through the land, and the unmistakable tone of the British press, at once surprise, and irritate, and disappoint them. The American journals, nevertheless, pretend to think it is a mere vulgar excitement, and that the press is "only indulging in its habitual bluster."

December 16th. I met Mr. Seward at a ball and cotillion party, given by M. [Miguel Maria] de Lisboa [Minister from Brazil]; and as he was in very good humour, and was inclined to talk, he pointed out to the Prince de Joinville and all who were inclined to listen, and myself, how terrible the effects of a war would be if Great Britain forced it on the United States. "We will wrap the whole world in flames!" he exclaimed. "No power so remote that she will not feel the fire of our battle and be burned by our conflagration." It is inferred that Mr. Seward means to show fight. One of the guests, however, said to me, "That's all bugaboo talk. When Seward talks that way, he means to break down. He is most dangerous and obstinate when he pretends to agree a good deal with you." The young French princes,[23] and the young and pretty Brazilian and American ladies, danced and were happy, notwithstanding the storms without.

Next day I dined at Mr. Seward's. Mr. Seward was in the best spirits and told one or two rather long, but very pleasant, stories. Now it is evident he must by this time know Great Britain has resolved on the course to be pursued, and his good humour, contrasted with the irritation he displayed in May and June, is not intelligible.

---

[23]The French princes were the Comte de Paris, pretender to the throne of France, and the Duc de Chartres, his brother. Exiled by Napoleon III, both young men offered their services to the Union cause. Their uncle, François d'Orléans, Prince de Joinville, accompanied the princes to the United States and served in an unofficial capacity on McClellan's staff.

The Americans are irritated by war preparations on the part of England, in case the Government of Washington do not accede to their demands; and, at the same time, much annoyed that all European nations join in an outcry against the famous project of destroying the Southern harbours.

December 20th. Lord Lyons had two interviews with Mr. Seward, read the dispatch, which simply asks for surrender of Mason and Slidell and reparation, but he received no indication from Mr. Seward of the course he would pursue. Mr. Lincoln has "put down his foot" on no surrender. "Sir," exclaimed the President, to an old Treasury official the other day, "I would sooner die than give them up." "Mr. President," was the reply, "your death would be a great loss, but the destruction of the United States would be a still more deplorable event." Mr. Seward will, however, control the situation, and the Cabinet will very probably support his views; and Americans will comfort themselves, in case the captives are surrendered, with a promise of future revenge and with the reflection that they have avoided a very disagreeable intervention between their march of conquest and the Southern Confederacy. The general belief of the diplomatists is, that the prisoners will not be given up and in that case Lord Lyons and the Legation will retire from Washington for the time, probably to Halifax, leaving Mr. [Edmund] Munson to wind up affairs and clear out the archives. But it is understood that there is no ultimatum, and that Lord Lyons is not to indicate any course of action should Mr. Seward inform him the United States Government refuses to comply with the demands of Great Britain.

Any humiliation which may be attached to concession will be caused by the language of the Americans themselves, who have given in their press, in public meetings, in the Lower House, in the Cabinet, and in the conduct of the President, a complete ratification of the act of Captain Wilkes, not to speak of the opinions of the lawyers, and the speeches of their orators, who declare "they will face any alternative, but that they will never surrender." The friendly relations which existed between ourselves and many excellent Americans are now rendered somewhat constrained by the prospect of a great national difference.

December 23rd. Constant interviews took place between the President and members of the Cabinet, and so certain are the people that war is inevitable that an officer connected with the executive of the Navy Department came in to tell me General Scott was coming over from Europe to conduct the Canadian campaign, as he had thoroughly studied the geography of the country, and that in a very short time he would be in possession of every strategic position on the frontier, and chaw up our reinforcements. Late in the evening, Mr. Olmsted called to say he had been credibly informed [that] Lord Lyons had quarrelled violently with Mr. Seward, had flown into a great passion with him, and so departed. The idea of Lord Lyons being quarrelsome, passionate, or violent, was preposterous enough to those who knew him; but the American papers, by repeated statements of the sort, have succeeded in persuading their public that the British Minister is a plethoric, red-faced, large-stomached man in top-boots, knee-breeches, yellow waistcoat, blue cut-away, brass button, and broad-brimmed white hat, who is continually walking to the State Department in company with a large bulldog, hurling defiance at Mr. Seward at one moment, and the next rushing home to receive dispatches from Mr. Jefferson Davis, or to give secret instructions to the British Consuls to run cargoes of quinine and gunpowder through the Federal blockade. I was enabled to assure Mr. Olmsted there was not the smallest foundation for the story; but he seemed impressed with a sense of some great calamity, and told me there was a general belief that England only wanted a pretext for a quarrel with the United States; nor could I comfort him by the assurance that there were good reasons for thinking General Scott would very soon annex Canada, in case of war.

December 26th. Senator Sumner dined with me, and after much evasion of the subject the English dispatch and Mr. Seward's decision turned up and caused some discussion. Mr. Sumner, who is Chairman of the Committee on Foreign Relations of the Senate, and in that capacity is in intimate *rapport* with the President, argues that the *Trent* affair can only be a matter for mediation. All along he has held this language and has maintained that at the very worst there is plenty of time for protocols, dispatches, and references, and more than once he said to me, "I hope you will keep the peace; help us to do so," the peace having been already broken by Captain Wilkes and the Government.

December 27th. This morning Mr. Seward sent in his reply to Lord [John] Russell's dispatch—*grandis et verbosa epistola* [a long and wordy letter]. The result destroys my prophecies, for, after all, the Southern Commissioners or Ambassadors are to be given up. Yesterday, indeed, in an undercurrent of whispers among the desponding friends of the South, there went a rumour that the Government had resolved to yield. What a collapse! What a bitter mortification! I had scarcely finished the perusal of an article in a Washington paper—which let it be understood is an organ of Mr. Lincoln—stating that "Mason and Slidell would *not* be surrendered, and assuring the people they need entertain no apprehension of such a dishonourable concession," when I learned beyond all possibility of doubt that Mr. Seward had handed in his dispatch, placing the Commissioners at the disposal of the British Minister. A copy of the dispatch will be published in the *National Intelligencer* tomorrow morning at an early hour, in time to go to Europe by the steamer which leaves New York.

December 28th. The *National Intelligencer* of this morning contains the dispatches of Lord Russell, M. [Antoine] Thouvenel,[24] and Mr. Seward. The bubble has burst. The rage of the friends of compromise, and of the South, who saw in a war with Great Britain the complete success of the Confederacy, is deep and burning, if not loud; but they all say they never expected anything better from the cowardly and braggart statesmen who now rule Washington.

Some time ago we were all prepared to hear nothing less would be accepted than Captain Wilkes taking Messrs. Mason and Slidell on board the *San Jacinto* and transferring them to the *Trent,* under a salute to the flag, near the scene of the outrage; but Mr. Seward, apprehensive that some outrage would be offered by the populace to the prisoners and the British flag, had asked Lord Lyons that the Southern Commissioners may be placed, as it were surreptitiously, in a United States boat and carried to a small seaport in the State of

[24]Lord John Russell and M. Antoine Edouard Thouvenel were the foreign ministers of Britain and France.

Maine, where they are to be placed on board a British vessel as quietly as possible; and this exigent, imperious, tyrannical, insulting British Minister had cheerfully acceded to the request. Mr. Conway Seymour, the Queen's messenger, who brought Lord Russell's dispatch, was sent back with instructions for the British Admiral to send a vessel to Providencetown for the purpose; as there was not the smallest prospect of any military movement taking place, I resolved to go northwards with him; and we left Washington accordingly on the morning of the 31st of December, and arrived at New York Hotel the same night.

[January 1–March 18, 1862.]   The illness which had prostrated some of the strongest men in Washington, including General McClellan himself, developed itself as soon as I ceased to be sustained by the excitement, such as it was, of daily events at the capital and by expectations of a move; and for some time an attack of typhoid fever confined me to my room and left me so weak that I was advised not to return to Washington till I had tried change of air. I remained in New York till the end of January, when I proceeded to make a tour in Canada, as it is quite impossible for any operation to take place on the Potomac, where deep mud, alternating with snow and frost, bound the contending armies in winter quarters.

On my return to New York, at the end of February, the North was cheered by some signal successes achieved in the West principally by gunboats, operating on the lines of the great rivers. The greatest results have been obtained in the capture of Fort Donelson and Fort Henry by Commander Foote's flotilla co-operating with the land forces. The possession of an absolute naval supremacy, of course, gives the North United States powerful means of annoyance and inflicting injury and destruction on the enemy; it also secures for them the means of seizing upon bases of operations wherever they please, of breaking up the enemy's lines, and maintaining communications. The long threatened encounter between Bragg and Brown has taken place at Pensacola, without effect, and the attempts of the Federals to advance from Port Royal have been successfully resisted. Sporadic skirmishes have sprung up over every border State; but, on the whole, success has inclined to the Federals in Kentucky and Tennessee.

On the 1st March, I arrived in Washington once more and found things very much as I had left them: the army recovering the effects of the winter's sickness and losses, animated by the victories of their comrades in western fields, and by the hope that the ever-coming tomorrow would see them in the field at last. In place of Mr. Cameron, an Ohio lawyer named [Edwin] Stanton has been appointed Secretary of War. He came to Washington a few years ago to conduct some legal proceedings for Mr. Daniel Sickles, and by his energy, activity, and a rapid conversion from Democratic to Republican principles, as well as by his Union sentiments, recommended himself to the President and his Cabinet.

The month of March passed without any remarkable event in the field. When the army started at last to attack the enemy—a movement which was precipitated by hearing that they were moving away —they went out only to find the Confederates had fallen back by interior lines towards Richmond, and General McClellan was obliged to transport his army from Alexandria to the peninsula of Yorktown, where his reverses, his sufferings, and his disastrous retreat, are so well known and so recent, that I need only mention them as among the most remarkable events which have yet occurred in this war.

I had looked forward for many weary months to participating in the movement and describing its results. Immediately on my arrival in Washington, I was introduced to Mr. Stanton, and the Secretary, without making any positive pledge, used words which led me to believe he would give me permission to draw rations and undoubtedly promised to afford me every facility in his power. Subsequently he sent me a private pass to the War Department to enable me to get through the crowd of contractors and jobbers; but on going there to keep my appointment, the Assistant Secretary of War told me Mr. Stanton had been summoned to a Cabinet Council by the President.

We had some conversation respecting the subject matter of my application, which the Assistant Secretary[25] seemed to think would be attended with many difficulties, in consequence of the number of correspondents to the American papers who might demand the same privileges, and he intimated to me that Mr. Stanton was little dis-

---

[25]It is not clear to which assistant secretary Russell is referring. Stanton's assistant secretaries of war included Peter Watson, John Tucker, and Thomas A. Scott.

posed to encourage them in any way whatever. Now this is undoubtedly honest on Mr. Stanton's part, for he knows he might render
himself popular by granting what they ask; but he is excessively vain
and aspires to be considered a rude, rough, vigorous Oliver Cromwell
sort of man, mistaking some of the disagreeable attributes and the
accidents of the external husk of the Great Protector for the brain and
head of a statesman and a soldier.

The American officers with whom I was intimate gave me to
understand that I could accompany them in case I received permission from the Government, but they were obviously unwilling to
encounter the abuse and calumny which would be heaped upon their
heads by American papers unless they could show the authorities did
not disapprove of my presence in their camp. Several invitations sent
to me were accompanied by the phrase, "You will of course get a
written permission from the War Department, and then there will be
no difficulty." On the evening of the private theatricals by which
Lord Lyons enlivened the ineffable dullness of Washington, I saw
Mr. Stanton at the Legation and he conversed with me for some time.
I mentioned the difficulty connected with passes. He asked me what
I wanted. I said, "An order to go with the army to Manassas." At his
request I procured a sheet of paper, and he wrote me a pass, took a
copy of it, which he put in his pocket and then handed the other to
me. On looking at it, I perceived that it was a permission for me to
go to Manassas and back, and that all officers, soldiers, and others,
in the United States service, were to give me every assistance and
show me every courtesy; but the hasty return of the army to Alexandria rendered it useless.

The *Merrimac* and *Monitor* encounter produced the profoundest
impression in Washington and unusual strictness was observed respecting passes to Fortress Monroe.[26]

[March 19–April 9.] I applied at the Navy Department for a
passage down to Fortress Monroe, as it was expected the *Merrimac*
was coming out again, but I could not obtain leave to go in any of
the vessels.

As soon as General McClellan commenced his movement, he sent

[26]The battle between the *Monitor* and the *Merrimack* occurred on March 9, 1862.

a message to me by one of the French princes, that he would have great pleasure in allowing me to accompany his headquarters in the field. I find the following, under the head of March 22nd:

"Received a letter from General Marcy, chief of the staff, asking me to call at his office. He told me General McClellan directed him to say he had no objection whatever to my accompanying the army, 'but,' continued General Marcy, 'you know we are a sensitive people, and that our press is exceedingly jealous. General McClellan has many enemies who seek to pull him down, and scruple at no means of doing so. He and I would be glad to do anything in our power to help you, if you come with us, but we must not expose ourselves needlessly to attack. The army is to move to the York and James rivers at once.' "

All my arrangements were made with General Van Vliet, the quartermaster-general of headquarters. I was quite satisfied from Mr. Stanton's promise and General Marcy's conversation that I should have no further difficulty. On the 26th March, I went to Baltimore in company with Colonel Rowan of the Royal Artillery, who had come down for a few days to visit Washington, intending to go on by steamer to Fortress Monroe, as he was desirous of seeing his friends on board the [H.M.S.] Rinaldo, and I wished to describe the great flotilla assembled there.

On arriving at Baltimore, we learned it would be necessary to get a special pass from General [John A.] Dix, and on going to the General's headquarters, his aide-de-camp informed us that he had received special instructions recently from the War Department to grant no passes to Fortress Monroe, unless to officers and soldiers going on duty, or to persons in the service of the United States. The aide-de-camp advised me to telegraph to Mr. Stanton for permission, which I did, but no answer was received, and Colonel Rowan and I returned to Washington, thinking there would be a better chance of securing the necessary order there.

Next day we went to the Department of War and were shown into Mr. Stanton's room—his secretary informing us that he was engaged in the next room with the President and other ministers in a council of war, but that he would no doubt receive a letter from me and send me out a reply. I accordingly addressed a note to Mr. Stanton, requesting he would be good enough to give an order to Colonel

Rowan, of the British army, and myself, to go by the mailboat from Baltimore to Monroe. In a short time Mr. Stanton sent out a note to the following words: "Mr. Stanton informs Mr. Russell no passes to Fortress Monroe can be given at present, unless to officers of the United States service." We tried the Navy Department, but no vessels were going down, they said; and one of the officers suggested that we should ask for passes to go down and visit *H.M.S. Rinaldo* exclusively, which could not well be refused, he thought, to British subjects, and promised to take charge of the letter for Mr. Stanton and to telegraph the permission down to Baltimore. There we returned by the afternoon train and waited, but neither reply nor pass came for us.

Next day we were disappointed also, and an officer of the *Rinaldo,* who had come up on duty from the ship, was refused permission to take us down on his return. So far as I know Mr. Stanton sent no reply to my last letter, and calling at his house on his reception night, the door was opened by his brother-in-law, who said, "The Secretary was attending a sick child and could not see any person that evening," so I never met Mr. Stanton again.[27]

The rest of the story may be told in a few words. It was perfectly well known in Washington that I was going with the army, and I presume Mr. Stanton, if he had any curiosity about such a trifling matter, must have heard it also. I am told he was informed of it at the last moment and then flew out into a coarse passion against General McClellan because he had dared to invite or to take anyone without his permission.[28] He sent down a dispatch to Van Vliet and summoned him at once to the War Office. When Van Vliet returned in a couple of hours, he made a communication to me that Mr. Stanton had given him written orders to prevent my passage. General

[27]James Hutchinson was the brother of Stanton's wife, Ellen Hutchinson Stanton. Russell's phraseology implies that Stanton was using the "sick child" excuse to avoid seeing him. That may not have been the case; Stanton's infant son was ill at the time and died four months later, in July 1862.

[28]Stanton's reaction was perhaps due more to his dislike of McClellan than to his desire to keep Russell from the fighting front. McClellan and Stanton had been on friendly terms before the latter's appointment as secretary of war. Once Stanton assumed his duties at the war office, he became convinced that McClellan's military ability was overrated, and the two men grew to dislike each other intensely.

Van Vliet assured me that he and General McDowell had urged every argument they could think of in my favour, particularly the fact that I was the specially invited guest of General McClellan, and that I was actually provided with a pass by his order from the chief of his staff.

I laid the statement of what had occurred before the President, who at first gave me hopes from the wording of his letter that he would overrule Mr. Stanton's order, but who next day informed me he could not take it upon himself to do so.

It was plain I had now but one course left. My mission in the United States was to describe military events and operations, or, in defect of them, to deal with such subjects as might be interesting to people at home. I went to America to witness and describe the operations of the great army before Washington in the field, and when I was forbidden by the proper authorities to do so, my mission terminated at once.

On the evening of April 4th, as soon as I was in receipt of the President's last communication, I telegraphed to New York to engage a passage by a steamer which left on the following Wednesday. Next day was devoted to packing up and to taking leave of my friends— English and American—whose kindnesses I shall remember in my heart of hearts, and the following Monday I left Washington, of which, after all, I shall retain many pleasant memories and keep souvenirs green forever. I arrived in New York late on Tuesday evening, and next day I saw the shores receding into a dim grey fog, and ere the night fell was tossing about once more on the stormy Atlantic, with the head of our good ship pointing, thank Heaven, towards Europe.

Biographical Notes

~

PROMINENT AMERICANS MENTIONED BY WILLIAM HOWARD RUSSELL

ADAMS, CHARLES FRANCIS (1807–1886). Union statesman. Son of John Quincy
Adams; graduated Harvard, 1826; Republican congressman from Massachusetts, 1859–1861; minister to Great Britain, 1861–1868.

ANDERSON, ROBERT (1805–1871). Union general. Graduated West Point, 1825;
served in Seminole and Mexican wars; taught tactics at West Point;
commander at Fort Sumter, 1861; commander of departments of Kentucky and the Cumberland, 1861–1862; retired, 1863.

BAKER, EDWARD D. (1811–1861). Union statesman and officer. Whig congressman from Illinois, 1849–1851; Republican senator from Oregon, 1860–
1861; served in Mexican War; commissioned colonel, 71st Pennsylvania, 1861; killed at Ball's Bluff, 1861.

BANCROFT, GEORGE (1800–1891). Historian and diplomat. Graduated Harvard,
1817; studied in various German universities; established Round Hill
School, 1822; published *History of the United States* (10 vols., 1834–1874);
secretary of navy, 1845–1846; advocated and established U.S. Naval
Academy, 1845; minister to Great Britain, 1846–1849; advised Lincoln
on matters of historical precedent; minister to Germany, 1867–1874.

BANKS, NATHANIEL P. (1816–1894). Union general. Democratic congressman from Massachusetts, 1853–1857; governor, 1858–1861; commissioned brigadier general, U. S. Volunteers, 1861; served on eastern front, 1861–1862; western front, 1862–1864.

BARRY, WILLIAM FARQUHAR (1818–1879). Union general. Graduated West Point, 1836; served in Seminole and Mexican wars; in charge of artillery at Fort Pickens, 1861; chief of artillery, eastern front, 1861–1864, and western front, 1864–1865.

BATES, EDWARD (1793–1869). Union statesman. National Republican congressman from Missouri, 1827–1829; judge St. Louis Land Court, 1853–1856; attorney general, 1861–1869.

BEAUREGARD, PIERRE G. T. (1818–1893). Confederate general. Graduated West Point, 1838; served in Mexican War; superintendent of West Point, 1861; resigned U.S. Army, 1861; commissioned brigadier general, C.S. Army, 1861; commander at Charleston and at Bull Run, 1861; various command posts in North Carolina and Virginia, 1862–1865.

BENJAMIN, JUDAH P. (1811–1884). Confederate statesman. Born in St. Croix, Virgin Islands; attended Yale; senator from Louisiana as Whig, 1853–1859; as Democrat, 1859–1861; attorney general, secretary of war, and secretary of state, 1861–1865.

BIGELOW, JOHN (1817–1911). Union editor and statesman. Graduated Union College, 1835; co-owner and editor of New York *Evening Post*, 1848–1861; consul-general at Paris, 1861–1865; minister to France, 1865–1866.

BLAIR, FRANCIS P., JR. (1821–1875). Union general and statesman. Graduated Princeton, 1841; served in Mexican War; Free-Soil and Republican congressman from Missouri, 1856–1858, 1860–1862; commissioned major general, 1862; served chiefly in western theater; Democratic vice-presidential nominee, 1868.

BLAIR, MONTGOMERY (1813–1883). Union statesman. Brother of Francis P. Blair, Jr.; Graduated West Point, 1835; served in Seminole War; Dred Scott's counsel before U.S. Supreme Court, 1856–1857; postmaster general, 1861–1864; joined Democratic party in Reconstruction era.

BRAGG, BRAXTON (1817–1876). Confederate general. Graduated West Point, 1837; served in Seminole and Mexican wars; resigned U.S. Army, 1856; commissioned major general, C.S. Army, 1861; commander of Gulf Coast defenses, 1861; of Army of Tennessee, 1862–1864; military adviser to Jefferson Davis, 1864–1865.

BROOKS, PRESTON S. (1819–1857). Statesman. Graduated South Carolina College; Democratic congressman from South Carolina, 1853–1856; noted chiefly for his assault on Charles Sumner in 1856.

BROWN, GEORGE W. (1835–?). Union naval officer. Appointed midshipman, 1849; lieutenant, 1856; served in African Squadron; special service on *Powhatan,* 1861; commander of *Ocorora* blockading Wilmington, North Carolina, 1862; commissioned lieutenant commander, 1862; commander, 1866; commander of Norfolk Navy Yard in postwar era.

BROWN, HARVEY (1796–1874). Union general. Graduated West Point, 1818; served in Seminole and Mexican wars; commander of Fort Pickens, 1861–1862; of New York harbor, 1862–1863; retired, 1863.

BROWNE, WILLIAM M. (?–1884). Confederate statesman and general. Born in England; newspaper editor in Washington, D.C., 1850s; assistant secretary of state, 1861; aide-de-camp to Jefferson Davis, 1861–1864; commissioned brigadier general, C.S. Army, 1864; commander of defenses of Savannah, 1864–1865.

BUCHANAN, FRANKLIN (1800–1874). Confederate admiral. Entered U.S. Navy, 1815; superintendent of U.S. Naval Academy, 1845–1847; served in Mexican War; commander of *Merrimack,* 1862; defeated at Mobile Bay, 1864.

BUCHANAN, JAMES (1791–1868). Statesman. Graduated Dickinson College, 1809; served in War of 1812; Federalist Pennsylvania state legislator, 1814–1815; National Republican congressman, 1821–1834; Democratic senator, 1837–1843; secretary of state, 1845–1849; minister to Great Britain, 1853–1856; U.S. president, 1857–1861.

BURNSIDE, AMBROSE E. (1824–1881). Union general. Graduated West Point, 1847; served in Mexican War; resigned U.S. Army, 1853; reentered and commissioned brigadier general, 1861; commander of Army of Potomac, 1862–1863; of Army of Ohio, 1863; of IX Corps, 1864–1865.

BUTLER, BENJAMIN F. (1818–1893). Union general and statesman. Graduated Colby College, 1838; Democratic New Hampshire legislator, 1853–1859; commissioned brigadier general, 1861; held various commands including Fort Monroe, New Orleans, departments of Virginia, North Carolina, and the James. Prominent Radical Republican politician from Massachusetts in postwar era.

CALHOUN, WILLIAM RANSOM (1827–1862). Confederate officer. Distant relative of John C. Calhoun; attended West Point; secretary, U.S. legation, Paris; captain and colonel in 1st Regiment South Carolina Regulars; killed in a duel, 1862.

CAMERON, SIMON (1799–1889). Union statesman. Newspaper editor; senator from Pennsylvania as Democrat, 1849–1853; as Republican, 1857–1861; secretary of war, 1861; minister to Russia, 1862; senator, 1867–1877.

CAMPBELL, JOHN A. (1811–1889). Jurist and Confederate statesman. Associate justice, U.S. Supreme Court, 1853–1861; Confederate assistant secretary of war, 1862; commissioner to Hampton Roads Conference, 1865.

CHASE, SALMON P. (1808–1873). Union statesman. Graduated Dartmouth, 1826; Free Soil senator from Ohio, 1849–1854; Republican governor of Ohio, 1855–1859; senator, 1860; secretary of the treasury, 1861–1864; chief justice, U.S. Supreme Court, 1864–1873.

CHESNUT, JAMES, JR. (1815–1885). Confederate statesman and general. Graduated Princeton, 1835; Democratic senator from South Carolina, 1858–1860; member, Confederate Provisional Congress, 1861; Beauregard's aide-de-camp, 1861; Davis's aide-de-camp, 1862–1864; commissioned brigadier general, C.S. Army, 1864; commander of reserve forces in South Carolina, 1864–1865.

CLARK, CHARLES (1811–1877). Confederate general and statesman. Planter; served in Mexican War; commissioned brigadier general, 1861; wounded at Shiloh; resigned, 1863; governor of Mississippi, 1864–1865.

COBB, HOWELL (1815–1865). Confederate statesman and general. Attended University of Georgia; Democratic congressman from Georgia, 1843–1857; secretary of the treasury, 1857–1860; chairman, Confederate Constitutional Convention, 1861; commissioned brigadier general, 1862; commander, District of Georgia.

CRAWFORD, MARTIN J. (1820–1883). Confederate statesman. Attended Mercer University; Democratic congressman from Georgia, 1855–1861; member, Confederate Provisional Congress, 1861; commissioner to U.S. government, 1861; aide-de-camp to Howell Cobb, 1862–1865.

CRITTENDEN, JOHN J. (1787–1863). Statesman. Graduated College of William & Mary, 1806; senator from Kentucky as National Republican, 1817–1819; as Whig, 1835–1848; 1855–1861; opposed secession; known chiefly for Crittenden Compromise measures of 1860–1861.

CULLUM, GEORGE W. (1809–1892). Union general. Graduated West Point, 1833; served as engineer in fortifications and construction; commissioned brigadier general, 1861; main service during war in Missouri, Tennessee, and Mississippi; superintendent of West Point, 1864–1866.

DAHLGREN, JOHN A. (1809–1870). Union admiral. Inventor of Dahlgren gun; commander of Washington Navy Yard, 1861–1862; chief of ordnance,

1862–1863; commander of South Atlantic Blockading Squadron, 1863–1865.

DANA, CHARLES A. (1819–1897). Journalist. Attended Harvard; participated in Brook Farm experiment, 1841–1846; city editor, *New York Tribune,* 1847–1862; assistant secretary of war, 1863–1864; editor, *New York Sun,* 1868.

DAVIS, JEFFERSON (1808–1889). Confederate statesman. Graduated West Point, 1828; resigned U.S. Army, 1835; reentered and served in Mexican War; Democratic senator from Mississippi, 1847–1851; 1857–1861; secretary of war, 1853–1857; president of Confederate States, 1861–1865; imprisoned at Fort Monroe, 1865–1867; spent remainder of life writing history of Confederacy.

DAVIS, VARINA HOWELL (1826–1906). Wife of Jefferson Davis. Attended Madame Greenland's school in Philadelphia; socially prominent in Washington during 1850s; staunchly defended Davis during war; often regarded with suspicion because of northern education; authored memoir of husband, 1890.

DAYTON, WILLIAM L. (1807–1864). Union statesman. Graduated Princeton, 1825; Whig senator from New Hampshire, 1842–1851; Republican vice-presidential nominee, 1856; minister to France, 1861–1864.

DEAS, ZACHARIAH C. (1819–1882). Confederate general. Nephew of James Chesnut, Jr.; attended Columbia College; served in Mexican War; appointed colonel Alabama Infantry, 1861; aide-de-camp to Joseph E. Johnston; commissioned brigadier general, 1862; served mainly in Tennessee, Georgia, and the Carolinas.

DOUGLAS, STEPHEN A. (1813–1861). Statesman. Democratic congressman and senator from Illinois, 1843–1861; as chairman of Senate Committee on Territories, guided Compromise of 1850 and Kansas-Nebraska Act through Congress; broke with Buchanan administration over Kansas, 1857; northern Democratic presidential nominee, 1860; toured South and North, giving speeches against secession, 1860–1861.

ELLIS, JOHN W. (1820–1861). Confederate statesman. Graduated University of North Carolina, 1841; Democratic state legislator North Carolina, 1844–1848; judge of North Carolina Superior Court, 1848–1858; governor, 1858–1861; advocated seizure of forts along Cape Fear estuary.

FOOTE, ANDREW H. (1806–1863). Union admiral. Entered U.S. Navy, 1822; flag officer in command of western flotilla, 1862; important role in seizure of Forts Donelson and Henry and Island No. 10; appointed rear admiral, 1862; chief of Bureau of Equipment and Recruiting, 1862–1863.

FORSYTH, JOHN (1812–1877). Confederate statesman and journalist. Graduated Princeton, 1832; editor, *Columbus* (Ga.) *Times,* 1841–1847; served in Mexican War; editor, Mobile *Register,* 1853–1856; minister to Mexico, 1856–1858; mayor of Mobile, 1860–1866; commissioner to U.S. government, 1861.

FOX, GUSTAVUS VASA (1821–1883). Union statesman and naval officer. Appointed midshipman, 1838; served in Mexican War; resigned U.S. Navy, 1856; Lincoln's special commissioner to investigate conditions at Fort Sumter, 1861; first assistant secretary of the Navy, 1861–1865.

FRÉMONT, JOHN C. (1813–1880). Union general. Army engineer noted for exploration of Far West; Republican presidential nominee, 1856; commissioned major general, 1861; commander Western Department, 1861; of Mountain Department, 1862; resigned, 1862.

GARNETT, ROBERT S. (1819–1861). Confederate general. Graduated West Point, 1841; served on frontier and in Mexican War; resigned U.S. Army, 1861; commissioned brigadier general, C.S. Army, 1861; killed at Corrick's Ford, Virginia, 1861.

GREELEY, HORACE (1811–1872). Journalist. Founded *New York Tribune,* 1841; known as advocate of reform, especially antislavery; Liberal Republican and Democratic presidential nominee, 1872.

GWIN, WILLIAM (1805–1885). Statesman. Graduated Transylvania University, 1828; Democratic congressman from Mississippi, 1841–1843; senator from California, 1850–1855, 1857–1861; Confederate sympathizer.

HALLECK, HENRY W. (1815–1872). Union general. Graduated West Point, 1839; authored books on military tactics; served in Mexican War; retired U.S. Army, 1854; reentered and commissioned major general, 1861; commander of Western Department, 1862; Lincoln's military adviser, 1862–1864; chief of staff, 1864–1865.

HAMLIN, HANNIBAL (1809–1891). Union statesman. Democratic congressman from Maine, 1843–1847; senator as Democrat, 1847–1857; as Republican, 1857–1861; U. S. vice-president, 1861–1865; senator, 1869–1881; minister to Spain, 1881–1882.

HARDEE, WILLIAM J. (1815–1873). Confederate general. Graduated West Point, 1838; served in Seminole and Mexican wars; resigned U.S. Army, 1861; commissioned brigadier general, C.S. Army, 1861; served chiefly in Tennessee and Georgia; evacuated Savannah and Charleston to Union forces in 1864 and 1865.

HAY, JOHN (1838–1905). Union statesman. Graduated Brown University, 1858; private secretary to Lincoln, 1860–1865; first secretary, U.S. legation, Paris, 1865–1867; assistant secretary of state, 1878–1881; minister to Great Britain, 1897–1898; secretary of state, 1898–1905; coauthor, with John Nicolay and John Hay, of *Abraham Lincoln: A History* (10 vols., 1890).

HICKS, THOMAS (1798–1865). Union statesman. Unionist governor of Maryland, 1857–1862; credited with keeping the state in the Union; Unionist senator, 1864–1865.

HUGER, BENJAMIN (1805–1877). Confederate general. Graduated West Point, 1825; served in Mexican War; resigned U.S. Army, 1861; appointed brigadier general, C.S. Army, 1861; served in Peninsula Campaign, 1862; inspector of artillery and ordnance in western theater for duration.

JACKSON, THOMAS J., "Stonewall" (1824–1863). Confederate general. Graduated West Point, 1846; served in Mexican War; resigned U.S. Army, 1851; taught at Virginia Military Institute, 1851–1861; commissioned brigadier general, C.S. Army, 1861; served in Virginia theater at first and second battles of Bull Run, Peninsula Campaign, Shenandoah Valley Campaign, Antietam, Fredericksburg, and Chancellorsville; mortally wounded by own men at Chancellorsville, 1863.

JOHNSTON, JOSEPH E. (1807–1891). Confederate general. Graduated West Point, 1829; served in Black Hawk, Seminole, and Mexican wars as well as on frontier; resigned U.S. Army, 1861; commissioned brigadier general, C.S. Army, 1861; credited with Confederate victory at first battle of Bull Run; wounded at Seven Pines, 1862; returned to duty, 1862; served chiefly in western theater, 1863–1865; surrendered western Confederate army to Sherman, 1865.

KEITT, LAWRENCE (1824–1864). Confederate statesman and officer. Graduated South Carolina College, 1843; Democratic congressman from South Carolina, 1853–1860; Confederate congressman, 1861–1862; commissioned colonel of South Carolina Volunteers, 1862; died from wounds received at Cold Harbor, 1864.

KENNER, DUNCAN (1813–1887). Confederate statesman. Confederate senator from Louisiana, 1862–1865; largest slaveholder in Confederate Congress, owning 473 slaves; sent by Jefferson Davis to Europe with offer to abolish slavery in return for diplomatic recognition by England and France, 1865.

LANE, JAMES H. (1814–1866). Union statesman. Served in Mexican War; Democratic congressman from Indiana, 1853–1855; leader of Free-State party in Kansas Territory; Republican senator from Kansas, 1861–1866; troops under his command served briefly as Lincoln's bodyguard, 1861.

LAWTON, ALEXANDER R. (1815–1896). Confederate general. Graduated West Point, 1839; resigned U.S. Army, 1840; lawyer and railroad president in

Georgia; commissioned brigadier general, C.S. Army, 1861; commander of Fort Pulaski, 1861; served in Peninsula Campaign and second battle of Bull Run, 1862; quartermaster general, 1864–1865.

LEE, ROBERT E. (1807–1870). Confederate general. Graduated West Point, 1829; served in Mexican War; superintendent of West Point, 1852–1855; refused command of U.S. Army and resigned, 1861; military adviser to Jefferson Davis, 1861–1862; commander Army of Northern Virginia, 1862–1865; commander-in-chief of all Confederate armies, 1865; president of Washington (later Washington and Lee) University, 1865–1870.

LETCHER, JOHN (1813–1884). Confederate statesman. Graduated Washington University, 1833; Democratic congressman from Virginia, 1851–1859; governor of Virginia, 1860–1864.

LINCOLN, ABRAHAM (1809–1865). Union statesman. Whig Illinois state legislator, 1834–1840; congressman, 1847–1849; leader of Republican party in Illinois, 1856–1860; candidate for U.S. Senate, 1855, 1858; U.S. president, 1861–1865.

LINCOLN, MARY TODD (1818–1882). Wife of Abraham Lincoln. Married, 1842; White House years plagued by rumors of extravagance and southern sympathy.

LOVEJOY, OWEN (1811–1864). Union statesman. Brother of Elijah Lovejoy, antislavery martyr; graduated Bowdoin College, 1832; Republican congressman from Illinois, 1859–1864.

LUCAS, JAMES J. (1831–1914). Confederate officer. Graduated South Carolina Military Academy, 1851; Democratic state legislator, 1856, aide-de-camp to Governor Pickens, 1861; commanded Lucas's battalion in South Carolina, 1861–1865; director of Atlantic Railroad Company in postwar era.

LYON, NATHANIEL (1818–1861). Union general. Graduated West Point, 1841; served in Seminole and Mexican wars; also on frontier and in Kansas; stationed at St. Louis Arsenal, 1861; commissioned brigadier general, U.S. Volunteers, 1861; killed at Wilson's Creek, 1861.

McCLELLAN, GEORGE BRINTON (1826–1885). Union general. Graduated West Point, 1846; served in Mexican War; U.S. military observer in Crimean War; resigned U.S. Army, 1857; vice-president Illinois Central Railroad, 1857–1861; commissioned major general, 1861; commander Army of Potomac, 1861–1862; dismissed from command following Antietam, 1862; Democratic presidential nominee, 1864; governor of New Jersey, 1878–1881.

McCULLOCH, BENJAMIN (1811–1862). Confederate general. Served in Mexican War; colonel in Texas Rangers, 1850s; appointed brigadier general, 1861; commander of Arkansas Department; killed at Pea Ridge, 1862.

McDOWELL, IRWIN (1818–1885). Union general. Graduated West Point, 1838; served in Mexican War and on frontier; staff officer in Washington; appointed brigadier general, 1861; commander Army of Potomac, 1861; defeated at first battle of Bull Run, 1861; commander I Corps, Army of Potomac; also commander, Army of Rappahannock and III Corps, Army of Virginia, 1861–1864, and Department of the Pacific, 1865.

MAGOFFIN, BERIAH (1815–1885). Statesman. Graduated Centre College, 1833; Kentucky state judge, 1840–1850; state legislator, 1850; governor of Kentucky, 1859–1862; private law practice in postwar years.

MANNING, JOHN L. (1816–1889). Confederate statesman. Graduated South Carolina College, 1837; South Carolina state legislator, 1840s; governor of South Carolina, 1852–1856; aide-de-camp to Beauregard, 1861–1865.

MANSFIELD, JOSEPH KING FENNO (1803–1862). Union general. Graduated West Point, 1822; served in Mexican War; inspector general, U.S. Army, 1853; commander, Department of Washington, 1861–1862; mortally wounded at Antietam, 1862.

MASON, JAMES M. (1798–1871). Confederate statesman. Graduated University of Pennsylvania, 1818; Democratic congressman from Virginia, 1837–1839; senator, 1847–1861; Confederate representative to Great Britain, 1861–1865.

MAURY, DABNEY H. (1822–1900). Confederate general. Graduated West Point, 1846; served in Mexican War and on frontier; resigned U.S. Army, 1861; appointed colonel, C.S. Army, 1861; brigadier general, 1862; served chiefly on western front.

MAURY, MATTHEW F. (1806–1873). Confederate naval officer. Uncle of Dabney Maury; authored books on navigation and commerce; commissioned commander, 1861; served in Europe purchasing and outfitting cruisers for C.S. Navy.

MEIGS, MONTGOMERY C. (1816–1892). Union general. Graduated West Point, 1836; duty limited to engineering assignments, 1836–1861; commissioned brigadier general and named quartermaster general, 1861; served as quartermaster general for duration.

MILES, WILLIAM PORCHER (1822–1899). Confederate statesman. Graduated Charleston College, 1842; mayor of Charleston, 1855–1857; Democratic congressman, 1857–1860; member, Confederate Provisional Congress,

1861; Confederate congressman, 1861–1864; president, University of South Carolina, 1880–1882.

NELSON, WILLIAM, "BULL" (1824–1862). Union general. Served in U.S. Navy during Mexican War; appointed brigadier general, U.S. Volunteers, 1861; commanded 4th Division, Army of Ohio, 1861; Army of Kentucky, 1862; killed in 1862; Nelson was called "Bull" because he was 6 feet, 4 inches tall and weighed over 250 pounds.

NOTT, JOSIAH D. (1804–1873). Physician. Graduated University of Pennsylvania, 1827; established Mobile Medical School, 1858; most noted for craniological research and writings on *Moral and Intellectual Diversity of Races* (1857) and *Types of Mankind* (1854).

OGLESBY, RICHARD (1824–1899). Union general and statesman. Served in Mexican War; commissioned colonel, 2nd Brigade, Cairo Military District; commander at Cairo, Illinois, 1861–1862; promoted to brigadier general, 1862; held commands in Army of Tennessee, 1862–1864; governor of Illinois, 1865–1869, 1872–1873; senator, 1873–1879.

OLMSTED, FREDERICK LAW (1822–1903). Landscape architect and journalist. Attended Yale; studied engineering; traveled in Europe and China; commissioned by *New York Times* to write unbiased impressions of slavery and South; designed and superintended building of Central Park, New York City, 1857–1861; general secretary, U.S. Sanitary Commission, 1861–1863; spent postwar years as horticultural architect.

PETIGRU, JAMES L. (1798–1863). Statesman. Graduated South Carolina College, 1809; served in War of 1812; opposed nullification, 1832–1833; not elected to public office because of Unionist views; opposed secession, 1860–1861; gave half-hearted support to Confederate cause.

PETTUS, JOHN J. (1813–1867). Confederate statesman. Served in Creek War; Democratic Mississippi state legislator; governor of Mississippi, 1860–1864; removed to Arkansas in 1865 and lived as a recluse.

PHILLIPS, PHILLIP (1807–1884). Confederate statesman. Democratic congressman from Alabama, 1853–1855; private law practice in Washington, D.C., 1855–1861; wife, Eugenia, was imprisoned in 1861 for Confederate sympathies; she was deported to the South in 1862; Phillips returned to the South in 1861.

PICKENS, FRANCIS W. (1805–1869). Confederate statesman. Graduated South Carolina College, 1824; Democratic congressman, 1834–1843; minister to Russia, 1858–1860; governor of South Carolina, 1860–1862.

PICKETT, GEORGE E. (1825–1875). Confederate general. Graduated West Point, 1846; served in Mexican War and on frontier; resigned U.S. Army, 1861;

commissioned brigadier general, C.S. Army, 1862; served mainly on Virginia front; most noted for "Pickett's Charge" at Gettysburg.

PILLOW, GIDEON J. (1806–1878). Confederate general. Served in Mexican War; appointed brigadier general, 1861; suspended for permitting surrender of Fort Donelson to U.S. Grant, 1862.

PORTER, DAVID DIXON (1813–1891). Union admiral. Joined U.S. Navy, 1829; served in Mexican War; appointed commander, 1861; commanded Mississippi Squadron, 1862; participated in Vicksburg and Red River campaigns, capture of Fort Fisher; promoted to vice-admiral, 1866; superintendent of U.S. Naval Academy, 1866–1870.

PORTER, FITZ-JOHN (1822–1901). Union general. Graduated West Point, 1845; served in Mexican War and on frontier; appointed brigadier general, U.S. Volunteers, 1861; commanded various units in Army of Potomac, 1861–1863; cashiered from service for disobedience, 1863; reinstated, 1886.

PRENTISS, BENJAMIN M. (1819–1901). Union general. Served in Illinois militia and Mexican War; appointed brigadier general, 1861; served chiefly in western theater.

PRYOR, ROGER A. (1828–1919). Confederate statesman and general. Graduated University of Virginia, 1848; Democratic congressman from Virginia, 1859–1861; member Confederate Congress, 1861–1862; commissioned brigadier general, 1862; captured near Petersburg, 1864; released after Appomattox.

RAYMOND, HENRY J. (1820–1869). Union statesman and journalist. Graduated University of Vermont, 1840; assistant editor, *New York Tribune*, 1841–1848; editor, *New York Enquirer*, 1848–1850; Republican state legislator, 1850–1851; established *New York Times*, 1851; lieutenant governor of New York, 1854; Republican congressman, 1865–1867.

RECTOR, HENRY M. (1816–1899). Confederate statesman. U.S. marshal for Arkansas, 1842–1845; Democratic state legislator, 1848–1852; governor, 1860–1862.

RHETT, ROBERT BARNWELL (1800–1875). Confederate statesman and journalist. Democratic congressman from South Carolina, 1837–1849; senator, 1850–1852; delegate to Confederate Provisional Congress, 1861; editor, Charleston *Mercury*.

ROMAN, ANDRÉ B. (1795–1866). Confederate statesman. Graduated St. Mary's College, Baltimore, 1815; Louisiana state legislator, 1818–1831; governor, 1831–1835; 1839–1843; president, New Orleans Drainage Company, 1843–1866; president, Louisiana Constitutional Conventions,

1845 and 1852; opposed secession but supported Confederacy; commissioner to U.S. government, 1861.

SCOTT, WINFIELD (1786–1866). Union general. Served in War of 1812 and Mexican War; general-in-chief, U.S. Army, 1841–1861; only non-West Pointer of southern birth (Virginia) in the Regular Army to remain loyal to the Union.

SEWARD, FREDERICK W. (1830–1915). Union statesman and journalist. Graduated Union College, 1849; staff of Albany (N.Y.) *Evening Journal*, 1851–1861; assistant secretary of state, 1861–1869, 1877–1879.

SEWARD, WILLIAM HENRY (1801–1872). Union statesman. Graduated Union College, 1820; Whig governor of New York, 1838–1842; senator as Whig, 1849–1855; as Republican, 1855–1861; secretary of state, 1861–1869.

SEYMOUR, HORATIO (1810–1886). Union statesman. Secretary to Governor William Marcy of New York, 1833–1839; Democratic state legislator, 1841–1842; 1844–1845; mayor of Utica, 1842–1843; governor, 1853–1855, 1863–1865; Democratic presidential nominee, 1868.

SHERMAN, WILLIAM T. (1820–1891). Union general. Graduated West Point, 1840; served in Mexican War; resigned U.S. Army, 1853; superintendent of Louisiana Military Academy, 1853–1861; commissioned brigadier general, U.S. Army, 1861; saw action at first battle of Bull Run, 1861; served chiefly in western theater, 1861–1865; most noted for his "March to the Sea" from Atlanta to Savannah, Georgia, November–December, 1864.

SICKLES, DANIEL E. (1825–1914). Union general. Democratic senator from New York, 1857–1861; appointed brigadier general, 1861; served on eastern front for duration.

SIGEL, FRANZ (1824–1902). Union general. German immigrant; graduated German Military Academy; appointed brigadier general, 1861; commanded units in Missouri, 1861–1862; on eastern front, 1862–1865.

SLIDELL, JOHN (1793–1871). Confederate statesman. Graduated Columbia College, 1810; Democratic congressman from Louisiana, 1843–1845; minister to Mexico, 1845; senator, 1853–1861; Confederate representative to France, 1861–1865.

SMITH, CALEB B. (1808–1864). Union statesman. Attended Miami (Ohio) University, 1825–1826; Whig congressman from Indiana, 1843–1849; secretary of interior, 1861–1863; U.S. district court judge, 1863–1864.

SMITH, TRUMAN (1791–1884). Union statesman. Graduated Yale, 1815; Whig Connecticut state legislator, 1831–1834; congressman, 1839–1843; 1845–1849; senator, 1849–1854; judge in Court of Arbitration in New York, 1862–1870.

SMITH, WILLIAM FARRAR, "BALDY" (1824–1903). Union general. Graduated West Point, 1845; taught at West Point; appointed brigadier general, 1861; served in eastern theater, 1861–1863, 1864–1865; in western theater, 1863–1864.

SPRAGUE, KATE CHASE (1840–1899). Daughter of Salmon P. Chase; wife of Senator William Sprague of Rhode Island. Social leader in Washington during the war; known for her efforts to secure the presidency for her father in 1868; divorced from Sprague in 1882; lived in poverty in later life.

STANTON, EDWIN M. (1814–1869). Union statesman. Lawyer; attorney general, 1860; secretary of war, 1862–1868; noted for efficiency with which he ran War Department and for his role in Andrew Johnson's impeachment trial, 1868.

SUMNER, CHARLES (1811–1874). Union statesman. Graduated Harvard, 1833; senator from Massachusetts as Free-Soiler, 1851–1857; as Republican, 1857–1874; noted for assault upon by Preston Brooks in 1856 and role in Reconstruction politics; traveled widely in Europe, 1856–1860, and had many friends among the English upper classes.

TATTNALL, JOSIAH (1795–1871). Confederate naval officer. Appointed midshipman during War of 1812; served in Mexican War; resigned captain, U.S. Navy, 1861; appointed captain, C.S. Navy, 1861; commanded defenses of Georgia and South Carolina, 1861; assigned command of *Merrimack,* 1862; naval defense of Savannah, 1863–1865.

TILDEN, SAMUEL J. (1814–1886). Union statesman. Attended Yale and New York University; noted corporation lawyer from 1843; coowner *New York Morning News;* Democratic state legislator, 1846; opposed Lincoln's election in 1860 and took little part in wartime activities; chairman of New York Democratic Committee, 1866; prosecuted "Tweed Ring"; governor of New York, 1874–1876; Democratic presidential nominee, 1876.

TOOMBS, ROBERT (1810–1885). Confederate statesman and general. Graduated Union College, 1828; Democratic congressman from Georgia, 1845–1853; senator, 1853–1861; secretary of state, 1861; appointed brigadier general, 1861; served in minor commands.

TRESCOT, WILLIAM HENRY (1822–1898). Historian, diplomat. Graduated College of Charleston, 1841; lawyer and planter; authored *A Few Thoughts on the Foreign Policy of the United States* (1849) and *The Position and Course of the South* (1850); secretary, U.S. legation, London, 1850–1854; assistant secretary of state, 1860; aide-de-camp to governors Andrew Magrath and Roswell Ripley of South Carolina during war; served U.S. government in various diplomatic posts in postwar era.

TWIGGS, DAVID E. (1790–1862). Confederate general. Entered U.S. Army during War of 1812; also saw service in Black Hawk, Seminole, and Mexican wars; dismissed for surrendering Union forces and supplies in Texas, 1861; commissioned major general, C.S. Army, 1861; command limited to District of Louisiana.

TYLER, DANIEL (1799–1882). Union general. Graduated West Point, 1819; served in garrison duty and as military attaché in France; resigned U.S. Army, 1834; reentered, 1861; commissioned brigadier general, 1862; commanded units at Blackburn's Ford, first battle of Bull Run, and Corinth, 1861–1862; commanded District of Delaware, 1862–1863; resigned, 1864.

VALLANDIGHAM, CLEMENT L. (1820–1871). Union statesman. Democratic congressman from Ohio, 1858–1863; noted chiefly for his opposition to the Civil War, his military trial, and his banishment to the Confederacy in 1863.

VAN VLIET, STEWART (1815–1901). Union general. Graduated West Point, 1840; served in Seminole and Mexican wars; garrison duty, 1848–1861; commissioned brigadier general, 1861; chief quartermaster, Army of Potomac, 1861–1862; served in New York as supply officer, 1862–1865; continued in service until 1881.

VIELÉ, EGBERT (1825–1902). Union general. Graduated West Point, 1847; served in Mexican War and on frontier; authored studies on topography and military subjects, 1850s; commissioned brigadier general, 1861; military governor of Norfolk, Virginia, 1862; resigned, 1863.

WALKER, LEROY POPE (1817–1884). Confederate statesman. Attended University of Alabama; state legislator, 1833–1840, 1850–1856; member Alabama secession convention, 1861; secretary of war, 1861; appointed brigadier general, 1861; served in departments of Alabama and West Florida, resigned, 1862.

WASHBURNE, ELIHU B. (1816–1887). Union statesman. Attended Harvard, 1839; Whig-Republican congressman from Illinois, 1853–1869.

WEED, THURLOW (1797–1882). Journalist and political organizer. Owner and editor of Albany (N.Y.) *Evening Journal*, 1830–1863; active in anti-Masonic, Whig, and Republican politics; supported William Seward for public office; adviser to Lincoln on political appointments.

WELLES, GIDEON (1802–1878). Union statesman. Democratic newspaper editor and minor politician before the war; secretary of the navy, 1861–1869.

WHITING, WILLIAM H. (1824–1865). Confederate general. Planned defense of Charleston harbor, 1861; served in Peninsula Campaign, Jackson's Valley Campaign; commander at Petersburg, 1864–1865; killed in battle of Fort Fisher, 1865.

WIGFALL, LOUIS T. (1816–1874). Confederate statesman and general. Attended South Carolina College; served in Seminole War; Democratic senator from Texas, 1859–1861; member of Confederate Congress, appointed brigadier general, 1861; fled to England during war.

WILKES, CHARLES (1798–1877). Union admiral. Entered U.S. Navy as midshipman, 1818; commanded expedition to Antarctica, 1838; another to Pacific Northwest, 1841–1842; noted for involvement in *Trent* affair, 1861; promoted to commander, 1862; to admiral, 1866.

WILSON, HENRY (1812–1875). Union statesman. Republican senator from Massachusetts, 1855–1873; U.S. vice-president, 1873–1875.

Index

Hamlin, Hannibal, 51, 329, 346
Harpers Ferry, 23, 95, 188, 234,
  259; described, 297–298
Harper's Monthly, 134n
Hatteras expedition, 305
Hay, John M., 51, 231, 258, 323,
  346
Hébert, Paul, 167
Helper, Hinton R., 35n
Heyward, Edward, 102, 103
Hicks, Thomas, 108, 347
Hodgson, William, 111
Hudson, Edward M., 308
Huger, Benjamin, 91, 347
Hurlburt, William H., 37
Hutchinson, James, 329n

Illinois Central Railroad, 14, 22,
  209, 216, 218, 219, 239, 307
Ingomar, 202
Intercoastal waterway: described,
  157–158
Irish, 26–27, 30, 112

Jackson, Andrew, 60, 329 and note
Jackson, James T., 163
Jackson, Miss.: described, 194
Jackson, Thomas J ("Stonewall"),
  226, 284n, 347
J. C. Cotton, 173
Johnston, Joseph E., 259, 284 and
  note, 285, 310, 347
Joinville, Prince de, 331n

Kane, George B., 221n
Keitt, Lawrence, 132, 347
Kenly, John, 221n
Kenner, Duncan, 187, 190, 347
Keyes, Erasmus, 302, 303

King, Henry C., 100
King, Preston, 233
King, Susan Petigru, 101
Knights of the Golden Circle, 118
  and note

Lane, James H., 109 and note, 347
Latham, Milton S., 258
Lawton, Alexander, 108, 110, 111,
  347
Lawton, Sarah, 108
Leander, 146
Lee, Robert E., 9, 109, 123, 235,
  310, 348
Leopard, 145
Letcher, John, 95, 348
Lincoln, Abraham, 8, 9, 13 and
  note, 29, 30n, 48 and note, 56n,
  58n, 59, 61, 64, 70, 71, 78, 83,
  90, 96, 109, 110, 116, 123,
  130n, 147, 153, 158, 163, 166,
  186, 193n, 207, 209, 216, 219,
  239, 254–255, 258, 278, 288,
  289, 290, 294, 300, 302, 306,
  308, 309, 311, 314, 320, 323,
  332, 334, 340, 348; described,
  89, 44–49, 317–318; humor of,
  50–51, 325
Lincoln, Mary Todd, 20, 55, 70,
  289, 309 and note, 311, 320,
  322, 348; described, 48–49, 55
Lind, Jenny, 253
Lisboa, Migul de, 331
London Herald, 316n
London Times, 3, 4, 6, 10, 12, 13,
  14, 23, 47, 121, 166, 301, 308,
  325
Louisiana: anti-Jewish prejudice in,
  167
Lovejoy, Owen, 329, 348
Lucas, James, 80, 348

About the Editor

Eugene H. Berwanger is Professor of History at Colorado State University; he previously taught at Illinois College in Jacksonville and Miles College in Birmingham, Alabama. He received his undergraduate degree from Illinois State University at Normal and his Ph.D. from the University of Illinois in Urbana. In 1984 he served as Senior Fulbright Lecturer at the University of Genoa, Italy. Colorado State University presented him with the Oliver P. Pennock Award for outstanding teaching and significant publication in 1983.

A specialist in United States history between 1830 and 1877, Professor Berwanger is author of *The Frontier Against Slavery: Western Anti-Negro Prejudice and the Slavery Extension Controversy* (1967); *As They Saw Slavery* (1973); and *The West and Reconstruction* (1981). In addition he revised Roy F. Nichols's *The Stakes of Power, 1845–1877* (1982). He has also contributed articles to various scholarly journals.